IoT Security: Threat Detection, Analysis and Defense

IoT Security: Threat Detection, Analysis and Defense

Guest Editors

Olivier Markowitch
Jean-Michel Dricot

MDPI

Basel • Beijing • Wuhan • Barcelona • Belgrade • Novi Sad • Cluj • Manchester

Guest Editors
Olivier Markowitch
Computer Sciences Department
Université Libre de Bruxelles
Brussels
Belgium

Jean-Michel Dricot
Cybersecurity Research Center
Université Libre de Bruxelles
Brussels
Belgium

Editorial Office
MDPI AG
Grosspeteranlage 5
4052 Basel, Switzerland

This is a reprint of the Special Issue, published open access by the journal *Future Internet* (ISSN 1999-5903), freely accessible at: https://www.mdpi.com/journal/futureinternet/special_issues/IoTS_TDAD.

For citation purposes, cite each article independently as indicated on the article page online and as indicated below:

Lastname, A.A.; Lastname, B.B. Article Title. *Journal Name* **Year**, *Volume Number*, Page Range.

ISBN 978-3-7258-5347-2 (Hbk)
ISBN 978-3-7258-5348-9 (PDF)
https://doi.org/10.3390/books978-3-7258-5348-9

Contents

About the Editors

Olivier Markowitch

Olivier Markowitch is a full professor in Computer Sciences of the Faculty of Sciences at the Université Libre de Bruxelles in Belgium. He is one of the coordinators of the Master in Cybersecurity program in Belgium and is currently working on the design and analysis of cryptographic protocols.

Jean-Michel Dricot

Jean-Michel Dricot is a professor at the engineering school of the Université Libre de Bruxelles in Belgium. He is one of the coordinators of the Master in Cybersecurity program in Belgium and is currently working on the hardware security of Internet of Things and, more generally, on network security.

future internet

Editorial

IoT Security: Threat Detection, Analysis, and Defense

Olivier Markowitch [1,*] and Jean-Michel Dricot [2,*]

[1] Computer Science Department and Cybersecurity Research Center, Faculty of Sciences, Université Libre de Bruxelles, Boulevard du Triomphe CP 212, 1050 Brussels, Belgium
[2] Cybersecurity Research Center, Ecole Polytechnique de Bruxelles, Université Libre de Bruxelles, 50 Avenue Franklin Roosevelt CP 165/56, 1050 Brussels, Belgium
* Correspondence: olivier.markowitch@ulb.be (O.M.); jean-michel.dricot@ulb.be (J.-M.D.)

In recent years, the rapid growth of Internet of Things (IoT) technologies has created numerous opportunities across fields such as smart cities, transportation, energy, and healthcare. However, the growth of IoT technology also introduces significant security and privacy challenges, leading to research on intrusion detection in IoT environments, privacy-preserving data analysis, firmware vulnerability analysis, and secure communication protocols. The complexity and diversity of IoT ecosystems necessitate new techniques, architectures, and frameworks to detect, analyze, and counter emerging threats. This Special Issue of *Future Internet*, titled "IoT Security: Threat Detection, Analysis and Defense", highlights papers and research reviews that explore the current state of the art in IoT system security.

After a thorough screening and peer-review process, ten papers were accepted for publication. These papers are categorized into two groups: (1) papers presenting emerging techniques and frameworks for intrusion detection, privacy preservation, and further securing operations in IoT, and (2) surveys and systematic analyses that aggregate knowledge and discuss future directions.

The first group focuses on innovative architectures and algorithms that aim to detect and mitigate attacks within IoT environments.

Lazea et al. [1] present a methodology for constructing "equi-width" histograms directly on homomorphically encrypted IoT data, thereby facilitating privacy-preserving analytics without the need to expose raw data. Their approach, based on the TFHE scheme, is optimized for secure computation. This approach is evaluated through the lens of an encrypted outlier detection use case.

Fatema et al. [2] introduce Federated XAI IDS, which integrates federated learning to develop an explainable intrusion detection system that safeguards privacy. Trained collaboratively across multiple decentralized devices on the CIC-IoT-2023 dataset, the framework achieves high accuracy while ensuring that sensitive network data remain local and interpretable.

Cibrario Bertolotti et al. [3] examine SlowROS attacks targeting the ROS Master component in industrial automation systems. They demonstrate how prolonged idle connection timeouts can be exploited to disrupt system-wide operations, bypassing built-in kernel protections.

In the domain of vehicular cybersecurity, Althunayyan et al. [4] propose a Hierarchical Federated Learning framework for intrusion detection in in-vehicle networks. The system's incorporation of multiple edge aggregators mitigates the risk of single points of failure and enhances scalability.

Tseng et al. [5] explore multi-class intrusion detection using Transformer models on the CIC-IoT-2023 dataset. Their Transformer-based approach performs well in binary classification, particularly in multi-class scenarios.

For resource-constrained environments such as smart homes, Javed et al. [6] implement a lightweight, two-layered IDS that operates both on-device and in the cloud. Their XGBoost-based solution efficiently detects MITM and DoS attacks on microcontroller-powered devices, making it suitable for real-time deployment.

The second group provides broader perspectives and foundational insights.

He et al. [7] surveyed energy-aware security mechanisms for IoT technologies, identifying the interplay between energy efficiency and security, reviewing current privacy-preserving approaches, and outlining future directions for sustainable IoT protection.

Bagheri et al. [8] address the issue of smart grid security through a PUF-based authentication and key agreement protocol that combines physical unclonable functions with elliptic curve cryptography.

Zhou et al. [9] provide a critical revisit of IoT firmware emulation and its application to fuzzing. By examining recent works, they identify fundamental challenges, systematically classify solutions according to the issues they address, and perform a comparative analysis of emulation fidelity and bug detection capabilities. They also highlight key research gaps for future exploration.

Finally, Papadopoulos et al. [10] provide a comprehensive review of recent advancements in federated learning. Their analysis emphasizes FL's role in privacy preservation and data decentralization while identifying existing challenges in securing models against adversarial attacks.

We sincerely thank all authors for their contributions and the reviewers for their efforts in ensuring the Special Issue was of the highest quality. Together, the papers represent the dynamic and changing field of IoT security research, providing implementation strategies, theoretical advances, and recommendations for addressing the security and privacy challenges of these connected systems.

Conflicts of Interest: The authors declare no conflict of interest.

References

1. Lazea, D.; Hangan, A.; Cioara, T. Building Equi-Width Histograms on Homomorphically Encrypted Data. *Future Internet* **2025**, *17*, 256. [CrossRef]
2. Fatema, K.; Dey, S.K.; Anannya, M.; Khan, R.T.; Rashid, M.M.; Su, C.; Mazumder, R. Federated XAI IDS: An Explainable and Safeguarding Privacy Approach to Detect Intrusion Combining Federated Learning and SHAP. *Future Internet* **2025**, *17*, 234. [CrossRef]
3. Cibrario Bertolotti, I.; Durante, L.; Cambiaso, E. Analyzing Impact and Systemwide Effects of the SlowROS Attack in an Industrial Automation Scenario. *Future Internet* **2025**, *17*, 167. [CrossRef]
4. Althunayyan, M.; Javed, A.; Rana, O.; Spyridopoulos, T. Hierarchical Federated Learning-Based Intrusion Detection for In-Vehicle Networks. *Future Internet* **2024**, *16*, 451. [CrossRef]
5. Tseng, S.-M.; Wang, Y.-Q.; Wang, Y.-C. Multi-Class Intrusion Detection Based on Transformer for IoT Networks Using CIC-IoT-2023 Dataset. *Future Internet* **2024**, *16*, 284. [CrossRef]
6. Javed, A.; Ehtsham, A.; Jawad, M.; Awais, M.N.; Qureshi, A.-u.-H.; Larijani, H. Implementation of Lightweight Machine Learning-Based Intrusion Detection System on IoT Devices of Smart Homes. *Future Internet* **2024**, *16*, 200. [CrossRef]
7. He, P.; Zhou, Y.; Qin, X. A Survey on Energy-Aware Security Mechanisms for the Internet of Things. *Future Internet* **2024**, *16*, 128. [CrossRef]
8. Bagheri, N.; Bendavid, Y.; Safkhani, M.; Rostampour, S. Smart Grid Security: A PUF-Based Authentication and Key Agreement Protocol. *Future Internet* **2024**, *16*, 9. [CrossRef]

9. Zhou, W.; Shen, S.; Liu, P. IoT Firmware Emulation and Its Security Application in Fuzzing: A Critical Revisit. *Future Internet* **2025**, *17*, 19. [CrossRef]
10. Papadopoulos, C.; Kollias, K.-F.; Fragulis, G.F. Recent Advancements in Federated Learning: State of the Art, Fundamentals, Principles, IoT Applications and Future Trends. *Future Internet* **2024**, *16*, 415. [CrossRef]

future internet

MDPI

Article

Building Equi-Width Histograms on Homomorphically Encrypted Data

Dragoș Lazea , Anca Hangan * and Tudor Cioara

Computer Science Department, Technical University of Cluj-Napoca, Memorandumului 28, 400114 Cluj-Napoca, Romania; dragos.lazea@cs.utcluj.ro (D.L.); tudor.cioara@cs.utcluj.ro (T.C.)
* Correspondence: anca.hangan@cs.utcluj.ro

Abstract: Histograms are widely used for summarizing data distributions, detecting anomalies, and improving machine learning models' accuracy. However, traditional histogram-based methods require access to raw data, raising privacy concerns, particularly in sensitive IoT applications. Encryption-based techniques offer potential solutions; however, they secure the data in transit or storage, requiring decryption during analysis, which exposes raw data to potential privacy risks. In this paper, we propose a method for constructing privacy-preserving histograms directly on homomorphically encrypted IoT data, leveraging the Fast Fully Homomorphic Encryption over the Torus (TFHE) scheme implemented in the Concrete framework. To overcome the challenges posed by homomorphic encryption, we redesign the traditional histogram construction algorithm, optimizing it for secure computation by addressing constraints related to nested loops and conditional statements. As an evaluation use case, we have considered an outlier detection mechanism based on histogram frequency counts, ensuring that all data and computations remain encrypted throughout the process. Our method achieves results consistent with plaintext-based outlier detection while maintaining reasonable computational overhead compared to those reported in the existing literature.

Keywords: histogram computation; histogram-based outlier detection; homomorphic encryption; internet of things; privacy

1. Introduction

In today's interconnected world, IoT devices have become integral to daily life, enhancing convenience, efficiency, and automation. From smart controllers and meters to wearables and connected homes, they transform industries and drive smart city development. IoT platforms aggregate sensor data, analyze patterns, and support decision-making with AI advancements further evolving these devices into intelligent systems [1,2]. As IoT adoption grows, so does its impact on urban planning, healthcare, and energy management [3,4]. As IoT devices generate vast amounts of data at high frequencies to support control processes, data analysis becomes essential for proactive interventions and enhanced reliability in various applications across different domains [2,5,6].

In this context, understanding data distributions is crucial for detecting anomalies, optimizing data compression, and improving machine learning accuracy. Histograms are valuable tools in this regard, as they provide summaries of large datasets as well as approximations of data distributions, making it easier and faster to analyze the underlying patterns and compute aggregate statistics [7–10]. At the same time, the large-scale integration of IoT data from heterogenous devices may increase the vulnerability to cyberattacks and device malfunctions. Integrating heterogeneous IoT data increases cybersecurity risks, making privacy protection essential to prevent infrastructure breaches and data leaks [11]. However, traditional histogram-based methods often rely on raw data analysis, posing privacy concerns, especially for sensitive information [8,9].

Differential privacy (DP) is one of the leading methods for privately sharing histograms with untrusted parties in the state of the art. It is used on a wide variety of IoT data, ranging from smart homes to industrial sensors, particularly in tasks related to anomaly detection [12,13]. DP histograms can be constructed by adding noise to histograms created using various methods [14,15]. To deal with trade-offs between accuracy and privacy, some approaches focus on building DP sketches to generate approximate private histograms [16,17]. The authors build new differentially private constructs, such as Misra–Gries sketches or the Approximate-Estimate sketches in a streaming setting, introducing less noise than similar solutions. However, despite its advantages, differential privacy-based techniques add noise to histogram bins, which can reduce accuracy, and defining the right privacy budget is a non-trivial task requiring extensive fine-tuning. Multi-party computation (MPC) can be used to compute histograms collaboratively across multiple parties without revealing individual data and adding noise to the data or the result. In such approaches, differential privacy is applied to the final output for additional protection; however, the tradeoff lies in the communication overhead, as parties must exchange many messages during computation [18–20]. The construction of histograms using lightweight masked encryption is explored in [21]. The authors introduce a scheme for secure frequency histogram estimation, allowing a central server to utilize histograms without identifying which values originated from specific users. While such solutions can be computationally efficient, they require at least partial decryption or assume plaintext access before analysis.

In this context, homomorphic encryption (HE) schemes are promising solutions for building privacy-preserving histograms. They enable the processing and execution of operations directly on encrypted IoT data ensuring that the IoT data remains encrypted throughout the entire process [22]. However, homomorphic encryption schemes have limitations which make them difficult to use in the context of histogram building processes. The supported operations are primarily restricted to addition and multiplication and pose constraints on the range and type of operands, which are typically limited to integer values [23–27]. Additional challenges related to secure computations such as comparisons, divisions or exponentiation over the encrypted domain still need to be addressed [28,29]. Overall, encryption/decryption mechanisms and HE data processing generate very large computational overheads that may negatively influence the system's responsiveness, making it difficult to address the trade-off between privacy and system operation [30]. Finally, noise induced by the encryption scheme can affect the data analysis accuracy, especially when dealing with small deviations from the IoT device's normal raw data values [31,32].

Therefore, in this paper we propose a solution for building histograms on homomorphic encrypted data generated by IoT devices without relying on partial or total decryption. To leverage the flexibility of the Fast Fully Homomorphic Encryption over the Torus (TFHE) scheme implemented in Concrete [33,34], we redesign the traditional histogram construction algorithm and address its limitations in handling nested loops and conditional statements. To assess the effectiveness of the private histogram, we implement an outlier detection use case, where outliers are identified using a thresholding rule applied to histogram counts, with all computations performed on encrypted data. The proposed privacy-preserving outlier detection mechanism has consistent results with the corresponding mechanism that operates on plain data, without needing to decrypt the results for decision-making. Moreover, the computational overheads are kept within reasonable limits.

The key contributions of this paper are as follows:

- A privacy-preserving method for constructing histograms on homomorphically encrypted data, enabling outlier detection without requiring decryption.
- Adaptation of traditional histogram construction and histogram-based outlier detection techniques for the Fast Fully Homomorphic Encryption over the Torus (TFHE) scheme in Concrete. We address challenges related to input size constraints and computational depth by vectorizing key operations, including addition, value placement in buckets, labeling abnormal buckets based on threshold frequency, and identifying outliers by their range and assigned bucket labels.
- Performance evaluation and analysis of computational overhead trade-offs across different configuration setups, assessing their impact on the effectiveness of privacy-preserving histograms in IoT environments.

2. Equi-Width Histograms on Homomorphically Encrypted Data

Different types of histograms, such as equi-depth, equi-width, and dynamic-width, offer varying levels of effectiveness depending on the characteristics of the underlying data distribution [35]. Equi-depth histograms are more effective for skewed data, whereas equi-width histograms perform better on uniformly distributed data. However, the adaptability of equi-depth histograms comes with increased complexity in both construction and maintenance. In this work, we chose to implement equi-width histograms because of their lower computational cost.

Equi-width histograms capture the overall data distribution by grouping data points into fixed-width buckets. In such histograms, buckets have the same size (range), but the number of values that fit in each of them is variable. Each bucket can be represented as a tuple:

$$b = (low, high, count), low, high, count \in \mathbb{N}, \quad (1)$$

where low and $high$ give the range of values which fit in the bucket and count is the number of data points within the $[low, high)$ range.

Next, we present the implementation of equi-width histogram computation on encrypted data and illustrate its effectiveness in detecting outliers in IoT data. The overview of our approach is depicted in Figure 1. The proposed framework simulates a real-world setting where outlier detection is performed on encrypted IoT data using prior measurement distribution. To this end, we first preprocess the raw IoT data by scaling and converting it to integer values within the range $[0, 100]$, as many homomorphic encryption frameworks do not support floating point operations. Next, we homomorphically encrypt the data and construct an encrypted equi-width histogram, which is then used for outlier detection across three different configuration scenarios described in the evaluation section.

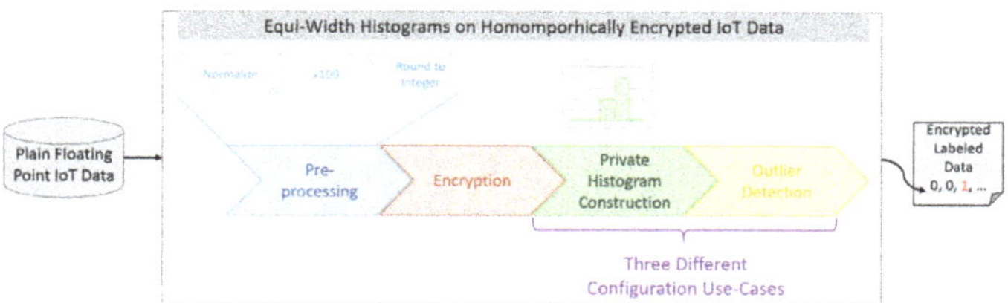

Figure 1. Pipeline of the proposed framework for privacy-preserving outlier detection in IoT data using private equi-width histograms.

For the implementation, we chose the TFHE scheme in Concrete [33,34] due to its superior flexibility in converting various operations into table lookups, outperforming other FHE schemes [36–39]. A key advantage is its support for function composition [40], enabling secure multi-step computations without decryption. Additionally, Concrete allows limited floating point operations [41], but its Compile tool only supports integer inputs and outputs, as computations rely on table lookups' mapping integers to integer results.

In Concrete, data is encrypted using Learning With Errors (LWE), which implies a series of constraints not only on the allowed operations and on the way that functions are implemented, but also on the size of the plain values. Moreover, this learning-based approach of translating arithmetic operations into table lookup operations is a probabilistic model which is prone to errors. The main drawback of Concrete is that it may not provide the expected answer in all test cases, but its default failure probability is very low (1 in 100,000).

As a fully homomorphic encryption scheme, TFHE implemented in Concrete overcomes the drawback of the traditional encryption schemes in which the data is temporarily encrypted during transmission between the client and the server. The server decrypts it upon receipt, executes the necessary operations on the plaintext, re-encrypts the result, and returns it to the client. In Concrete, the only private key holder is the client, and the server-side operations are entirely performed on encrypted data, using the public evaluation key, which is mathematically related to the client's private key.

2.1. Private Histogram Construction

First, we define a function to determine whether a given value falls within a bucket defined by a specific range. While this may seem like a straightforward operation, implementing it directly on homomorphically encrypted data presents significant challenges. Homomorphic encryption imposes strict limits on the number of operations that can be performed on the same ciphertext, and conventional loops using a counter variable are not feasible, especially when the number of iterations is large. This restriction exists because each iteration increases the computational depth on the ciphertext, potentially exceeding the allowed limit. As only foreach loops and vectorial operations are allowed without any restrictions, alternative procedures need to be implemented to ensure compliance with the constraints imposed by the encryption scheme. Therefore, we implement the range-checking procedure in a vectorized manner, allowing us to efficiently determine whether a given data point x falls within a set of buckets, represented as lists of low values, $low[]$, and of high values, $high[]$.

Given an input value x and two lists containing, on the same position, the minimum (low) and, respectively, the maximum ($high$) value of each bucket, applying the previously defined procedure in a vectorial approach involves iteratively checking whether x falls within the range defined by the corresponding low and high values. The result of each comparison is appended to a new list $r[]$, maintaining the same index as the original range lists. Therefore, the vectorized implementation returns a list of the same size as the $low[]$ and $high[]$ lists containing a single value of 1 at the position corresponding to the bucket where x fits, while all the other elements of the result list are equal to 0.

This vectorial approach to determine the bucket in which each value of the input fits can be formally described as a map operation, which takes a data sample and the lists containing the ranges of buckets as inputs and returns another vector as output, where each element of the output vector is the result of applying the *isInBucket* function to the corresponding elements of the input vectors, as follows:

$$isInBucket : \mathbb{N}^3 \rightarrow \{0,1\}, isInBucket(x, low, high) = \begin{cases} 1, & \text{if } x \in [low, high) \\ 0, & \text{otherwise} \end{cases} \tag{2}$$

$$\begin{aligned} r = vectorialIsInBucket(x, low, high) &= map(isInBucket(x, low, high)) \\ &= [isInBucket(x, low_0, high_0), \cdots, isInBucket(x, low_{n-1}, high_{n-1})] \end{aligned} \tag{3}$$

where x is a scalar and low and $high$ are lists. Algorithm 1 shows the vectorial implementation of the procedure.

Algorithm 1 Vectorial is in bucket.

Require: x ▷ New sampled data from IoT devices
Require: $low[], high[]$ ▷ Lists of bucket bounds in histogram
Ensure: $r[]$ ▷ List with 1 at the position of the matching bucket
$r \leftarrow []$
for $i = 0$ to $low.length - 1$ **do**
  r.append(isInBucket($x, low[i], high[i]$))
end for
return r

Using the vectorial approach to determine the bucket in which the given value fits, we can compute the histogram of an input dataset by adding the result vectors for each value in the input set, as shown in Algorithm 2. To achieve this, we use the vectorial addition operation which is defined as the element-wise addition of their corresponding components.

Algorithm 2 Building equi-width histogram on homomorphically encrypted data.

Require: $x[]$ ▷ New sampled data stream from IoT devices
Require: $low[], high[]$ ▷ Lists of bucket bounds in histogram
Ensure: $h[]$ ▷ Equi-width histogram
$h \leftarrow [0, 0, \ldots, 0]$
for all $x_i \in x$ **do**
  $h \leftarrow h +$ vectorialIsInBucket($x_i, low, high$)
end for
return h

For two given vectors $\mathbf{v}$ and $\mathbf{u}$ of size n, the result of the vectorial addition is another vector, $\mathbf{w}$, of the same size, defined as follows:

$$\mathbf{w} = \mathbf{u} + \mathbf{v} = [u_0, u_1, \cdots, u_{n-1}] + [v_0, v_1, \cdots, v_{n-1}] = [u_0 + v_0, u_1 + v_1, \cdots, u_{n-1} + v_{n-1}] \tag{4}$$

Generalizing the above relation for the case of m vectors, $\mathbf{u}^{(j)}, j = \overline{1,m}$, each having n components, the result of the vectorial addition is:

$$\begin{aligned} \mathbf{w} = \mathbf{u}^{(1)} + \mathbf{u}^{(2)} + \cdots + \mathbf{u}^{(m)} &= [u_0^{(1)}, u_1^{(1)}, \cdots, u_{n-1}^{(1)}] + [u_0^{(2)}, u_1^{(2)}, \cdots, u_{n-1}^{(2)}] + \cdots + [u_0^{(m)}, u_1^{(m)}, \cdots, u_{n-1}^{(m)}] \\ &= [u_0^{(1)} + u_0^{(2)} + \cdots + u_0^{(m)}, u_1^{(1)} + u_1^{(2)} + \cdots + u_1^{(m)}, \cdots, u_{n-1}^{(1)} + u_{n-1}^{(2)} + \cdots + u_{n-1}^{(m)}] \end{aligned} \tag{5}$$

The vectorial addition can be performed only on vectors having the same number of components, since the components of the sum are the element-wise sums of the components of all input vectors. Therefore, for a given input list of elements, if we perform an element-wise addition of the results given by the vectorial range check function for each element, we determine the equi-width histogram of the input set, as depicted in Figure 2.

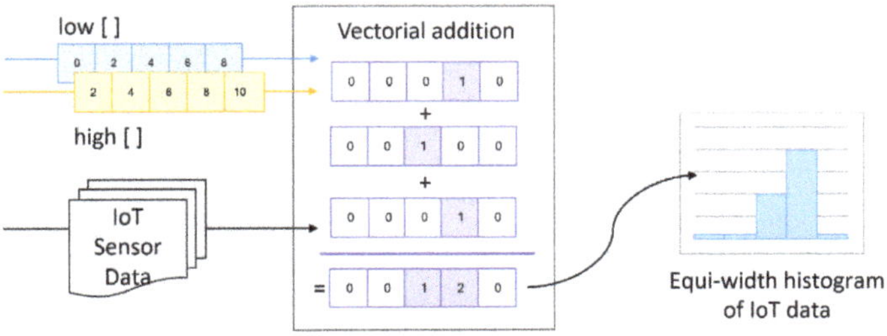

Figure 2. Vectorial approach of constructing equi-width histograms.

2.2. *Detecting Outliers in Encrypted Data Using Private Histograms*

As homomorphic encryption schemes impose significant limitations in terms of available operations, performing more complex data analysis on homomorphically encrypted data is a challenging task. In this section, we show how our private equi-width histogram can be utilized for detecting outliers in homomorphically encrypted IoT sensor data streams by analyzing the distribution of data across buckets. Since outliers typically appear less frequently than normal values, data points can be labeled based on the number of elements within the same bucket.

Therefore, to bypass the limitations of existing homomorphic encryption schemes, a mainly additive and comparison-based simple thresholding approach can be applied, where data falling into buckets with low counts is classified as an outlier. Values that belong to low-frequency buckets are identified as outliers, whereas values in high-frequency buckets are considered normal.

As in the case of constructing a private histogram, we adopt a vectorized approach for outlier detection on FHE-encrypted data, leveraging frequency-based labeling. Specifically, we define a procedure that, given an input value and a bucket, determines whether the value falls within the bucket and whether the bucket's element count is below a predefined threshold (as shown in Algorithm 3). By vectorizing this procedure, we enable repeated application across an entire IoT sensor dataset, while adhering to the constraints of fully homomorphic encryption.

To accomplish this, we define a map operation that processes an IoT data sample alongside lists representing bucket ranges, element counts per bucket, and a predefined threshold. This operation outputs a list in which each element corresponds to the result of applying the $isInAbnormalBucket$ function (defined below) to the respective elements of the input lists. The function determines whether a given data point falls within a bucket and if the bucket's element count is below the specified threshold, as follows:

$$isInAbnormalBucket : \mathbb{N}^5 \rightarrow \{0,1\}, isInAbnormalBucket(x, low, high, count, th) = \\ = \begin{cases} 1, & \text{if } x \in [low, high) \text{ and } count < th \\ 0, & \text{otherwise} \end{cases} \tag{6}$$

$$\begin{aligned} r = vectorialIsInAbnormalBucket(x, low, high, count, th) = \\ = map(isInAbnormalBucket(x, low, high, count, th)) \\ = [isInAbnormalBucket(x, low_0, high_0, count_0, th), \cdots, isInAbnormalBucket(x, low_{n-1}, high_{n-1}, count_{n-1}, th)] \end{aligned} \tag{7}$$

where x and th are scalars and *low*, *high*, and *count* are lists defining the buckets in the histogram. This approach is formally defined in Algorithm 3.

Algorithm 3 Vectorial is in abnormal bucket.

```
Require: x                                ▷ New data sample
Require: low[], high[]                    ▷ Bucket bounds in histogram
Require: count[]                          ▷ Element counts per bucket
Require: th                               ▷ Threshold for outlier detection
Ensure: r[]      ▷ Vector with 1 at the index of the abnormal bucket if any
r ← []
for i = 0 to low.length − 1 do
    r.append(isInAbnormalBucket(x, low[i], high[i], count[i], th))
end for
return r
```

To compute the binary label of a specific value, we perform a reduce operation on the result provided by the *vectorialIsInAbnormalBucket* procedure by summing all the elements in the list. Reducing a list by summing is a recursive vectorial operation which is defined as follows:

$$reduce(L, \oplus) = \begin{cases} 0, & \text{if } L = [\,] \\ x + reduce(L', \oplus), & \text{if } L = [x] + L' \end{cases} \quad (8)$$

where L is the original list, x is the first element of the list, and L' is the rest of the list. This operation generates a single value that is the sum of all the elements of the list, by adding the first element to the sum of the rest of the list, until the list is empty (see Algorithm 4). For an empty list, the reduce-by-summing operation returns 0.

Algorithm 4 Equi-width histogram-based outlier detection on homomorphically encrypted data.

```
Require: x[]                 ▷ New sampled data stream from IoT devices
Require: low[], high[]                    ▷ Bucket bounds in histogram
Require: count[]                          ▷ Element counts per bucket
Require: th                 ▷ Frequency threshold for outlier detection
Ensure: a[]                     ▷ Vector of outliers detected per sample
a ← [ ]
for all x_i ∈ x do
    r ← vectorialIsInAbnormalBucket(x_i, low, high, count, th)
    a.append(∑ r)
end for
return a
```

The vectorial approach of labeling an input value involves iteratively checking if the value is in each of the buckets defined by three lists: one for minimum values, one for maximum values, and one for the current element count in each bucket. When the bucket in which the value must be placed is determined, the number of values that it contains is compared to a given threshold.

The result of the vectorial procedure is a list of the same size as the lists containing the range limits for the buckets. It contains at most one element set to 1, positioned at the index of the bucket where the value fits, but only if the bucket's element count is below the threshold. If no such bucket meets the condition, all elements in the output list are 0. This mechanism is depicted in Figure 3.

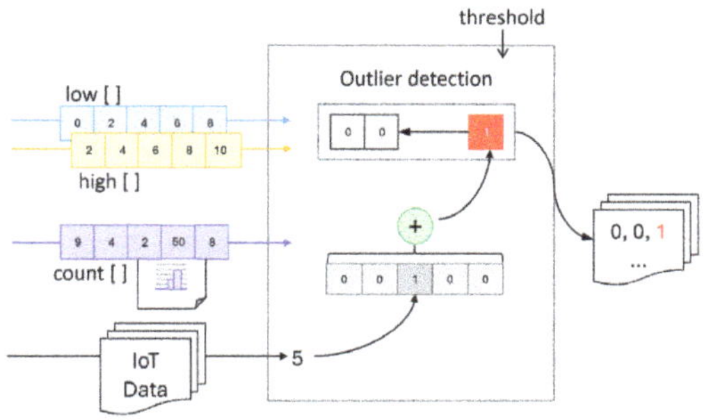

Figure 3. Vectorial approach of detecting outliers using equi-width histograms.

2.3. *Threat Model Definition and Assumptions*

Our privacy-preserving histogram construction technique targets edge–cloud deployments in IoT environments, where sensitive data collected from distributed sensors is encrypted using homomorphic encryption and aggregated before being transmitted to the cloud. The data sources (i.e., sensors) are considered to be trusted entities. We assume that sensor data is encrypted at the source immediately upon collection using the private encryption keys managed by a trusted HE controller. Data is then transmitted to more capable but untrusted edge/cloud processors, where the histogram building and outlier detection modules are deployed, as shown in Figure 4. These edge/cloud processors are not granted access to private encyption/decryption keys, but only to the evaluation public key to perform the histogram construction and anomaly detection. The HE controller is the only trusted entity responsible for distributing keys, validating computation circuits, and enforcing policies. Only a single trusted controller governs each deployment.

In such a deployment, we consider several potential risks, including the execution of tampered circuits by malicious edge nodes, replay attacks aiming to skew the histogram, and statistical inference from aggregate outputs. To mitigate these threats, all data is encrypted at the source using homomorphic encryption, and we assuume that only validated, signed computation circuits approved by the trusted controller are allowed to run. Additionally, we assume the existence of authenticated channels over which the encrypted data is transmitted, and that policy enforcement is centralized under a single trusted HE controller that governs key management and computation integrity. However, this setup introduces a single point of failure, as the HE controller is solely responsible for key management, policy enforcement, and circuit validation.

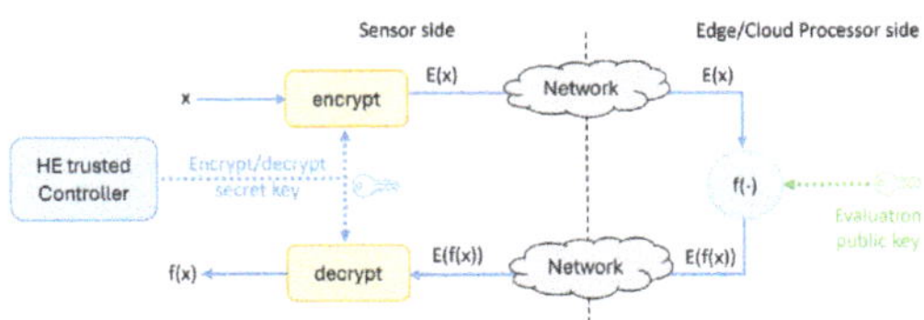

Figure 4. Deployment sketch and threat model.

3. Evaluation Results

We implemented the proposed solution in Python 3.10.6, using the Concrete Homomorphic Encryption library [40]. The code is available on GitHub (version 2.38.0) [42]. All experiments were conducted in a laboratory environment and were not deployed in a real-world setting, such as the one described in Section 2.3. The evaluation was performed on a computer equipped with an Intel(R) Core(TM) i7-10750H CPU @ 2.60 GHz (6 physical cores, 12 logical processors) and 16 GB of RAM. While this setup provides a reasonable baseline for assessing the computational performance of our methods, it does not reflect the constraints typically found on edge devices. Therefore, further optimization and testing would be required for deployment in resource-constrained environments. Nonetheless, the trained circuits generated with Concrete could be deployed on more powerful edge or fog computing nodes.

To evaluate our prototypes, we use the data provided by IoT devices in a city district, specifically an electricity production dataset [43] containing measurements recorded by smart meters on an hourly basis. Since the values measured by the IoT meters are floating point values between 0 and 9.91 kW and our models can operate only on integer data which has a limited binary representation, we preprocess the electric power data by scaling it to integer values between 0 and 100 to meet the constraints of our prototypes. To achieve this, we normalize the data to ensure it fits into a limited range, multiply the normalized values by 100, and round the result to the nearest integer, as shown in Figure 1. By applying this normalization-based data preprocessing, we aim at converting the data to small integers while not disturbing the general distribution of the values. As the device measures the produced electric power, the values are higher at midday and lower during the morning and the evening (see reference values in Figure 5). The distribution of the data is preserved by the data preprocessing flow that we use. This preprocessing strategy also supports generalizability to other types of IoT data, such as temperature, motion, or air quality, since these values can similarly be normalized and scaled to the $[0, 100]$ range before encryption, allowing our modules to operate on a broad range of sensor inputs.

To simulate a real-world scenario in which the data received from IoT devices is already encrypted, we encrypted benchmark data using homomorphic encryption and then fed it to the outlier detection method in three use cases. However, in practice, the models would be pre-trained on data within the expected range of the IoT devices, without requiring this additional encryption step.

We ran multiple experiments on encrypted data to assess the performance of our outlier detection method on encrypted data under various challenges, including sensor noise, adversarial inputs, communication issues, and device malfunctions—such as sensors persistently reporting constant value regardless of environmental conditions. To this aim, we artificially introduced anomalies in the preprocessed data by adding noise values to simulate various kinds of abnormal situations which can be encountered in an IoT sensor-based system. To ensure that the data used at building the equi-width histogram reflects the expected behavior of the monitored phenomenon, we consider the average of the data recorded by the electric smart meter during five consecutive days as the reference data.

This histogram-based approach of detecting outliers based on a frequency threshold performs best on catching anomalies in data containing significant variations and samples which exceed the range of the reference data. However, the major assumption this technique makes is that outliers have a considerably lower frequency compared to normal data; this method does not catch constant anomalies when the value repeatedly reported by the sensor is present within the reference data used at building the histogram.

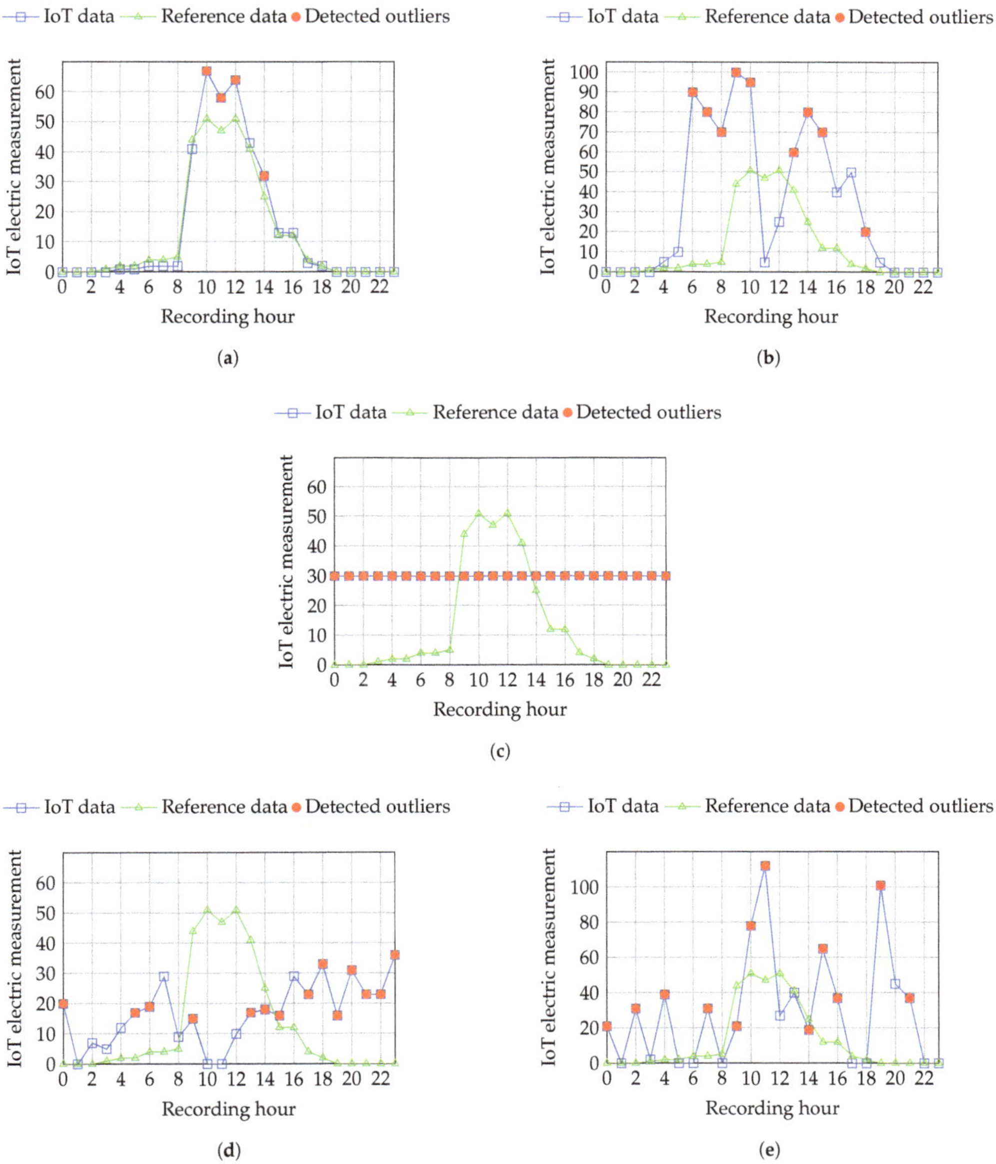

Figure 5. Results provided by our privacy-preserving outlier detection method on different kinds of variations which simulate various abnormal situations encountered in an IoT system: (**a**) measurements not matching with the reference histogram, (**b**) unusual data pattern with significant variations (spikes), (**c**) constant values reported by a faulty IoT smart meter, (**d**) data produced by a noisy IoT sensor, (**e**) noisy data exceeding the maximum value we have considered.

Determining the frequency threshold used at deciding if observations are outliers or not is crucial in ensuring a high detection precision. Overly high threshold values result in a larger number of bins being considered to contain outliers, increasing the number of false positives and thus lowering precision, while a low value of the threshold leads to a large number of false negative samples. Furthermore, the threshold value should also be selected according to the number of buckets in the histogram, as a large number of buckets implies lower frequencies inside buckets. Therefore, to determine an appropriate frequency threshold for detecting outliers, we performed a sensitivity analysis by varying the number of histogram buckets and frequency thresholds to evaluate how these parameters influence detection precision. Specifically, we computed precision scores for each combination and tried to identify the optimal match depending on the dataset, as shown in Figure 6 for data depicted in Figure 5b. Our analysis revealed that the precision generally decreases when both the number of buckets in the histogram and the threshold increase.

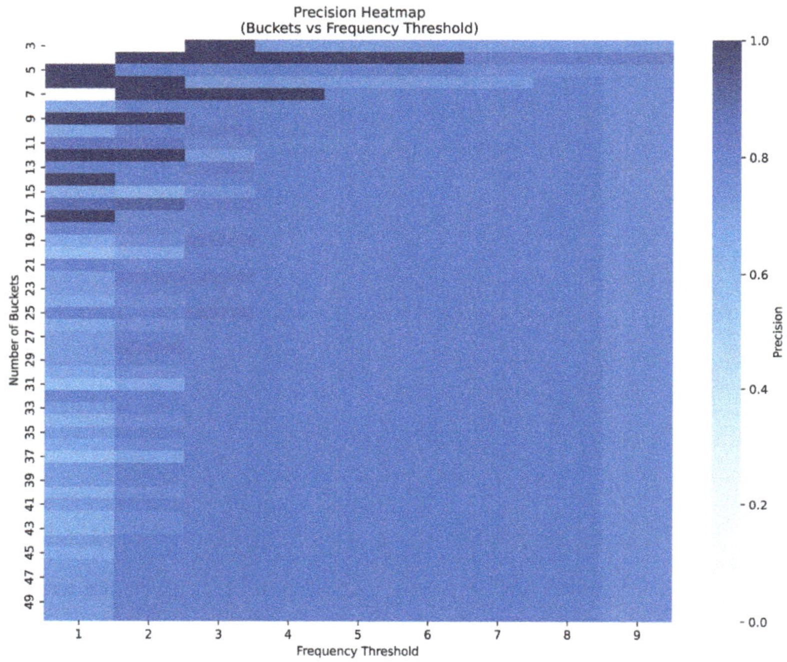

Figure 6. Sensitivity analysis of number of buckets and frequency threshold for data in Figure 5b.

Figure 5 depicts the results of our method on various types of variations, including real measurements from the IoT smart meter as well as artificially modified data representing several abnormal behaviors. As shown in Table 1, both the cryptographic and non-cryptographic methods detect the same number of outliers, indicating that our privacy-preserving histogram-based outlier detector achieves the same precision as the traditional method operating on raw data. The corresponding performance metrics for both the plaintext and cryptographic techniques are summarized in Table 2. However, it is important to note that the accuracy of the private histogram outlier detection technique heavily depends on the training data. When presented with data in ranges that have not been seen during training, the private histogram may produce errors or fail to detect certain outliers as expected.

In the following, we discuss and compare the complexity and execution time of our outlier detection solution for encrypted data considering three different configuration use cases depicted in Figure 7. The complexity of our configurations is determined in terms of basic operations, such as clear addition, encrypted addition, encrypted negation, and programmable bootstrap, which is used to reduce the amount of noise within the encrypted representation to allow performing multiple operations on the same encrypted operands. The relative complexity of the circuits gives a hint about which circuit is faster (lower complexity will determine a lower execution time), as presented in [44]. To ensure the relevance and reliability of the reported results, we conducted approximately five runs for each of the experiments described below. The execution times and operation counts reported for our histogram construction and outlier detection circuits represent the average values computed across these runs. However, the results across all runs showed minimal variance, with the computed values remaining consistently close.

Table 1. Comparison of outlier detection between non-cryptographic and cryptographic methods performance on various types of outliers.

Outlier Type (in Figure 5)	# Outliers in Dataset	# Normal Samples in Dataset	# Outliers Detected by Non-Cryptographic Method	# Outliers Detected by Cryptographic Method
Figure 5a	3	21	4	4
Figure 5b	12	12	9	9
Figure 5c	24	0	24	24
Figure 5d	22	2	14	14
Figure 5e	13	11	12	12

Table 2. Performance metrics of our outlier detection method.

Data (in Figure 5)	Precision $\frac{TP}{TP+FP}$	Recall $\frac{TP}{TP+FN}$	F1 Score $\frac{2\times Precition \times Recall}{Presicion+Recall}$
Figure 5a	0.75	1.0	0.86
Figure 5b	1.0	0.75	0.86
Figure 5c	1.0	1.0	1.0
Figure 5d	1.0	0.64	0.78
Figure 5e	1.0	0.92	0.96

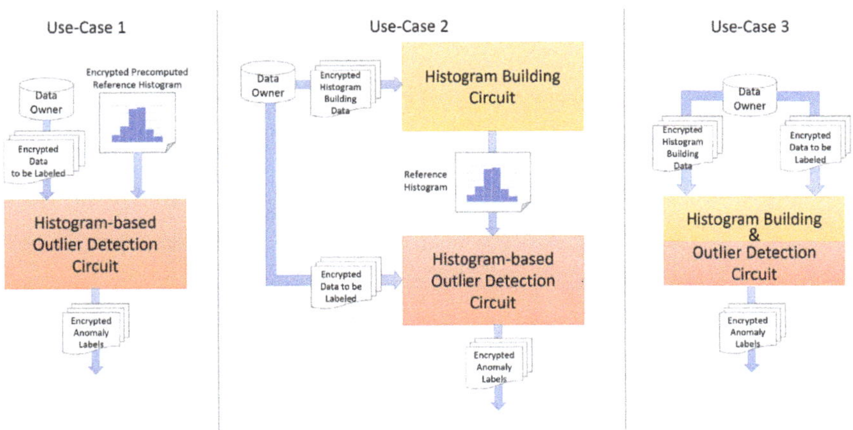

Figure 7. Configuration use cases for our outlier detection solution.

3.1. First Configuration Use Case (UC-1)

UC-1 assumes the availability of a previously computed histogram of IoT sensor data for the normal behavior of the device. This histogram, along with new IoT sensor data, serves as input for the outlier detection circuit. In this setup, the expected data variance over the selected time interval is a key factor. To account for this, we construct a reference histogram using hourly mean energy measurements recorded over several past days. UC-1 is designed to evaluate the outlier detection circuit independently, focusing on identifying outliers in encrypted data without addressing the construction of the data distribution.

In our evaluation, we aim to determine how the size of the plain input data samples affects the size of the encrypted inputs, results, and secret keys. As all the values used in computations are preprocessed to fit in $[0, 100]$, they can all be represented using 8 bits. Therefore, when computing the size of the plain inputs, we consider that the size of each value is 1 Byte. Thus, since the measurements are recorded on an hourly basis and each bucket is represented by a tuple containing three values, namely (low, high, count), the size of the clear inputs can be expressed, in bytes, as follows:

$$sizeof(Data) + sizeof(Histogram) + sizeof(threshold) = 24 \times \text{No. of days} + 3 \times \text{No. of buckets} + 1 \quad (9)$$

We measured the variation of the size of encrypted inputs, outputs, and secret keys with the size of the plain inputs, expressed as pairs of number of days considered, each containing 24 measurements, and the number of buckets in the reference histogram used to detect outliers. The actual size of the inputs, expressed in bytes, can be determined using relation 9. The size of the encrypted inputs is correlated to the size of the raw inputs, but the size of the encrypted data is considerably higher. The size of the encrypted output also increases with the size of plain inputs and depends only on the number of measurements to be labeled, as the module outputs an encrypted label associated with each input measurement. However, the size of the secret keys is not correlated with the size of input data, and it has the same order of magnitude, regardless of the size of the inputs. As depicted in Figure 8a, even if the size of the encrypted inputs increases almost linearly with the size of the clear inputs, the overhead introduced by the encryption is significant ($\times 10^6$).

The complexity of the model can be expressed in terms of operations performed during the outlier detection process. This complexity for UC-1 is highly dependent on the size of the input samples. As previously described, in our case, the length of the input is determined by the number of buckets in the histogram and the number of IoT data samples we want to process. We measured the variation of different types of operations with the size of the inputs. As expected, the number of operations performed increases when the size of the data input increases. However, since we propose an additive algorithm operating on encrypted data, encrypted addition is the most frequently performed operation. The number of programmable bootstrap operations, used to reduce the noise and to allow repeated computations on the same ciphertext, also significantly increases with the size of the inputs as the number of values that must be repeatedly operated on grows.

A synthetic view of the operation-based complexity variation is depicted in Figure 8b. We consider the total number of operations as a measure of the complexity of the model. In this global view, the complexity of our prototype in UC-1 doubles when either the number of buckets or the number of measurements doubles, resulting in an almost linear variation.

We evaluate the performance of our prototype by measuring the compile time, which is the time needed to train the model using a set of plain input samples, the time taken by the model to generate the keys, and the time taken to generate the encrypted labels associated with the input encrypted measurements. Figure 8c depicts the variation of all time components considered for UC-1 configuration, with the size of inputs. The time required for key generation is significantly lower than both the compilation and detection (execution) times. Meanwhile, compilation and detection times follow a similar pattern, increasing exponentially as the input size grows.

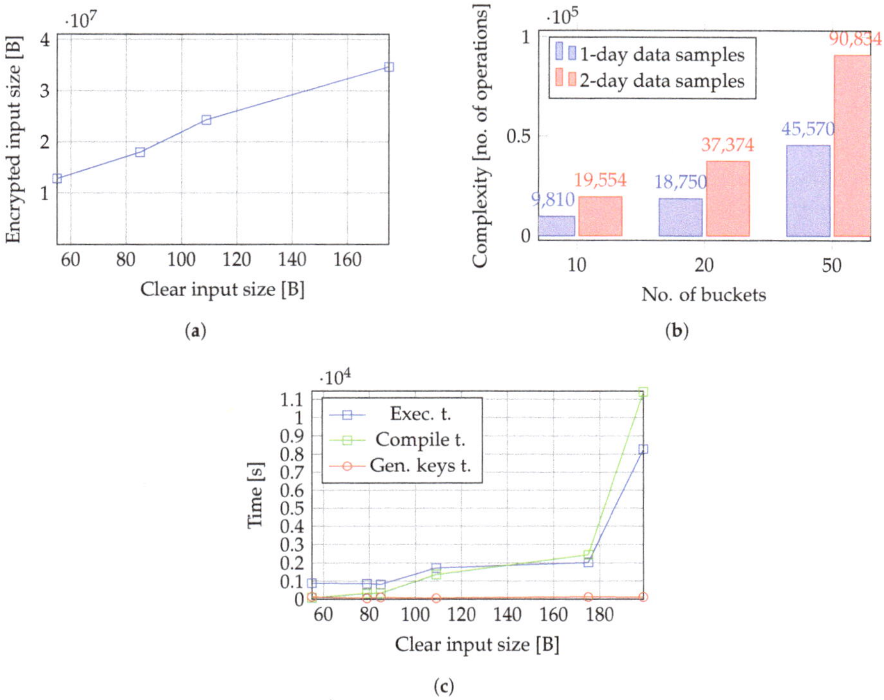

Figure 8. UC-1 configuration analysis: (**a**) correlation between the size of encrypted inputs and the size of clear inputs; (**b**) variation of complexity for different number of buckets and size of input data; (**c**) compile, execution, and key generation times variation with the size of the plain input data.

3.2. Second Configuration Use Case (UC-2)

UC-2 focuses on evaluating the histogram construction and outlier detection phases of our privacy-preserving solution. This approach ensures a more accurate representation of the data distribution, which may shift over time due to seasonality and other external factors. As a result, the reference histogram needs to be periodically updated. This histogram, along with the data to be labeled, is then fed into the outlier detection circuit. This use case allows for independent analysis of the two key phases in the proposed outlier detection process. Transferring the reference histogram between two circuits requires either decrypting and re-encrypting it with the second circuit's key or securely sharing encryption keys via a trusted third party. While the Concrete library supports storing keys on disk and loading them for use in another circuit, this method introduces potential security risks by exposing sensitive data, making it more vulnerable to exploitation.

We measured the complexity of both the histogram construction and outlier detection modules concerning the size of encrypted inputs, outputs, and secret keys. The encrypted input size is similar for both modules. However, the encrypted output size is significantly larger for the outlier detection circuit. This increase is due to its strong dependence on input size, as the output consists of encrypted binary labels corresponding to each input value. Furthermore, the encrypted input and output sizes of the outlier detection circuit are comparable to the input size in UC-1, as both use the same circuit. Given that 24 measurements are sampled per day and each bucket range is represented as a $(low, high)$ value pair, the size of the clear inputs for the histogram construction phase can be expressed as follows:

$$sizeof(DataRef) + sizeof(BucketsRange) = 24 \times \text{No. of days} + 2 \times \text{No. of buckets} \tag{10}$$

The size of the plain inputs of the outlier detection phase is equal to the size of the inputs in UC-1 (see (9)). The overhead introduced by encrypting the inputs is around $\times 10^6$ in the case of both circuits in UC-2, as Figure 9 shows. The relationship between encrypted and plain input sizes is linear for the histogram construction prototype and nearly linear for the outlier detection prototype.

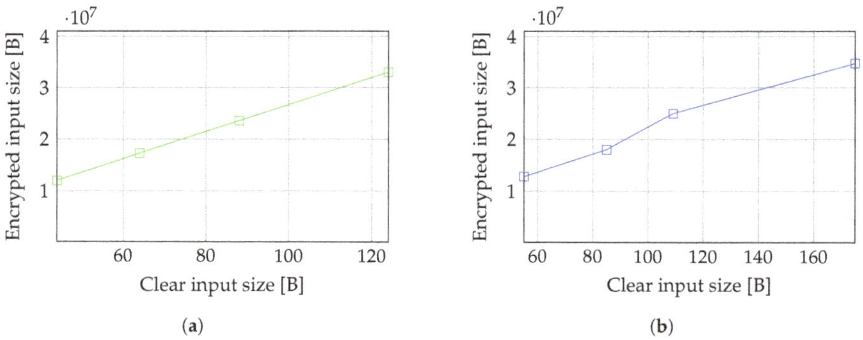

Figure 9. Correlation of encrypted input size with the size of clear inputs for both histogram building and outlier detection phases in UC-2: (**a**) histogram building phase encrypted input size, (**b**) outlier detection phase encrypted input size.

We evaluated the operation-based complexity of both models, displaying the number of operations of each type performed by each circuit. Similar to UC-1, encrypted addition is the most frequent operation, as both circuits rely primarily on vectorial addition. While the total number of operations is higher during the outlier detection phase leading to increased circuit complexity, it remains comparable to the complexity of the model in UC-1. As shown in Figure 10, the operational complexity of both circuits, as well as the total number of operations performed in our prototype circuits for UC-2, approximately doubles when either the size of the data to be labeled or the number of buckets doubles. However, running the models in UC-2 with a 50-bucket histogram and two full days of data samples proved infeasible in our experimental setup, as it required excessive computation time and exceeded the available processing power.

The performance of the circuits in UC-2 in terms of compile (training), generating keys, and building histogram or outlier detection time is synthetically presented Figure 10. The compile time is considerably lower for the histogram building prototype, while the time taken to generate the keys and the execution (building histogram or outlier detection) time are comparable between the two circuits.

The execution time generally increases with the size of inputs and, implicitly, with the number of operations performed on input values. However, for both histogram building and outlier detection circuits, the execution time and key generating time shows a local minimum when the size of inputs is $(\#days, \#buckets) = (2, 20)$, as depicted in Figure 11, while, in the case of training (compile) time, the local minimum is encountered at an input of size $(\#days, \#buckets) = (2, 10)$.

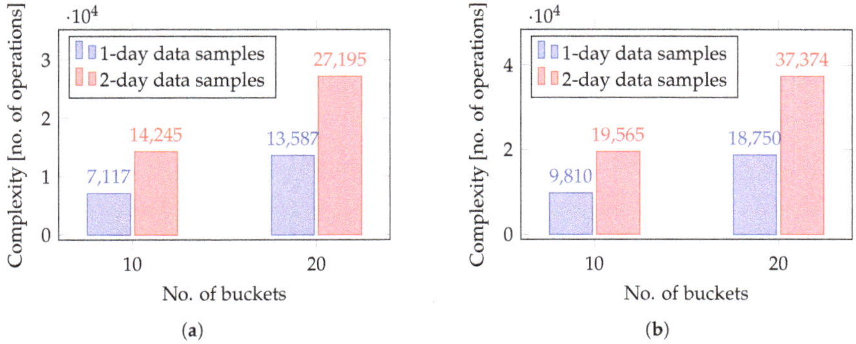

Figure 10. Variation of complexity in configuration UC-2 for different number of buckets and size of input data: (**a**) histogram building phase operation complexity, (**b**) outlier detection phase operation complexity.

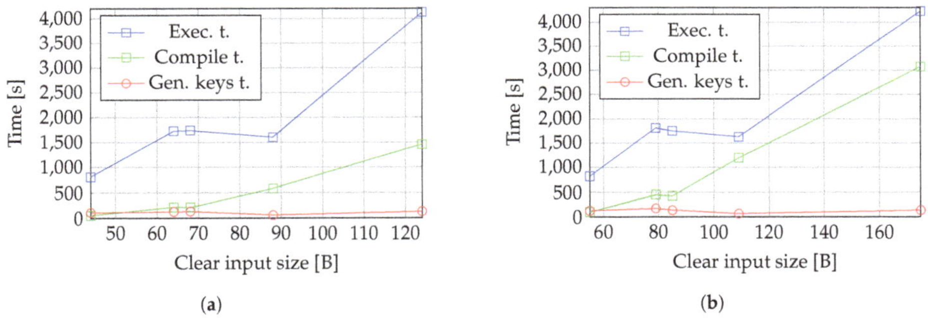

Figure 11. Variation of execution time, compile time, and key generation time for both histogram building and outlier detection phases of UC-2 with the size of the plain input data: (**a**) histogram building phase time variation, (**b**) outlier detection phase time variation.

3.3. Third Use Case (UC-3)

UC-3 aims to increase the security of the overall process by computing the histogram and detecting outliers using the same circuit. However, this results in a higher complexity of the circuit and slower execution. In this scenario, the global complexity of the technique is evaluated.

As in UC-1 and UC-2, the complexity of the model regarding the size of encrypted inputs increases with the size of data, while the size of the encrypted outputs is influenced only by the number of buckets in the equi-width histogram. However, as more operations are performed in the model that we define in UC-3, we notice a slight increase in the size of secret keys compared to the size of secret keys generated in UC-1 and UC-2. The total size of the inputs is expressed for UC-3 in a totally similar way to the size of inputs corresponding to UC-1 and UC-2 (see relations (9) and (10)). As in UC-2, performing experiments on a 50-bucket histogram using 2-full-days data samples is not feasible in UC-3.

Since in UC-3, we compute the reference histogram and detect outliers using a single model, the size of inputs is considerably higher than in the case of circuits defined in UC-1 and

UC-2. Therefore, the overhead introduced by encrypting the inputs is even higher than in UC-1 and UC-2, reaching an increase of almost $\times 2 \cdot 10^6$ in the size of inputs, as shown in Figure 12a.

Integrating both the histogram building and outlier detection phases into the same model, as defined in UC-3, increases the computational complexity of the circuit. This results in higher overall complexity due to the greater number of operations performed. The number of operations of each type performed by our prototype in UC-3 is roughly the sum of the operations from the circuits that separately handle histogram construction and outlier detection in UC-2. Consequently, the complexity of the circuit used in UC-3 provides a comprehensive view of the overall complexity of the proposed privacy-preserving outlier detection technique.

Similar to UC-1 and UC-2, the effect of the number of samples to be labeled and the number of buckets in the reference histogram on the model's operation count is consistent. As shown in Figure 12b, doubling both the number of data samples and the number of buckets results in models with comparable operational complexity.

We measured the time variation of the model in UC-3 relative to input size. Although the circuit in UC-3 is a combination of the two circuits from UC-2, the compile time, key generation time, and execution time of the UC-3 circuit do not simply add up to the sum of the corresponding times for the two individual circuits in UC-2. The execution and compile time for UC-3 follow the same pattern as the corresponding time components in UC-2. A local minimum can be identified for an input size of $(\#days, \#ofbuckets) = (2, 10)$ for this prototype, as depicted in Figure 12c. However, taking into consideration the high complexity of the model in terms of both input size and number of operations, the training and execution (i.e., histogram construction and outlier detection) are slower than in UC-1 and UC-2.

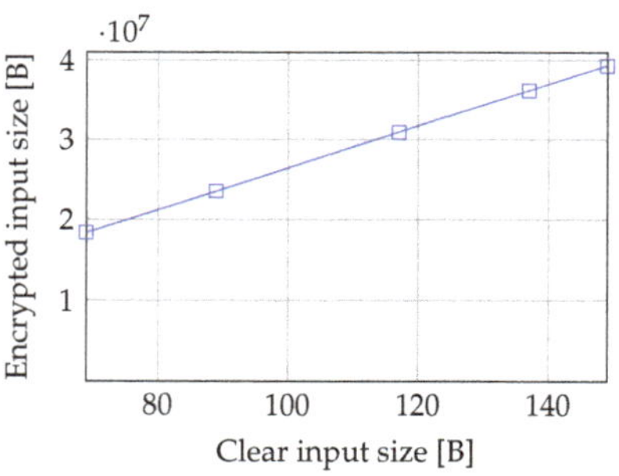

(a)

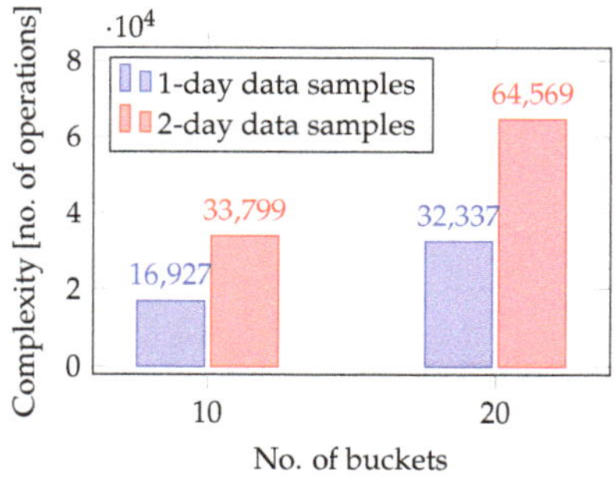

(b)

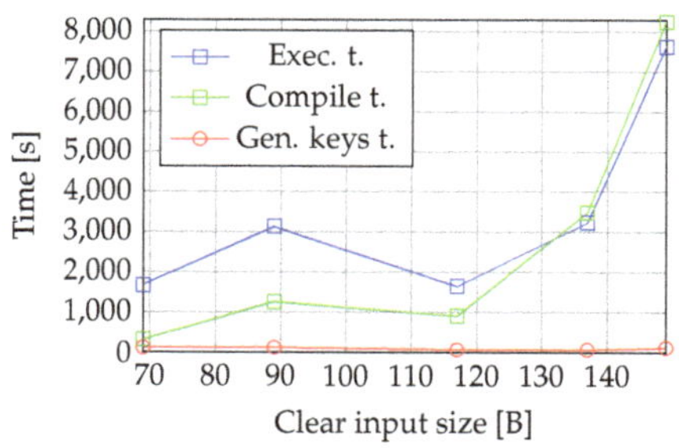

(c)

Figure 12. UC-3 configuration analysis: (**a**) correlation between the size of encrypted inputs and the size of clear inputs; (**b**) variation of complexity for different number of buckets and size of input data; (**c**) compile, execution, and key generation times variation with the size of the plain input data.

4. Conclusions

In this paper, we introduce a solution for building equi-width histograms and detecting outliers on homomorphically encrypted data generated by IoT devices. To address constraints such as the limited set of operations that can be performed on encrypted data, we leverage the TFHE scheme implemented in Concrete, a fully homomorphic encryption variant optimized for practical applications. Our approach incorporates a redesigned histogram-based technique tailored for encrypted IoT data streams, enabling the detection of sensor readings that statistically deviate from previous measurements and are therefore considered anomalous. We have implemented the main operations of the equi-width histograms' outlier detection algorithm adapted for the TFHE homomorphic encryption scheme. The customization involves vectorizing additive operations, value placement in buckets, and labeling abnormal buckets based on a threshold frequency.

The proposed solution effectively constructs histograms and detects outliers on fully homomorphic encrypted data streams without decryption. While operations on encrypted numbers introduce significant execution overhead, they remain practical for offline processing. Labelling 24 to 48 sensor measurements can take minutes to hours, depending on input size and histogram complexity. Communication between the client and outlier detector is minimal, and deploying the detector closer to the edge reduces cloud traffic. The experiments were conducted in a laboratory setting using standard hardware. The proposed solution's performance in an actual deployment still needs to be investigated, as in real-world conditions, it may be affected by more limited memory capacity, lower processing power, and stricter energy constraints typical of edge computing nodes.

Using the TFHE scheme and Concrete library offers advantages such as encrypted data operations, ready-to-deploy circuits, and efficient key management. However, limitations persist, including restrictions on computational depth, arithmetic precision, and function complexity. Errors may arise due to reliance on precomputed lookup tables, but these are generally less impactful than potential IoT sensor noise.

Processing encrypted IoT data is constrained by computational overhead, requiring careful data scaling to fit within limited bit representations. Vectorial operations offer a more flexible alternative to iterative methods. Our experiments used small integer values (8-bit) to ensure feasible outlier detection configurations.

Lastly, designing computations on encrypted data is rigid. Changes in input size or operations necessitate circuit recompilation and model retraining, which can take several hours. More complex algorithms result in larger, costlier circuits, increasing execution time.

While encrypted data processing introduces additional execution time and homomorphic encryption imposes constraints on operation size and precision, these trade-offs are inherent to secure computation. Additionally, adapting to changes in input size or operations requires recompilation and retraining, which may limit flexibility. However, our solution remains highly effective for constructing cryptographic equi-width histograms on homomorphically encrypted data and can be successfully applied to IoT data outlier detection, ensuring compliance with data protection regulations. The promising results highlight its potential for advancing privacy-preserving analytics.

Author Contributions: Conceptualization, D.L., A.H. and T.C.; methodology, A.H. and T.C.; software, D.L.; validation, D.L. and A.H.; data curation, D.L.; writing—original draft preparation, D.L., A.H. and T.C.; writing—review and editing, D.L., A.H. and T.C.; visualization, D.L., A.H. and T.C.; supervision, A.H. and T.C.; project administration, T.C.; funding acquisition, T.C. All authors have read and agreed to the published version of the manuscript.

Funding: This research received funding from the European Union's Horizon Europe research and innovation program under the Grant Agreement number 101136216. Views and opinions expressed are, however, those of the author(s) only and do not necessarily reflect those of the European Union or the European Climate, Infrastructure, and Environment Executive Agency. Neither the European Union nor the granting authority can be held responsible for them.

Data Availability Statement: The original contributions presented in this study are included in the article. Further inquiries can be directed to the corresponding author.

Conflicts of Interest: The authors declare no conflicts of interest.

Abbreviations

The following abbreviations are used in this manuscript:

TFHE	Fully Homomorphic Encryption over the Torus
IoT	Internet of Things
LWE	Learning With Errors

References

1. Soori, M.; Arezoo, B.; Dastres, R. Internet of things for smart factories in industry 4.0, a review. *Internet Things Cyber-Phys. Syst.* **2023**, *3*, 192–204. [CrossRef]
2. Villegas-Ch, W.; Govea, J.; Jaramillo-Alcazar, A. Iot anomaly detection to strengthen cybersecurity in the critical infrastructure of smart cities. *Appl. Sci.* **2023**, *13*, 10977. [CrossRef]
3. Diraco, G.; Rescio, G.; Caroppo, A.; Manni, A.; Leone, A. Human action recognition in smart living services and applications: Context awareness, data availability, personalization, and privacy. *Sensors* **2023**, *23*, 6040. [CrossRef]
4. Farrokhi, A.; Farahbakhsh, R.; Rezazadeh, J.; Minerva, R. Application of Internet of Things and artificial intelligence for smart fitness: A survey. *Comput. Netw.* **2021**, *189*, 107859. [CrossRef]
5. Diro, A.; Kaisar, S.; Vasilakos, A.V.; Anwar, A.; Nasirian, A.; Olani, G. Anomaly detection for space information networks: A survey of challenges, techniques, and future directions. *Comput. Secur.* **2024**, *139*, 103705. [CrossRef]
6. Li, C.; Wang, J.; Wang, S.; Zhang, Y. A review of IoT applications in healthcare. *Neurocomputing* **2024**, *565*, 127017. [CrossRef]
7. Mousavi, H.; Zaniolo, C. Fast and accurate computation of equi-depth histograms over data streams. In Proceedings of the 14th International Conference on Extending Database Technology, Uppsala, Sweden, 21–24 March 2011; pp. 69–80.
8. Goldstein, M.; Dengel, A. Histogram-based outlier score (hbos): A fast unsupervised anomaly detection algorithm. *KI-2012 Poster Demo Track* **2012**, *1*, 59–63.
9. Ge, L.; Parhi, K.K. Robust clustering using hyperdimensional computing. *IEEE Open J. Circuits Syst.* **2024**, *5*, 102–116. [CrossRef]
10. Yuan, H.; Cong, G.; Li, G. Nuhuo: An effective estimation model for traffic speed histogram imputation on a road network. *Proc. VLDB Endow.* **2024**, *17*, 1605–1617. [CrossRef]
11. Sasi, T.; Lashkari, A.H.; Lu, R.; Xiong, P.; Iqbal, S. A comprehensive survey on IoT attacks: Taxonomy, detection mechanisms and challenges. *J. Inf. Intell.* **2024**, *2*, 455–513. [CrossRef]
12. Cunningham, T.; Cormode, G.; Ferhatosmanoglu, H. Privacy-preserving synthetic location data in the real world. In Proceedings of the 17th International Symposium on Spatial and Temporal Databases, Online, 23–25 August 2021; pp. 23–33.
13. Waites, C.; Cummings, R. Differentially private normalizing flows for privacy-preserving density estimation. In Proceedings of the 2021 AAAI/ACM Conference on AI, Ethics, and Society, Virtual, 19–21 May 2021; pp. 1000–1009.
14. Cai, Z.; Zheng, X.; Wang, J.; He, Z. Private data trading towards range counting queries in internet of things. *IEEE Trans. Mob. Comput.* **2022**, *22*, 4881–4897. [CrossRef]
15. Tosa, A.; Hangan, A.; Sebestyen, G.; István, Z. In-Storage Computation of Histograms with differential privacy. In Proceedings of the 2021 International Conference on Field-Programmable Technology (ICFPT), Auckland, New Zealand, 6–10 December 2021; IEEE: Piscataway, NJ, USA, 2021; pp. 1–4.
16. Lebeda, C.J.; Tetek, J. Better differentially private approximate histograms and heavy hitters using the Misra-Gries sketch. In Proceedings of the 42nd ACM SIGMOD-SIGACT-SIGAI Symposium on Principles of Database Systems, Seattle, WA, USA, 18–23 June 2023; pp. 79–88.
17. Wang, X.; Mo, L.; Zheng, X.; Dang, Z. Streaming Histogram Publication Over Weighted Sliding Windows Under Differential Privacy. *Tsinghua Sci. Technol.* **2024**, *29*, 1674–1693. [CrossRef]

18. Bell, J.; Gascon, A.; Ghazi, B.; Kumar, R.; Manurangsi, P.; Raykova, M.; Schoppmann, P. Distributed, private, sparse histograms in the two-server model. In Proceedings of the 2022 ACM SIGSAC Conference on Computer and Communications Security, Los Angeles, CA, USA, 7–11 November 2022; pp. 307–321.
19. Braun, L.; Gascón, A.; Raykova, M.; Schoppmann, P.; Seth, K. Malicious security for sparse private histograms. *Cryptology ePrint Archive* **2024**.
20. Liebenow, J.; Imort, T.; Fuchs, Y.; Heisel, M.; Käding, N.; Rupp, J.; Mohammadi, E. PrivAgE: A Toolchain for Privacy-Preserving Distributed Aggregation on Edge-Devices. *KI-Künstl. Intell.* **2024**, *38*, 183–188. [CrossRef]
21. Su, Y.; Li, J.; Li, J.; Su, Z.; Meng, W.; Yin, H.; Lu, R. Robust and lightweight data aggregation with histogram estimation in edge-cloud systems. *IEEE Trans. Netw. Sci. Eng.* **2024**, *11*, 2864–2875. [CrossRef]
22. Shrestha, R.; Kim, S. Integration of IoT with blockchain and homomorphic encryption: Challenging issues and opportunities. In *Advances in Computers*; Elsevier: Amsterdam, The Netherlands, 2019; Volume 115, pp. 293–331.
23. Zhang, C.; Yin, A.; Zuo, W.; Chen, Y. Privacy preserving anomaly detection based on local density estimation. *Math. Biosci. Eng.* **2020**, *17*, 3478–3497. [CrossRef]
24. Alabdulatif, A.; Kumarage, H.; Khalil, I.; Yi, X. Privacy-preserving anomaly detection in cloud with lightweight homomorphic encryption. *J. Comput. Syst. Sci.* **2017**, *90*, 28–45. [CrossRef]
25. Chen, S.; Susilo, W.; Zhang, Y.; Yang, B.; Zhang, M. Privacy-preserving anomaly counting for time-series data in edge-assisted crowdsensing. *Comput. Stand. Interfaces* **2023**, *85*, 103707. [CrossRef]
26. Li, R.; Ishimaki, Y.; Yamana, H. Fully homomorphic encryption with table lookup for privacy-preserving smart grid. In Proceedings of the 2019 IEEE International Conference on Smart Computing (SMARTCOMP), Washington, DC, USA, 12–15 June 2019; IEEE: Piscataway, NJ, USA, 2019; pp. 19–24.
27. Itokazu, K.; Wang, L.; Ozawa, S. Outlier Detection by Privacy-Preserving Ensemble Decision Tree U sing Homomorphic Encryption. In Proceedings of the 2021 International Joint Conference on Neural Networks (IJCNN), Virtual, 18–22 July 2021; IEEE: Piscataway, NJ, USA, 2021; pp. 1–7.
28. Bourse, F.; Sanders, O.; Traoré, J. Improved secure integer comparison via homomorphic encryption. In Proceedings of the Cryptographers' Track at the RSA Conference, San Francisco, CA, USA, 24–28 February 2020; Springer: Berlin/Heidelberg, Germany, 2020; pp. 391–416.
29. Babenko, M.; Golimblevskaia, E. Euclidean division method for the homomorphic scheme ckks. In Proceedings of the 2021 IEEE Conference of Russian Young Researchers in Electrical and Electronic Engineering (ElConRus), St. Petersburg, Moscow, Russia, 26–29 January 2021; IEEE: Piscataway, NJ, USA, 2021; pp. 217–220.
30. Zhang, L.; Li, C.; Hu, Q.; Lang, J.; Huang, S.; Hu, L.; Leng, J.; Chen, Q.; Lv, C. Enhancing privacy in large language model with homomorphic encryption and sparse attention. *Appl. Sci.* **2023**, *13*, 13146. [CrossRef]
31. Li, R.; Bhattacharjee, S.; Das, S.K.; Yamana, H. Look-up table based FHE system for privacy preserving anomaly detection in smart grids. In Proceedings of the 2022 IEEE International Conference on Smart Computing (SMARTCOMP), Helsinki, Finland, 20–24 June 2022; IEEE: Piscataway, NJ, USA, 2022; pp. 108–115.
32. Shen, M.; Tang, X.; Zhu, L.; Du, X.; Guizani, M. Privacy-preserving support vector machine training over blockchain-based encrypted IoT data in smart cities. *IEEE Internet Things J.* **2019**, *6*, 7702–7712. [CrossRef]
33. Zama. What Is Concrete? 2024. Available online: https://docs.zama.ai/concrete/ (accessed on 19 February 2024).
34. Chillotti, I.; Gama, N.; Georgieva, M.; Izabachène, M. TFHE: Fast fully homomorphic encryption over the torus. *J. Cryptol.* **2020**, *33*, 34–91. [CrossRef]
35. Ioannidis, Y. The history of histograms (abridged). In Proceedings of the 2003 VLDB Conference, Berlin, Germany, 9-12 September 2003; Elsevier: Amsterdam, The Netherlands, 2003; pp. 19–30.
36. Microsoft. Microsoft SEAL. 2024. Available online: https://github.com/Microsoft/SEAL?tab=readme-ov-file (accessed on 19 February 2024).
37. Brakerski, Z.; Gentry, C.; Vaikuntanathan, V. (Leveled) fully homomorphic encryption without bootstrapping. *ACM Trans. Comput. Theory (TOCT)* **2014**, *6*, 1–36. [CrossRef]
38. Cheon, J.H.; Kim, A.; Kim, M.; Song, Y. Homomorphic encryption for arithmetic of approximate numbers. In Proceedings of the Advances in Cryptology—ASIACRYPT 2017: 23rd International Conference on the Theory and Applications of Cryptology and Information Security, Hong Kong, China, 3–7 December 2017; Proceedings, Part i 23; Springer: Berlin/Heidelberg, Germany, 2017; pp. 409–437.
39. Fan, J.; Vercauteren, F. Somewhat practical fully homomorphic encryption. *Cryptology ePrint Archive* **2012**.
40. Concrete. Composition. 2024. Available online: https://docs.zama.ai/concrete/2.5/tutorials/composition (accessed on 19 February 2024).
41. Concrete. Floating Points. 2024. Available online: https://docs.zama.ai/concrete/explanations/advanced-features/floating_points (accessed on 19 February 2024).

42. HEADpy. HEADpy. 2024. Available online: https://github.com/dragoslazea/HEADpy (accessed on 22 March 2024).
43. De Mulder, C. 2021 Electricity and Heat Demand Data for a City District (Belgium). Zenodo, Published 20 January 2022. Available online: https://zenodo.org/records/5155659 (accessed on 19 February 2024).
44. Concrete. Depth and Complexity of Circuit. 2024. Available online: https://community.zama.ai/t/depth-and-complexity-of-circuit/485 (accessed on 19 February 2024).

future internet

MDPI

Article

Federated XAI IDS: An Explainable and Safeguarding Privacy Approach to Detect Intrusion Combining Federated Learning and SHAP †

Kazi Fatema [1,*], Samrat Kumar Dey [2], Mehrin Anannya [1], Risala Tasin Khan [1], Mohammad Mamunur Rashid [2], Chunhua Su [3,*] and Rashed Mazumder [1,*]

1 Institute of Information Technology, Jahangirnagar University, Dhaka 1342, Bangladesh; mehrin.anannya@juniv.edu (M.A.); risala@juniv.edu (R.T.K.)
2 School of Science & Technology, Bangladesh Open University, Gazipur 1705, Bangladesh; samrat.sst@bou.ac.bd (S.K.D.); mamunur@bou.ac.bd (M.M.R.)
3 Graduate School of Computer Science and Engineering, University of Aizu, Aizuwakamatsu 965-8580, Fukushima Prefecture, Japan
* Correspondence: kazifatema1975@gmail.com (K.F.); chsu@u-aizu.ac.jp (C.S.); rmiit@juniv.edu (R.M.)

† This article is an extended version of the preliminary version that was presented on the 2nd International Conference on Data Security and Privacy Protection, Xi'an, China, 25–28 October 2024. Fatema, Kazi, Mehrin Anannya, Samrat Kumar Dey, Chunhua Su, and Rashed Mazumder. Securing Networks: A Deep Learning Approach with Explainable AI (XAI) and Federated Learning for Intrusion Detection. In *International Conference on Data Security and Privacy Protection* Springer Nature Singapore: Singapore, 2024; pp. 260–275.

Abstract: An intrusion detection system (IDS) is a crucial element in cyber security concerns. IDS is a safeguarding module that is designed to identify unauthorized activities in network environments. The importance of constructing IDSs has never been this significant with the growing number of attacks on network layers. This research work was intended to draw the attention of the authors to a different aspect of intrusion detection, considering privacy and the contribution of the features on attack classes. At present, the majority of the existing IDSs are designed based on centralized infrastructure, which raises serious concerns about security as the network data from one system are exposed to another system. This act of sharing the original network data with another server can worsen the current arrangement of protecting privacy within the network. In addition, the existing IDS models are merely a tool for identifying the attack categories without analyzing a further emphasis of the network feature on the attacks. In this article, we propose a novel framework, FEDXAIIDS, converging federated learning and explainable AI. The proposed approach enables IDS models to be collaboratively trained across multiple decentralized devices while ensuring that local data remain securely on edge nodes, thus mitigating privacy risks. The primary objectives of the proposed study are to reveal the privacy concerns of centralized systems and identify the most significant features to comprehend the contribution of the features to the final output. Our proposed model was designed, fusing federated learning (FL) with Shapley additive explanations (SHAPs), using an artificial neural network (ANN) as a local model. The framework has a server device and four client devices that have their own data set on their end. The server distributes the primary model constructed using an ANN among the local clients. Next, the local clients train their individual part of the data set, deploying the distributed model from the server, and they share their feedback with the central end. The central end then incorporates an aggregator model named FedAvg to assemble the separate results from the clients into one output. At last, the contribution of the ten most significant features is evaluated by incorporating SHAP. The entire research work was executed on CICIoT2023. The data set was partitioned into four parts and distributed among the four local ends. The proposed method demonstrated efficacy in intrusion detection, achieving 88.4% training and

88.2% testing accuracy. Furthermore, UDP has been found to be the most significant feature of the network layer from the SHAP analysis. Simultaneously, the incorporation of federated learning has ensured the safeguarding of the confidentiality of the network information of the individual ends. This enhances transparency and ensures that the model is both reliable and interpretable. Federated XAI IDS effectively addresses privacy concerns and feature interpretability issues in modern IDS frameworks, contributing to the advancement of secure, interpretable, and decentralized intrusion detection systems. Our findings accelerate the development of cyber security solutions that leverage federated learning and explainable AI (XAI), paving the way for future research and practical implementations in real-world network security environments.

Keywords: cyber security; FedXAIIDS (Federated Explainable IDS); intrusion detection system (IDS); XAI (explainable AI); Shapley additive explanation (SHAP); ANN

1. Introduction

In the digital age, cyber security—the practice of safeguarding frameworks, networks, and confidential data from unwelcome inspection, distress, and emerging cyber hazards [1]—has become an essential battle line. Since people, organizations, and governments grow more interconnected and dependent on digital infrastructure, it is crucial to guarantee data availability, confidentiality, and integrity. In order to safeguard their valuable assets and lower risks, companies need to proactively create multilayer protection measures in response to evolving cyber threats. Within the ever-changing field of cyber security, safeguarding private data from a continuously increasing spectrum of cyber attacks is essential. In order to discover and prevent undesirable activity in network traffic, intrusion detection systems (IDS) are essential. They are the first line of defense against malicious attacks. An intrusion detection system (IDS) scans over malicious activity or unauthorized access through analysis of traffic dynamics, applications and session behavior, and signature-based features [2]. By emphasizing anomalies and recognized attack patterns, IDS alerts help organizations promptly address possible security risks.

In this new age of interconnected world, approximately 50% of startups disclose experiencing information theft, underscoring the urgency of robust IDS solutions in institutional security frameworks [3]. The integration of deep learning (DL) and machine learning (ML) along with IDS has acquired substantial traction due to their superior classification accuracy. Nonetheless, conventional machine learning-based intrusion detection systems encounter considerable privacy and security vulnerabilities, owing to their dependence on centralized data storage and transmission [4]. Additionally, The challenges of developing effective IDS systems include the substantial quantity of network information and the prevalence of imbalanced data sets, where minor yet critical attack types are often underrepresented [5]. The current advances in deep learning, particularly the use of the transformer technique, have demonstrated significant potential in identifying anomalies and interpreting the order for advanced performance in decoding complicated patterns [6], which significantly prevents complicated network intrusion in IDS.

However, there are serious concerns regarding confidentiality, with the use of deep learning-based IDS frameworks, especially when models are trained using private network traffic data. These issues can be effectively addressed via federated learning (FL), which permits for decentralized coordinated infrastructure refinement while maintaining the privacy and security of confidential information [7]. This research introduces a federated learning-based intrusion detection system that employs artificial neural networks as the local-end prediction system and incorporates Shapley additive explanations in order to enhance comprehensibility. The decentralized training approach guarantees confidentiality while facilitating visibility in detecting threats to networks. This piece of literature is the expanded version of the initial manuscript previously laid out in [8].

Explainable artificial intelligence (XAI) has significantly enhanced intrusion detection systems (IDSs) by providing accountability, understanding, and integrity in decision-making. Traditional IDS models, particularly those based on deep learning, frequently function as "black boxes", complicating security analysts' understanding of their predictions. Shapley additive explanations (SHAPs) have emerged as a powerful XAI approach, offering feature attribution scores that elucidate the influence of different input characteristics on the conclusions of the models. Employing SHAP in intrusion detection systems aids researchers and practitioners in identifying significant attack patterns, reducing false positives, and enhancing model robustness. Research, including [9], demonstrates that SHAP provides equitable and consistent feature importance ratings, making it an ideal method for enhancing the interpretability of IDS. Moreover, SHAP facilitates feature selection and optimization, hence enhancing generalization and efficiency in IDSs that are constructed deploying FL, where privacy preservation is paramount [10]. Utilizing SHAP in FL-based IDS confidentiality security insights while safeguarding raw data, hence maintaining user privacy and delivering actionable knowledge for cyber defense.

The CICIoT2023 data set [11], a real-world data set with contemporary attack types, has been used for experiments. The system's performance and generalizability in a range of intrusion scenarios, as well as its capacity to identify known and new network threats, have been the main areas of focus. In addition, the integration of explainable artificial intelligence (XAI) techniques, particularly SHAP, will provide essential transparency within the IDS framework. This comprehensibality constitutes an essential towards instilling assurance in AI-driven frameworks, specifically when legal and regulatory compliance is a factor in the deployment of network security solutions.

In this study, an artificial neural network (ANN) is incorporated as the local framework, as it is capable of adopting complicated, non-linear relationships within the high dimensional feature that is the nature of network traffic. Other ML frameworks such as support vector machines (SVMs), decision trees (DTs), and convolutional neural networks (CNNs) have been incorporated into IDS. However, several studies have demonstrated comparatively higher success rate in various IDS benchmarks [12]. On the other hand, SVM model can be impressively effective on high-dimensional spaces but can produce high computational costs for larger data sets, and it can struggle with highly complicated patterns compared to an ANN [13]. Though decision trees are interpretable frameworks, they can be vulnerable to overfitting and struggle with complicated trends like ANNs [14]. Furthermore, CNN models excel in handling spatial data, and they have been incorporated into IDS for transforming network traffic into image representations. However, ANNs, specifically RNNs and their classifications and feedforward neural networks, can perform more effectively than CNNs [15]. Moreover, we chose to incorporate a basic ANN into our proposed FEDXAIIDS to balance the computational complexity of the framework with training efficiency in a distributed system.

Additionally, we incorporated the CICIoT2023 data set, as it provides large coverage on attack classes extracted from a real-life IoT scenario [11]. This data set is more updated than the earlier edition of the IDS data set, CICIDS2017 and CICIDS2018, which did not encounter particular IoT attacks that may have represented the IoT network more accurately [16]. On the other hand, ToN-IoT did not cover the same margin of the device to enlist the attacks [17]. Thus, we came to the decision to use CICIoT2023 for our proposed architecture.

The new study builds on the foundations laid by focusing on explainable AI and federated learning, while the earlier work concentrated on these conventional approaches. The goal is to improve the privacy, efficacy, and interpretability of IDS solutions. This research builds upon prior work with the CIC_IDS_2018 data set, where the challenge of imbalanced data sets was addressed by developing an IDS using balanced data and exploring unorthodox categorization methods incorporating the Dendritic Cell Algorithm (DCA) [18].

In order to improve transparency and interpretability and facilitate a more thorough comprehension of model decisions, explainable artificial intelligence (XAI) approaches can be incorporated into the IDS framework. By elucidating the reasoning behind certain results, this transparency contributes to the development of trust in AI-driven frameworks, which is crucial for fulfilling legal and regulatory obligations.

This research attempts to tackle important network security issues by designing and deploying a sophisticated intrusion detection system (IDS) that integrates explainable artificial intelligence (XAI), federated learning (FL), and machine learning (ML). This study aims to achieve the following goals:

1. To assess the efficacy of an intrusion detection system utilizing cutting-edge machine learning methodologies, federated learning for decentralized training, and explainable artificial intelligence for enhanced interpretability and transparency.
2. To minimize computational overhead by utilizing federated learning, which allows decentralized data processing and eliminates the need for central data aggregation.
3. To reduce the dangers of single points of failure and centralized data breaches by implementing a distributed, node-based architecture in federated learning.
4. To ensure the reliability and trustworthiness of IDS predictions by employing explainable AI, which provides insights into model decisions and fosters greater user trust in automated systems.

This research work was structured in the following manner: Section 2 highlights relevant research on XAI, federated learning, and IDS. Section 3 details the proposed methodology, including model architecture and SHAP-based interpretability. Section 4 discusses the experimental setup, along with the results and analysis. Section 5 discusses key findings, and Section 6 finishes with contributions and future study directions.

2. Literature Review

This section analyzes a number of significant research works that paved the way for the proposed framework. The growing popularity of Internet of Things (IoT) networks has generated considerable security concerns, prompting the creation of effective IDSs. Recent improvements in FL represent a viable approach, facilitating decentralized learning while safeguarding data privacy. This section examines current research initiatives that combine FL with DL. Several research works and their limitations with performance evaluation of the federated learning based architecture have been presented in the Table 1.

Table 1. A tabular representation of the FL-based infrastructure and its corresponding challenges.

Authors	FL Technique Used (Yes/No)	Framework	Limitation	Performance Evaluation
Sinh-Ngoc et al. [19]	No	Employed CNN architecture for categorization.	This study entirely focused on detecting only the DoS type of malicious activities	Achieved a 99.8% detection rate.
Bertoli et al. [20]	Yes	Constructed a multilayered autonomous FL architecture that integrates an autoencoder with an energy flow classifier, enabling enhanced feature extraction and classification performance while maintaining privacy in a distributed learning environment.	A new privacy concern was generated	90% success rate on CICIDS2018.
Toldinas et al. [21]	No	The initial processing technique that combines a predetermined number of network flow feature records. Three independent ML methodologies, federated transfer learning, traditional transfer learning, and federated learning, were used on NIDS, employing deep learning for image classification.	Focused on detecting DDoS attack	99.7% success rate.
Markovic et al. [22]	Yes	Implemented a federated learning (FL) model that utilizes the shared model incorporating RF, enabling learning across multiple consumers collaboratively while safeguarding the privacy of information.	This framework does not perform well while implemented on an entire data set	91.7% accurateness on CICIDS2017
Lazzarini et al. [23]	Yes	Developed an IDS incorporating FL, a shallow ANN, as the regional framework and FedAvg as the aggregation method.	Computationally expensive, as MLP, DNN, CNN, and LSTM were integrated in the proposed framework	98.7% success rate on CICIDS2017.

Torre et al. [24] initiated an IDS built on FL adopting a 1D convolutional neural network (CNN) to secure IoT networks. This framework enhances privacy through Diffie–Hellman key exchange, dynamic security, and homomorphic cryptography. Almadhor et al. [25] introduced a federated deep neural network (FDNN) for detecting and preventing distributed denial-of-service (DDoS) integrating explainable artificial intelligence (XAI) in IoT networks. Their methodology employed FDNNs trained across three client devices over multiple rounds without sharing raw data. Furthermore, XGBoost was used with Shapley additive explanations (SHAPs) to select features, which improved model comprehensibility. This method successfully preserved robustness, scalability, and confidentiality while obtaining high detection accuracy. To further optimize FL-based IDSs, Alsaleh et al. [26] offered a semi-distributed FL model that clusters IoT devices and assigns a cluster head to reduce communication overhead. The model incorporated bidirectional LSTM (BiLSTM), long short-term memory (LSTM), and Wasserstein generative adversarial networks (WGANs) to enhance intrusion detection, particularly focusing on DDoS attacks in scenarios with scarce resources. Their evaluation implementing the CICIoT2023 data set revealed BiLSTM as the most efficient model due to its optimized size. Testing on WUSTL-IIoT-2021, Edge-IIoTset, and BoT-IoT further confirmed its superior detection accuracy. An unorthodox secure and authenticated structure built on federated learning employing Blockchain (SA-FLIDS) was initiated by Bensaid et al. [27] to enhance security in advanced healthcare systems that are enabled via fog-IoMT. Experimental results using the CICIoT2023 and EdgeIIoTset data sets demonstrated the framework's strong resilience against adversarial attacks while preserving the confidentiality of the data and deducting the expenses of communication. Sun et al. [28] addressed the dilemma of attack-class dispersion in FL-based IDSs by proposing FedMADE, an adaptive collaborative framework. FedMADE groups IoT gadgets based on the trends on the traffic and incorporates local approaches according to their significance to the entire evaluation. This approach significantly improved the accuracy of minority attacks' classification to 71.07% compared to existing FL methods for non-IID data. Additionally, FedMADE exhibited robustness against poisoning attacks while incurring only a 4.7% latency overhead (5.03 s per iteration) contrasting with FedAvg, without uploading computational weigh on IoT gadgets. These research works collectively underline the efficacy of FL-based IDSs in intensifying cyber security within IoT networks. The combination of deep learning simulations, privacy-preserving techniques, and blockchain technology shows great promise for protecting modern IoT systems. However, issues such as communication overhead, data disparity, and adversarial resilience remain critical areas for further research and optimization.

Deep learning (DL) and machine learning (ML) have become foundational approaches to constructing IDS, significantly improving network confidentiality by spotting various attacks and anomalies. Several ML techniques are widely used for their robustness and efficiency. Support vector machines (SVMs) are valued for handling high-dimensional data, while decision trees (DTs) offer simplicity and interpretability. Random forest (RF), an association of decision trees, amplifies efficacy and deduces overfitting. Naive Bayes (NB) provides probabilistic classification with efficiency in large data sets, and K-nearest neighbors (KNNs) excel in instance-based learning for classification tasks. In DL, CNNs are highly efficient at pooling out complex hierarchical patterns from structured data, while gradient boosting (GB) and another updated version of GB, extreme gradient boosting (XGB), iteratively improve weak learners for superior predictive performance. These techniques [19,29,30] have demonstrated considerable success in advancing IDS capabilities. However, evolving cyber threats pose ongoing challenges, including scalability, real-time detection, and addressing imbalanced data, which require further research and innovation to enhance future IDS frameworks.

Apart from traditional techniques, bio-inspired frameworks have been quite effective for IDS. Though there have been fewer works in this genre, some have proved the significance of bio-inspired techniques, particularly in anomaly detection. In an article [31], a bi-layer structure, with the initial stage eliminating recursive patterns and incorporating RF-based methodology (RF-RFE) and optimization approaches that are inspired by a biological style, is employed in the following layer. In an article [32], the support vector machine was optimized using Whale Optimization (WO), Grey Wolf Optimization (GWO), and Firefly Optimization (FO) algorithms. However, the detection rates of the irregularities using the optimized methodologies did not demonstrate optimal efficiency. In an article [33], a novel combination of deep learning and the Dendritic Cell Algorithm (DeepDCA) was integrated into the framework alongside a neural network that normalizes itself (SNN). However, the implementation utilized a relatively outdated and less diverse data set.

In addition to traditional methods, FL has become a popular architecture for developing intrusion detection systems (IDSs), offering distributed training without allowing access to original data. Various studies have explored different FL-based approaches, including RF-based federated learning [22], shallow artificial neural networks (ANNs) with FedAvg for aggregation [23], CNNs and RNNs [34], and combinations of a multi-layer perceptron (MLP) with a CNN [35].

Euclides et al. introduced the CICIoT2023 data set, which has been widely used in experiments involving ML algorithms for classification [11]. Notable studies include [36], which proposed a convoluted structure depending on LSTM for attack detection, and Fray et al., who explored DL models with different stages and functions that activate the model [37]. Maryam et al. deployed unbiased ML algorithms to detect irregularities, and [38] emphasized fairness and accuracy in model predictions. These efforts highlight the evolution of IDS using FL and advanced machine learning techniques.

Although there exist advanced FL-based IDSs, these systems have their limitations, such as most of the infrastructure focusing only on identifying one type of malicious action, such as DDoS [25] or DoS [26], some being computationally costly [23,26,27], and some not performing well when the data volume grows [22]. On the other hand, centralized ML or DL approaches have always been prone to vulnerability in maintaining confidentiality and sometimes result in overfitting. Additionally, bio-inspired approaches such as DeepDCA [33] or combined optimization techniques have proven themselves promising, but their scalability and compatibility with FL environments are still subject to skepticism. Furthermore, the implementation of XAI has been isolated, rather than combined with a model, and the experimental surface is still narrow. At present, the most urgent limitation is the lack of an architecture that can ensure privacy, explainability, and effective efficiency. Our study focused on this challenge and tried to build an architecture that can address these issues, implementing the CICIoT2023 data set.

3. Methodology

In this section of the article, the methodology of the entire research work is presented. This section highlights the research approach, encompassing data set compilation, data analysis, prior processing, and the proposed framework.

The section includes an illustration of the attack diversity in Figure 1, a visual representation of data preparation in Figure 2, an architectural depiction of the proposed framework in Figure 3, and the pictorial representation of local architecture in Figure 4.

3.1. Data Set Compilation

In this work, the CICIoT2023 [11] data set was used for the proposed model. The data set was created to meet the growing demand for reliable security analytics applications in real-world IoT contexts. The experimental setup comprises a complete IoT architecture with 105 networked devices that simulate a genuine operational environment. Within this network, 33 different cyberattacks were carried out, each meticulously planned to mirror the changing threat landscape of IoT security. We have distributed the data set in four parts containing 467,449 data at each end, containing 340,557 data of DDoS, 81,205 data of DoS, 26,268 data of Mirai, 3113 data of Recon, 11,011 Benign data, and 5275 data of other classes combined. In order to provide diversity and authenticity in attack situations, compromised IoT devices were intentionally used as hostile entities, attacking other IoT devices in the network. The data set encompasses a wide range of harmful activities, with the goal of serving as a standard for the research community in developing and assessing intrusion detection and mitigation solutions. The assault diversion is shown in Figure 1.

The recorded attacks are systematically categorized into seven major classes, each representing a fundamental aspect of IoT security threats:

I. Distributed Denial of Service (DDoS): Large-scale flooding assaults meant to harm multiple IoT gadgets simultaneously to exhaust computational resources and disrupt network availability.

II. Denial of service (DoS): single-source attack tactics designed to overwhelm a specific IoT device, making it unresponsive to valid queries.

III. Reconnaissance (Recon): passive and active network scanning techniques are used to obtain information on vulnerable IoT devices, services, and network setups.

IV. Web-based attacks: exploitation of IoT web interfaces using security holes in IoT web interfaces, including SQL infiltration, command insertion, and cross-website scripting to gain unauthorized access.

V. Brute-force attacks: systematic password-guessing attacks targeting IoT authentication mechanisms to compromise credentials and gain illicit control over devices.

VI. Spoofing attacks: identity forging techniques, such as ARP and IP spoofing, are used to masquerade as legitimate IoT organizations in order to eavesdrop or manipulate communications.

VII. Mirai-based attacks: malware-driven attacks use the Mirai botnet to exploit vulnerabilities in IoT device security, allowing for large-scale infections and subsequent coordinated cyber attacks.

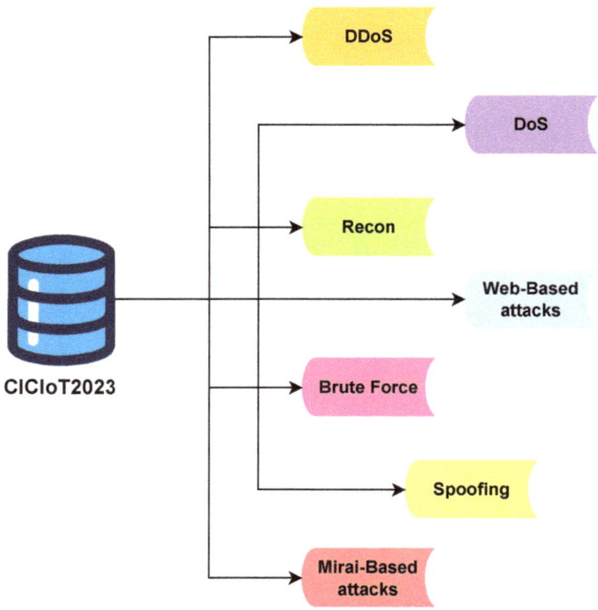

Figure 1. Pictorial representation of the experimented data set with the attack categories.

This data set is a crucial asset for cyber security research, allowing for the creation and testing of advanced machine learning models, intrusion detection systems, and anomaly detection approaches designed specifically for IoT security applications.

3.2. Data Investigation & Pre-Processing

At this level of the suggested approach, the data set is thoroughly inspected if the data are in an eligible format for use. In order to achieve an impactful work, the data sets were pre-processed in several steps.

Proper handling of missing values is important because they could result in errors during model building. In this study, no additional data cleaning technique was needed, as the data set was pre-processed during its generation to discard the incomplete packets that contained null feature values. Additionally, the timestamp feature was eliminated, as it adds no significance to network behavior and, rather, acts as ordering elements. Therefore, the remaining features were ready to be utilized to assess the efficacy of several machine learning models [11]. In our study, we opted for no balancing technique implemented, as we wanted to sustain the real-nature of network traffic. We wanted to observe the performance of the proposed framework in a real-life-like scenario. Apart from that, several researchers have pointed out different perspectives on using balancing techniques. For example, in the paper [39], the authors clarified that the significance of the balancing technique is hardly impactful in the resultant of the framework, specifically in binary class detection. Figure 2 is the step-by-step illustration of the techniques that were employed in this study. The details of the pre-processing is visually represented in Figure 2 and described below.

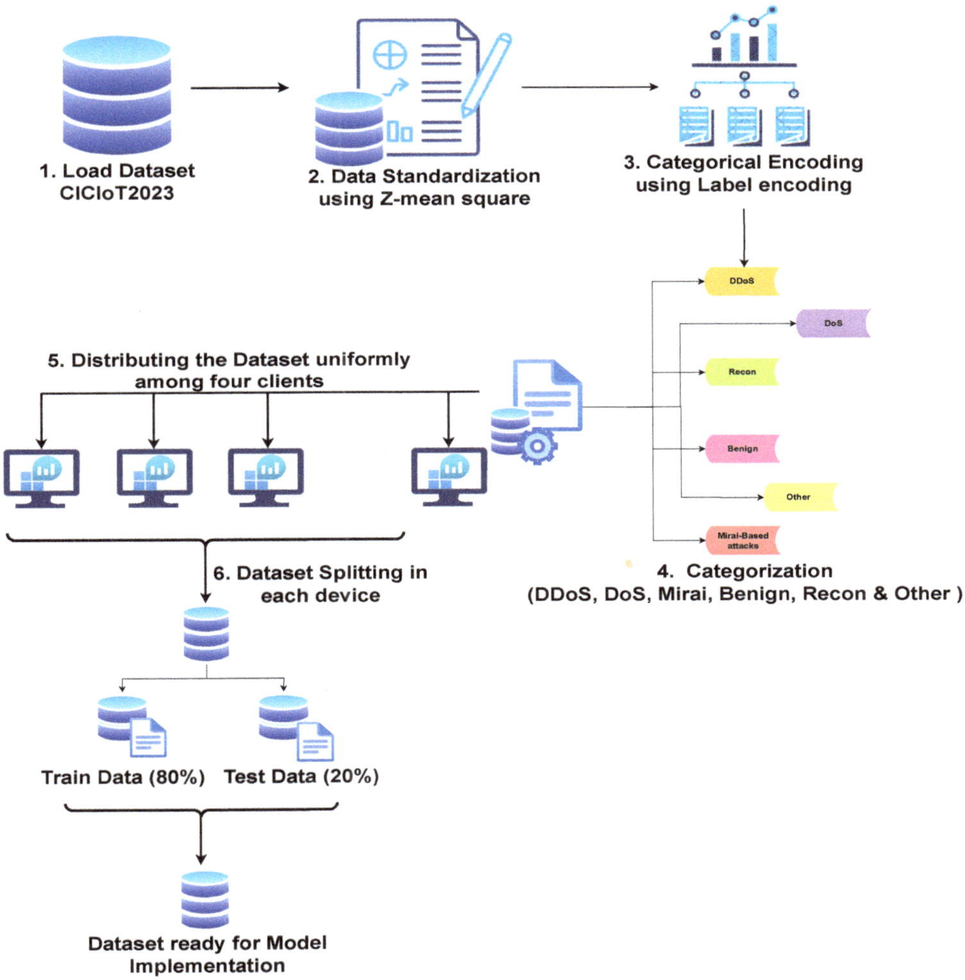

Figure 2. Detailed steps of data preparation for the proposed experiment.

3.2.1. Data-Type Correcting

In order to ensure precise calculations, inconsistent data types (e.g., numeric columns erroneously saved as strings) were transformed into their correct formats.

a. Data standardizing: Standardizing the data is a transformation process that increases the integrity and quality of the data that is used in future calculations. For this study, we used Z-index standardization shown in Equation 1. This method normalizes the data to have zero mean and unit variance.

$$Z = \frac{X - \mu}{\sigma} \tag{1}$$

Here:

- Z denotes the standardized merit,
- X signifies the initial data instance,
- μ represents the mean value of the data,
- σ indicates the standard deviation of the results.

b. Categorical encoding: Any machine learning algorithm requires numerical input to perform mathematical operations, so categorical encoding converts categorical data, which contains arbitrary labels or discrete components, into a numerical format. For the encoding technique, we used label encoding in this study to convert the attack classes labels to numeric values, such as converting label DDoS to class "0". Unlike one-hot encoding, label encoding preserves the ordinal nature of categorical variables, allowing for interaction between dummy variables while providing a meaningful numeric representation of the synonyms. It treats categorical features as a variable to keep the categorical variables' interpretability and thus helps in efficient data processing, such as the given in Equation 2.

$$f(x_i) = y_i \tag{2}$$

Here,

- $f(x_i)$ denotes the function for encoding categorical values to numeric values;
- x_i represents the set of categorical data;
- y_i represents the set of converted numerical data.

3.2.2. Class-Conversion

A robust representation of class conversion is essential in machine learning, as it simplifies the model derived from complex data sets, enhances model performance, and facilitates improved interpretability. The data are simplified and expedited for training due to consolidating classes, which aggregates like assault types. This approach addresses data imbalance by integrating minor attack types into a more significant segment. Moreover, it decreases bias and enhances generalization. Simultaneously, it aligns with the purpose of real-world intrusion detection and increases the significance of cyber-security. In the proposed study, CICIoT2023 was classified into Benign with 1101 data, DDoS with 340,557 data, DoS with 1205 data, Mirai with 26,268 data, Recon with 3113 data, and Other, which consisted of 5275 data after the above mentioned pre-processing steps.

3.2.3. Data Set Splitting

At the last step of pre-processing, the selected data sets were partitioned into two segments. One part was for training, consuming 80 percent of the data, and another part was for an evaluation test, consuming 20 percent of the data.

3.3. *Proposed Framework*

Our extensive research work experimented with ML frameworks in a prior study with another data set, CIC_IDS_2018 and DL, in conjugation with FL and XAI with the CICIoT2023 data set in this study. We implemented an explainable AI-based DL model on the CICIoT2023 data set. The description of the models is given below. The illustration of Figure 3 depicts the process of a federated learning model. It specifies the procedure of initializing a server, disseminating the global framework to local end nodes, changing the model regionally, and transmitting revisions back to the server. The server subsequently incorporates the updates with the federated averaging (FedAvg) mechanism. The diagram illustrates the allocation of models and upgrades to features between the server and remote nodes, where multiple users (Client-1, Client-2, Client-3, and Client-4) utilize their data sets to enhance the effectiveness of the models. The remainder of this section will proceed to explore the suggested framework in greater depth. The conceptualization of the proposed framework was developed based on our earlier work [8]. The following contents provide a detailed, step-by-step discussion of Figure 3.

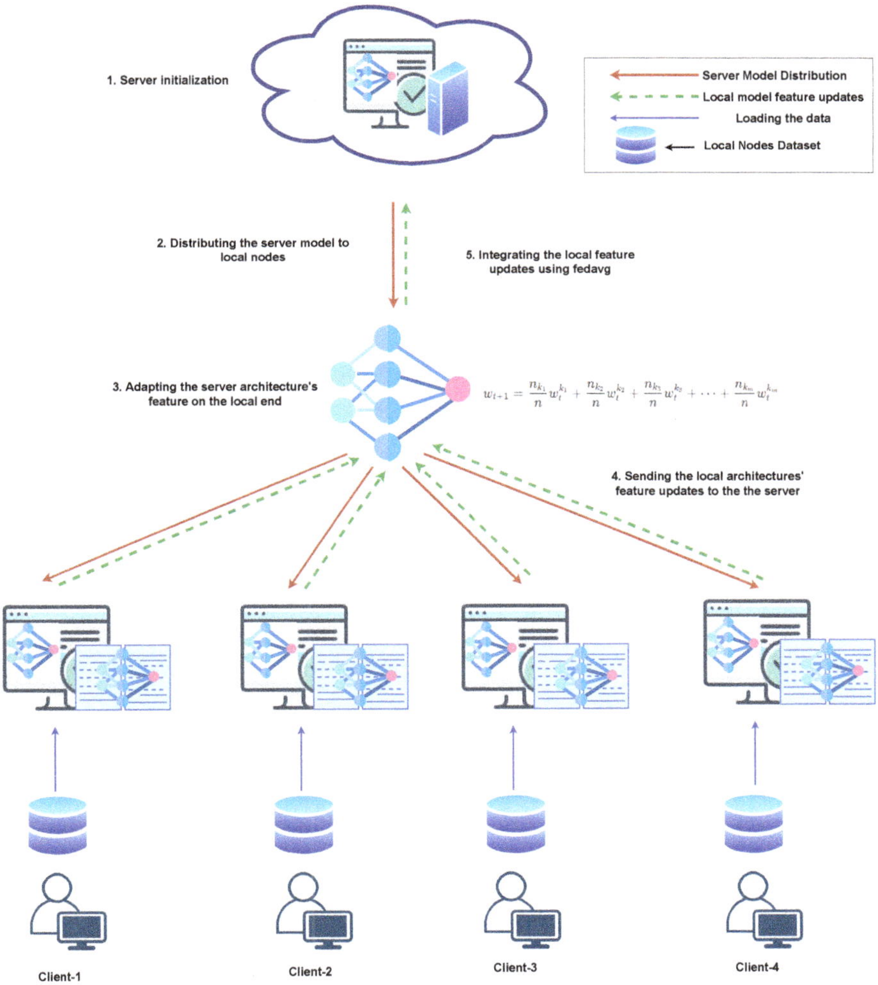

Figure 3. Proposed architectural diagram of FedXAIIDS.

3.3.1. FedXAIIDS

The proposed federated learning (FL) model for intrusion detection leverages a distributed architecture, incorporating the devices attached to the local end. These gadgets regionally implement the frameworks on their particular data set. Later, the computing device at the server end integrates these trained schemes. For this study, the CICIoT2023 data set was distributed across four clients to simulate a federated environment. The following stages define the operation of the proposed model.

1. Initialization: In FL, initialization implies the procedure of establishing the initial universal model prior to the commencement with instruction across various client endpoints. Our experiments started with this initialization; a centralized computer establishes a global architecture and disseminates it to all collaborating peers.
2. Local model training: In our next step, each client initiates local training utilizing their specific data upon acquiring the global framework. At this stage, every collaborating client autonomously trains a replica of the global framework on its own data set prior to transmitting updates to the central server. The depiction of the regional architecture is shown in Figure 4. Every client develops a distinct ANN architecture and explains its results utilizing SHAP. ANN is modeled after the architecture of the human brain, utilizing layers of interconnected neurons. In this work, the ANN framework is fabricated as follows:
    (a) Input layer: The input layer in an artificial neural network (ANN) with 64 neurons representing the 64 features of the data set, where each neuron processes a corresponding feature. Using the activation strategy of ReLU (3),

    $$f(X) = \max(0, X) \tag{3}$$

    It passes only positive values, ensuring efficient learning and faster convergence. Each feature has calculated weighted inputs while making negative inputs are 0. Due to its simplicity and non-linearity, ReLU allows for sparse activation and, therefore, scalability, making it suitable for more complicated tasks such as intrusion detection.
    (b) Dropout layer: Two dropout layers with a fifty percent reduction in rate are utilized, and that helps reduce overfitting by randomly adjusting fifty percent of the units used for input to zero throughout each training iteration. This technique minimizes reliance on single neurons, allowing the network to learn more robust properties.
    (c) Hidden layer: The model has two hidden layers to improve learning and feature abstraction. The first hidden layer is made up of 128 neurons with ReLU activation, which allows the network to record complicated patterns using non-linear transformations. The second hidden layer has 64 neurons and uses ReLU activation to reduce dimensionality while retaining abstraction for better computational efficiency. This layered structure strikes a compromise between learning capacity and processing speed, allowing for deeper pattern identification and more effective generalization.
    (d) Output layer: The layer that is designed to provide outcomes, contains six neuronal cells, each corresponding to one of the six categories of interest in the classifying task. The activation function of softmax is employed, transforming the output into the distribution of probabilities among every category. The softmax function guarantees the sum of probabilities is 1 and enables the model to simply make the most likely class prediction and give more probability to

whatever output is more relevant, which makes it popular for multi-class classification problems.

(e) Loss function: This framework employs a loss function approach that is known as categorical cross-entropy, quantifying the disparity between the actual label distribution and the projected distribution of probabilities. This method is used when there is multi-class classification, and it penalizes when the prediction is neither close to the labels nor close to the class by solving a loss of negative log likelihood of the actual class. Preventing this loss can help tune the model so that it is more left-leaning or right-leaning, which improves its accuracy, resulting in predicted probability aligning better with actual labels.

(f) Optimizer: This model employs Adam optimizing techniques with a primary learning ratio of 0.001 to take advantage of momentum and adaptation rates for improved training. Adam adapts the learning rates for each individual parameter, which leads to quicker convergence and resilient performance across different types of issues, making it frequently employed in deep learning models.

3. Global aggregator: The centralized computer consolidates modifications to the model from each client to formulate a unified framework utilizing federated averaging (FedAvg) (4). This method involves the server systematically calculating a weighted average of the parameters (weights) that are achieved from client models according to the magnitude of their local data. The method has shown its efficacy in several fields, for example, a mobile healthcare application [40], IoT-based intrusion detection [41], and picture categorization employing non-IID data [42]. FedAvg enhances the global model by integrating varied local insights while maintaining data privacy, establishing it as a fundamental technique in FL [43]. The calculation is as follows [43],

$$\theta^{(t+1)} = \sum_{k=1}^{K} \frac{n_k}{N} \theta_k^{(t)} \quad (4)$$

where

- $\theta^{(t+1)}$ represents the new global model parameters;
- K denotes the number of participating clients;
- n_k is the number of local training samples for client k;
- $N = \sum_{k=1}^{K} n_k$ is the total number of training samples across all selected clients;
- $\theta_k^{(t)}$ represents the locally updated model parameters from client k at round t.

4. Explainable AI (XAI) integration: Explainability is a crucial characteristic for analyzing different machine learning and deep learning models. In this experiment, the explainable AI technique SHAP was deployed on the global end of the framework, after combining all results from local frameworks. SHAP is a model-agnostic technique that leverages the interpretability of the implemented model in the experiment. SHAP incorporates the Shapely values, which are inspired by game theory, to calculate the contribution of each feature to the projected result [9]. In this study, each characteristic of the data set is represented as a player of a collaborative game, and the result of the proposed framework is considered as the outcome of that game. After that, the SHAP evaluated the Shapely value for all the features separately by calculating the average marginal significance among all possible combinations of features. Therefore, the library for SHAP was implemented to assess the SHAP values for the testing subset of the experimental data set, CICIoT2023. In this proposed framework, Kernel SHAP, an approach that was introduced in the article [9], was deployed to interpret

predictions and represent the interpretability of CICIoT2023. This method enables us to achieve insights about the features that are prominently influencing the outcome of the proposed framework.

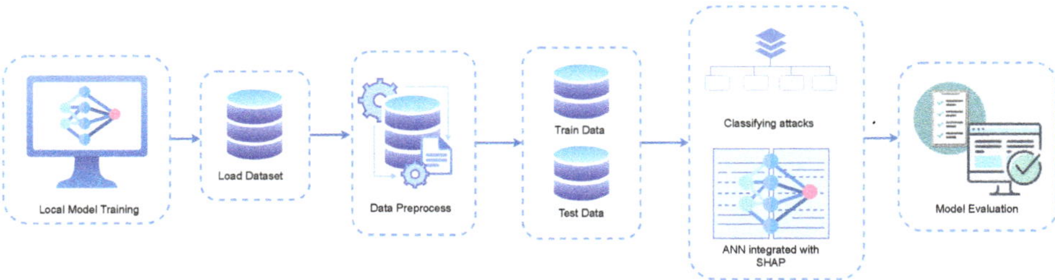

Figure 4. Visual representation of local architecture from [8].

3.4. *Evaluative Metric*

The properties employed for the suggested framework in this investigation include precision, accuracy, and recall, alongside the F1-score.
Confusion matrix: The confusion matrix is an evaluation parameter that is used for classification models. It is represented as a table that summarizes the prediction by comparing real target values with the predicted values from the model. It comprises TP—true positive, TN—true negative, FP—false positive, and FN—false negative.

$$\text{Confusion Matrix} = \begin{bmatrix} TP & FN \\ FP & TN \end{bmatrix} \tag{5}$$

Accuracy: The metric that indicates how frequently an ML approach correctly projects an outcome is known as accuracy. The division of the number of correct predictions by the total estimation quantity is implemented to evaluate the accuracy.

$$ACCURACY = \frac{TP + TN}{FP + TP + FN + TN} \tag{6}$$

Recall: The capacity to identify all pertinent instances within the data set is termed recall. It is defined as the ratio of actual positives to the total of true positives and false negatives in the genre of mathematics.

$$RECALL = \frac{TP}{FN + TP} \tag{7}$$

Precision: The metric that represents the efficacy of an ML approach is known as precision. It reflects the accuracy of the algorithms' positive predictions. It is the ratio of genuine successes to the total number of positive projections.

$$PRECISION = \frac{TP}{FP + TP} \tag{8}$$

F1-score: the balanced average of accuracy and recall is termed the F1-score. Accuracy and recall are aggregated into a single statistic in order to enhance the comprehension of the efficacy of the suggested framework.

$$F1\text{-}SCORE = \frac{2 \times RECALL \times PRECISION}{PRECISION + RECALL} \tag{9}$$

Loss: A function called a loss function is a formula of algebra that quantifies the variance between the envisioned results derived from the computerized model and the actual target values. The loss function evaluates the degree to which the forecasts of the model align with the factual information.

$$\text{Loss} = -\sum_{i=1}^{n}\sum_{c=1}^{C} y_{i,c}\log(\hat{y}_{i,c}) \tag{10}$$

4. Experimental Result

The research experiment was conducted on a portable computer with the configuration features of a Core i5 processor, 4 GB of main memory, and 2.4 GHz of CPU momentum that was running Microsoft Windows 11. The programming environment utilized Jupyter Notebook and Kaggle Notebook, both with Python 3. Furthermore, the Colab at Google acted as a program framework to conduct the experiment. In the following section, the outputs are discussed and compared with other frameworks.

FedXAIIDS

The envisioned infrastructure built on FL was allocated among four end-users along with the global framework. The findings were assembled from the local ends utilizing the aggregator strategy of FedAvg. The resultant products produced during the testing cycles are illustrated in Figure 5.

Figure 5. Accuracy trends of federated learning clients over five iterations.

Figure 5 depicts the accuracy trends of a federated learning model across many clients over a number of repetitions of the local training and sharing of the feedback with a global server. The horizontal axis depicts the number of repetitions, indicating the advancement of training, and the vertical axis represents accuracy in percentage terms, representing the model's performance. Every curve in the figure displays an individual client; the blue line denotes client-1, the orange line denotes client-2, the green line denotes client-3, and the red line represents another client, showcasing how their respective models improve over time. The accuracy deviations could be attributed to differences in data distributions, local model updates, or computing resources. The graph in Figure 5 illustrates the converging behavior of federated learning, demonstrating whether all clients attain equal performance levels or if there are differences because of disparities in data or system-related constraints. From Figure 5, we can observe that client-1 achieved 87.5% accuracy in its first time execution of the model; then, it grew gradually, by 88%, 88.06%, 88.18%, and 88.31%, in the second, third, fourth and fifth time executions, respectively. On the other hand, client-2 acquired 87.81%, 88.06%, 88.31%, 88.43%, and 88.5% in the first time execution to the fifth time execution, respectively. On the other hand, client-3 showed an efficacy of 88%, 88.31%, 88.5%, 88.56%, and 88.68% in each execution and also performed the best among all the local clients. Finally, client-4 achieved a success rate of 87.56% in the first execution of the model on its end, and then it achieved 88.18%, 88.37%, 88.5%, and 88.63% in its second, third, fourth, and fifth time runs on the model, respectively. In conclusion, we can state from Figure 5, that each local client performed better with each time execution of the model, and client-3 showed the highest efficacy growth over time. This approach is important in federated learning because it helps evaluate model consistency across clients, discover potential fairness issues, and ensure that no client suffers a great disadvantage during training. The detected trends can also be used to inform optimization tactics, such as modifying learning rates, enhancing aggregation approaches, and dealing with straggler effects.

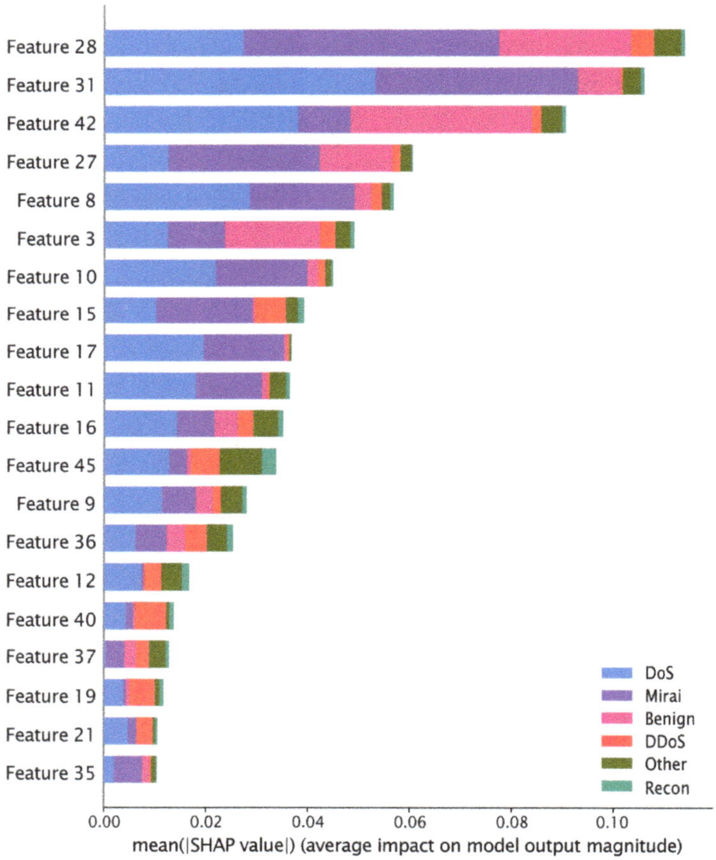

Figure 6. SHAP value representation of significant features on the projected output for each class ranked by decreasing significance.

The feature importance visualisations that were created using the SHAP framework are summarised in Figure 6. From Figure 7a, we can observe that the suggested method has an 88.4% achievement rate during the training session and an 88.2% achievement rate during the testing session. Furthermore, Figure 7b represents the loss calculation of the model after aggregating all models with a loss value of 26.6% in the training phase and a 27.7% loss value in the testing phase. In the suggested framework, SHAP was employed in order to clarify the significance of the attributes on the anticipated output. The proposed framework was trained with the Adam optimizer having a learning rate of 0.001, which adjusts the learning rates during training and enhances the convergence stability. On the other hand, the input features were standardized, incorporating the StandardScaler technique, and no missing or null values were discovered in the data set, which ensures a clean data set, providing less information loss with a balanced feature set for learning. Additionally, a categorical cross-entropy was incorporated as a loss function, which is suitable for multi-class categorization, promoting accurate probability estimation among all output categories. In addition, the dropout layers were employed in the framework, as it mitigates overfitting and contributes to the generalization capability of the proposed architecture. These parameters cooperated all together to achieve low loss values and efficient classification performance.

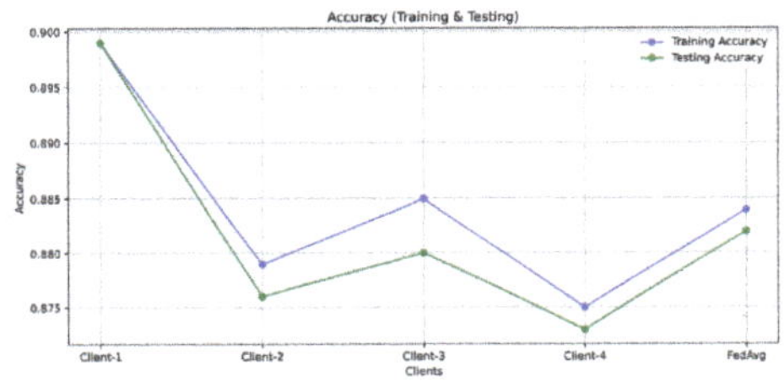

(**a**)

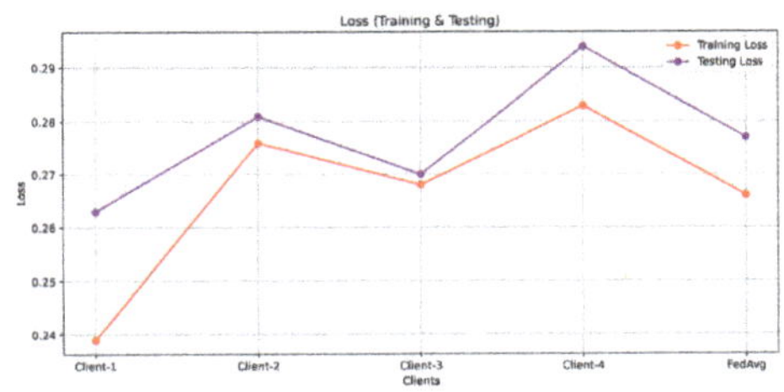

(**b**)

Figure 7. Experimental findings of FedXAIIDS. (**a**) Accuracy graph for participants of FedXAIIDS of both training and testing sessions. (**b**) Loss graph for participants of FedXAIIDS of both training and testing sessions.

Moreover, the proposed framework achieved a precision of 0.886, a recall of 0.678, and an F1-Score of 0.698. During the testing phase, the model achieved consistent behavior with a precision of 0.8908, a recall of 0.684, and an F1-score of 0.705. The comparatively high precision indicates that, when the experimented structure detects an instance as intrusion, it is likely to be correct, minimizing the false positives. The average recall value indicates that the framework might miss some incidents of false negatives despite being cautious in identifying malicious behavior. On the other hand, the value of the F1-score indicates the balance between precision and recall, and it demonstrates a consistent generalization ability across observed and unseen components. The limitation of our model is the low output value, which indicates that this framework still needs fine-tuning, a parameter reset, and other appropriate techniques' incorporation to enhance the output parameter values. However, the strength of the proposed model lies in discovering the most significant features while breaching the network. In the future, we can reduce the dimensionality of the data set, focusing only on the significant features that we enlisted by deploying the SHAP framework. Thus, we may obtain better output values than the current ones.

In Figure 6, a summary of the feature importance visualizations that were derived from the SHAP framework is shown. SHAP estimates the average influence of every feature on the overall dimension of the output of the model across all classes. On the x-axis, the mean "SHAP value" is demonstrated, which displays the average quantity of the contribution of a feature to the evaluation of the model. In our experiment, the features' contribution is shown as a positive influence on the overall framework. This metric shows the overall effect of each feature on the projected accuracy of the model, providing a global measure of feature relevance. On the other hand, the y-axis enlists the characteristics of the data in a decreasing sequence, meaning a start from the most influenced class to the least influenced class. The classes are Class 0—DDoS, Class 1—DoS, Class 2—Mirai, Class 3—Benign, Class 4—Other, and Class 5—Recon. In the figure, the classes are represented by the following colors: DDoS—red, DoS—blue, Mirai—purple, Benign—magenta, Other—olive green, and Recon-dark teal. The width of each color represents the impact of that particular feature on each class. From Figure 6, we can observe that the 10 most significant features of CICIoT2023 are feature 28—UDP, 31—ICMP, 42—Magnitude, 27—TCP, 8—fin_flag_number, 3—Protocol type, 10—rst_flag_number, 15—ack_count, 17—fin_count, and 11—psh_flag_number. Furthermore, feature 28 has the most influence on identifying the attack classes on the CICIoT2023 data set.

5. Discussion

In this section, the proposed model is compared with several frameworks that were implemented on CICIoT2023. In this study, we implemented FEDXAIIDS as the baseline model on CICIoT2023, and our comparison study focused on the performance of different frameworks on the CICIoT2023 data set. The findings in Table 2 show that FedXAIIDS is effective in addressing major intrusion detection concerns, particularly in terms of privacy preservation, explainability, and decentralized learning. While the recommended framework attained a training efficacy of 88.4% and a testing efficacy of 88.2% on the CICIoT2023 data set, which are lower than some centralized approaches, its advantages in security, interpretability, and real-world applicability make it a superior choice for modern cyber security frameworks. FedXAIIDS, unlike standard IDS models, uses federated learning (FL) to ensure that sensitive network data are dispersed across edge devices. This considerably decreases the danger of data breaches and ensures compliance with severe privacy requirements such as the GDPR (General Data Protection Regulation).

In an article [44], the proposed framework achieved impressive efficacy of 100% for sql injection attacks and a 98.25% success rate for brute-force attacks, but the limitation of this work was that it only focused on identifying two attacks. The majority of works have prioritized evaluating accuracy, ignoring the need for a justification of the gained accuracy, while FEDXAIIDS properly justifies the achieved accuracy by evaluating feature contribution utilizing SHAP. Despite yielding high accuracy, 99.41% for multi-attack and 99.83% for binary classification, the proposed model of the article [45] is computationally expensive for using multiple techniques in a single architecture. Similarly, ref. [46] implies a 1D to 3D synaptic transformation on a large data set, CICIoT2023, to achieve 97.69% accuracy while increasing the computational overhead. In the article [47], the authors experimented and autoencoder-based feedforward neural network with the success rate of 99.55%, but it is a centralized system that still involves a privacy issue. Ji et al. [48] proposed a CPS-based framework integrating Adaboost and RF, achieving 98.27% accuracy while adopting a centralized method that does not protect the confidentiality of end-to-end devices. On the other hand, Torre et el. [24] overcame the privacy issue by applying Diffie–Hellman key exchange and homomorphic encryption, achieving 97.31% accuracy while maintaining unclarity about the number of attack types it is identifying. The most competitive article with our work is the article [25], with the framework of FDNN with XAI having a success rate of 99.78%, but it only focused on classifying different types of DDoS attacks, while JiaMing et al. proposed NIDS-FGPA with Pailier encryption to resolve security issues, having a success rate of 99.2% on CICIoT2023 but computational complexity [1].

Additionally, the primary objective of the current experiment was to ensure interpretability by calculating SHAP values, but our future research might look at utilizing top-ranked features that SHAP discovered for dimensionality reduction. This framework might even increase or sustain performance while supporting the development of a more computationally efficient infrastructure.

Table 2. Comparison of the evaluation of Experiment-2 with current studies on CICIoT2023.

Ref	Year	Federated Learning Applied	Method	Data Set	Performance Metrics (Accuracy)
A. Adamova et al.	2025	Yes	Implemented federated learning on SQL injection and brute-force attacks.	CICIOT2023	100% accuracy in predicting SQL injection attacks and 98.25% accuracy for brute-force attacks [44].
R. Saadouni et al.	2025	No	Incorporated VGG16 along with BBinary Greylag Goose Optimization (BGGO) and Random Forest Classifier [45].	CICIOT2023	99.41% accuracy for multiclass classification and 99.83% for binary classification.
H. Chen et al.	2025	No	Proposed synaptic structures transformation from 1D to 3D. Additionally, imbalance categorization issue is mitigated implement a unique strategy for calculating loss.	CIC_IDS_2017, CICIOT2023	demonstrated a 88.48% on CICIDS2017 and a 97.69% on CICIoT2023 [46].
J. J. Shirley et al.	2025	No	Deployed autoencoder along with a feedforward neural network (AE-FNN) [47].	CICIOT2023	99.55% accuracy in binary classification and 90.91% in multiclass classification.
R. Ji et al.	2025	No	Introduced a hybrid IDS Cyber-Physical Systems (CPSs), integrating AdaBoost and RF techniques [48].	CICIOT2023	accuracy of 98.27%, with recall, precision, and F1-score all at 0.98 and a false detection rate of 0.0006, along with a testing time of 0.1563 s
Sabrina et al.	2025	Yes	Proposed a secure gradient-exchange algorithm utilizing FL and blockchain, incorporating CNN1D and multi-head attention.	CICIOT2023	accuracy of 79.92%, 77.41% identification percentage, and 2.55% of false detection rate [49].
Qawsar et al.	2025	Yes	Introduced a hybrid learning infrastructure integrating CNN, LSTM, GRU, and a capsule network [50].	CICIoT 2023 and UNSW_NB15	accuracy of 99.82% on CICIoT 2023 and 95.55% on UNSW_NB15.
Torre et al.	2025	Yes	Presented an FL-based using 1D-CNN incorporating differential privacy, Diffie–Hellman key exchange, and homomorphic encryption [24].	TONIoT, IoT23, BoTIoT, CICIoT2023, CICIoMT2024, RTIoT2022, and Edge-IIoT	The model achieved an estimated accurateness of 97.31%, across the various data sets.
Ahmad et al.	2024	Yes	This study proposes using federated deep neural networks (FDNNs) and explainable AI (XAI) [25].	DDoS-ICMP-Flood, DDoS-UDP-Flood, DDoS-TCP-Flood, DDoS-PSHACK-Flood, DDoS-SYN-Flood, DDoS-RSTFINFlood, DDoS-SynonymousIP-Flood, DoS-UDP-Flood, DoS-TCP-Flood, and DoS-SYN-Flood.	The model achieved 99.78% accuracy.
JiaMing et al.	2025	Yes	Proposed an NIDS-FGPA NIDS-FGPA with Paillier encryption for secure training and uses GSA to optimize updates and reduce overhead.	Edge-IIoTset and CICIoT2023	Edge-IIoTset and CICIoT2023 data sets exhibit accurateness of 94.5% and 99.2%, correspondingly [51].
FedXAIIDS	2025	Yes	Federated XAI IDS(FedXAIIDS) uses Federated Learning (FL) and SHAP for a privacy-preserving, explainable IDS. An ANN is distributed across four federated clients, aggregated with FedAvg on CICIoT2023.	CICIOT2023	SHAP enhances interpretability, and the model achieved 88.4% training and 88.2% testing accuracy, balancing security, privacy, and trustworthiness.

From the above discussion, we can observe that our proposed framework performed worse in accuracy than the other compared frameworks, which is a vulnerable point in the proposed study. But the proposed infrastructure is computationally lower in cost, as we opted for an ANN as a local framework in an FL environment. Moreover, the significant factor about our proposed infrastructure, FEDXAIIDS, is that our model has generated a set of significant features implementing XAI and particularly showed their contribution to the detection of different attack classes. According to the SHAP analysis plot, we have observed that the feature 28-UDP has the most significance in detecting any attack class. Moreover, we can use this clue in the future to implement an intrusion prevention system (IPS). Furthermore, in future work, we aim to explore different XAI techniques, as well as build a real-life network scenario to incorporate the model in real time.

6. Conclusions

This research introduced Federated XAI IDS, a novel explainable and privacy-preserving intrusion detection system (IDS) that effectively addresses the key limitations of traditional IDS, including high inaccurate positive detection and inaccurate negative detection percentage, a lack of interpretability, and data privacy concerns. By leveraging federated learning (FL) and Shapley additive explanations (SHAPs), our approach ensures that IDS models can be collaboratively trained across multiple decentralized devices while preserving data privacy by keeping sensitive information on local edge nodes. This decentralized paradigm mitigates the security risks associated with centralized approaches, making it a commendatory solution for modern network circumstances. The proposed IDS framework utilizes an artificial neural network (ANN) distributed across four federated clients, with model aggregation performed using FedAvg on the CICIoT2023 data set. The output highlighted the efficiency of this approach, achieving 88.4% training accuracy and 88.2% testing accuracy. Additionally, SHAP was incorporated to analyze feature importance, providing a transparent perspective of the most significant attributes influencing model predictions. The ability to rank and interpret feature significance enhances model trustworthiness and supports cyber security professionals in making informed decisions. Though our accuracy is lower than that of other current studies, SHAP analysis ensured the efficiency our results, and our findings demonstrate that Federated XAI IDS successfully tackles two critical challenges in intrusion detection, explainability, and privacy preservation. By integrating federated learning with explainable AI (XAI), this work offers a scalable, interpretable, and secure IDS solution suited for modern cyber security applications, particularly in scenarios where sensitive data cannot be centrally shared. Moreover, it was found in the proposed method that the most significant feature in contributing to detect intrusion is UDP. This information can pave the way to build an efficient intrusion prevention system to protect the system from any kind of breaching in the first place. For a future extension of this work, we will experiment with different federated aggregation tactics, as well as XAI methods, to analyze the performance efficiency shift and significant features. Additionally, we would like to implement the framework on a real-life network system to test its eligibility to work in an actual network layer as a realistic implementation, and an assessment in extensive and diverse networks will confirm the resilience and applicability of our methodology.

Author Contributions: Conceptualization, K.F. and R.M.; Methodology, K.F. and S.K.D.; Validation, S.K.D. and C.S.; Formal analysis, S.K.D.; Investigation, K.F., M.A., and R.T.K.; Resources, M.A. and R.T.K.; Data curation, M.A. and M.M.R.; Writing—original draft, K.F.; Writing—review & editing,

M.M.R., C.S. and R.M.; Supervision, R.M. and S.K.D. All authors have read and agreed to the published version of the manuscript.

Funding: This research work is partially funded by the University Grants Commision (UGC) of Bangladesh with Grant number: 37.01.0000.073.12.009.23.458.

Data Availability Statement: The data that support the findings of this study are openly available in the University of New Brunswick Canadian Institute for Cybersecurity (CIC) at https://www.unb.ca/cic/datasets/iotdataset-2023.html accessed on 20 May 2025.

Acknowledgments: This study is the extended version of our earlier work that was published at a conference [8]. Additionally, in the writing of this publication, we employed AI-assisted technologies, namely OpenAI's ChatGPT-4, to facilitate language refining, paraphrasing, section structuring, and a summary of background literature. All text was rigorously examined, amended, and verified by the authors to guarantee precision, originality, and alignment with our study aims. The AI technologies were not employed for the generation of novel scientific insights, experimental outcomes, or data analysis.

Conflicts of Interest: The authors have no conflicts of interest to declare.

Abbreviations

This document employs the following abbreviations:

IDS	Intrusion Detection System
FL	Federated Learning
XAI	eXplainable AI
AI	Artificial Intelligence
SHAP	SHapley Additive exPLanation
ML	Machine Learning
DL	Deep Learning
ANN	Artificial Nueral Network
FedXAIIDS	Federated Explainable IDS
CNN	Convolutional Neural Network
LSTM	Long Short-Term Memory

References

1. Wang, S.; Asif, M.; Shahzad, M.F.; Ashfaq, M. Data privacy and cybersecurity challenges in the digital transformation of the banking sector. *Comput. Secur.* **2024**, *147*, 104051. [CrossRef]
2. Otoum, Y.; Nayak, A. As-ids: Anomaly and signature based ids for the internet of things. *J. Netw. Syst. Manag.* **2021**, *29*, 23. [CrossRef]
3. Okoye, C.C.; Nwankwo, E.E.; Usman, F.O.; Mhlongo, N.Z.; Odeyemi, O.; Ike, C.U. Securing financial data storage: A review of cybersecurity challenges and solutions. *Int. J. Sci. Res. Arch.* **2024**, *11*, 1968–1983. [CrossRef]
4. Agrawal, S.; Sarkar, S.; Aouedi, O.; Yenduri, G.; Piamrat, K.; Alazab, M.; Bhattacharya, S.; Maddikunta, P.K.R.; Gadekallu, T.R. Federated learning for intrusion detection system: Concepts, challenges and future directions. *Comput. Commun.* **2022**, *195*, 346–361. [CrossRef]
5. Karatas, G.; Demir, O.; Sahingoz, O.K. Increasing the performance of machine learning-based IDSs on an imbalanced and up-to-date dataset. *IEEE Access* **2020**, *8*, 32150–32162. [CrossRef]
6. Waswani, A.; Shazeer, N.; Parmar, N.; Uszkoreit, J.; Jones, L.; Gomez, A.; Kaiser, L.; Polosukhin, I. Attention is all you need. In Proceedings of the NIPS, Long Beach, CA, USA, 4–9 December 2017.
7. Adadi, A.; Berrada, M. Peeking inside the black-box: A survey on explainable artificial intelligence (XAI). *IEEE Access* **2018**, *6*, 52138–52160. [CrossRef]
8. Fatema, K.; Anannya, M.; Dey, S.K.; Su, C.; Mazumder, R. Securing Networks: A Deep Learning Approach with Explainable AI (XAI) and Federated Learning for Intrusion Detection. In *Data Security and Privacy Protection;* Springer: Berlin/Heidelberg, Germany, 2024; pp. 260–275.
9. Lundberg, S. A unified approach to interpreting model predictions. *arXiv* **2017**, arXiv:1705.07874.

10. Dong, T.; Li, S.; Qiu, H.; Lu, J. An interpretable federated learning-based network intrusion detection framework. *arXiv* **2022**, arXiv:2201.03134.
11. Neto, E.C.P.; Dadkhah, S.; Ferreira, R.; Zohourian, A.; Lu, R.; Ghorbani, A.A. CICIoT2023: A real-time dataset and benchmark for large-scale attacks in IoT environment. *Sensors* **2023**, *23*, 5941. [CrossRef]
12. Hodo, E.; Bellekens, X.; Hamilton, A.; Tachtatzis, C.; Atkinson, R. Machine learning methods for cyber security intrusion detection: Overview, issues, and open challenges. *Int. J. Commun. Syst.* **2016**, *29*, 2056–2085.
13. Li, W.; Liao, X.; Wang, W.; Zhang, W. Intrusion detection system based on SVM with feature selection. *Int. J. Commun. Syst.* **2012**, *25*, 934–945.
14. Singh, G.; Singh, L. Network anomaly detection using hybrid decision tree. *Int. J. Innov. Technol. Explor. Eng. (IJITEE)* **2019**, *8*, 2451–2456.
15. Yin, C.; Zhu, Y.; Fei, J.; He, X. A deep learning approach for intrusion detection using recurrent neural networks. *IEEE Access* **2017**, *5*, 21954–21961. [CrossRef]
16. Maseer, Z.K.; Yusof, R.; Bahaman, N.; Mostafa, S.A.; Foozy, C.F.M. Benchmarking of machine learning for anomaly based intrusion detection systems in the CICIDS2017 dataset. *IEEE Access* **2021**, *9*, 22351–22370. [CrossRef]
17. Sarhan, M.; Layeghy, S.; Portmann, M. Evaluating standard feature sets towards increased generalisability and explainability of ML-based network intrusion detection. *Big Data Res.* **2022**, *30*, 100359. [CrossRef]
18. Fatema, K.; Dey, S.K.; Bari, R.; Mazumder, R. A Novel Two-Stage Classification Architecture Integrating Machine Learning and Artificial Immune System for Intrusion Detection on Balanced Dataset. In Proceedings of the International Conference on Information and Communication Technology for Intelligent Systems, Las Vegas, NV, USA, 22–23 May 2024; Springer: Singapore, 2024; pp. 179–189.
19. Nguyen, S.N.; Nguyen, V.Q.; Choi, J.; Kim, K. Design and implementation of intrusion detection system using convolutional neural network for DoS detection. In Proceedings of the 2nd International Conference on Machine Learning and Soft Computing, Phu Quoc Island, Vietnam, 2–4 February 2018; pp. 34–38.
20. de Carvalho Bertoli, G.; Junior, L.A.P.; Saotome, O.; dos Santos, A.L. Generalizing intrusion detection for heterogeneous networks: A stacked-unsupervised federated learning approach. *Comput. Secur.* **2023**, *127*, 103106. [CrossRef]
21. Toldinas, J.; Venčkauskas, A.; Damaševičius, R.; Grigaliūnas, Š.; Morkevičius, N.; Baranauskas, E. A novel approach for network intrusion detection using multistage deep learning image recognition. *Electronics* **2021**, *10*, 1854. [CrossRef]
22. Markovic, T.; Leon, M.; Buffoni, D.; Punnekkat, S. Random forest based on federated learning for intrusion detection. In Proceedings of the IFIP International Conference on Artificial Intelligence Applications and Innovations, Hersonissos, Greece, 17–20 June 2022; Springer: Berlin/Heidelberg, Germany, 2022; pp. 132–144.
23. Lazzarini, R.; Tianfield, H.; Charissis, V. Federated learning for IoT intrusion detection. *Ai* **2023**, *4*, 509–530. [CrossRef]
24. Torre, D.; Chennamaneni, A.; Jo, J.; Vyas, G.; Sabrsula, B. Toward Enhancing Privacy Preservation of a Federated Learning CNN Intrusion Detection System in IoT: Method and Empirical Study. *ACM Trans. Softw. Eng. Methodol.* **2025**, *34*, 1–48. [CrossRef]
25. Almadhor, A.; Altalbe, A.; Bouazzi, I.; Hejaili, A.A.; Kryvinska, N. Strengthening network DDOS attack detection in heterogeneous IoT environment with federated XAI learning approach. *Sci. Rep.* **2024**, *14*, 24322. [CrossRef]
26. Alsaleh, S.; Menai, M.E.B.; Al-Ahmadi, S. A Heterogeneity-Aware Semi-Decentralized Model for a Lightweight Intrusion Detection System for IoT Networks Based on Federated Learning and BiLSTM. *Sensors* **2025**, *25*, 1039. [CrossRef]
27. Bensaid, R.; Labraoui, N.; Ari, A.A.A.; Saidi, H.; Emati, J.H.M.; Maglaras, L. SA-FLIDS: Secure and authenticated federated learning-based intelligent network intrusion detection system for smart healthcare. *PeerJ Comput. Sci.* **2024**, *10*, e2414. [CrossRef] [PubMed]
28. Sun, S.; Sharma, P.; Nwodo, K.; Stavrou, A.; Wang, H. FedMADE: Robust Federated Learning for Intrusion Detection in IoT Networks Using a Dynamic Aggregation Method. In Proceedings of the International Conference on Information Security, Arlington, VA, USA, 23–25 October 2024; Springer: Berlin/Heidelberg, Germany, 2024; pp. 286–306.
29. Al-Imran, M.; Ripon, S.H. Network intrusion detection: An analytical assessment using deep learning and state-of-the-art machine learning models. *Int. J. Comput. Intell. Syst.* **2021**, *14*, 200. [CrossRef]
30. Arslan, R.S. FastTrafficAnalyzer: An efficient method for intrusion detection systems to analyze network traffic. *Dicle Üniversitesi Mühendislik Fakültesi Mühendislik Dergisi* **2021**, *12*, 565–572. [CrossRef]
31. Tonni, Z.A.; Mazumder, R. A Novel Feature Selection Technique for Intrusion Detection System Using RF-RFE and Bio-inspired Optimization. In Proceedings of the 2023 57th Annual Conference on Information Sciences and Systems (CISS), Baltimore, MD, USA, 22–24 March 2023; pp. 1–6.
32. Haque, N.I.; Khalil, A.A.; Rahman, M.A.; Amini, M.H.; Ahamed, S.I. Biocad: Bio-inspired optimization for classification and anomaly detection in digital healthcare systems. In Proceedings of the 2021 IEEE International Conference on Digital Health (ICDH), Chicago, IL, USA, 5–10 September 2021; pp. 48–58.

33. Aldhaheri, S.; Alghazzawi, D.; Cheng, L.; Alzahrani, B.; Al-Barakati, A. DeepDCA: Novel network-based detection of IoT attacks using artificial immune system. *Appl. Sci.* **2020**, *10*, 1909. [CrossRef]
34. Rashid, M.M.; Khan, S.U.; Eusufzai, F.; Redwan, M.A.; Sabuj, S.R.; Elsharief, M. A federated learning-based approach for improving intrusion detection in industrial internet of things networks. *Network* **2023**, *3*, 158–179. [CrossRef]
35. Liu, W.; Xu, X.; Wu, L.; Qi, L.; Jolfaei, A.; Ding, W.; Khosravi, M.R. Intrusion detection for maritime transportation systems with batch federated aggregation. *IEEE Trans. Intell. Transp. Syst.* **2022**, *24*, 2503–2514. [CrossRef]
36. Yaras, S.; Dener, M. IoT-Based Intrusion Detection System Using New Hybrid Deep Learning Algorithm. *Electronics* **2024**, *13*, 1053. [CrossRef]
37. Becerra-Suarez, F.L.; Tuesta-Monteza, V.A.; Mejia-Cabrera, H.I.; Arcila-Diaz, J. Performance Evaluation of Deep Learning Models for Classifying Cybersecurity Attacks in IoT Networks. *Proc. Inform.* **2024**, *11*, 32. [CrossRef]
38. Khan, M.M.; Alkhathami, M. Anomaly detection in IoT-based healthcare: machine learning for enhanced security. *Sci. Rep.* **2024**, *14*, 5872. [CrossRef]
39. Boateng, A.; Odoom, C.; Mensah, E.T.; Fobi, S.M.; Maposa, D. Predictive Analysis of Misuse of Alcohol and Drugs using Machine Learning Algorithms: The Case of using an Imbalanced Dataset from South Africa. *Appl. Math* **2023**, *17*, 261–271.
40. Brisimi, T.S.; Chen, R.; Mela, T.; Olshevsky, A.; Paschalidis, I.C.; Shi, W. Federated learning of predictive models from federated electronic health records. *Int. J. Med. Inform.* **2018**, *112*, 59–67. [CrossRef] [PubMed]
41. Liu, Y.; Zhang, Y.; Kang, J.; Yu, R.; Deng, Q. Secure Federated Learning for Autonomous Driving. *IEEE Trans. Veh. Technol.* **2020**, *69*, 7131–7140.
42. Zhao, Y.; Li, M.; Lai, L.; Suda, N.; Civin, D.; Chandra, V. Federated learning with non-iid data. *arXiv* **2018**, arXiv:1806.00582. [CrossRef]
43. McMahan, B.; Moore, E.; Ramage, D.; Hampson, S.; y Arcas, B.A. Communication-efficient learning of deep networks from decentralized data. In Proceedings of the Artificial Intelligence and Statistics, Fort Lauderdale, FL, USA, 20–22 April 2017; pp. 1273–1282.
44. Adamova, A.; Zhukabayeva, T.; Mukanova, Z.; Oralbekova, Z. Enhancing internet of things security against structured query language injection and brute force attacks through federated learning. *Int. J. Electr. Comput. Eng. (2088-8708)* **2025**, *15*, 1187. [CrossRef]
45. Saadouni, R.; Gherbi, C.; Aliouat, Z.; Harbi, Y.; Khacha, A.; Mabed, H. Securing smart agriculture networks using bio-inspired feature selection and transfer learning for effective image-based intrusion detection. *Internet Things* **2025**, *29*, 101422. [CrossRef]
46. Chen, H.; Wang, Z.; Yang, S.; Luo, X.; He, D.; Chan, S. Intrusion detection using synaptic intelligent convolutional neural networks for dynamic Internet of Things environments. *Alex. Eng. J.* **2025**, *111*, 78–91. [CrossRef]
47. Shirley, J.J.; Priya, M. An Adaptive Intrusion Detection System for Evolving IoT Threats: An Autoencoder-FNN Fusion. *IEEE Access* **2025**, *12, 4201–4217. [CrossRef]*
48. Ji, R.; Selwal, A.; Kumar, N.; Padha, D. Cascading Bagging and Boosting Ensemble Methods for Intrusion Detection in Cyber-Physical Systems. *Secur. Priv.* **2025**, *8*, e497. [CrossRef]
49. Sakraoui, S.; Ahmim, A.; Derdour, M.; Ahmim, M.; Namane, S.; Dhaou, I.B. FBMP-IDS: FL-based blockchain-powered lightweight MPC-secured IDS for 6G networks. *IEEE Access* **2024**, *12*, 105887–105905. [CrossRef]
50. Gulzar, Q.; Mustafa, K. Enhancing network security in industrial IoT environments: A DeepCLG hybrid learning model for cyberattack detection. *Int. J. Mach. Learn. Cybern.* **16**, 2025, 1–19. . [CrossRef]
51. Wang, J.; Yang, K.; Li, M. NIDS-FGPA: A federated learning network intrusion detection algorithm based on secure aggregation of gradient similarity models. *PLoS ONE* **2024**, *19*, e0308639. [CrossRef]

future internet

Article

Analyzing Impact and Systemwide Effects of the SlowROS Attack in an Industrial Automation Scenario

Ivan Cibrario Bertolotti [1], Luca Durante [1] and Enrico Cambiaso [2,*]

[1] Istituto di Elettronica e di Ingegneria dell Informazione e delle Telecomunicazioni (IEIIT), Consiglio Nazionale delle Ricerche (CNR), 10129 Turin, Italy; ivan.cibrariobertolotti@cnr.it (I.C.B.); luca.durante@cnr.it (L.D.)

[2] Istituto di Elettronica e di Ingegneria dell Informazione e delle Telecomunicazioni (IEIIT), Consiglio Nazionale delle Ricerche (CNR), 16152 Genoa, Italy

* Correspondence: enrico.cambiaso@cnr.it

Abstract: The ongoing adoption of Robot Operating Systems (ROSs) not only for research-oriented projects but also for industrial applications demands a more thorough assessment of its security than in the past. This paper highlights that a key ROS component—the ROS Master—is indeed vulnerable to a novel kind of Slow Denial of Service (slow DoS) attack, the root reason of this vulnerability being an extremely high idle connection timeout. The effects of vulnerability exploitation have been evaluated in detail by means of a realistic test bed, showing how it leads to a systemwide and potentially dangerous disruption of ROS system operations. Moreover, it has been shown how some basic forms of built-in protection of the Linux kernel can be easily circumvented, and are therefore ineffective against this kind of threat.

Keywords: cybersecurity; denial of service; slow DoS attack; industrial security; ROS; critical infrastructure protection

1. Introduction

Nowadays, the Robot Operating System (ROS) enjoys widespread popularity in industrial operational technology environments due to its open-source nature, its ease of use, and the support of leading stakeholders [1]. Being used for different applications, such as edge robotics [2] or Industry 4.0 and Industrial Internet of Things (IIoT, in short) [3,4], today, ROS represents a leading protocol in the industrial sector [5]. In virtue of this, investigating its potential security weaknesses becomes essential to protect it from external threats that might disrupt manufacturing plants and lead to possible economic loss and equipment damage, not to mention the possible harm to human safety.

In the cybersecurity panorama, denial of service (DoS) threats are perpetrated to make a network service unreachable by its intended users. Considering such threats, conventional flooding-based approaches require a huge amount of attack resources, whereas other menaces, such as slow DoS, use limited attack bandwidth. slow DoS threats are therefore particularly relevant from this point of view because they can exhaust some kind of resource of the system they target while effectively deceiving detection mechanisms. In fact, proper protection against last-generation distributed DoS threats, such as slow DoS threats [6], is still an open research challenge.

This work investigates the susceptibility of an ROS system deployed in an industrial context to a slow DoS threat and evaluates its adverse effects on the overall system behavior. To this purpose, we evaluate and validate SlowROS, an innovative slow DoS threat that targets the ROS Master, a mandatory component that is invariably present in all ROS systems. To the best of our knowledge, the literature on industrial security does not cover slow DoS threats targeting the ROS protocol. In addition, to date, there are no known ROS vulnerabilities related to the exploitation of slow DoS-oriented approaches.

The contributions of this paper are the following: *(i)* address the lack of extensive analysis of the impact of slow DoS-like attacks on industrial protocols; *(ii)* evaluate the efficacy of the SlowROS threat by executing proper tests on a real network scenario; *(iii)* attempt to identify the optimal attack setup in terms of attack timeout: by doing this, in Section 6.2 we will find that the ROS Master does not implement any connection-closure timeout; and *(iv)* discuss possible protection approaches able to counter SlowROS.

In detail, after providing an overview of the state of the art and related work in Section 2, the paper continues with some basic information about ROS in Section 3. The slow DoS attack to ROS is discussed in Section 4, while the test bed used to demonstrate it is described in Section 5. Section 6 presents and comments on the experimental results while Section 7 outlines possible protection approaches to counter slow DoS attacks. Finally, Section 8 concludes the paper.

2. Related Work

For the sake of clarity, the discussion of the related work has been split into two parts. The first, in Section 2.1, concerns slow DoS attacks in general, regardless of the specific protocol or system they are directed against. The second part, in Section 2.2, summarizes the ROS security analysis work carried out since its inception.

2.1. slow DoS

slow DoS attacks are introduced in [6], defining them as "denial of service attacks which make use of low attack bandwidth to accomplish their purpose". Particularly, the aim of [6] is to properly categorize slow DoS attacks, considering available threats, born both in the wild and as a result of research activities. The work identifies a set of server timeouts the attacker can potentially exploit to deploy a successful slow DoS attack. Among these timeouts, the Δ_{req} timeout, exploited by threats like Slowloris [7] or SlowComm [8], is the same timeout targeted by the threat subject of this work.

Other work has instead been focused on targeting specific protocols. While the most popular attack in this context, Slowloris [9], is able to target HTTP/HTTPS only, other threats are aimed at disrupting different services. In this context, an evolution of Slowloris is proposed in [10], introducing a new threat targeting HTTP/2 by sending specific HTTP requests to the server. Differently, ref. [11] proposes SlowTT, a slow DoS attack targeting the MQTT protocol. By following a similar approach, in this paper, we aim at targeting the ROS protocol through a dedicated attack. Although a preliminary version of the work appears in [12], the current work extends the concept previously introduced by considering attack optimization strategies and by identifying, evaluating, and overcoming the limits of the previously introduced threat.

Today, the protection from distributed slow DoS attacks represents an open research challenge. Even though identifying threats executed from a single malicious node is trivial [13], detecting distributed attacks is particularly challenging, as the network traffic they generate appears to be legitimate upon analysis [14]. In addition, as the payload exchanged during an ongoing attack complies with the exploited protocol, distinguishing between a malicious slow DoS scenario and a "legitimate" flash crowd is arduous [15]. Indeed, both situations generate a surge in traffic, making it difficult to differentiate between malicious intent and legitimate high-demand behavior [16].

Although an efficient detection of slow DoS attacks is not straightforward, multiple research works propose solutions in this context. Particularly, refs. [7,17,18] propose a literature analysis on the topic, while [16] introduces a detection system able to distinguish flash crowds from denial of service attacks, by exploiting network flows correlation. Similarly, analogies between network flows are investigated in [19] for slow DoS detection purposes. Instead, ref. [20] introduces a detection system based on user behavior forecasting. As authors analyze traffic patterns and related delays, a malicious user may tune the attack to mimic user timings and exploit randomization techniques to bypass detection. Ref. [21] makes use of artificial intelligence algorithms to detect slow DoS attacks, also considering encrypted traffic. Other similar approaches consider deep learning [22,23], fuzzy logic [24], or neural networks [25]. Most of the mentioned works focus on the ability to successfully identify an attack, without considering detection times. To this aim, ref. [13] proposes a detection system able to identify running slow DoS attacks shortly after it begins. Given the novelty of the SlowROS threat considered in this paper, although approaches similar to the ones mentioned could in principle be deployed to detect the attack, to the best of our knowledge, specific solutions able to efficiently identify a running SlowROS threat are still missing in the literature.

2.2. ROS Security

The security of ROS 1 has been the subject of a fair amount of scrutiny by researchers and practitioners alike, especially since it gained traction for industrial applications. Initially, researchers [26–28] focused on the lack of enforceable authentication and encryption between ROS nodes, which makes them susceptible to replay attacks and service hijacking. However, they did not consider denial of service (DoS) attacks specifically and did not provide any details about their execution.

Later work [29,30] discussed ROS penetration testing and demonstrated more elaborate attacks that crash or disable some ROS nodes, thus making the services they provide unavailable to other nodes and, eventually, making the ROS system as a whole inoperable. Although the final result of those attacks is similar to the ones presented in this paper, in their case, the attack strategy is radically different. In fact, they leverage specific software vulnerabilities (for instance, CVE exploits), rather than a slow DoS attack strategy. Even a recent comprehensive review of ROS security [31] still does not mention slow DoS attacks at all.

Moreover, the official "Python library reference" [32] warns that the `xmlrpc.server` module—used by the ROS communication layers—is not robust against *maliciously crafted* data. However, it does not mention the possibility of perpetrating attacks by means of *legitimate* data as the slow DoS attack proposed in this work does.

Finally, a query performed on the Common Vulnerabilities and Exposures (CVEs) list at the time of this writing with "ROS" as the search term [33] returned 114 records. Of them, 82 were disputed, and hence, were not further considered. Of the remaining 32, 19 pertained to other products with a similar name (for instance, the Rugged Operating System by Siemens) and 2 were about ROS 2, leaving 11 records related to ROS 1. A further refinement of the query including "`noetic`" as the search term eventually returned two records, CVE-2020-16124 and CVE-2021-37146.

CVE-2020-16124 discusses an integer overflow or wraparound vulnerability in the XML-RPC library, while CVE-2021-37146 reports an infinite loop in the XML-RPC server that may be triggered by a malicious RPC call. Neither of those vulnerabilities nor their underlying operating principle have been exploited for the attack discussed in this paper, thus confirming that the attack is, in fact, novel.

The mitigation techniques discussed so far in the literature belong to three broad categories. The first category aims at *preventing* attacks, for instance, by means of additional security-oriented components, like Rosbridge and SROS. Rosbridge is a WebSocket–ROS bridge that grants web applications controlled access to ROS nodes, and can indeed prevent attackers from reaching the ROS system directly from the Internet. However, it may be ineffective against insider threats, which act from the private side of the industrial network. SROS adds TLS support to the existing ROS protocols but is currently still experimental and has no longer been maintained since 2022 [34]. The recommendation of restricting access to the ROS network by isolating it from the Internet, advocated by the official ROS documentation [35], belongs to the same category. Nonetheless, this policy may be hard to enforce, considering that a relatively recent study [36] found a plethora of ROS systems that were indeed publicly reachable.

The second category of mitigation techniques aims at *detecting* attacks instead, usually by means of machine learning algorithms [37–39]. To the best of the authors' knowledge, none of the existing work considers slow DoS attacks, focusing instead on data injection attacks [37] or on traditional DoS attacks [38] involving large amounts of illegitimate data. The use of deep reinforcement learning to identify vulnerabilities in ROS-based robot navigation is explored in [39] but without explicitly considering DoS attacks.

The last mitigation technique simply consists of *switching* to ROS 2, also because the most recent version of ROS (Noetic Ninjemys, often abbreviated as `noetic`) is meant to be the last version of ROS before the transition to ROS 2 and will reach its End-Of-Life (EOL) date in mid-2025. Nevertheless, assessing and analyzing ROS security as performed in this work still makes sense despite this impending transition due to its rather significant installed base in real-world applications. Even more importantly, the slow pace at which ROS 2 is replacing it [40] suggests that the final phase-out of ROS and its replacement by ROS 2 will undoubtedly require a significant amount of time beyond 2025, also considering the unavoidable inertia of industrial equipment procurement and production lines commissioning. Finally, since ROS 2 relies on the Data Distribution Service (DDS) standard [41] for communication, it is indeed affected by its own vulnerabilities [42], which have recently led to an ICS advisory [43].

3. ROS Primer

This section contains a brief introduction to ROS, encompassing its evolution and fundamental concepts. It then describes in more detail the protocol used by the ROS Master, the ROS agent whose vulnerability has been exploited for the work being discussed in this paper.

3.1. History

In a nutshell, ROS is a set of open-source libraries and tools that provide commonly used robot control functionalities and algorithms. Although, strictly speaking, ROS is not an operating system per se because it relies on "true" operating systems such as Linux as a foundation, it still provides hardware abstraction and platform-independent robotic device control and access, along with a comprehensive message passing subsystem based on the publisher–subscriber communication paradigm and a modular, high-level software packaging framework.

In embryonic form, ROS development began in late 2006 in the context of the Stanford Personal Robotics Program [44]. One of the main initial goals—maintained through the whole project history—was to facilitate code reuse so that researchers would focus more on designing and developing innovative robot control software, rather than re-implementing the underlying middleware infrastructure anew whenever they moved to a new project or new hardware.

Even though ROS was initially geared towards robotic research and hobbyists' projects, it gained more and more industrial interest with time, fueled by initiatives like the ROS Industrial Consortium [1], whose charter is to extend ROS to work effectively with industrial relevant hardware and applications. Current consortium members include leading robot OEM manufacturers, end-users such as large international manufacturing companies, and research institutes worldwide.

The most recent released version of ROS, Noetic Ninjemys (often abbreviated `noetic`), was released in mid-2020 and is meant to be the last version of ROS before the transition to ROS 2, slated for mid-2025 when `noetic` will reach its End-Of-Life (EOL) date. Despite this impending transition, `noetic` is the ROS release to be considered in this work.

3.2. Basic Concepts

From the software organization and communication standpoint, an ROS system is composed of a set of cooperating processes structured in a *computation graph*. Within the graph, each *node* is a process responsible for a portion of data processing. Links in the graph represent communication paths among nodes. Since ROS encourages fine-grained modularity, a typical ROS system consists of multiple nodes. Nodes are written with the help of a client library that depends on the programming language being used. For instance, nodes written in Python (both version 2 and 3 are supported) use the `rospy` library.

The basic unit of communication among nodes is the *message*, a simple data structure comprising typed fields. ROS supports the most common primitive types, like Booleans, integers, and floating-point values. They can be placed into arrays and structures, which can then be nested arbitrarily.

The main ROS message transport system is based on the publisher–subscriber paradigm. In this approach, nodes send out data of possible interest to others by publishing messages to a certain *topic*. Interested nodes subscribe to the topic to receive them. Each topic supports a single message type and has a unique *name* in the system, which both publishers and subscribers use to refer to it. There may be multiple publishers and subscribers to the same topic, and an individual node may publish and subscribe to multiple topics, thus establishing a many-to-many communication relationship.

To better accommodate one-to-one, synchronous, request–reply interactions between nodes, ROS also supports the concept of *service*. A service has a unique name, like a topic, and has two message structures associated to it, one for requests and one for replies. A server node that offers a service registers it under a unique name. Client nodes locate a server by looking up the name of the service it offers, send a request message to it, and wait for a reply. From the programmer's perspective, this kind of interaction is usually seen as a Remote Procedure Call (RPC).

In both cases, the ability to resolve a name and determine which nodes are related to it as publishers–subscribers of a topic or as service provider is crucial, also considering that ROS nodes are not a priori aware of each other's existence and position in the computation graph. This role is fulfilled by the ROS *master*, whose identity is expressed by a Uniform Resource Identifier (URI) and is assumed to be well known to all other nodes.

The master acts as a centralized store of registration information about topics and services for other nodes to use. For instance, publishers of a certain topic contact the master to inform it of their presence. The master keeps the list of publishers of a certain topic up to date so that subscribers can acquire this information as needed. The master may also call nodes back when the registration information changes, thus enabling nodes to adapt to a dynamically changing communication graph topology.

It is work noting that, although the ROS master plays the role of a *broker*, unlike other kinds of brokers, it is not directly involved in publisher–subscriber data transfer. In order to do that, nodes will indeed make use of the information they acquired from the master but will then use it to establish a direct peer-to-peer data connection.

The last ROS component to be discussed here is the *parameter server*. It acts as a centralized store of (key, data) pairs that all ROS nodes may obtain and set at will. In the pair, key uniquely identifies a certain parameter and data is its value. Parameters are often used to store settings for an ROS application as a whole and make them globally accessible. Although the parameter server was originally meant to be used sparingly and mostly during initialization, to retrieve parameters that are not going to change while the system is operational, ROS `noetic` actually calls it much more frequently as better explained in Section 6.4.

Most importantly for the threat to be discussed in Section 4, the parameter server is currently implemented as part of the ROS master process and hence shares network communication resources with it. As a consequence, any attack that hinders network access by the master also affects the parameter server in the same fashion.

3.3. ROS Master Protocol

ROS nodes interact with the master via the XML-RPC protocol [45]. XML-RPC is a connection-oriented protocol that uses HTTP [46] POST requests to transport XML-encoded [47] RPC requests and receive responses. ROS layers the master APIs on top of XML-RPC by defining suitable RPC method names, along with their parameters and return values. In turn, HTTP runs over a TCP [48] connection initiated by a ROS client node and accepted by the master.

As an example relevant to the discussion in Section 4, Figure 1 shows the request and response messages exchanged between an ROS node on host `bravo` and the master on `alfa` to register the node as a publisher of a certain topic. For simplicity, the figure omits all details about TCP connection establishment and segmentation.

The ROS node sends an HTTP POST request to the master at `alfa:11311`, which contains an XML-RPC `methodCall` to the ROS method `registerPublisher`. Its four arguments are the unique identifiers of the publisher (`/talker_39066_1706698579110`), the name of the topic it publishes (`/chatter`), the data type of the topic messages (`std_msgs/String`, corresponding to the basic string type), and the URI of the publisher (`http://bravo:40717/`), which may be used to contact it.

If there are no HTTP-layer errors, the master always returns the HTTP status `200 OK` in its response. The XML-RPC `methodResponse`, as required by the ROS master API upon successful RPC completion, contains a single `<value>` enclosed in a `<param>` and then in a `<params>`. If the XML-RPC layer detects an error, the `methodResponse` would instead contain a `<fault>` that, in turn, would contain additional information about the error itself.

The `<value>` in the response represents the return value(s) of the method. For the `registerPublisher` method, the return values are an integer ROS-layer status code (`1` indicates that the request has been fulfilled successfully), a human-readable message that summarizes the operation just performed, and an `<array>` that contains the URIs of the current subscribers to the topic. In this case, the array is empty because there were no subscribers when the publisher registered itself.

— Request —

```
POST /RPC2 HTTP/1.1
Host: alfa:11311
Accept-Encoding: gzip
Content-Type: text/xml
User-Agent: Python-xmlrpc/3.8
Content-Length: 380

<?xml version='1.0'?>
<methodCall>
<methodName>
registerPublisher
</methodName>
<params>
<param>
<value>
<string>
/talker_39066_1706698579110
</string>
</value>
</param>
<param>
<value>
<string>
/chatter
</string>
</value>
</param>
<param>
<value>
<string>
std_msgs/String
</string>
</value>
</param>
<param>
<value>
<string>
http://bravo:40717/
</string>
</value>
</param>
</params>
</methodCall>
```

— Response —

```
HTTP/1.1 200 OK
Server: BaseHTTP/0.6 Python/3.8.10
Date: Wed, 31 Jan 2024 10:56:19 GMT
Content-type: text/xml
Content-length: 311

<?xml version='1.0'?>
<methodResponse>
<params>
<param>
<value>
<array>
<data>
<value>
<int>
1
</int>
</value>
<value>
<string>
Registered [/talker_39066_1706698579110] as publisher of [/chatter]
</string>
</value>
<value>
<array>
<data>
</data>
</array>
</value>
</data>
</array>
</value>
</param>
</params>
</methodResponse>
```

Figure 1. Message exchange to register a new ROS publisher. HTTP headers are shown in red, XML-RPC encapsulation elements in green, and ROS-specific fields in blue.

4. Attack Context and Description

4.1. Underlying Protocol Mechanisms

In the TCP protocol, a three-way handshake procedure determines how connections between the client and the server are established [49]. Although the way network packets are exchanged during such a procedure may be familiar, the local activities executed on the hosts may need further discussion.

In particular, referring to Figure 2, before sending the first `SYN` packet to the server [49], the client allocates a local socket for the connection. When the server receives the `SYN` packet, it does not immediately allocate a dedicated socket yet. At this point, it merely allocates an in-kernel state vector to keep track of the connection state and puts it in the so-called TCP SYN queue while the handshake proceeds towards full connection establishment.

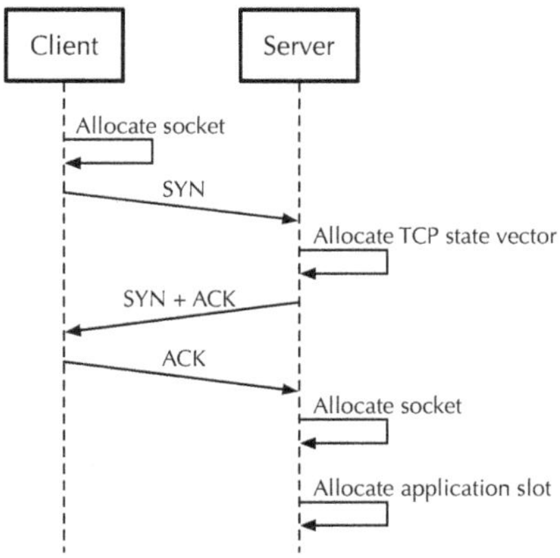

Figure 2. Analysis of the 3-way handshake procedure during a TCP connection between a client and a ROS Master service.

The socket is in fact allocated on the server only at the end of the three-way handshake, when the `ACK` packet has been received and the server has eventually been informed about the new connection by the successful completion of an `accept()` system call. After accepting the new connection, the server also usually allocates an application slot for it, to store all the information the server needs for its management.

4.2. Kernel Behavior and System Limits in TCP Connection Handling

Important constraints on the maximum number of concurrent connections a server can support come from the internal logic of the server itself, besides several kernel parameters related to protocol stack resource management. For instance, connections that require a large quantity of server-side memory to be handled may exhaust the total amount of memory allotted to the server well before hitting against any other system limit.

Moreover, flaws in the server implementation, like the failure to release sockets upon normal or abnormal connection closure, may lead to premature socket exhaustion. Unfortunately, memory requirements and implementation quality are usually very specific to a certain kind/version of a server, and can hardly be generalized. In addition, while testing the ROS Master implementation, we found no indication of any memory or socket leak. Its memory allocation level stayed well below the upper limit as well.

For all these reasons, in this paper, we focus only on system-level limits that depend on the Linux kernel configuration, and hence, impose an upper bound to the number of concurrent TCP connections that a certain server can successfully support, regardless of its internal structure. While such a choice may represent a limit for slow DoS categories like delayed or long responses DoS, it has no impact on our long request attack [6].

Furthermore, we also assume there is a one-to-one correspondence between established TCP connections and sockets in the ROS Master. This is not strictly true for the *partially* established TCP connections outlined in Section 4.1, that is, connections that went through the first two stages of the three-way TCP handshake and are waiting for the final ACK from the initiator.

For these connections, the in-kernel protocol stack has already allocated a state vector but, since processes are not made aware of incoming connections until they are *fully* established, no sockets in the user space have been assigned to them yet. However, the `net.ipv4.tcp_max_syn_backlog` parameter (128 by default on the nodes described in Section 5) determines the maximum number of *partially* established TCP connections that the kernel allows for the whole system. This limit prevents both crashes and protocol stack memory exhaustion due to this reason.

Two other kernel and process parameters apply to the different stages an incoming TCP connection may be in. In particular, we have the following:

1. When they have been fully established from the TCP/IP protocol stack point of view, incoming connections enter the backlog of the listening socket, waiting to be accepted by the server by means of an `accept()` system call. The actual limit to the backlog length is primarily set by the server through the second parameter of `listen()`, but a kernel parameter sets an upper bound to what the server may ask for. The parameter is `net.core.somaxconn`, and its default value is 4096 on the nodes used in our test bed.
2. As also discussed in Section 4.1, when the server eventually tries to accept an incoming connection, a new socket must be allocated for it within the `accept()`. Linux, like many other operating systems, represents a socket in user space with a file descriptor. Therefore, the maximum number of connections a server can accept is also limited by the maximum number of open file descriptors the server is allowed to have.

Unlike the previous two, the maximum number of file descriptors a process may open is not set by a kernel parameter but is primarily a per-process limit that can be set by means of the `setrlimit` (set resource limit) system call [50]. Resource limits are uniquely identified by a symbolic constant, `RLIMIT_NOFILE` in this particular case, which becomes the first argument of `setrlimit`. The second argument represents the desired value of the limit being set, encoded in a `struct rlimit`. The shell command `ulimit -n` provides a more user-friendly interface to the same underlying system call. The default value of the file descriptor limit is 1024 on the nodes used in this paper.

Therefore, if we call f the value of `RLIMIT_NOFILE` and b the listening socket backlog length, in a congestion scenario like a slow DoS one, assuming that a server accepts incoming connections as soon as they come in and has no other internal constraints, the following occurs:

- The server accepts the first $f - k$ incoming connections, where k represents the number of file descriptors already opened by the server for other purposes.
- Then, b more connections are established at the TCP level but stay in the listening socket backlog.
- Eventually, further connections requests are postponed by the TCP/IP protocol stack, which stops acknowledging incoming SYNs.

4.3. *slow DoS Attack Description and Analysys*

If we consider the ROS protocol as mentioned above, it is a TCP-based application layer protocol used to manage communication inside of an industrial IoT network, based on a publish–subscribe approach. In more detail, the ROS protocol makes use of HTTP REST-based APIs, including XML-formatted data.

Considering such aspects, the slow DoS Attack examined in this paper is going to act in two stages: (i) At first, a specific amount of simultaneous connections with the server is established in order to seize all available connection slots that the (application) server is able to support. (ii) Then, each connection is kept alive as long as possible in order to prevent its closure by the server. Such typical behavior of slow DoS Attacks [6] leads to a denial of service on the server and attempts to keep it as long as possible.

In detail, the number of connections that the attacker has to simultaneously establish and keep alive depends on the application server configuration. Although for specific daemon software, such as the Apache web service, such a value can be set up, it may not have an impact on the attack success, while, by increasing such a value, the attacker would require more resources to accomplish its goal.

Instead, in order to keep the connection as long as possible, different approaches are possible: in our case, by implementing a so-called *Long Request DoS*, we split the transmission of the request payload in multiple cycles, sending a predefined payload to the server, split into multiple portions on each round. In particular, the considered payload transmitted by the attacker may vary and may exploit different functionalities/methods provided by the ROS server. In our case, we adopt a payload similar to the one reported in Figure 3.

```
POST /RPC2 HTTP/1.1
Host: {ros_server_host}:11311
Accept-Encoding: gzip
Content-Type: text/xml
User-Agent: Python-xmlrpc/3.8
Content-Length: {payload_length}

<?xml version='1.0'?>
<methodCall>
<methodName>registerPublisher</methodName>
<params>
<param>
<value><string>/talker_{id}</string></value>
</param>
<param>
<value><string>/chatter</string></value>
</param>
<param>
<value><string>std_msgs/String</string></value>
</param>
<param>
<value><string>http://{endpoint}/</string></value>
</param>
</params>
</methodCall>
```

Figure 3. Payload content sent by the attack to the ROS publisher. HTTP headers are shown in red, XML-RPC encapsulation elements in green, and ROS-specific fields in blue.

For the sake of readability, we indent content in the figure, whereas when sending data over the network, the content is not indented. Token and field separators—the `\r\n` sequence between HTTP headers and any amount of white space between XML syntactic elements—are not shown, either. Moreover, although XML tags and ROS-specific fields are split into multiple lines in Figure 1, we do not consider such formatting in Figure 3 to better represent the actual payload sent by the attacker. We also replace specific information (such as the value of the HTTP Host parameter) with generic tags to provide a more general payload applicable independently on the target.

It should be noted that any payload compliant to the protocol is valid to perpetrate a successful attack. In addition, payloads not compliant to the ROS protocol may lead to a successful DoS as well [8].

As the payload sent by the attacker typically is a legitimate payload compliant to the ROS protocol, it is not trivial to detect an ongoing attack, by analyzing the data exchanged by the client and the server. In addition, although in this paper we consider, for simplicity, a single attacking host, whose detection of the malevolent aims at the network layer would be trivial, it is quite simple for a real attacker to distribute the threat to multiple malicious nodes, coordinated to perpetrate a common attack against a simple server. In such a case, the detection of an ongoing attack would be more difficult.

Figure 4 summarizes the prospective attack sequence as a whole. The attacker is shown on the left and regular ROS nodes on the right. The ROS Master and parameter server are represented as two separate entities in the middle of the figure, although, as discussed in Section 3.2, they are implemented within the same process. The sequence consists of the following steps, whose number is also recalled in the figure for clarity:

1. In the system initialization and setup phase, regular ROS nodes interact with the ROS Master to register themselves as publishers and/or subscribers. The attacker does not interfere with this phase.
2. ROS nodes typically do not interact with the ROS master anymore when the system enters the operational phase. Instead, they exchange process data through dedicated point-to-point TCP connections and may query the ROS parameter server. As also mentioned in Section 3.2, in the ROS version considered in this paper, parameter server access is not as sporadic as it was supposed to be when ROS was designed. Even more importantly, its use is not at all confined to the setup phase.
3. At this point, the attacker opens a number of TCP connections to the ROS Master by conducting the three-way handshake shown in Figure 2 and, optionally, sending partial requests to it. As described in Section 4.1, the ROS Master has to allocate some resources for each open connection.
4. As the number of malicious connections keeps increasing, the ROS Master exhausts its resources. Most notably, it runs out of file descriptors as outlined in Section 4.2. Resource exhaustion affects not only the ROS Master but also the parameter server since they share the same pool of process-level file descriptors.
5. The final effect of the attack is that operational ROS nodes become unable to reach the parameter server. Moreover, any ROS node that attempts to recover and repeat the setup phase to become operational again can no longer communicate with the ROS Master to announce itself.

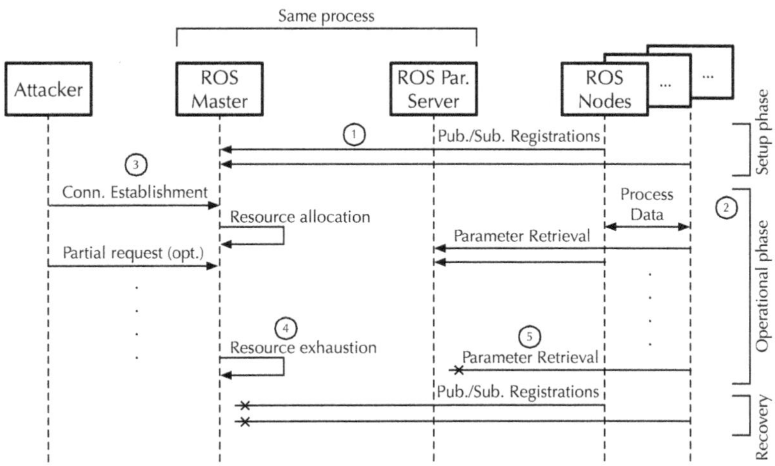

Figure 4. Sequence diagram of the attack scenario.

In order to evaluate the possibility of carrying out a successful attack along the lines just presented, also as a function of the payload sent and the attack approach adopted, in terms of timings and data sent at each round of attack, in the next section, we are going to define the testbed considered in our experimentation.

5. Test Bed

In order to validate the efficacy of the threat introduced in Section 4, we built a setup representing a full ROS-powered network. Overall, the test bed being presented and used to conduct and analyze the slow DoS attack is meant to represent a simplified, but still realistic, implementation of a typical industrial production line.

As shown in Figure 5, it consists of five nodes interconnected by means of a 100BaseTX shop-floor network, depicted as a green line. This network emulates a local plant network; its IP addresses are assigned statically and lie in the same `/24` subnet. More specifically, we have the following:

- Node `alice`, depicted on the right of the figure, is an Interbotix PincherX-100 robot arm (4 DOF plus gripper) controlled by an 8th Gen Intel NUC equipped with the Interbotix-provided distribution of Ubuntu 20.04 and ROS `noetic`. It corresponds to one of the regular ROS nodes depicted on the right side of Figure 4. The NUC runs the ROS joint control software and, possibly, additional ROS applications that implement any local robot arm control algorithms needed by the application at hand.
- Nodes `alpha`, `bravo`, and `charlie` are also regular ROS nodes, based on Raspberry PI 3 model B boards equipped with an off-the-shelf distribution of Ubuntu 20.04 and ROS `noetic`. They run ROS code that performs various higher-level system coordination and supervision functions. According to the guidelines presented in [51], `alpha` also hosts the centralized ROS Master and parameter server shown in the middle of Figure 4, which all ROS nodes query as described in Section 3. Node `charlie` is the malicious node that conducts the slow DoS attack. In our scenario, we assume this node has been compromised in some way to act malevolently and implement the attack sequence summarized in Figure 4.
- The gateway shown at the far left of Figure 5 grants external access to the shop-floor network, for instance, through a wired or WiFi connection to a plant-wide SCADA or MES network. This node usually incorporates a firewall that protects the shop-floor

network from unauthorized access, while still allowing control and supervision traffic to pass through. For instance, a SCADA system might obtain access to robot arm operating information and statistics by means of an OPC-UA/ROS software gateway installed at the shop-floor boundary, or use ROS directly for the same purpose. In the example attack described in this paper, the gateway represents the entry point leveraged by the remote attacker to inject malicious software into node `charlie`.

In the specific test bed version used in this paper, the ROS Master is implemented by means of the off-the-shelf `rosmaster` process found in the ROS `noetic` distribution. The joint control software running on `alice` is the `robot_state_publisher` application provided by Interbotix with the robot arm, whose communication functions to the ROS Master are also based on unmodified, lower-level software libraries from ROS `noetic`.

The high-level ROS application (also running on `alice`) is simulated by a Python application, derived from one of the ROS examples, which drives the gripper through a closed Cartesian trajectory in space indefinitely, until stopped by hand. Finally, system coordination and supervision functions are simulated by a telemetry application based on the standard `rostopic` tool, which runs on `bravo` and periodically reports the joints' position, velocity, and torque.

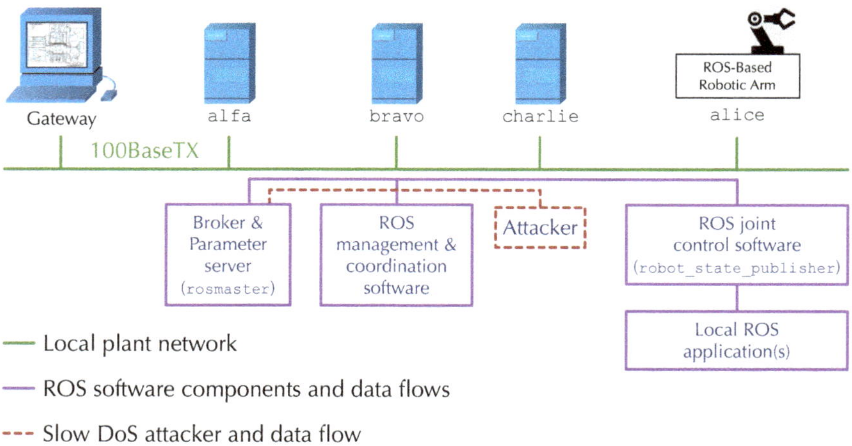

Figure 5. ROS Test bed for slow DoS attacks.

This rather conservative approach is meant to realize a "minimal working example" of the vulnerable industrial system and guarantees that neither application-specific nor vendor-specific code is involved in the communication between the ROS Master and the rest of the ROS software. This aspect will turn out to be crucial to ensure that the attack discussed in Section 4 does not depend on the specific test bed in use or any custom software that runs on it, and can hence be exploited on a variety of ROS-based systems.

6. Tests, Results, and Analysis

In this section, we report the results of the tests we executed in our test bed, with the aim to evaluate the performance of the considered SlowROS attack and define an optimal attack strategy.

6.1. Identifying the Maximum Number of TCP Connections the Server Can Simultaneously Manage

Understanding what is the maximum number of concurrent TCP connections a Linux process can successfully support is crucial to properly configure the attack described in Section 4. First of all, since the value of b defined in Section 4.2 partly depends on the server itself (`net.core.somaxconn` is merely its upper bound), we determined it by inspecting the source code of the ROS master used in the experiments, available at [52]. Namely, b is set at `xmlrpc.py::132` of the `ros_comm` ROS component as follows:

```
self.request_queue_size = min(socket.SOMAXCONN, 128)
```

Neglecting k, which is unknown for the time being, the maximum number of established connections c towards the ROS Master can be approximated by

$$c = f + \min(s, 128)\,, \quad (1)$$

where s is the value of `net.core.somaxconn`. We checked (1) with a set of experiments in which we measured the actual maximum number of established connections c' to the ROS Master for varying f and s, obtaining the results shown in Table 1.

Table 1. Maximum number of connections c' for varying f and s.

f	s	c (from (1))	c' (Measured)	k (calc.)
1024	4096	1152	1148	4
768	96	864	860	4
512	96	608	604	4
512	64	576	572	4
256	64	320	316	4

As shown in the table, the value of k derived from c and c' is consistently $k = 4$. This confirms both the validity of (1) and the experiments accuracy, given that we expect the server to use three file descriptors for its standard input, output, and error streams plus one more for the listening socket. Additional tests were executed to analyze the behavior of the server as a function of its load. In detail, by varying the number of legitimate clients connected during the attack (denoted as c_l), we measured that c' assumes the value $c - k - c_l$.

Once the number of concurrent connections the server is able to manage was determined, we attempted to identify another relevant attack parameter, namely, the time interval to be adopted by the attacker to slow data transmission down as much as possible, as described in the next section. For all subsequent tests, the ROS Master was configured according to the first row of Table 1.

6.2. Identification of the Connection Timeout Used by the ROS Master

As anticipated, a first, crucial step needed to evaluate the feasibility and success probability of the SlowROS threat is to determine the value of the server-side timeout T_i adopted by the ROS Master. Namely, servers are typically programmed to close pending connections on their own initiative when a specific inactivity timeout T_i expires. Under normal conditions, such expiration typically occurs when communicating with badly connected nodes or nodes interrupting the communication without advising it.

A correct identification of T_i enables the attacker to optimize the network resources it spends to keep its connections awake, hence maintaining the DoS state. To do this, the attacker shall send some more data on each connection every T_c, namely, the Wait

Timeout [6], where $T_c \leq T_i - \epsilon$. On the one hand, $\epsilon > 0$ shall be a time buffer large enough to accommodate transmission timing inaccuracies due, for instance, to network latency or unpredictable delays, as well as T_i measurement. On the other hand, according to the general bandwidth-saving requirement typical of slow DoS attacks, ϵ shall also be as small as possible. In other words, the attacker shall send some data just before T_i expires but not more often than needed. Indeed, keeping those illegitimate connections alive without letting the server close them denies legitimate users the ability to connect to the service and use it.

The test strategy put into effect for T_i identification in this work assumes that T_i is fixed, as, to the best of our knowledge, is typically the case. It involves establishing a single connection with the ROS Master, possibly transmitting some data, and then waiting until the peer closes the connection. Sending different amounts of valid (and possibly invalid) data in different tests is crucial to detect whether T_i is fixed or changes depending on the specific, incoming data-dependent state the server's protocol stack is brought in.

To avoid indefinite waits, the test program only waits for the connection to be closed for up to T_{max} before exiting. When this occurs (i.e., the connection is not closed by the server within T_{max}), the test is unable to determine T_i precisely, but it can still be safely stated that T_{max} is a lower bound of T_i, that is, it must be $T_i \geq T_{max}$.

Since there may be different timeout settings depending on the protocol layer currently in charge of handling the partial payload received by the ROS Master, several different tests were performed, truncating the full message listed in Figure 3 at various points before suspending the transmission and waiting for further ROS Master's actions as further detailed in the following.

Table 2 summarizes the results obtained with $T_{max} = 3600$ s. From left to right, the columns represent the following:

- A numeric identifier used to refer to the test.
- Brief description of the scenario considered.
- Information about the application payload being sent by the test program, if any. When sending a partial payload, it simply refers to a range of lines of Figure 3. When sending an altered payload, details of the alteration are reported in the scenario description: for instance, in test 4, the partial payload being sent consists of lines 1–8 of Figure 3 plus an invalid XML-RPC token.
- Information on the measured connection closure time T_i.
- The time required by the server to return either an error indication or a method response, from the reception of the connection closure packet from the client.
- The final application server response when the connection is closed, for both HTTP and XML protocol layers, which does not affect T_i assessment but will be further discussed in Section 6.3.

Table 2. Tests for ROS Master Timeout Identification, $T_{max} = 3600$ s.

# Scenario	Payload	T_i	Response Time (ms)	Response upon Close HTTP	XML
1 Basic	*none*	$\geq T_{max}$	—	*none*	*N/A*
2 POST only	1–1	$\geq T_{max}$	1.44	HTTP/1.1 500	*N/A*
3 Full HTTP header	1–7	$\geq T_{max}$	1.45	HTTP/1.1 200	<fault>
4 Invalid XML-RPC request	1–8	$\geq T_{max}$	1.16	HTTP/1.1 200	<fault>
5 Partial XML-RPC request	1–11	$\geq T_{max}$	1.84	HTTP/1.1 200	<fault>
6 Ending newline missing	1–25	$\geq T_{max}$	3.42	HTTP/1.1 200	<methodResponse>
7 Full, valid request	1–35	$\geq T_{max}$	—	HTTP/1.1 200 *(immediate)*	*none*

The rationale behind the partial payloads used for the tests is that, in test 1, nothing is sent, to make the server process wait for HTTP headers. Differently, in test 2, the server receives a valid POST request and reassembles the remaining HTTP headers. Instead, in test 3, the server waits for an XML-RPC request to start, while in test 4, the server reassembles an XML-RPC request that contains an invalid token.

Test 5 is similar to test 4, but the partial XML-RPC request sent to the server is valid. In test 6, a fully valid XML-RPC request is sent to the server, but the request is one byte shorter than what the HTTP Content-Length says. All in all, these tests stops the HTTP/XML-RPC payload reassembly and interpretation process performed by the server at different stages to determine the T_i of each stage.

Finally, in test 7, the test program sends a full XML-RPC request whose length is consistent with the HTTP Content-Length, followed by silence. This test's goal is to clarify whether the server behaves differently for what concerns T_i while waiting for the very first XML-RPC request (as it does in test 1) rather than the next.

As reported in Table 2, we find that in no tests did the ROS master close the connection on its own initiative, leading to the important conclusion that $T_i \geq 3600\,\mathrm{s}$. Considering that a timeout of 3600 s is typically considered quite high for this kind of protocol; this observation paved the way to suspecting that T_i might be infinite, at least in some cases.

To further validate this hypothesis, test 1 was repeated with a longer timeout, that is, $T_{max} = 10^9\,\mathrm{s}$. Also in this case, the server did not close the connection until the test program was manually interrupted after about 11.85 days. Despite the manual interruption, the connection was closed with an FIN rather than a RST because the test program still terminated it with a `close()` system call, corresponding to an orderly connection shutdown from the transport point of view.

This result confirms that, for all intents and purposes, the ROS Master connection inactivity timeout can be considered infinite, at least for completely inactive connections, that is, connections on which no data have been sent after establishment. It is worth mentioning that a direct communication between the attacker and the victim takes place as shown in Figure 5. A more accurate characterization of T_i was not performed because it would serve no practical purpose at this stage.

Variant of tests 1–7 were then executed to check whether or not the ROS Master implements any *dynamic* connection closure strategy, for instance, whether it starts closing idle connections when it detects a possible overload condition on the number of open connections. As determined in Section 6.1, in its default configuration (corresponding to the first row of Table 1) the ROS Master supports up to $c' = 1148$ connections. Considering there is always one active connection to the ROS Master whenever a fully functional ROS system is brought up (due to the presence of a mandatory subscriber to the ROS logging topic `/rosout`), the test programs now opens $c' - 1 = 1147$ connections to the ROS Master instead of one, in order to bring the total number of established connections to the ROS Master exactly to c'.

Event log and traffic analysis confirmed that the ROS Master did not attempt to close any connections, thus confirming the apparent lack of dynamic connection closure and all results reported in Table 1. Last, but not the least, manual inspection of the ROS code base under analysis confirmed the absence of any time- or load-dependent connection timeout mechanism. If this were not the case or, more generally, when confronted with a closed-source ROS Master implementation, a dynamic adjustment of T_c based on real-time connection closure monitoring would become necessary.

Summarizing, we found that the ROS protocol is, at least in our scenario, vulnerable to different attack approaches, occurring at different stages of the communication with the

ROS Master. In addition, its extremely high T_i value gives a vantage point to the adversary, enabling it to perpetrate a potentially successful attack even with a minimum amount of network resources. In detail, we found that once the attack is initiated, the DoS state is potentially maintained indefinitely, even without any action by the attacker, which may even be disconnected by the network for a long time, leaving the server under the DoS state. Considering the executed tests, in the next section, we further analyze the server response to the different scenarios introduced in Table 2.

6.3. Response of the ROS Master Service to Different Malicious Payloads

As outlined in the previous section, some of the test programs aimed at determining T_i also send to the ROS Master a (possibly partial) payload before eventually closing the connection. The server's responses, summarized in the rightmost column of Table 2, provide valuable information on how the software modules responsible for implementing the protocol layers on the server side exchange data.

Firstly, when the test program sends either no data at all (test 1) or a complete, valid request from both the HTTP and XML-RPC viewpoints (test 7), the server does not send any response when the client closes the connection. Instead, as expected, in the same test, the server sends back a normal reply containing an indication of success at both the HTTP and XML-RPC layers upon receiving the request. This suggests that none of the software layers involved in the communication perform any action besides housekeeping upon connection closure.

In test 2, the server replies with an HTTP error (namely, 500 Internal Server Error). This is consistent with the HTTP layer trying to parse an incomplete set of HTTP headers, in which some mandatory information is missing. In tests 3–5, the HTTP layer responds with a success indication (200 OK) because it obtains a valid set of HTTP headers, but the XML-RPC layer reports a fault because the request it obtains from the HTTP layer is incomplete or invalid. In all cases, the fault indication reflects the issue in the request. More specifically, we have the following:

- In test 3, the XML-RPC fault indication contains the error "no element found" from the XML parser because empty XML-RPC requests are forbidden.
- In test 4, the parser reports a syntax error that pinpoints the invalid token present in the request.
- In test 5, the parser is unable to find the end of the dangling `<params>` clause.

Interestingly, the reply the server sends in test 6 contains a success indication at both the HTTP and XML-RPC layers, although the actual requests for the length are shorter than what is declared in the HTTP Content-Length. Hence, the fact that the request is actually incomplete (a well-known fact at the HTTP layer) is not properly forwarded to the XML-RPC layer, which then proceeds to parse it as normal.

Another important, counterintuitive conclusion that can be drawn from tests 2–6 is that, regardless of everything else, the ROS master tries to process any partial payload it may have received from a client when the client closes the connection. The reason behind this behavior has not been further investigated because it falls outside the scope of the present work but may be conducive to other kinds of attack, such as delayed or long-response DoS [6].

6.4. Systemwide Effects of the Attack

For the reasons outlined at the end of Section 3.2, the consequences of the attack presented in this paper go far beyond a disruption of the publisher–subscriber registration and notification mechanism that the ROS Master implements. If this were the case, the impact of the attack would still be significant but also somewhat limited in scope because it would just prevent *new* publishers and subscribers from registering, without interfering with *existing* ROS nodes that already entered the operational phase after a successful registration. So, for example, the attack would prevent a remote monitoring ROS subscriber (typically instantiated on demand) from accessing and displaying system information but would not affect the core robot control nodes.

However, as also mentioned in Section 3.2, in ROS `noetic` both the ROS Master and the parameter server are part of the same process, an implementation choice that the ROS specification does not explicitly forbid. As a consequence, any DoS attack that depletes some process-wide resource, such as file descriptors, also prevents ROS nodes from accessing system parameters.

Finally, the `JointStateListener` of ROS `noetic` queries the parameter server on every control cycle to retrieve the `tf_prefix` parameter from the closest namespace by means of the method `getTFPrefix()` (file `joint_state_listener.cpp`, line 91). Being a standard component, the `JointStateListener` is going to be present in virtually all ROS `noetic`-based systems.

These observations are crucial to understand why an attack involving solely the ROS Master eventually leads to a full, systemwide lockup like the one discussed in [12], instead of having more localized and less severe effects.

This discussion also calls attention to the importance of chain effects in cyber attacks, which are rather common and make their ultimate effects hard to predict. In this particular case, the combination of the following make the attack perimeter way larger than it could have been anticipated by intuition: *(a)* A DoS attack against a very specific ROS component (the ROS Master); *(b)* A legitimate implementation choice fully within the ROS specification boundaries (putting the ROS Master and parameter server together in the same process); *(c)* A coding peculiarity within a crucial ROS node (leading to the retrieval of a parameter on every robot control cycle)

By considering instead how the attack effects on the targeted server might vary depending on the actual deployment of TCP flooding countermeasures, in the next section, we discuss how a malicious user could bypass potential connection request flooding mitigation approaches.

6.5. Connection Request Flooding Bypass

While conducting the experiments discussed previously, care was taken not to trigger any connection request flooding protection mechanism built in the Linux TCP/IP protocol stack. These mechanisms typically activate when the connection request rate exceeds a certain threshold and are worth further investigation because, although they were likely not specifically designed with slow DoS threats in mind, they might still falsify experiment results and mitigate or disrupt the slow DoS attack itself.

To this purpose, we performed a set of tests similar to the ones discussed in Section 6.1, in which our attacking node tried to establish $c' = 1148$ connections to the ROS Master, with a varying connection request rate, that is, with a varying time interval T_{SYN} between consecutive SYNs. The client did not send any data after connection establishment and just closed the connection after $T_{max} = 3600$ s. By means of suitable probes located in the test bed, we measured the number of SYN retransmissions, as well as the difference between the number of successfully established connections on the test program (client) and ROS Master (server) side. The values of T_{SYN} used for the experiments were primarily chosen to highlight the knees of the two curves, to be discussed in the following. Multiple experiments were performed at around $T_{SYN} \simeq 0.6$ ms to assess and confirm result repeatability. The minimum value $T_{SYN} \simeq 0.1$ ms corresponds to the maximum connection request rate attainable by the test program on the machine used as attacker. Figure 6 depicts the results.

As shown in the figure, under normal operating conditions (T_{SYN} above about 2.5 ms) the number of SYN retransmissions is negligible (<1%) with respect to the total number of connections. Moreover, both the client and the server agree on how many connections have been established, that is, the difference between the number of connections registered by the protocol stack on the two sides is zero. This is in fact the condition under which all experiments discussed previously have been performed.

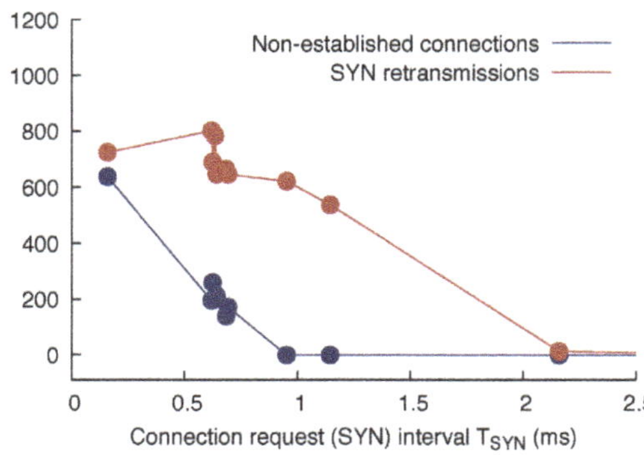

Figure 6. SYN retransmissions and number of non-established connections on the server side as a function of the connection request period.

In the approximate range 1 ms $\leq T_{SYN} <$ 2.5 ms, a significant increment of the number of SYN retransmissions can be observed, which gradually grows up to about 60% of the total number of connections. However, as shown, this does not lead to any discrepancy on the number of established connections registered on the client versus the server side. A likely reason for this behavior is server-side network buffer overload, which leads the server to drop part of the incoming SYNs. Then, client-side retransmissions lead the server to fully recover from these drops.

Instead, a significant pattern from the slow DoS attack's point of view emerges when T_{SYN} falls below 1 ms. While the number of SYN retransmissions further increases up to about 75% of the total number of connections as T_{SYN} decreases, the number of established connections on the server side also becomes systematically lower, and lower than the number of connections on the client side. When this happens, the server-side kernel starts reporting that it detected, and is reacting to, a "SYN flooding" [53].

From the practical point of view, triggering this protection means that the server-side protocol stack tricks the client into thinking that the expected number of connections has been established—by completing the three-way TCP handshake as normal—but these connections are neither registered in the protocol stack nor passed up into user space. As a result, they do not contribute to the depletion of any server resources, thus mitigating any slow DoS attack that might be in progress.

We were able to validate this last statement further by analyzing the client–server traffic. We observed that, when the client eventually closes its connections by sending FINs, the server responds with a FIN/ACK for the connections that are considered established on both sides, whereas it responds with RST to the connections established only on the client side. According to the TCP specification, the transmission of RST instead of FIN confirms that the corresponding connection was never established on the server side.

The mitigation has indeed a significant impact because, at the maximum connection request rate reached in our experiments ($T_{SYN} = 158\,\mu s$), about 55% of the connections "established" by the client are silently discarded and never reach the ROS Master. What makes the SYN flooding protection mechanism even more relevant in this context is that it is part of the standard TCP/IP protocol stack and does not depend on the installation and configuration of any dedicated kernel modules and utilities like, for instance, Iptables [54]. Therefore, it can be assumed to be ubiquitously present on virtually all Linux-based systems.

Unfortunately, from the victim's point of view, the SYN flooding protection can, however, be easily circumvented exactly as we did for our experiments, that is, by ensuring that the attacker's connection request rate stays sufficiently low. This approach is also in line with the typical stealthiness goal of slow DoS attacks that, among other requirements, stipulates a carefully controlled and limited peak bandwidth usage.

As a final remark, the actual T_{SYN} thresholds for the two behaviors just described (about 2.5 ms and 1 ms, respectively) may likely depend on the specific hardware capabilities and software configuration of the server operating system. This aspect has not been further investigated in the present work and will be the subject of future work concerning attack strategy optimization.

7. Countermeasures and Protection

If we consider the protection from the SlowROS attack discussed in this paper, although the approaches found in the literature and mentioned in Section 2 could be adapted to this aim, a dedicated detection and mitigation system able to protect from the considered threat is still missing. Nevertheless, in Section 6.5 we analyzed how protection systems embedded on many Linux-based operating systems can apply some kind of mitigation, identifying the attack as a SYN flood attack. Although the mitigation could be effective to protect from specific executions of SlowROS, we demonstrated that a malicious user could still fine-tune the attack and slow down the connection establishment procedure by means of specific delays (i.e., T_{SYN}), thus bypassing the restriction. As an additional benefit, such an approach would also lead to a reduction in the attack bandwidth. In other words, since the protection can easily be circumvented by the attacker, it should not be considered an efficient countermeasure.

Other protection approaches may filter network connections through dedicated firewall rules, embedded on the targeted host or on an intermediary firewall. To this aim, it is possible to use tools like Iptables or nfw [55] to block single node attacks, by limiting the number of concurrent connections a single node is allowed to establish with the server [56] and forcibly closing open connections, regardless of the server-side timeout settings described in Section 6.2. Such an approach is effective to counter slow DoS scenarios, even though it it may be ineffective against distributed attacks and artificially reduce server capacity. Indeed, in such a case, the attacking group of nodes may not be sufficient, in terms of the number of attacking bots, to lead a denial of service on the victim.

Another mitigation option may involve the implementation of a server-side timeout, used to close connections that do not respect minimum bandwidth requirements. Such an approach is implemented, for instance, by the `reqtimeout` module for the Apache web server [57]. By following this direction, let B be the bandwidth required for a single connection. During a flooding-based attack, B is supposed to assume particularly high values. On the contrary, in a slow DoS scenario, B is extremely low. As normal/legitimate flows are characterized by "in-between" values of B, it could be possible to implement a flow-control threshold T_B^s that lets connections stay alive only if $B > T_B^s$, hence being able to counter slow DoS threats. Typically, such an approach is adopted to implement $B < T_B^f$, with T_B^f being the threshold used to filter flooding-based threats. Therefore, generally speaking, implementing two lower and upper thresholds T_B^s and T_B^f may filter anomalous traffic. Nevertheless, identifying proper T_B^s and T_B^f values may not be trivial, as they depend on the behavior of the underlying network components. In addition, referring to T_B^f in particular, accurately defining when to apply the thresholds, in terms of time from the establishment of the connection, may not be trivial as well, as it may lead to temporary denial of service states. Therefore, although such an approach may represent a good choice for web server protection, the identification of an appropriate bandwidth threshold(s) to adopt may be complex, due to the nature of the ROS traffic. In addition, it is important to consider that such an approach may interrupt malicious connections only after the denial of service state has been experienced. Further variants of the mitigation technique may consider the use of dynamic thresholds, varying as a function of the number of currently established connections.

Instead, relying on various forms of server-side payload syntax checking is going to be ineffective because, as shown in Section 4, the slow DoS threat described in this paper only transmits legitimate payloads to the server. Finally, reimplementing the ROS Master and parameter server as two separate processes would avoid the chain effect discussed in Section 6.4. However, new publishers and subscribers would still be unable to contact the ROS Master and make themselves known to the system while an attack is ongoing.

8. Conclusions

This paper discussed and evaluated SlowROS, an innovative slow DoS threat directed towards the ROS Master, a mandatory ROS 1 component. In spite of the impending transition to ROS 2, improving ROS security is still quite relevant for the reasons given in Section 2.2. Among them, the most important one is that the deployment of ROS 2 is advancing more slowly than anticipated [40]. Hence, the possible security-related implications of the ROS/ROS 2 transition has been left to future work.

By means of a realistic experimental test bed, it was shown that the attack effect unexpectedly went well beyond the single component being targeted, as it could seem at first sight. Instead, it caused a systemwide service disruption that eventually affects all ROS nodes. Table 3 summarizes all test scenarios.

Table 3. Summary of test scenarios.

Scenario	Paper Section	Strategy	DoS?
1	Section 6.2	Single connection, $T_{max} = 10^9$ s	X
2	Section 6.2	Multiple connections, no payload, $T_{max} = 3600$ s	✓
3	Section 6.3	Multiple connections, partial/malformed payload, $T_{max} = 3600$ s	✓
4	Section 6.3	Multiple connections, full payload, $T_{max} = 3600$ s	✓
5	Section 6.5	Multiple connections, $T_{SYN} < 1$ ms (SYN flooding)	X

While designing SlowROS, the inner workings of the ROS Master and its underlying protocols were also thoroughly investigated. Besides being important for the design itself, the analysis led to an accurate characterization of the ROS Master connection timeout. Notably, one relevant discovery was related to the particularly high idle connection timeout adopted by the server. Future work on the topic may address such an aspect through additional tests. This characterization is crucial to saving bandwidth and making the SlowROS attack harder to detect.

Moreover, the ROS Master response to different kinds of payloads, both legitimate and invalid, has been determined. This information is useful to devise future, stealthier variations of SlowROS. Finally, the information gained about the Linux TCP/IP protocol stack was leveraged to circumvent its SYN flooding detection and protection mechanism.

Author Contributions: Conceptualization, I.C.B. and E.C.; methodology, I.C.B. and E.C.; software, I.C.B. and E.C.; validation, I.C.B. and E.C.; data curation, I.C.B. and E.C.; writing—original draft preparation, I.C.B. and E.C.; writing—review and editing, I.C.B. and E.C.; project administration, L.D.; funding acquisition, L.D. All authors have read and agreed to the published version of the manuscript.

Funding: This work was partially supported by project SERICS (PE00000014) under the MUR National Recovery and Resilience Plan funded by the European Union—NextGenerationEU.

Data Availability Statement: The raw data supporting the conclusions of this article will be made available by the authors on request.

Conflicts of Interest: The funders had no role in the design of the study; in the collection, analyses, or interpretation of data; in the writing of the manuscript; or in the decision to publish the results.

References

1. ROS Industrial Consortium. Consortium Home Page. Available online: https://rosindustrial.org (accessed on 28 January 2025).
2. Dechouniotis, D.; Spatharakis, D.; Papavassiliou, S. Edge robotics experimentation over next generation iiot testbeds. In Proceedings of the NOMS 2022-2022 IEEE/IFIP Network Operations and Management Symposium, Budapest, Hungary, 25–29 April 2022; pp. 1–3.
3. Ayaida, M.; Messai, N.; Valentin, F.; Marcheras, D. Talkrobots: A middleware for robotic systems in industry 4.0. *Future Internet* **2022**, *14*, 109. [CrossRef]
4. Lin, H.I.; Hwang, Y.C. Integration of robot and IIoT over the OPC unified architecture. In Proceedings of the 2019 International Automatic Control Conference (CACS), Keelung, Taiwan, 13–16 November 2019; pp. 1–6.
5. Profanter, S.; Tekat, A.; Dorofeev, K.; Rickert, M.; Knoll, A. OPC UA versus ROS, DDS, and MQTT: Performance evaluation of industry 4.0 protocols. In Proceedings of the 2019 IEEE International Conference on Industrial Technology (ICIT), Melbourne, Australia, 13–15 February 2019; pp. 955–962.
6. Cambiaso, E.; Papaleo, G.; Chiola, G.; Aiello, M. Slow DoS attacks: Definition and categorisation. *Int. J. Trust. Manag. Comput. Commun.* **2013**, *1*, 300–319. [CrossRef]
7. Rios, V.; Inacio, P.; Magoni, D.; Freire, M. Detection of Slowloris Attacks using Machine Learning Algorithms. In Proceedings of the 39th ACM/SIGAPP Symposium on Applied Computing, Avila, Spain, 8–12 April 2024; pp. 1321–1330.
8. Cambiaso, E.; Papaleo, G.; Aiello, M. Slowcomm: Design, development and performance evaluation of a new slow DoS attack. *J. Inf. Secur. Appl.* **2017**, *35*, 23–31. [CrossRef]
9. Sabri, S.; Ismail, N.; Hazzim, A. Slowloris DoS attack based simulation. In Proceedings of the IOP Conference Series: Materials Science and Engineering, Bapatla, India, 7–8 May 2021; Volume 1062, p. 012029.
10. Tripathi, N.; Hubballi, N. Slow rate denial of service attacks against HTTP/2 and detection. *Comput. Secur.* **2018**, *72*, 255–272. [CrossRef]
11. Vaccari, I.; Aiello, M.; Cambiaso, E. SlowTT: A slow denial of service against IoT networks. *Information* **2020**, *11*, 452. [CrossRef]
12. Cambiaso, E.; Durante, L.; Cibrario Bertolotti, I. SlowROS: Investigating the possibility to perpetrate Slow DoS Attacks against Robot Operating System. In Proceedings of the 8th International Conference on Communication and Network Technology (ICCNT), Florence, Italy, 16–18 September 2024.
13. Aiello, M.; Cambiaso, E.; Mongelli, M.; Papaleo, G. An on-line intrusion detection approach to identify low-rate DoS attacks. In Proceedings of the 2014 International Carnahan Conference on Security Technology (ICCST), Rome, Italy, 13–16 October 2014; pp. 1–6.
14. Kemp, C.; Calvert, C.; Khoshgoftaar, T.M. Detection methods of slow read DoS using full packet capture data. In Proceedings of the 2020 IEEE 21st International Conference on Information Reuse and Integration for Data Science (IRI), Las Vegas, NV, USA, 11–13 August 2020; pp. 9–16.
15. Wen, S.; Jia, W.; Zhou, W.; Zhou, W.; Xu, C. CALD: Surviving various application-layer DDoS attacks that mimic flash crowd. In Proceedings of the 2010 Fourth International Conference on Network and System Security, Melbourne, Australia, 1–3 September 2010; pp. 247–254.
16. Yu, S.; Zhou, W.; Jia, W.; Guo, S.; Xiang, Y.; Tang, F. Discriminating DDoS attacks from flash crowds using flow correlation coefficient. *IEEE Trans. Parallel Distrib. Syst.* **2011**, *23*, 1073–1080. [CrossRef]

17. Alashhab, A.A.; Zahid, M.S.M.; Azim, M.A.; Daha, M.Y.; Isyaku, B.; Ali, S. A survey of low rate DDoS detection techniques based on machine learning in software-defined networks. *Symmetry* **2022**, *14*, 1563. [CrossRef]
18. Wu, Z.; Li, W.; Liu, L.; Yue, M. Low-rate DoS attacks, detection, defense, and challenges: A survey. *IEEE Access* **2020**, *8*, 43920–43943.
19. Lysenko, S.; Bobrovnikova, K.; Matiukh, S.; Hurman, I.; Savenko, O. Detection of the botnets' low-rate DDoS attacks based on self-similarity. *Int. J. Electr. Comput. Eng.* **2020**, *10*, 3651–3659. [CrossRef]
20. Savchenko, V.; Ilin, O.; Hnidenko, N.; Tkachenko, O.; Laptiev, O.; Lehominova, S. Detection of slow DDoS attacks based on user's behavior forecasting. *Int. J. Emerg. Trends Eng. Res. (IJETER)* **2020**, *8* , 2019–2025. [CrossRef]
21. Garcia, N.; Alcaniz, T.; González-Vidal, A.; Bernabe, J.B.; Rivera, D.; Skarmeta, A. Distributed real-time SlowDoS attacks detection over encrypted traffic using Artificial Intelligence. *J. Netw. Comput. Appl.* **2021**, *173*, 102871. [CrossRef]
22. Muraleedharan, N.; Janet, B. A deep learning based HTTP slow DoS classification approach using flow data. *ICT Express* **2021**, *7*, 210–214.
23. Nugraha, B.; Murthy, R.N. Deep learning-based slow DDoS attack detection in SDN-based networks. In Proceedings of the 2020 IEEE Conference on Network Function Virtualization and Software Defined Networks (NFV-SDN), Virtual, 9–12 November 2020; pp. 51–56.
24. de Miranda Rios, V.; Inácio, P.R.; Magoni, D.; Freire, M.M. Detection of reduction-of-quality DDoS attacks using Fuzzy Logic and machine learning algorithms. *Comput. Netw.* **2021**, *186*, 107792. [CrossRef]
25. Xu, C.; Shen, J.; Du, X. Low-rate DoS attack detection method based on hybrid deep neural networks. *J. Inf. Secur. Appl.* **2021**, *60*, 102879. [CrossRef]
26. Jeong, S.Y.; Choi, I.J.; Kim, Y.J.; Shin, Y.M.; Han, J.H.; Jung, G.H.; Kim, K.G. A Study on ROS Vulnerabilities and Countermeasure. In Proceedings of the Companion of the 2017 ACM/IEEE International Conference on Human-Robot Interaction, Vienna, Austria, 6–9 March 2017; HRI '17, pp. 147–148. [CrossRef]
27. Abeykoon, I.; Feng, X. Challenges in ROS Forensics. In Proceedings of the 2019 IEEE SmartWorld, Ubiquitous Intelligence & Computing, Advanced & Trusted Computing, Scalable Computing & Communications, Cloud & Big Data Computing, Internet of People and Smart City Innovation (SmartWorld/SCALCOM/UIC/ATC/CBDCom/IOP/SCI), Leicester, UK, 19–23 August 2019; pp. 1677–1682. [CrossRef]
28. Teixeira, R.R.; Maurell, I.P.; Drews, P.L. Security on ROS: Analyzing and exploiting vulnerabilities of ROS-based systems. In Proceedings of the 2020 Latin American Robotics Symposium (LARS), 2020 Brazilian Symposium on Robotics (SBR) and 2020 Workshop on Robotics in Education (WRE), Virtual, 10–13 November 2020; pp. 1–6. [CrossRef]
29. Dieber, B.; White, R.; Taurer, S.; Breiling, B.; Caiazza, G.; Christensen, H.; Cortesi, A. Penetration Testing ROS. In *Robot Operating System (ROS): The Complete Reference (Volume 4)*; Koubaa, A., Ed.; Springer International Publishing: Cham, Switzerland, 2020; pp. 183–225. [CrossRef]
30. Basan, E.; Sushkin, N.; Khabarov, O.; Makarevich, O.; Azarov, I. Analysis of Attacks on Robotic Operation System. In Proceedings of the International Workshop on Advanced in Information Security Management and Applications (AISMA 2021), CEUR Workshop Proceedings, Stavropol and Krasnoyarsk, Russia, 1 October 2021; pp. 41–48.
31. Mokhamed, T.; Dakalbab, F.M.; Abbas, S.; Talib, M.A. Security in Robot Operating Systems (ROS): Analytical review study. In Proceedings of the 3rd International Conference on Distributed Sensing and Intelligent Systems (ICDSIS 2022), Dubai, United Arab Emirates, 19–21 October 2022; pp. 79–94. [CrossRef]
32. van Rossum, G.; the Python Development Team. *The Python Library Reference—Release 3.12.3*; Python Software Foundation: Beaverton, OR, USA, 2024.
33. MITRE Corporation. Common Vulnerabilities and Exposures (CVE) List. Available online: https://cve.mitre.org/cgi-bin/cvekey.cgi?keyword=ros (accessed on 28 January 2025).
34. Open Source Robotics Foundation, Inc. SROS Documentation. Available online: https://wiki.ros.org/SROS (accessed on 28 January 2025).
35. Open Source Robotics Foundation, Inc. ROS.org Documentation. Available online: http://wiki.ros.org/Documentation (accessed on 28 January 2025).
36. DeMarinis, N.; Tellex, S.; Kemerlis, V.P.; Konidaris, G.; Fonseca, R. Scanning the Internet for ROS: A View of Security in Robotics Research. In Proceedings of the 2019 International Conference on Robotics and Automation (ICRA), Montreal, QC, Canada, 20–24 May 2019; pp. 8514–8521. [CrossRef]
37. Antunes, R.A.; Dalmazo, B.L.; Drews, P.L.J. Detecting Data Injection Attacks in ROS Systems using Machine Learning. In Proceedings of the 2022 Latin American Robotics Symposium (LARS), 2022 Brazilian Symposium on Robotics (SBR), and 2022 Workshop on Robotics in Education (WRE), São Paulo, Brazil, 18–21 October 2022; pp. 1–6. [CrossRef]

38. Zaim, H.Ç.; Yolaçan, E.N.; Yavanoğlu, U. Intelligent Attack Detection in ROS-based Systems. In Proceedings of the 2023 IEEE International Conference on Big Data (BigData), Sorrento, Italy, 15–18 December 2023; pp. 5946–5950. [CrossRef]
39. Qiu, Q.; Zhang, X.; Yao, S.; Chen, Y.; Chen, G.; Hua, B.; Ji, J. Training a Non-Cooperator to Identify Vulnerabilities and Improve Robustness for Robot Navigation. *IEEE Robot. Autom. Lett.* **2023**, *8*, 4465–4472. [CrossRef]
40. Portugal, D.; Rocha, R.P.; Castilho, J.P. Inquiring the robot operating system community on the state of adoption of the ROS 2 robotics middleware. *Int. J. Intell. Robot. Appl.* **2024**, 1–26.
41. Object Management Group, Inc. DDS Security, Version 1.1. 2018. Available online: https://www.omg.org/spec/DDS-SECURITY/1.1/About-DDS-SECURITY (accessed on 24 May 2024).
42. Trend Micro Research, TXOne, ADLINK, Alias Robotics, and ZDI. Defending the Supply Chain: Why the DDS Protocol Is Critical in Industrial and Software Systems. 2022. Available online: https://www.trendmicro.com/en_us/research/22/a/defending-the-supply-chain-why-dds-is-critical-in-industrial-and-software-systems.html (accessed on 24 May 2024).
43. America's Cyber Defense Agency. ICS ADVISORY—Multiple Data Distribution Service (DDS) Implementations (Update A). 2022. Available online: https://www.cisa.gov/news-events/ics-advisories/icsa-21-315-02 (accessed on 24 May 2024).
44. Wyrobek, K.A.; Berger, E.H.; Van der Loos, H.M.; Salisbury, J.K. Towards a personal robotics development platform: Rationale and design of an intrinsically safe personal robot. In Proceedings of the 2008 IEEE International Conference on Robotics and Automation, Pasadena, CA, USA, 19–23 May 2008; pp. 2165–2170. [CrossRef]
45. Winer, D. XML-RPC Specification. Available online: https://xmlrpc.com/spec.md (accessed on 28 January 2025).
46. Internet Engineering Task Force (IETF). HTTP/2, RFC 9113. Available online: https://datatracker.ietf.org/doc/html/rfc9113 (accessed on 28 January 2025).
47. World Wide Web Consortium (W3C). Extensible Markup Language (XML). Available online: https://www.w3.org/XML/ (accessed on 28 January 2025).
48. Internet Engineering Task Force (IETF). Transmission Control Protocol (TCP), RFC 9293. Available online: https://datatracker.ietf.org/doc/html/rfc9293 (accessed on 28 January 2025).
49. Shebaro, B. SYN, SYN-ACK, and beyond: Learning by networking. *J. Comput. Sci. Coll.* **2020**, *35*, 44–51.
50. ISO/IEC/IEEE. *International Standard ISO/IEC/IEEE 9945, Information Technology—Portable Operating System Interface (POSIX®) Base Specifications, Issue 7*; International Organization for Standardization: Geneva, Switzerland, 2009.
51. Malavolta, I.; Lewis, G.; Schmerl, B.; Lago, P.; Garlan, D. How do you Architect your Robots? State of the Practice and Guidelines for ROS-based Systems. In Proceedings of the 2020 IEEE/ACM 42nd International Conference on Software Engineering: Software Engineering in Practice (ICSE-SEIP), Seoul, Republic of Korea, 27 June–19 July 2020; pp. 31–40.
52. Open Source Robotics Foundation, Inc. Source code of the Ros_comm Component. Available online: https://github.com/ros/ros_comm (accessed on 28 January 2025).
53. Yang, C.H.; Wu, J.P.; Lee, F.Y.; Lin, T.Y.; Tsai, M.H. Detection and Mitigation of SYN Flooding Attacks through SYN/ACK Packets and Black/White Lists. *Sensors* **2023**, *23*, 3817. [CrossRef] [PubMed]
54. Netfilter Core Team. The netfilter.org "Iptables" Project", 1999–2021. Available online: https://www.netfilter.org/projects/iptables/index.html (accessed on 20 June 2024).
55. Bewasana, D.A.D.; Harumnanda, M.S.A.; Priambodo, D.F. Securing Networks with Port Knocking: An Experimental Study on Ubuntu and Kali. In Proceedings of the 2023 3rd International Conference on Electronic and Electrical Engineering and Intelligent System (ICE3IS), Yogyakarta, Indonesia, 9–10 August 2023; pp. 92–97.
56. Oktivasari, P.; Zain, A.R.; Agustin, M.; Kurniawan, A.; arbi Murad, F.; fabian Anshor, M. Analysis of effectiveness of iptables on web server from Slowloris attack. In Proceedings of the 2022 5th International Conference of Computer and Informatics Engineering (IC2IE), Jakarta, Indonesia, 13–14 September 2022; pp. 215–219.
57. Treglia, P. PiSecurityCheck: Server Security Check in a Hand. In Proceedings of the 2024 47th MIPRO ICT and Electronics Convention (MIPRO), Opatija, Croatia, 20–24 May 2024; pp. 1549–1554.

future internet

MDPI

Article

Hierarchical Federated Learning-Based Intrusion Detection for In-Vehicle Networks

Muzun Althunayyan [1,2,*], Amir Javed [1,*], Omer Rana [1] and Theodoros Spyridopoulos [1]

[1] School of Computer Science and Informatics, Cardiff University, Cardiff CF10 3AT, UK; ranaof@cardiff.ac.uk (O.R.); spyridopoulost@cardiff.ac.uk (T.S.)
[2] Computer Sciences and Information Technology College, Majmaah University, Al Majma'ah 11952, Saudi Arabia
* Correspondence: althunayyanms@cardiff.ac.uk (M.A.); javeda7@cardiff.ac.uk (A.J.)

Abstract: Intrusion detection systems (IDSs) are crucial for identifying cyberattacks on in-vehicle networks. To enhance IDS robustness and preserve user data privacy, researchers are increasingly adopting federated learning (FL). However, traditional FL-based IDSs depend on a single central aggregator, creating performance bottlenecks and introducing a single point of failure, thereby compromising robustness and scalability. To address these limitations, this paper proposes a Hierarchical Federated Learning (H-FL) framework to deploy and evaluate the performance of the IDS. The H-FL framework incorporates multiple edge aggregators alongside the central aggregator, mitigating single-point failure risks, improving scalability, and efficiently distributing computational load. We evaluate the proposed IDS using the H-FL framework on two car hacking datasets under realistic non-independent and identically distributed (non-IID) data scenarios. Experimental results demonstrate that deploying the IDS within an H-FL framework can enhance the F1-score by up to 10.63%, addressing the limitations of edge-FL in dataset diversity and attack coverage. Notably, H-FL improved the F1-score in 16 out of 24 evaluated scenarios. By enabling the IDS to learn from diverse data, driving conditions, and evolving threats, this approach substantially strengthens cybersecurity in modern vehicular systems.

Keywords: CAN bus; cyberattack; IDS; federated learning; in-vehicle network

1. Introduction

The number of connected and autonomous vehicles (CAVs) is experiencing rapid growth globally. This surge in reliance on electronics and software within modern automotive systems introduces cybersecurity risks that were not previously considered in their design and engineering [1]. A recent report estimates that the global market for connected vehicles will grow to approximately USD 244 billion by 2030 [2]. The controller area network (CAN) bus has emerged the primary protocol for in-vehicle communication because of its simplicity and efficiency. However, it lacks essential security features such as authentication and encryption [3], making it vulnerable to cyberattacks that can have severe consequences, including loss of life [4,5]. Intrusion detection systems (IDSs) are an effective method for detecting these threats within in-vehicle networks. Despite significant advancements in machine learning and deep learning for IDSs, challenges related to data privacy and communication efficiency remain. Federated learning (FL) offers a promising solution by enabling local model training while preserving the privacy of raw data [6]. FL addresses key limitations of centralized IDS approaches and is particularly well suited for in-vehicle networks for several compelling reasons:

- Privacy Preservation:Regulations such as the general data protection regulation (GDPR), California consumer privacy act (CCPA), personal information protection and electronic documents act (PIPEDA), and Brazilian general data protection law

(LGPD) safeguard sensitive data from unauthorized movement. FL enhances privacy by transmitting only learned parameters to the cloud server instead of raw data, thereby improving data protection [7].

- Reduced latency: By processing data locally and only sending model updates, FL reduces latency compared to traditional centralized approaches that require sending raw data to a central server [7].
- Compliance with guidelines: According to the 2020 guidelines of the International Telecommunication Union, an in-vehicle IDS must have the ability to regularly update its set of rules [8]. FL facilitates these updates by allowing continuous learning and model refinement.
- Adaptability to new attacks: FL enhances IDS adaptability to new, unseen attacks by updating local models with those trained on newly identified threats. These continuous updates ensure effective responses to evolving threats.
- Diverse driving scenarios: FL facilitates the training of a universal model that encompasses various driving scenarios, vehicle states, and driving behaviors.

Numerous studies have developed FL-based IDSs for in-vehicle networks [9–14]. However, they all utilize the standard FL architecture. To the best of our knowledge, this is the first study to introduce the H-FL framework for an in-vehicle IDS and to deploy and evaluate IDS performance within this architecture. The aim of this paper is to introduce and deploy our proposed IDS in [15] in the H-FL environment, evaluating its performance. The main contributions are summarized as follows:

- Deployment and evaluation of our proposed multistage IDS in an H-FL environment.
- Distribution of data across clients with three levels of non-IID data distributions, making the scenario more realistic.
- Performance evaluation of the IDS in the H-FL environment for both seen and unseen attack detection.
- Assessing IDS performance under different levels of non-IID data distribution.

The remainder of this paper is organized as follows. Section 2 provides context and background on FL, followed by a discussion of related work. Section 3 describes our overall methodology, followed by experimental results and evaluation in Section 4. Finally, Section 5 concludes the paper.

2. Background and Related Work

This section begins by providing background information on cloud-based FL and HFL, followed by a review of related works on in-vehicle IDSs deployed using an FL approach. It then examines non-IID data distributions, how these works allocated data across clients, and the limitations of existing studies.

2.1. Cloud-Based FL and Hierarchical FL

The standard cloud-based FL architecture comprises a cloud server and numerous clients, as shown in Figure 1. Clients (vehicles) download a global model from the cloud server, undergo multiple rounds of local training, and then send the model weights back to the server for aggregation. The iteration continues until the model achieves the desired level of accuracy. In cloud-based FL, the number of participating clients can reach into the millions [16], which can cause communication with the cloud server to become slow and unpredictable due to factors like network congestion, ultimately leading to inefficiencies in the training process [16,17]. In contrast, H-FL architecture consists of a cloud server, multiple edge servers, and numerous clients. In H-FL, clients update their local parameters and send them to the nearest edge server for edge aggregations, following a similar approach as in cloud-based FL. The difference is that after several rounds of edge aggregations, multiple edge servers send their parameters to a cloud server for cloud aggregation. This design allows more clients to participate in the framework. Moreover, H-FL significantly reduces the costly communication with the cloud by leveraging efficient client–edge interactions, leading to considerable decreases in both runtime and the number of necessary local iterations [18].

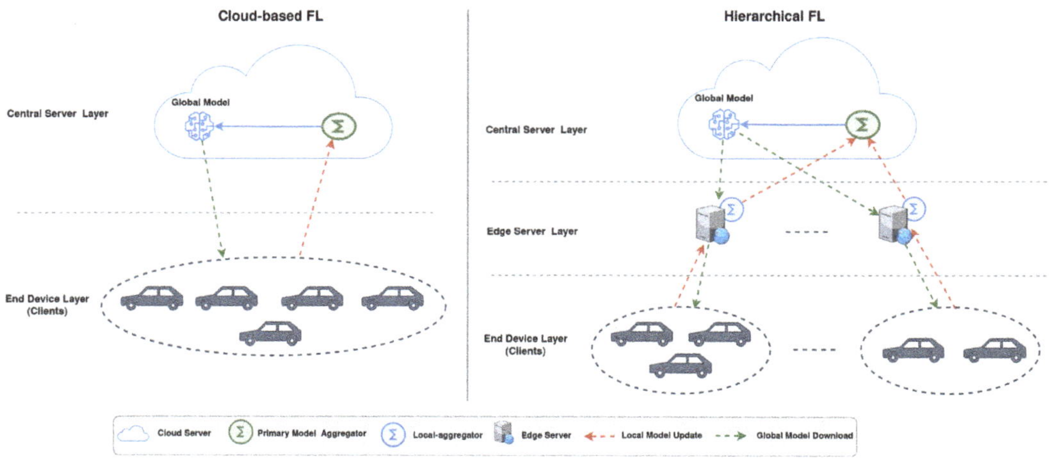

Figure 1. Cloud-based FL and H-FL.

2.2. Federated Learning-Based Intrusion Detection Systems

Driss et al. [9] introduced an FL-based framework to identify attacks in vehicular sensor networks. Given the resource constraints of smart sensing devices in vehicular networks, the authors emphasized the significance of adopting lightweight security approaches. To address this issue, they utilized a set of Gated Recurrent Units with an ensemble method based on Random Forest to aggregate the global machine learning models. They distributed the dataset equally among clients.

Shibly et al. [10] presented an FL-based IDS for enhancing security in autonomous systems. The authors personalized the model for each client participating in the FL process. The study integrates both supervised and unsupervised FL-based IDS to analyze patterns in CAN buses. Moreover, to create a more generalized model, local clients have the option to refine the global model using their local data and deploy it during inference.

Yu et al. [11] introduced an FL-based IDS based on Long Short-Term Memory (LSTM) for in-vehicle networks. They utilized the periodicity of CAN communications to predict the arbitration IDs of new messages. The 11-bit arbitration ID is transformed into vectors using one-hot encoding, and these vectors are utilized by the LSTM to predict the subsequent arbitration ID. Data are evenly distributed among clients, with each client holding 1000 instances for training and 200 instances for testing. A comparison between the FL-based and a centralized IDS revealed a 0.071 accuracy loss for the FL-based IDS. However, the authors suggested that this loss could be mitigated through a cumulative error scheme.

Zhang et al. [12] developed an anomaly detection system utilizing a graph neural network, capable of detecting CAN bus intrusions within a minimal 3-millisecond timeframe. They constructed a two-stage classifier cascade consisting of a classifier designed for anomaly detection in one class, and another classifier for categorizing attacks into multiple classes. To address novel anomalies from unseen classes, an openmax layer is integrated into the multi-class classifier.

Yang et al. [13] introduced an IDS for in-vehicle networks utilizing federated deep learning. The proposed approach leverages the periodicity of network messages, employs the ConvLSTM model, and trains the model through federated deep learning. To simulate a non-IID environment, clients were assigned varying data samples (ranging from 50 to 3500), although specific details regarding data distribution among clients and the distribution of samples across all classes were not provided.

Taslimasa et al. [14] proposed ImageFed, a practical IDS designed to preserve privacy, which utilizes federated Convolutional Neural Networks. To simulate a non-IID setting, data were distributed to vehicles using a Dirichlet (μ) distribution, with (μ) values varying from 0.1 to 0.7. To assess ImageFed's resilience, they examined two potential scenarios leading to performance decline in FL: non-IID clients and limited availability of training data. Table 1 summarizes previous works and highlights our contribution. In cases where the aggregation function is not explicitly indicated, as in [9,10], we assume that FedAvg is the method employed.

Although previous works have deployed their in-vehicle IDSs in an FL environment, they exhibit some limitations. Firstly, all the proposed FL-based in-vehicle IDSs in the literature utilized a standard cloud-based FL architecture to deploy and evaluate their proposed IDSs, relying solely on one central aggregator. However, this standard FL architecture can limit the IDS's adaptability and effectiveness in detecting diverse, evolving threats. Additionally, it leads to network congestion and communication delays due to the time required to share the model between the central aggregator and a large number of vehicles, potentially millions [16]. Furthermore, relying on one aggregator poses a risk as a single point of failure [19], compromising the IDS's robustness and scalability. To address these issues, we propose an H-FL framework that incorporates multiple edge aggregators in addition to the central aggregator. This approach enables the IDS to learn from a broader range of driving scenarios and evolving threats while distributing the computational load and reducing latency. This approach aims to overcome the limitations of relying solely on a central aggregator [19].

2.3. Non-Independent and Identically Distributed Data Distributions

Non-IID data occur when the training data on each client in FL vary significantly, resulting in differing data distributions among clients [17]. In real-world applications, such data are typically non-IID because of variations in user behavior, preferences, and environments. Managing non-IID data is a major challenge in FL [20]. However, previous works [9–12] did not account for non-IID data and instead employed divisions where clients received either an equal number of samples or samples from all classes (i.e., types of attacks). This approach contradicts the nature of FL scenarios characterized by non-IID data distributions [7] and assumes an unrealistic data distribution [21]. Non-IID data distributions are only considered in [13,14]. In [13], nine candidate clients are assumed, each possessing varying numbers of data samples (50, 100, 150, 1000, 1500, 2000, 2500, 3000, 3500), but the data distribution among clients and the distribution of samples across all classes are not clarified. In [14], to achieve a non-IID setting, data are allocated to vehicles using a Dirichlet (μ) distribution, with the (μ) parameter adjusted from 0.1 to 0.7.

However, the majority of studies [9–11] did not consider the data heterogeneity (non-IID data) in CAN bus data when they distributed the data across clients, thus rendering their findings unrealistic [21]. This consideration is essential for two reasons: first, in real-world deployments, vehicles will not have uniform distributions of both attack and normal data; second, testing with varying non-IID levels enables a more comprehensive evaluation of IDS performance and robustness across diverse data distributions. To address these issues, we have adopted H-FL with a realistic non-IID data distribution. H-FL incorporates a central aggregator with multiple edge aggregators instead of having one central aggregator. Furthermore, both experimental results and theoretical analysis have shown that H-FL architecture leads to faster convergence and lower training time and energy consumption of the end devices compared with the conventional FL-based framework [18]. To the best of our knowledge, no prior work has deployed and evaluated the performance of an in-vehicle IDS in an H-FL environment to detect known and unknown attacks.

Table 1. FL-based IDSs for in-vehicle networks.

Ref.	Fed. Learning	U Attacks	Non-IID	Aggregation Function	Dataset	FL Implementation
[14]	Standard	x	✓	FedAvg	car-hacking [22]	PyTorch
[11]	Standard	x	x	FedAvg	HCRL CAN Intrusion Detection [23]	N/A
[10]	Standard	x	x	FedAvg	car-hacking [22], NAIST CAN attack dataset [24]	Keras, TensorFlow
[12]	Standard	✓	—	FedAvg, FedProx	READ [25]	N/A
[9]	Standard	x	x	FedAvg	Car Hacking: Attack & Defense Challenge 2020 [26]	Keras, TensorFlow
[13]	Standard	x	✓	FedAvg	HCRL CAN Intrusion Detection [23]	N/A
Our work	Hierarchical	✓	✓	FedAvg	car-hacking [22]	Flower

U Attacks: Unknown Attacks.

3. Materials and Methods

In this section, we outline the methodologies used in our experiments, including the experimental setup, the proposed H-FL architecture, dataset description, in-vehicle IDS, data partitioning across multiple FL clients, data preprocessing, model initialization and pre-training, local training, aggregation, and evaluation methods.

3.1. Experimental Setup

The implementation was conducted in Visual Studio Code. The experimental setup used a 64-bit Windows 11 Pro for Workstations operating system with an AMD Ryzen Threadripper PRO 5995WX processor, featuring 64 cores at 2701 MHz, 128 logical processors, and 128 GB of RAM. The construction, training, and evaluation of the deep learning model were conducted with Flower framework [27], TensorFlow (version 2.13.1), and Python (version 3.8.10). Flower is an open-source FL framework to build AI applications capable of training on data distributed across numerous devices. We selected Flower for its ability to seamlessly transition from conventional to federated machine learning frameworks, its compatibility with popular platforms such as TensorFlow and PyTorch, its support for diverse privacy requirements, and its flexibility in facilitating the implementation of novel approaches with minimal engineering effort [28].

3.2. Hierarchical Federated Learning Architecture

The H-FL architecture consists of a main cloud server, several edge servers (aggregators), and numerous clients (vehicles), as depicted in Figure 2. The cloud server is connected to the edge servers, each of which interacts with vehicles in different geographical locations. In this paper, we utilize one main server, two edges, and five clients per edge. The H-FL process begins with the cloud server sending the initial model to the edge servers. Each edge server then selects a subset of clients for training using a suitable selection approach. The selected clients receive the initial model and perform edge aggregations over several rounds to generate an edge model. Once the edge servers complete their aggregations, they send their aggregated models' parameters to the cloud server. The cloud server aggregates these edge models to produce a global model, which is then sent back to the edge servers for further aggregation. A detailed description of the H-FL process is provided in Table 2. To handle the variability in CAN bus data across different vehicle makes and models, edge servers select clients based on similarities in their CAN bus data, such as make or model, within specific geographical areas. This approach ensures that the global model is trained on relevant and similar data, thereby improving accuracy.

The main server, located at 127.0.0.1:8088, initiates the process by distributing the pre-trained model to its connected clients (edges). Subsequently, each edge, serving as a server at addresses 127.0.0.1:8080 and 127.0.0.1:8081, respectively, relays the pre-trained model to its connected clients (vehicles). Each edge server then starts the standard FL process with the clients (vehicles) in its area, resulting in an edge model. These edge servers, now operating as clients, send their models back to the main server. The main server aggregates the received edge models into a global model, which it then redistributes to the edges. Finally, the edges, again functioning as servers, transmit the new global model to their clients (vehicles) to restart the FL cycle. Figure 3 illustrates this H-FL setup as implemented in Flower.

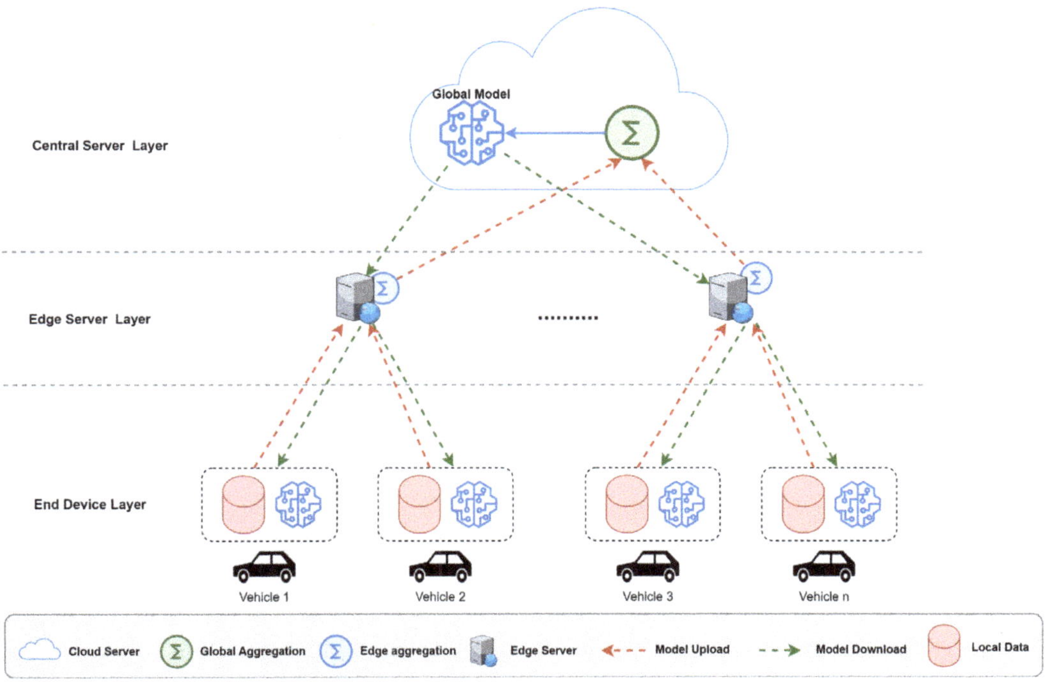

Figure 2. Architecture of the proposed H-FL method.

Table 2. Detailed description of the H-FL approach.

H-FL Process	
	Begin
Step 1	The central server $\mathcal{S}$ initializes a global model $\mathcal{GM}$
Step 2	$\mathcal{S}$ sends the $\mathcal{GM}$ to each local aggregator L_{Agg}
Step 3	Each L_{Agg} selects a subset of vehicles V_n
Step 4	L_{Agg} sends the $\mathcal{GM}$ to the selected V_n
Step 5	Each V_n trains the $\mathcal{GM}$ on local Data for K rounds
Step 6	Each V_n computes and sends the learned parameters to the corresponding L_{Agg}
Step 7	Each L_{Agg} aggregates the received local model parameters from V_n to obtain the edge aggregation model
Step 8	All L_{Agg} send the aggregated model parameters to $\mathcal{S}$ to build a new updated $\mathcal{GM}$
Step 9	The $\mathcal{S}$ aggregate edge aggregation model and build a new $\mathcal{GM}$
Step 10	Repeat steps 2–9 until achieving the desired performance
	End

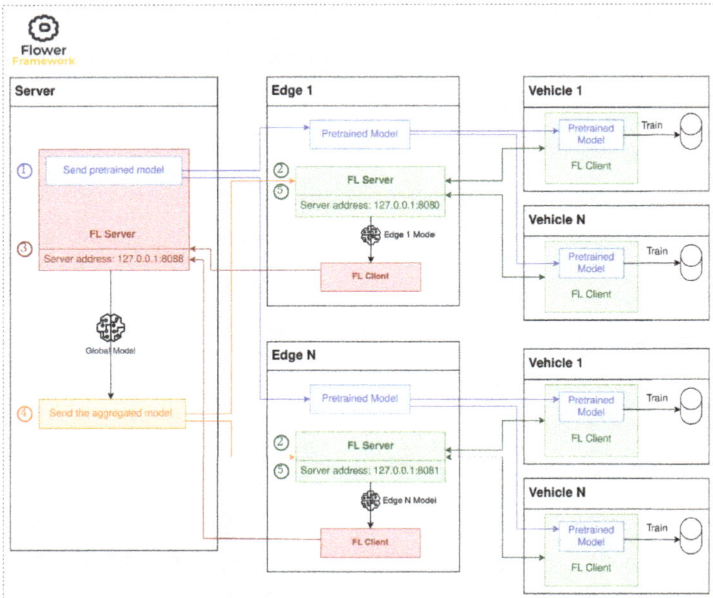

Figure 3. H-FL environment in Flower.

3.3. Dataset Description

To evaluate the performance of our IDS within the federated framework, we employed a benchmark car hacking dataset published by Song et al. [29]. We selected this dataset due to its widespread use in automotive security research and its status as the most frequently cited resource in the literature of the field [30]. The dataset contains normal data and four types of attacks: Denial of Service (DoS), frame fuzzification, engine RPM spoofing, and drive gear spoofing. It includes four files, one for each attack (DoS, frame fuzzification, gear spoofing, and RPM spoofing), with each file including normal as well as attack instances. Table 3 shows the number of instances for each type of attack as well as for normal data. For every CAN message, the dataset provides valuable information, including timestamp, CAN ID, DLC, data field, and flag. The timestamp records the exact time the message was captured since the system startup, while the CAN ID determines message priority, with lower values being prioritized. Additionally, the DLC defines the length of the data field, which can reach a maximum of 8 bytes. The flag indicates whether the message is normal or an attack. Table 4 provides an overview of the dataset's features, along with their descriptions and data types. To ensure the generalizability of our proposed H-FL architecture across diverse scenarios and to avoid reliance on a single dataset, we validated it using another benchmark dataset in automotive security research, the car hacking: attack & defense challenge 2020 dataset [26], which comprises normal traffic and three types of attacks: DoS, frame fuzzification, and spoofing [26].

Table 3. Dataset overview.

Attack Type	Attack Instances	Normal Instances
DoS	587,521	3,078,250
Frame Fuzzification	491,847	3,347,013
Gear	597,252	3,845,890
RPM	654,897	3,966,805
Total	2,331,517	14,237,958

Table 4. Data features, descriptions, and types.

Feature	Describtion	Type
Timestamp	Time	float
CAN ID	CAN message identifier	hexadecimal
DLC	The length of the data field, measured in bytes	integer
Data	Payload (64-bit)	hexadecimal
Flag	T or R, T: Attack, R: Normal	string

3.4. In-Vehicle Intrusion Detection System

In this paper, we evaluate the performance of our proposed IDS as detailed in [15]. The proposed IDS consists of a multistage approach, where the first stage is responsible for detecting and classifying known attacks using an Artificial Neural Network (ANN), while the second stage acts as an anomaly detector to identify novel, unknown attacks using a Long Short-Term Memory (LSTM) autoencoder. The first stage of our proposed in-vehicle IDS classifies traffic data as either normal traffic or any known attack class that the ANN model has been trained on. Any data classified as normal by the first model will be re-examined by the second model (LSTM autoencoder) to detect unseen attacks that bypassed the initial model, providing an additional layer of protection. The first stage is a signature-based multiclassifier model, while the second stage is an unsupervised anomaly detection model. Figure 4 shows the workflow of proposed multistage IDS. The proposed IDS achieves an F1-score of 0.95 and a 99.99% detection rate for previously unseen attacks, all within a compact model size of 2.98 MB, making it highly suitable for deployment in real-world applications. This efficient model size fits well within the memory constraints of vehicle-level systems, which typically have over 1 GB of available RAM [31]. More details about the proposed IDS can be found in [15].

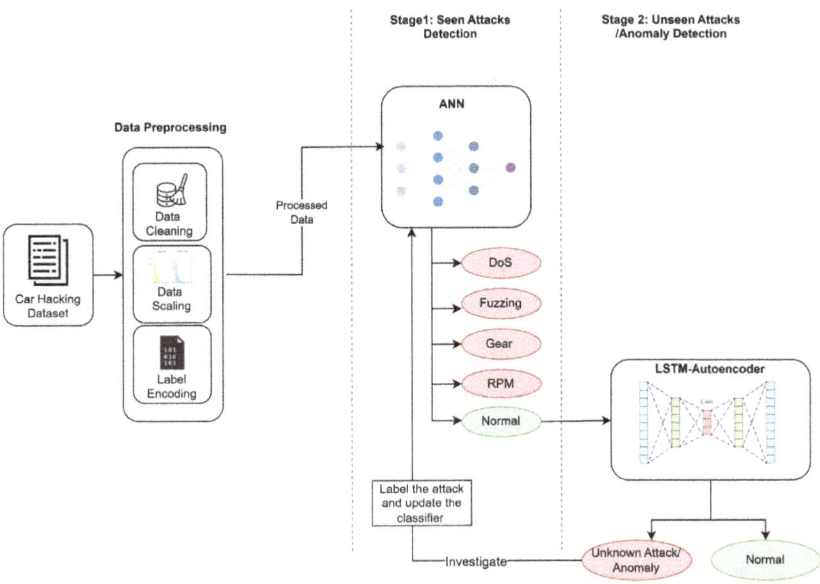

Figure 4. Workflow of the proposed multistage in-vehicle IDS.

3.5. Data Preprocessing and Partitioning

To replicate a real-world scenario where data are independently generated for each client, each FL client performs individual and independent data preprocessing before engaging in local model training, as depicted in Figure 5. However, certain preprocessing steps, such as removing missing data and label encoding, should occur before data partitioning. This approach ensures that each client receives a consistent and complete dataset, fostering a standardized training environment and maintaining uniform label representation throughout the FL process. Therefore, we divide the data preprocessing into two phases: initial data preprocessing and on-device data preprocessing. Initial data preprocessing occurs before data partitioning, while on-device preprocessing is performed on the device. This section will elaborate on each step: initial data preprocessing, data partitioning, and on-device data preprocessing.

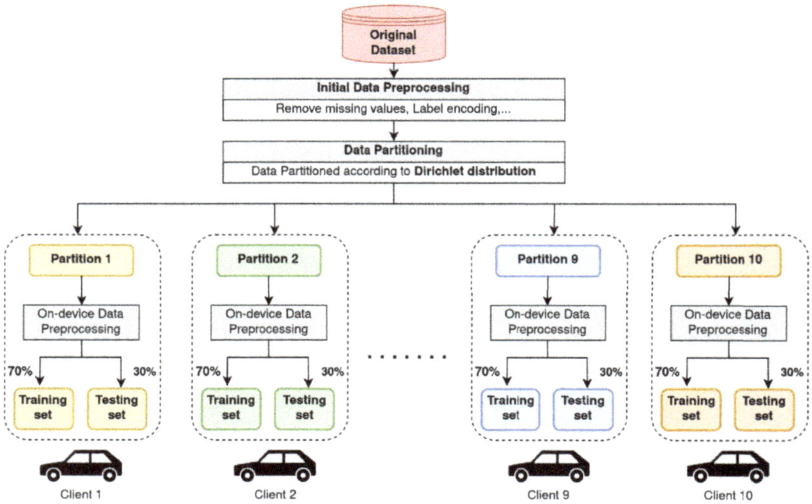

Figure 5. Data partitioning.

3.5.1. Initial Data Preprocessing

In the initial phase of data preprocessing, for each data file, we convert 'T' to the corresponding attack type, such as 'DoS', and 'R' to 'Normal' in the 'Flag' column. Then, we shift the 'Flag' field to the last column and fill non-available data bytes with (NaN) values. We combine the four data files into one. Given the extensive data points we have, we remove any row with these missing values (NAN) in the Data fields. Lastly, we use a label encoder to convert categorical values into numerical representations. This ensures consistent encoding across all clients, facilitating model training and aggregation.

3.5.2. Data Partitioning

After the initial data preprocessing step, we perform data partitioning to simulate the FL environment. In the context of CAN bus data, the data are horizontally structured, where the training data from participating clients shares a common feature space but exhibits distinct sample spaces. As illustrated in Figure 6, for instance, client 1 and client 2 contain dissimilar data while sharing the same set of features.

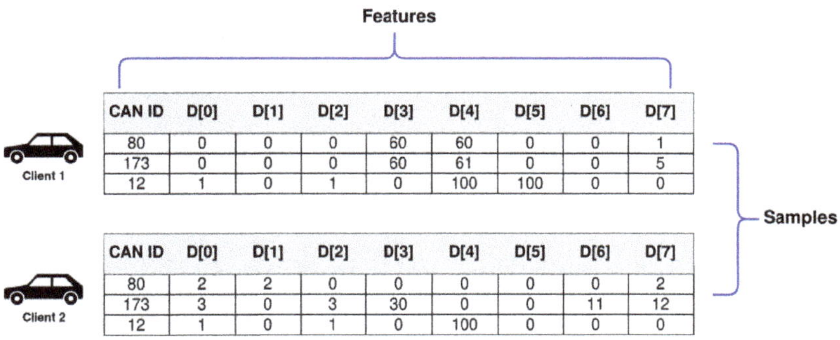

Figure 6. Horizontal CAN bus data.

To simulate a non-IID setting, we assign data to clients using Dirichlet $(Dir(\mu))$ distribution according to [20], where every client is assigned a share of the samples for each label. Dirichlet distribution is commonly used as a prior distribution in Bayesian statistics [32] and is an appropriate choice to simulate real-world data distribution [20]. An advantage of this approach is that we can flexibly change the imbalance level by varying the concentration parameter (μ). The parameter (μ) in $(Dir(\mu))$ regulates the degree of non-IID property among clients, where lower (μ) values signify a higher level of non-IID. We adjust (μ) to simulate diverse data distributions among clients, ranging from 0.1 (indicating the highest non-IID) to 0.7 (indicating the lowest non-IID). Figure 7 shows the data partition on car hacking dataset with different (μ) values. The number displayed in each rectangle represents the quantity of data samples of a class (DoS (0), frame fuzzification (1), drive gear spoofing (2), normal (3), and engine RPM spoofing (4)) for each client. However, we exclude (μ) = 0.1 due to its highly imbalanced data distribution, as shown in Figure 7a, where some clients lack normal data (3) for training, making it unrealistic. Data are distributed among two edges, each with five clients, for a total of ten clients. We chose ten clients, a common practice in the literature [12,33–35], to manage the increased computational demands associated with additional clients.

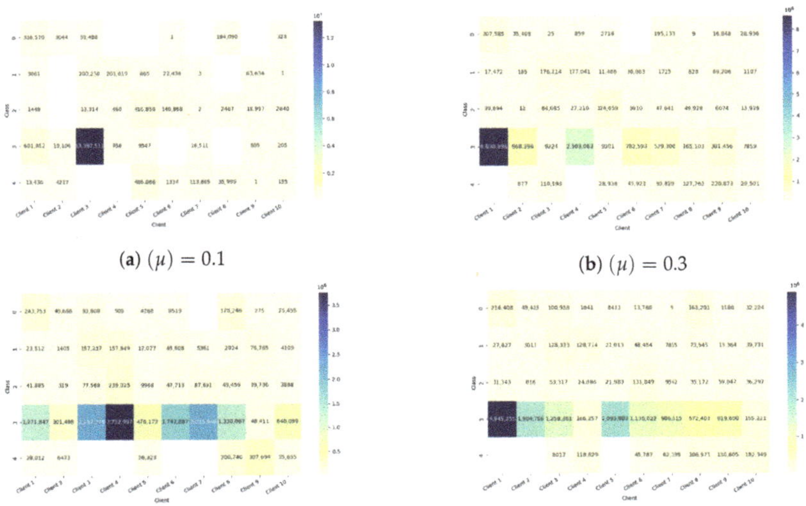

(a) $(\mu) = 0.1$ (b) $(\mu) = 0.3$

(c) $(\mu) = 0.5$ (d) $(\mu) = 0.7$

Figure 7. Dataset distribution based on Dirichlet(μ) distribution.

3.5.3. On-Device Data Preprocessing

For on-device data preprocessing, unwanted columns (Timestamp, DLC) are removed. Additionally, we convert the CAN ID and Data values from hexadecimal to decimal values per the machine learning requirement, and a normalization process is applied.

3.6. Model Initialization and Pre-Training

The model is initialized on the server side, followed by distributing a copy to each participating client. In this paper, we use a pre-trained model, as Chen et al. [36] demonstrates that pre-training models on a central server before distribution to edge devices enhance task accuracy, especially with non-IID client data. Additionally, many advantages arise from pre-training a model on a centralized dataset for FL. Firstly, it enhances generalization by enabling the model to capture general features and patterns, ensuring better adaptability to the diverse data distributions across devices. Furthermore, initializing a pre-trained model on a powerful centralized server can significantly reduce the time required to fine-tune the model for specific devices [37]. To pre-train the models, we extract a small data sample representing each class, amounting to 0.8% (less than 1%) of the entire original dataset, for use in pre-training. The remaining data are then partitioned across clients. Our approach builds on the methodology outlined in [31], employing K-Means clustering to capture underlying patterns and the Synthetic Minority Over-sampling Technique (SMOTE) to address class imbalance. The sampling process starts by grouping the data into clusters using K-Means. To ensure a representative subset, we apply a group-based sampling strategy, selecting 0.8% of data points from each cluster. This approach retains diversity in the sampled dataset while significantly reducing its size. The selected samples are subsequently excluded from the full dataset before partitioning the data among clients. As the sampled data often display label imbalance, SMOTE is applied to effectively balance the classes.

3.7. Local Training

On the vehicle side, we include all clients in the training and evaluation process to ensure consistency in the results. Clients receive the pre-trained model from the corresponding edge and train it on their private data locally for one epoch and fifty rounds. After each round, each client sends its local weight updates to the corresponding edge for aggregation.

3.8. Aggregation

In H-FL, there are two stages of aggregation: edge aggregation and server aggregation. Edge aggregation combines the models from the clients, while server aggregation merges the results from edge aggregation to produce a global model. An aggregation strategy refers to the process of combining local models from clients into a centralized global model. In this paper, we use for both edge server aggregation, the standard aggregation strategy, and federated averaging (FedAvg) [17] according to the following equation:

$$w^{g}_{t+1} \leftarrow \sum_{k=1}^{K} \frac{n_k}{n} w^{k}_{t+1} \qquad (1)$$

Accordingly, the edge server calculates the weighted average of local w_k^{t+1} based on the number of samples each local vehicle used in one round (n_k) over the total training samples (n). Similarly, the cloud server calculates the weighted average of the total training samples (n) under each edge server.

3.9. Evaluation

In FL, there are two ways to evaluate the model: on the server side or the client side. In this paper, we chose to employ client-side evaluation over server-side evaluation because it enables us to assess models across a larger set of data, often leading to more realistic evaluation outcomes [38].

4. Results and Evaluations

4.1. Evaluation Metrics

For a robust assessment of model performance, it is important to choose metrics that align with the dataset type and class distribution. In the context of imbalanced intrusion datasets, relying solely on accuracy is considered unreliable [39]. Hence, we opted for the evaluation metrics of F1-score, precision, and recall for our model. Furthermore, given the unequal distribution of the data based on the label, we use the weighted average to consider the size of each class. This is an important consideration, as it ensures that the distribution of instances in each class is taken into account [40]. Additionally, the training time for each model, network load, and memory requirements for each client are also evaluated.

4.2. Performance Results and Analysis

We evaluate the performance of the proposed IDS within an H-FL architecture using two datasets, each with three non-IIDlevels, resulting in a total of 24 scenarios: 12 for dataset 1 and 12 for dataset 2. Figure 8 shows the average F1-score performance of the ANN model and the proposed cascaded IDS across different non-IID levels in the car hacking dataset [29]. As depicted in Figure 8a, the ANN classifier's performance improved at all non-IID levels except when ($\mu = 0.5$), where it slightly decreased after applying the H-FL model. In contrast, the F1-score for the cascaded multistage IDS increased across all non-IID levels, as shown in Figure 8b. Notably, the H-FL improved the F1-score in 10 out of 12 scenarios in the car hacking dataset.

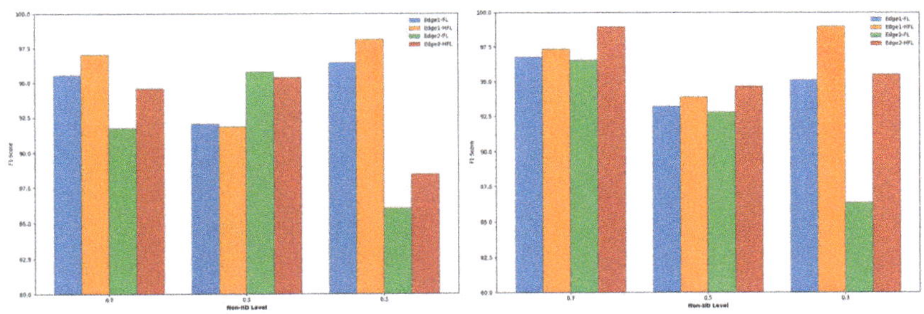

(**a**) ANN model (**b**) Proposed multistage-IDS

Figure 8. Average F1-score results non-IID levels across communication rounds for car hacking dataset [29].

This indicates that deploying the model in an H-FL architecture significantly enhanced performance, enabling it to more effectively identify both known and unknown attacks by not only learning from participating clients' data but also from a broader range of client data and evolving threats. The reasoning behind this is that an edge-FL approach, when applied to a limited number of vehicles with specific data and attack scenarios, confines the learning process to the vehicles participating within that particular edge-FL network. This restriction can limit the model's ability to generalize to diverse attack patterns not represented in the local FL process. In contrast, H-FL aggregates models from multiple edge servers across different areas into a central server, then redistributes the global model back to the edges and ultimately to all participating vehicles. This process enables vehicles to leverage insights from a broader range of data and attack scenarios across various regions, enhancing the IDS's adaptability to new and varied threats, and ultimately increasing robustness and accuracy in attack detection across the network.

Figure 8b also reveals a notable difference between Edge 1 and Edge 2, primarily due to the high imbalance in data distribution when ($\mu = 0.3$), compared to ($\mu = 0.5$) and ($\mu = 0.7$). Across all non-IID distributions, the H-FL approach consistently outperforms the edge-FL approach, with percentage increases ranging from 0.57% to 10.63%, highlighting a significant performance improvement with the H-FL method. The increase may vary based on the clients selected under each edge and non-IID level, as demonstrated by the Edge 2 results in Figure 8b. These results underscore the critical impact of the participating clients' data on performance. Detailed F1-score performance is available in Figures 9 and 10, which further illustrate the F1-score performance of the ANN model and the proposed cascaded IDS across various non-IID levels. Table 5 shows the average recall and precision of our IDS in an H-FL environment. The results indicate an increase in both recall and precision after deploying the H-FL model at nearly all non-IID levels. The best results are obtained when the data are distributed across clients with a low level of imbalance, such as at ($\mu = 0.7$). Figure 11 demonstrates the distributed loss across communication rounds. Results show that the model has different convergence speeds across non-IID levels.

Table 5. Average recall and precision of the proposed IDS model.

Non-IID	Edge 1 FL		Edge 1 H-FL		Edge 2 FL		Edge 2 H-FL	
	Recall	**Precision**	**Recall**	**Precision**	**Recall**	**Precision**	**Recall**	**Precision**
0.3	94.93	96.76	98.39	99.89	81.29	84.61	86.48	94.71
0.5	92.59	95.27	93.91	94.21	92.92	93.11	95.40	94.16
0.7	95.28	98.63	95.75	99.53	96.27	97.09	98.14	99.86

We also evaluated the performance of the proposed IDS using another dataset, the car hacking: attack & defense challenge 2020 dataset. Figure 12 shows that 50% of the scenarios demonstrated improvement, while the remaining 50% showed a decline. This is likely due to imbalanced data distributions between labels and data heterogeneity. Overall, H-FL improved the F1-score in 16 out of 24 evaluated scenarios across both datasets.

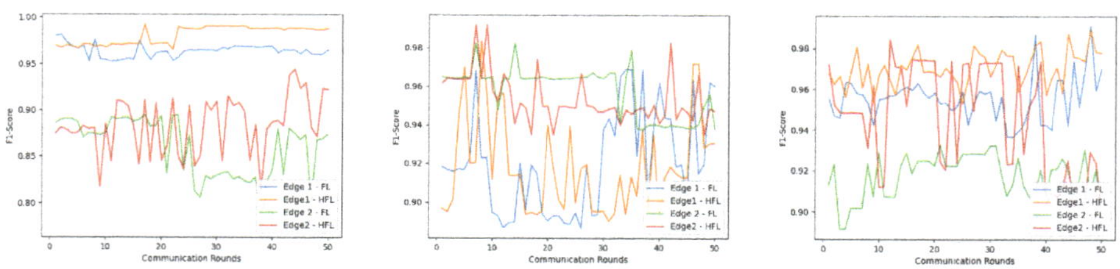

(a) (μ) = 0.3 (b) (μ) = 0.5 (c) (μ) = 0.7

Figure 9. F1-score of ANN model for different non-IID levels across communication rounds.

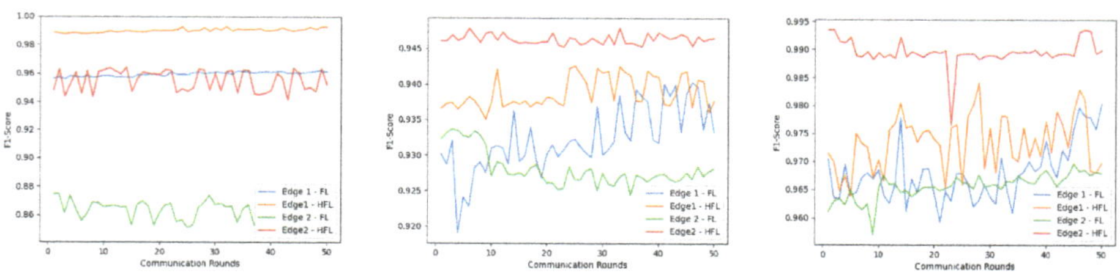

(a) (μ) = 0.3 (b) (μ) = 0.5 (c) (μ) = 0.7

Figure 10. F1-score of our proposed multistage-IDS for different non-IID levels across communication rounds.

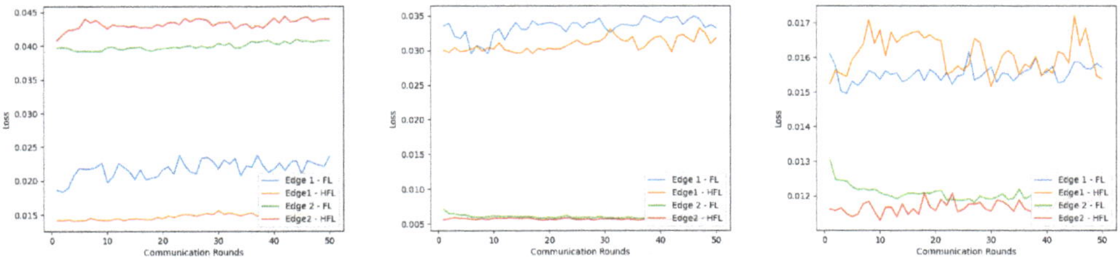

(**a**) $(\mu) = 0.3$ (**b**) $(\mu) = 0.5$ (**c**) $(\mu) = 0.7$

Figure 11. Distributed loss across communication rounds.

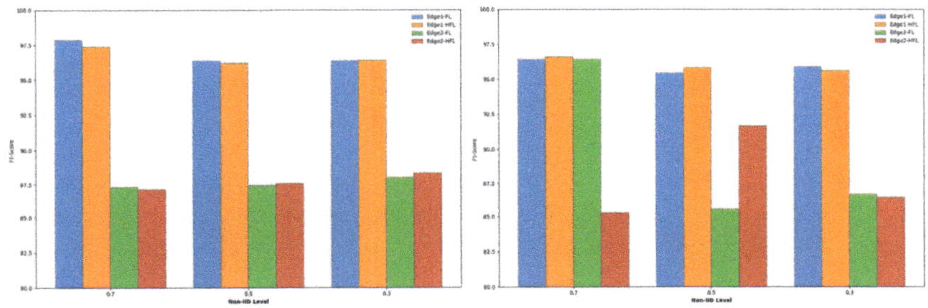

(**a**) ANN model (**b**) Proposed multistage-IDS

Figure 12. Average F1-score results non-IID levels across communication rounds for car hacking: Attack & Defense Challenge 2020 dataset [26].

Table 6 shows the average training time in seconds (S) for both the ANN and LSTM models, as well as the total training time for one round. The results indicate that training time depends on the number of training data, with Client 6 having the highest training time of 75.35 s due to its large training dataset, and the inverse being true for clients with smaller datasets.

Table 6. Average training time per client for one round.

Clients	Number of Training Data	Average ANN Training Time (S)	Average LSTM Training Time (S)	Total Training Time (S)
Client 0	75,341	1.45	4.49	5.94
Client 1	956,504	14.47	56.02	70.49
Client 2	140,115	2.53	10.61	13.14
Client 3	440,494	7.25	27.03	34.28
Client 4	410,876	6.88	27.09	33.97
Client 5	140,044	2.58	0.41	2.99
Client 6	1,118,686	16.71	58.64	75.35
Client 7	405,376	6.34	17.77	24.11
Client 8	131,100	2.39	7.55	9.94
Client 9	162,991	2.93	2.28	5.21

We also measured the network load by calculating the size of weights transferred between the server and edges, as well as between vehicles and edges. The weights size is 0.966 MB. As shown in Table 7, the network load for a single client in one round is twice the weights size, as each client sends its weights to the edge and receives the newly aggregated weights. In H-FL, the network load slightly increases because the main server sends the global model weights to the edges and receives the weights from each edge for aggregation. Although H-FL introduces an additional layer of communication between the server and edges, which is absent in standard FL, it reduces bottlenecks by distributing clients across edges, effectively dividing the network load and improving efficiency.

Table 7. Network load across different architectures.

Architecture	Edges	Clients	Rounds	Model Weights (MB)
Edge-FL/FL	1	1	1	1.932
H-FL	1	1	1	3.86
Edge-FL /FL	1	5	50	483.45
Edge- H-FL	1	5	50	968.8
FL	1	10	50	966.9
H-FL	2	10	50	970.76

One of the main challenges in implementing FL is the memory consumption of learning models trained locally on individual vehicles. High-end automobiles, such as those produced by Tesla, utilize advanced deep learning algorithms for tasks like object detection and various driver assistance features. To handle the substantial computational demands of data from cameras and sensors, these vehicles are equipped with dedicated GPUs. For example, Tesla's latest Model S and Model X are powered by AMD RDNA 2 GPUs, which provide 16–32 GB of memory for processing tasks [41]. Given that our IDS also relies on GPUs, we evaluate a vehicle's memory requirements by analyzing both the size of the learning models and the memory needed to process the dataset. The total model size is 2.98 MB. To optimize memory usage during training, we process the data in batches of 256 rather than loading the entire dataset at once. This approach significantly reduces the memory required for training data from 104.25 MB (for the full dataset) to just 0.02 MB per batch. Consequently, the model requires approximately 1 GB of memory for operation, which is well within the capabilities of current vehicle-level machines.

5. Conclusions and Future Works

The aim of this paper was to deploy and evaluate our proposed in-vehicle IDS [15] within the H-FL framework to address the limitations of the standard FL approach. We evaluated the performance of the IDS using two datasets with three non-IID levels to simulate real-world scenarios and assess the impact of different data distributions. Experimental results indicate that the H-FL framework, in most scenarios, improves F1-score results by up to 10.63% for both known and unknown attacks across diverse non-IID conditions, outperforming edge-FL, which is constrained by smaller, vehicle-specific datasets. However, in certain scenarios, the results showed a decline after applying H-FL, potentially due to the heterogeneity of data among the clients. Overall, H-FL improved the F1-score in 16 out of 24 evaluated scenarios in two datasets. This raises an important research question for future studies: How can we cluster vehicles to ensure the effectiveness of the H-FL framework? By applying clustering methods, vehicles could be grouped based on factors such as proximity, connectivity, or data similarity, which could improve overall training performance across all clients [42]. One limitation of this work is the use of a fixed number of clients for all experiments, whereas in real-world scenarios, the number of clients can vary significantly. Future work should include a more flexible evaluation framework that tests variations in client numbers to enhance the reliability and scalability of the proposed H-FL architecture.

Author Contributions: Conceptualization, M.A., A.J., O.R. and T.S.; Methodology, M.A.; Supervision, A.J. and O.R.; Writing—original draft, M.A.; Writing—review and editing, M.A. and A.J. All authors have read and agreed to the published version of the manuscript.

Funding: This research received no external funding.

Data Availability Statement: The datasets used in this paper are publicly available to everyone and can be obtained from https://ocslab.hksecurity.net/Datasets/car-hacking-dataset and https://ocslab.hksecurity.net/Datasets/carchallenge2020 (accessed on 1 November 2022) and has been cited in the manuscript.

Acknowledgments: We would like to acknowledge the scholarship and support provided by Majmaah University.

Conflicts of Interest: The authors declare no conflicts of interest.

References

1. Pickford, J.; Attale, R.; Shaikh, S.; Nguyen, H.N.; Harrison, L. Systematic Risk Characterisation of Hardware Threats to Automotive Systems. *J. Auton. Transp. Syst.* **2024**, *1*, 1–36. [CrossRef]
2. Grand View Research, Inc. Connected Car Market Size & Share Analysis Report. 2030. Available online: https://www.grandviewresearch.com/industry-analysis/connected-car-market (accessed on 7 August 2024).
3. Paul, A.; Islam, M.R. An artificial neural network based anomaly detection method in can bus messages in vehicles. In Proceedings of the 2021 International Conference on Automation, Control and Mechatronics for Industry 4.0 (ACMI), Rajshahi, Bangladesh, 8–9 July 2021; pp. 1–5. [CrossRef]
4. Young, C.; Zambreno, J.; Olufowobi, H.; Bloom, G. Survey of automotive controller area network intrusion detection systems. *IEEE Des. Test* **2019**, *36*, 48–55. [CrossRef]
5. Alfardus, A.; Rawat, D.B. Intrusion detection system for can bus in-vehicle network based on machine learning algorithms. In Proceedings of the 2021 IEEE 12th Annual Ubiquitous Computing, Electronics & Mobile Communication Conference (UEMCON), New York, NY, USA, 1–4 December 2021; pp. 944–949. [CrossRef]
6. Alsamiri, J.; Alsubhi, K. Federated Learning for Intrusion Detection Systems in Internet of Vehicles: A General Taxonomy, Applications, and Future Directions. *Future Internet* **2023**, *15*, 403. [CrossRef]
7. Hernandez-Ramos, J.L.; Karopoulos, G.; Chatzoglou, E.; Kouliaridis, V.; Marmol, E.; Gonzalez-Vidal, A.; Kambourakis, G. Intrusion Detection based on Federated Learning: A systematic review. *arXiv* **2023**, arXiv:2308.09522. [CrossRef]
8. Group, X.W. *Guidelines for an Intrusion Detection System for In-Vehicle Networks*; Technical Report X.1375; International Telecommunication Union: Geneva, Switzerland, 2020.
9. Driss, M.; Almomani, I.; e Huma, Z.; Ahmad, J. A federated learning framework for cyberattack detection in vehicular sensor networks. *Complex Intell. Syst.* **2022**, *8*, 4221–4235. [CrossRef]
10. Shibly, K.H.; Hossain, M.D.; Inoue, H.; Taenaka, Y.; Kadobayashi, Y. Personalized federated learning for automotive intrusion detection systems. In Proceedings of the 2022 IEEE Future Networks World Forum (FNWF), Montreal, QC, Canada, 10–14 October 2022; pp. 544–549. [CrossRef]
11. Yu, T.; Hua, G.; Wang, H.; Yang, J.; Hu, J. Federated-LSTM based Network Intrusion Detection Method for Intelligent Connected Vehicles. In Proceedings of the IEEE International Conference on Communications (ICC), Seoul, Republic of Korea, 16–20 May 2022. [CrossRef]
12. Zhang, H.; Zeng, K.; Lin, S. Federated graph neural network for fast anomaly detection in controller area networks. *IEEE Trans. Inf. Forensics Secur.* **2023**, *18*, 1566–1579. [CrossRef]
13. Yang, J.; Hu, J.; Yu, T. Federated AI-Enabled In-Vehicle Network Intrusion Detection for Internet of Vehicles. *Electronics* **2022**, *11*, 3658. [CrossRef]
14. Taslimasa, H.; Dadkhah, S.; Neto, E.P.; Xiong, P.; Iqbal, S.; Ray, S.; Ghorbani, A. ImageFed: Practical Privacy Preserving Intrusion Detection System for In-Vehicle CAN Bus Protocol. In Proceedings of the 2023 IEEE 9th Intl Conference on Big Data Security on Cloud (BigDataSecurity), IEEE Intl Conference on High Performance and Smart Computing, (HPSC) and IEEE Intl Conference on Intelligent Data and Security (IDS), New York, NY, USA, 6–8 May 2023. [CrossRef]
15. Althunayyan, M.; Javed, A.; Rana, O. A robust multi-stage intrusion detection system for in-vehicle network security using hierarchical federated learning. *Veh. Commun.* **2024**, *49*, 100837. [CrossRef]
16. Bonawitz, K.; Eichner, H.; Grieskamp, W.; Huba, D.; Ingerman, A.; Ivanov, V.; Kiddon, C.; Konečný, J.; Mazzocchi, S.; McMahan, B.; et al. Towards federated learning at scale: System design. *Proc. Mach. Learn. Syst.* **2019**, *1*, 374–388. [CrossRef]
17. McMahan, B.; Moore, E.; Ramage, D.; Hampson, S.; y Arcas, B.A. Communication-efficient learning of deep networks from decentralized data. In Proceedings of the Artificial Intelligence and Statistics, Fort Lauderdale, FL, USA, 20–22 April 2017; pp. 1273–1282. [CrossRef]
18. Liu, L.; Zhang, J.; Song, S.; Letaief, K.B. Client-edge-cloud hierarchical federated learning. In Proceedings of the ICC 2020-2020 IEEE International Conference on Communications (ICC), Dublin, Ireland, 7–11 June 2020; pp. 1–6. [CrossRef]
19. Rana, O.; Spyridopoulos, T.; Hudson, N.; Baughman, M.; Chard, K.; Foster, I.; Khan, A. Hierarchical and Decentralised Federated Learning. *arXiv* **2023**, arXiv:2304.14982. [CrossRef]
20. Li, Q.; Diao, Y.; Chen, Q.; He, B. Federated learning on non-iid data silos: An experimental study. In Proceedings of the 2022 IEEE 38th International Conference on Data Engineering (ICDE), Virtual, 9–12 May 2022; pp. 965–978. [CrossRef]
21. Zhao, Y.; Li, M.; Lai, L.; Suda, N.; Civin, D.; Chandra, V. Federated learning with non-iid data. *arXiv* **2018**, arXiv:1806.00582. [CrossRef]
22. Song, H.M.; Woo, J.; Kim, H.K. In-vehicle network intrusion detection using deep convolutional neural network. *Veh. Commun.* **2020**, *21*, 100198. [CrossRef]

23. Lee, H.; Jeong, S.H.; Kim, H.K. OTIDS: A novel intrusion detection system for in-vehicle network by using remote frame. In Proceedings of the 2017 15th Annual Conference on Privacy, Security and Trust (PST), Calgary, AB, Canada, 28–30 August 2017; pp. 57–5709. [CrossRef]
24. Hossain, M.D.; Inoue, H.; Ochiai, H.; Fall, D.; Kadobayashi, Y. LSTM-based intrusion detection system for in-vehicle can bus communications. *IEEE Access* **2020**, *8*, 185489–185502. [CrossRef]
25. Marchetti, M.; Stabili, D. READ: Reverse engineering of automotive data frames. *IEEE Trans. Inf. Forensics Secur.* **2018**, *14*, 1083–1097. [CrossRef]
26. Kang, H.; Kwak, B.I.; Lee, Y.H.; Lee, H.; Lee, H.; Kim, H.K. Car hacking and defense competition on in-vehicle network. In Proceedings of the Workshop on Automotive and Autonomous Vehicle Security (AutoSec), online, 25 February 2021; Volume 2021, p. 25. [CrossRef]
27. AI, F. Flower A Friendly Federated Learning Framework. 2024. Available online: https://flower.ai/ (accessed on 10 January 2024).
28. Beutel, D.J.; Topal, T.; Mathur, A.; Qiu, X.; Fernandez-Marques, J.; Gao, Y.; Sani, L.; Li, K.H.; Parcollet, T.; de Gusmão, P.P.B.; et al. Flower: A friendly federated learning research framework. *arXiv* **2020**, arXiv:2007.14390. [CrossRef]
29. Seo, E.; Song, H.M.; Kim, H.K. GIDS: GAN based intrusion detection system for in-vehicle network. In Proceedings of the 2018 16th Annual Conference on Privacy, Security and Trust (PST), Belfast, Ireland, 28–30 August 2018; pp. 1–6. [CrossRef]
30. Rajapaksha, S.; Kalutarage, H.; Al-Kadri, M.O.; Petrovski, A.; Madzudzo, G.; Cheah, M. Ai-based intrusion detection systems for in-vehicle networks: A survey. *ACM Comput. Surv.* **2023**, *55*, 1–40. [CrossRef]
31. Yang, L.; Moubayed, A.; Shami, A. MTH-IDS: A Multitiered Hybrid Intrusion Detection System for Internet of Vehicles. *IEEE Internet Things J.* **2022**, *9*, 616–632. [CrossRef]
32. Huang, J. Maximum likelihood estimation of Dirichlet distribution parameters. *CMU Tech. Rep.* **2005**, *18*, pp. 1–9.
33. Caldas, S.; Konečny, J.; McMahan, H.B.; Talwalkar, A. Expanding the reach of federated learning by reducing client resource requirements. *arXiv* **2018**, arXiv:1812.07210. [CrossRef]
34. Díaz, J.S.P.; García, Á.L. Study of the performance and scalability of federated learning for medical imaging with intermittent clients. *Neurocomputing* **2023**, *518*, 142–154. [CrossRef]
35. Tam, K.; Li, L.; Han, B.; Xu, C.; Fu, H. Federated noisy client learning. In *IEEE Transactions on Neural Networks and Learning Systems*; IEEE: New York, NY, USA, 2023. [CrossRef]
36. Chen, H.Y.; Tu, C.H.; Li, Z.; Shen, H.W.; Chao, W.L. On the importance and applicability of pre-training for federated learning. *arXiv* **2022**, arXiv:2206.11488. [CrossRef]
37. Kaur, I.; Jadhav, A.J. A Comprehensive Study on Model Initialization Techniques Ensuring Efficient Federated Learning. *arXiv* **2023**, arXiv:2311.02100. [CrossRef]
38. Framework, F. Use a Federated Learning Strategy. Available online: https://flower.ai/docs/framework/tutorial-series-use-a-federated-learning-strategy-pytorch.html (accessed on 24 March 2024).
39. Galar, M.; Fernandez, A.; Barrenechea, E.; Bustince, H.; Herrera, F. A review on ensembles for the class imbalance problem: Bagging-, boosting-, and hybrid-based approaches. *IEEE Trans. Syst. Man Cybern. Part C Appl. Rev.* **2011**, *42*, 463–484. [CrossRef]
40. Belarbi, O.; Spyridopoulos, T.; Anthi, E.; Mavromatis, I.; Carnelli, P.; Khan, A. Federated deep learning for intrusion detection in IoT networks. In Proceedings of the GLOBECOM 2023-2023 IEEE Global Communications Conference, Kuala Lumpur, Malaysia, 4–8 December 2023; pp. 237–242. [CrossRef]
41. Lambert, F. Tesla Is Using New Amd RDNA 2 Gpu in New Model S/X, Same as in Playstation 5. 2021. Available online: https://electrek.co/2021/06/01/tesla-amd-rdna-2-gpu-new-model-s-x-same-playstation-5/ (accessed on 18 November 2024).
42. Briggs, C.; Fan, Z.; Andras, P. Federated learning with hierarchical clustering of local updates to improve training on non-IID data. In Proceedings of the 2020 International Joint Conference on Neural Networks (IJCNN), Glasgow, UK, 19–24 July 2020; pp. 1–9.

future internet

MDPI

Article

Multi-Class Intrusion Detection Based on Transformer for IoT Networks Using CIC-IoT-2023 Dataset

Shu-Ming Tseng [1,*], Yan-Qi Wang [1] and Yung-Chung Wang [2]

[1] Department of Electronic Engineering, National Taipei University of Technology, Taipei 10608, Taiwan
[2] Department of Electrical Engineering, National Taipei University of Technology, Taipei 10608, Taiwan
* Correspondence: shuming@ntut.edu.tw

Abstract: This study uses deep learning methods to explore the Internet of Things (IoT) network intrusion detection method based on the CIC-IoT-2023 dataset. This dataset contains extensive data on real-life IoT environments. Based on this, this study proposes an effective intrusion detection method. Apply seven deep learning models, including Transformer, to analyze network traffic characteristics and identify abnormal behavior and potential intrusions through binary and multivariate classifications. Compared with other papers, we not only use a Transformer model, but we also consider the model's performance in the multi-class classification. Although the accuracy of the Transformer model used in the binary classification is lower than that of DNN and CNN + LSTM hybrid models, it achieves better results in the multi-class classification. The accuracy of binary classification of our model is 0.74% higher than that of papers that also use Transformer on TON-IOT. In the multi-class classification, our best-performing model combination is Transformer, which reaches 99.40% accuracy. Its accuracy is 3.8%, 0.65%, and 0.29% higher than the 95.60%, 98.75%, and 99.11% figures recorded in papers using the same dataset, respectively.

Keywords: Internet of Things; intrusion detection; deep learning; CIC-IoT-202; transformer

1. Introduction

In recent years, Internet of Things technology has developed rapidly, and we have entered a highly interconnected smart world. IoT devices have been integrated into various industries, including healthcare, agriculture, transportation, and manufacturing [1]. Experts predict that by 2025, the Internet of Things and its applications will have a huge economic impact, with the annual impact ranging from 3.9 trillion to 11.1 trillion [2]. However, this seamless connection also brings new challenges, one of which is security. The ever-increasing number of IoT devices makes them potential targets for attacks, so protecting these devices from improper access and attacks has become critical. In such an environment with diverse devices, there are bound to be devices that are more vulnerable to attacks. Such devices not only affect the security of the IoT system, but also affect the transmission channels in the system, and even cause a partial or complete failure of the transmission network [3]. With the advancement of artificial intelligence technology, machine learning (ML) and deep learning (DL) have made great progress and are now widely used in various fields such as wireless communications, computer vision, and healthcare systems [4]. Intrusion detection systems based on machine learning and deep learning are widely used in the Internet of Things environment [5].

Abbas et al. [1] used the CIC-IoT-2023 dataset and used DNN-based federated learning to detect the security of IoT devices through binary classification. The result accuracy rate is 99.0%. Wang et al. [6] compared six DL models, including DNN, CNN, RNN, LSTM, CNN + LSTM, and the CNN + RNN hybrid model, with the CSE-CIC-IDS2018 dataset. The results showed that the CNN + LTSM model performed well in both classifications. The results all have the highest accuracy rates, 98.84% and 98.85%, respectively. Ahmed et al. [7] compared their proposed Transformer architecture with RNN and LSTM with binary classification using the ToN_IoT dataset released in 2020. The results show that the proposed Transformer model performs excellently in terms of accuracy and precision, with an accuracy rate of 87.79%.

References [7,8] mention the time complexity of some of the models in our paper such as RNN, CNN, LSTM, etc. Reference [6] mentions most of the models' time complexity, in the same way as our paper but in a different dataset.

He et al. [9] proposed a transferable and adaptive network intrusion detection system (NIDS) based on deep reinforcement learning. The results reached 99.60% and 95.60% in the binary classification and multi-class classification of CIC-IoT2023, respectively. Jony et al. [10] used LSTM to conduct an experimental evaluation of the multi-class classification in CIC-IoT-2023, and the accuracy of the results reached 98.75%. Jaradat et al. [11] used four different machine learning methods to classify network attacks in CIC-IoT-2023, but they did not mention the classification tasks they used. Among them, Gradient Boost achieved the highest accuracy of 95%. Among the above-mentioned papers, only Abbas et al. [1] dealt with the problem of data imbalance in the dataset. Table 1 summarizes the key points of the above papers. The effectiveness of machine learning-based intrusion detection systems (ML-IDSs) depends largely on the quality of the dataset [12]. In this paper, we use the CIC-IoT-2023 dataset [13] released in 2023 to conduct IDS experiments. CIC-IoT-2023 is a unique and comprehensive collection of information designed specifically for IoT attacks. And we use multiple models, such as DNN, CNN, RNN, LSTM, CNN + LSTM, CNN + RNN, and Transformer, to identify whether the traffic is malicious. Classification tasks cover binary classification and multi-class classification. The main contributions of this study are detailed below.

(1) We use the CIC-IoT-2023 dataset [1,13] used by Abbas et al. This is currently the largest collection of IoT data recorded by real IoT devices. The number of data entries in this dataset reaches 46,686,579 and there are as many as 33 attack types. Among them, most of the examples in this dataset are related to common malicious attacks: DDoS and DoS attacks [14];
(2) We not only use the six DL models used in [6], but also use a Transformer model [15] to handle binary and multi-class classification tasks. Compared with [1,7], we further implement the multi-class classification on our model;
(3) On the ToN_IoT dataset, compared with [7], our Transformer model achieved an accuracy of 88.25%, which is 0.46% higher than the 87.79% of [7];
(4) Compared with [10,11,13], which also use the CIC-IoT-2023 dataset [16,17], the accuracy of our Transformer model in the multi-class classification reaches 99.40% accuracy; when compared with 95.60% [10], 98.75% [11], and 99.11% [13], our results are 3.8%, 0.65%, and 0.29% higher, respectively.

Table 1. Related works/baseline schemes.

Paper	Dataset	Classification	DL Method	Accuracy	Inference Time [1]
[1]	CIC-IoT-2023	Binary	DNN based on Federated Learning	99.00%	
[6]	CIC-IDS-2018	Binary, Multi-class	DNN, RNN, CNN, LSTM, CNN + LSTM, and CNN + RNN	98.85%	Multi-Class: LSTM: 3.451 (ms) CNN + LSTM: 4.31 (ms)
[7]	ToN-IoT	Binary	LSTM, RNN, and Transformer	87.79%	Binary Class LSTM: 27 (s) RNN: 35 (s)

Table 1. *Cont.*

Paper	Dataset	Classification	DL Method	Accuracy	Inference Time [1]
[9]	CIC-IoT-2023	Multi-class	Deep Reinforcement Learning	95.60%	
[10]	CIC-IoT-2023	Multi-class	LTSM	98.75%	
[11]	CIC-IoT-2023	Not Mentioned	Gradient Boost, MLP, Logistic Regression, and KNN	95.00%	
[13]	CIC-IoT-2023	Binary, Multi-class	DNN	99.44%, 99.11%	
[8]	KD999	Multi-class	CNN, Autoencoder, FCN RNN, U-Net, TCN, and TCN + LSTM	97.7%	Multi-Class CNN: 5 (min/epoch) TCN + LSTM: 11 (min/epoch)

[1] Inference time is copy from references.

The second part of this paper is methodology, which describes the dataset and data preprocessing methods in detail. The third part will introduce six neural network models and Transformer models, and the fourth part will show the experimental results. The fifth part is the conclusion of this paper.

2. Methodology

The system architecture diagram of this paper is shown in Figure 1, which is divided into two parts: data preprocessing and training evaluation. Next, we will introduce the details of the system architecture diagram one by one.

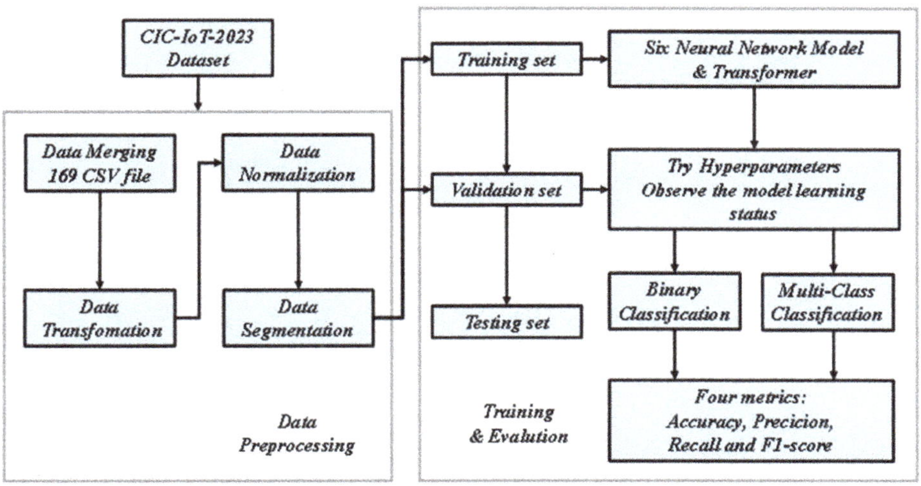

Figure 1. Architecture diagram of this paper.

2.1. CIC-IoT-2023

As of 2023, CIC-IoT-2023 stands out as the largest IoT dataset [16], derived from real IoT devices. The dataset contains data from 105 IoT devices, documenting 33 recorded attacks. Notably, these attacks were launched by malicious IoT devices targeting other IoT devices. In addition, CIC-IoT-2023 also contains multiple attack types that do not exist in other IoT datasets

Table 2 provides the number of each label containing benign traffic. This dataset contains a total of 46 features and 1 label. Different from the 84 features of CSE-CIC-IDS2018, CIC-IoT-2023 has 37 fewer features. In this experiment, no specific feature screening was performed, and all features were used directly to conduct the experiment.

Table 2. The number of each label containing benign traffic.

Label	Quantitys	Label	Quantitys	Label	Quantitys
DDoS-ICMP_Flood	7,200,504	Mirai-greeth_flood	991,866	DoS-HTTP_Flood	71,864
DDoS-UDP_Flood	5,412,287	Mirai-udpplain	890,576	Vulnerability Scan	37,382
DDoS-TCP_Flood	4,497,667	Mirai-greip_flood	751,682	DDoS-SlowLoris	23,246
DDoS-PSHACK_Flood	4,094,755	DDoS-ICMP_Fragmentation	452,489	DictionaryBruteForce	13,064
DDoS-SYN_Flood	4,059,190	MITM-ArpSpoofing	307,593	BrowserHijacking	5859
DDoS-RSTFINFlood	4,045,190	DDoS-UDP_Fragmentation	286,925	CommandInjection	5409
DDoS-SynonymousIP_Flood	3,598,138	DDoS-ACK_Fragmentation	285,104	SQL Injection	5245
DoS-UDP_Flood	3,318,595	Recon-HostDiscovery	178,911	XSS	3946
DoS-TCP_Flood	2,671,445	Recon-OSScan	134,378	Backdoor_Malware	3218
DoS-SYN_Flood	2,028,834	Recon-PortScan	98,259	Recon-PingSweep	2262
Benign	1,098,195	DDoS-HTTP_Flood	71,864	Uploading_Attack	1252

CIC-IoT-2023 Features

CIC-IoT-2023 has 46 features and those features are shown in Table 3.

Table 3. The features used in CIC-IoT-2023.

Feature	Name
1	Flow duration
2	Header Length
3	Protocol
4	Type
5	Duration
6	Rate Mrate Drate
7	fin flag number
8	syn flag number
9	rst flag number
10	psh flag number
11	ack flag number
12	ece flag number
13	cwr flag number
14	ack count
15	syn count
16	fin count
17	urg count
18	rst count
19	HTTP
20	HTTPS
21	DNS
22	Telnet
23	SMTP
24	SSH
25	IRC
26	TCP
27	UDP
28	DHCP
29	ARP
30	ICMP
31	IPv
32	LLC
33	Tot sum
34	Min
35	Max

Table 3. *Cont.*

Feature	Name
36	AVG
37	Std
38	Tot size
39	IAT
40	Number
41	Magnitude
42	Radius
43	Covariance
44	Variance
45	Weight
46	Flow duration

We chose all the above features because all of these features lack redundancy. This method ensures better accuracy.

2.2. Data Merging

Since the dataset is spread across 169 CSV files, it is necessary to merge these files into a single file before importing the data for processing and training. Therefore, as a first step, we will merge all 169 CSV files before proceeding to subsequent stages.

2.3. Data Transformation

In this part, the text labels must be converted to a numeric format so that the model can read the labels In the binary classification, there are two types of labels. The benign label assignment is 0, with a total of 1,098,195 records. The malicious attack label is 1, with a total of 45,588,384 records, making an overall total of 46,686,579 records. In the multi-class classification, we classify malicious attacks into seven categories. Including the benign traffic, there are a total of eight labels [17]. The distribution of converted tags is shown in Figure 2.

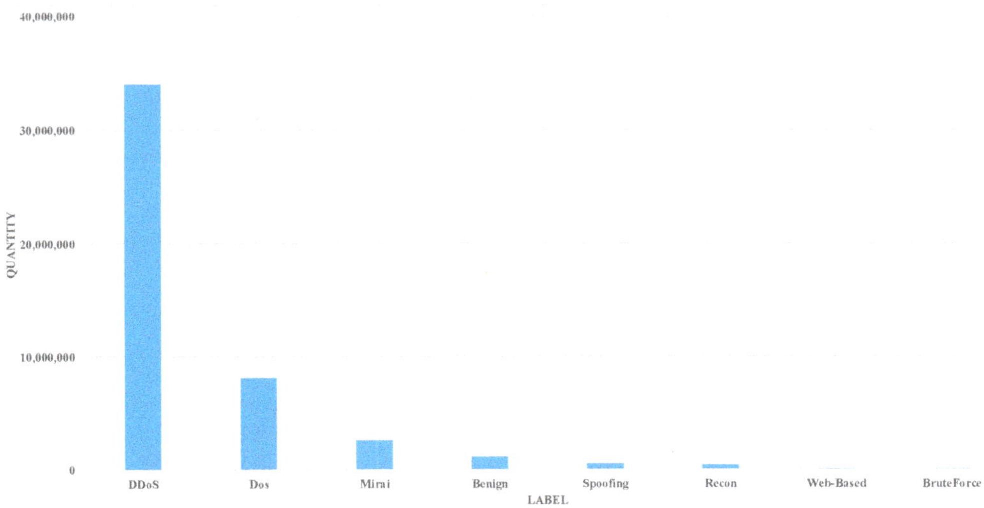

Figure 2. Distribution of converted labels containing benign traffic.

2.4. Data Normalization

In order to improve the performance of deep learning models, feature normalization techniques are usually used to achieve the above purposes. We transform the numerical values of the features so that they are relatively consistent. The method we use is Standard-Scaler technology, which is used to convert the value to a standard normal distribution with a mean of 0 and a standard deviation of 1. This specific method is to calculate the ratio of the difference between the original value and the mean and the standard deviation.

2.5. Data Segmentation

Since the dataset lacks predefined training and testing sets, we used the holdout method for segmentation in this experiment. This technique involves dividing the dataset into a training–validation set and a testing set based on a specified ratio. In this study, we allocate 80% of the dataset to the training–validation set and the remaining 20% to the test set. This partitioning strategy aims to make the model generalizable. Furthermore, in the training–validation set, 80% is designated as the training set, including 37,349,263 records, while the remaining 20% is designated as the validation set, with a total of 9,337,316 records. This distribution corresponds to a proportion of approximately 80% and 20% for the entire dataset [6].

3. Deep Learning Model

In the experiments of this paper, we use the six neural network models mentioned above [6]. In addition to this, we use the Transformer model [7,15] to conduct further experiments. Transformer's self-attention mechanism allows the model to process all positions in the sequence in parallel, unlike RNN, which needs to process them sequentially. This enables Transformer to more effectively utilize computing resources during training and inference and improve the model's training speed. We use brute force to try our best to exhaust various parameter settings to find the best model settings.

3.1. Neural Network

In the neural network, each neural network has six combinations, the hidden layer is set to layer 1 and layer 3, and the number of neurons is set to 256, 512, and 768, respectively. Detailed parameters are shown in Table 4.

Table 4. The number of neurons and units of each of the neural networks.

Layers	Neurons	Units
1	256	256
	512	512
	768	768
3	256	64 + 64 + 128
	512	128 + 128 + 256
	768	256 + 256 + 256

The various architectures of the neural network are shown in Figure 3. Part of the figure only shows one layer of the architecture of each deep learning network. But, we actually conducted experiments using one- and three-layer stacking architectures. At the output layer, it is worth noting that we will use excitation functions for the classification tasks, binary classification will use Sigmoid, and multivariate classification will use Softmax. We will describe the detailed parameter quantities of each neural network in the following sections.

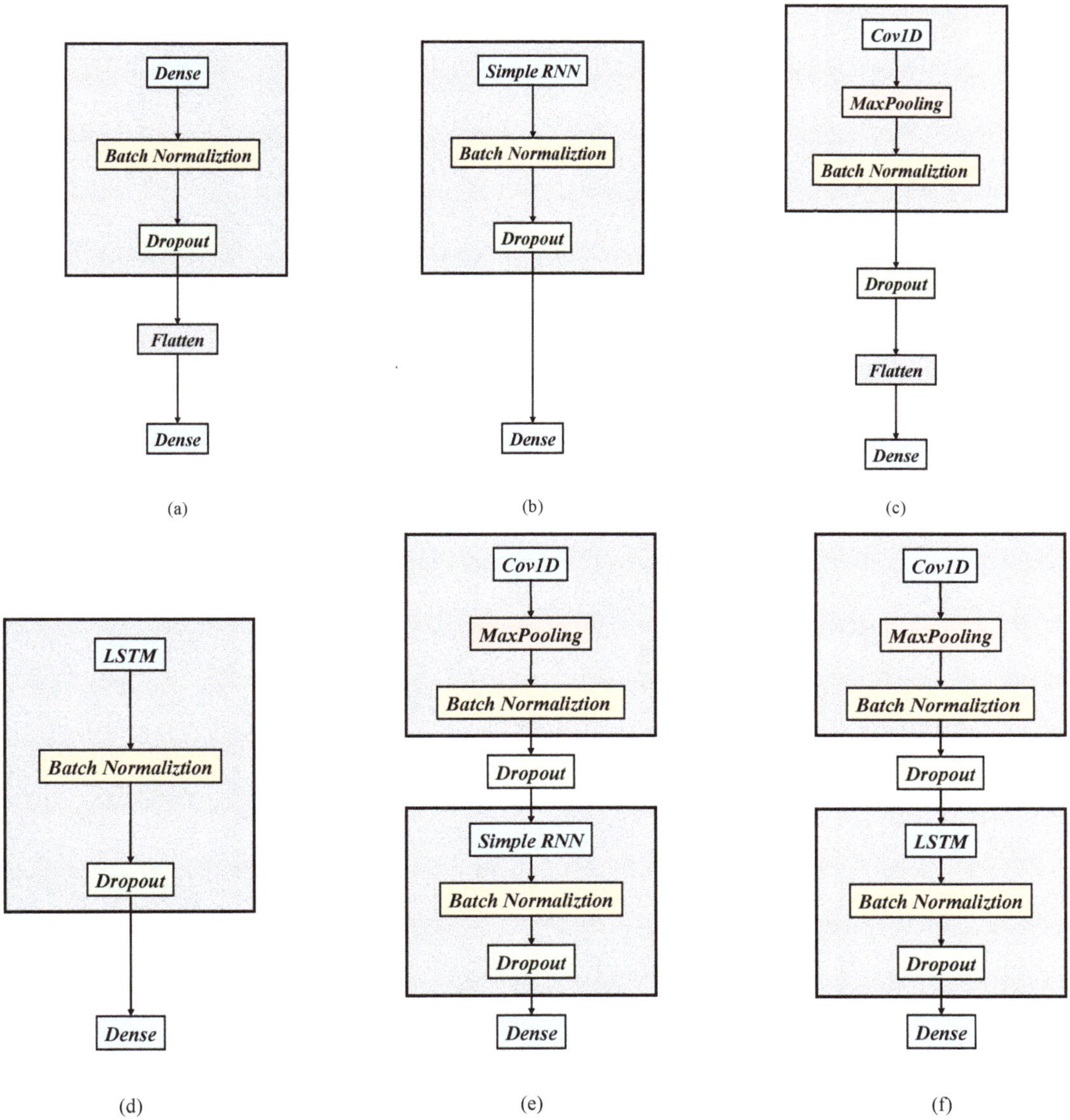

Figure 3. (**a**) Architecture diagram of DNN, (**b**) architecture diagram of RNN, (**c**) architecture diagram of CNN, (**d**) architecture diagram of LSTM, (**e**) architecture diagram of CNN + RNN, and (**f**) architecture diagram of CNN + LSTM.

3.1.1. DNN

The architecture of DNN is shown in Figure 3a, which mainly consists of the input Dense layer, Batch Normalization (BN) layer, Dropout layer, Flatten layer, and output Dense layer. The number of parameters in each layer and the corresponding number of nodes are shown in Table 5. In order to reduce the occurrence of overfitting, we add a BN layer and a Dropout layer to each layer, normalize each batch during the training process, and the Dropout layer randomly discards neurons at a certain proportion in each layer. Both effectively prevent neurons from becoming overly dependent on certain features.

Table 5. Number of parameters and nodes of DNN.

Layers	Neurons	Parameters	
		Binary	Multi-Class
1	256	13,313	15,112
	512	26,625	30,216
	768	39,937	45,320
3	256	19,521	19,976
	512	63,617	64,520
	768	146,945	148,744

3.1.2. RNN

The architecture of RNN is shown in Figure 3b. Similar to DNN, it also consists of a Simple RNN, BN layer, and Dropout layer. But, there is no Flatten layer in RNN. This is because, in RNN, the input can be a sequence, such as a text sentence or a time series, and the RNN layer is designed to be able to process sequence data. Therefore, there is no need to add a Flatten layer to convert the dimensions of the data. The number of parameters in each layer and the corresponding number of nodes are shown in Table 6.

Table 6. Number of parameters and nodes of RNN.

Layers	Neurons	Parameters	
		Binary	Multi-Class
1	256	78,849	80,648
	512	288,769	292,360
	768	629,761	635,144
3	256	44,097	44,552
	512	161,921	162,824
	768	343,553	345,352

3.1.3. CNN

The architecture of CNN is shown in Figure 3c, which mainly consists of Conv1D and MaxPooling layers. Unlike DNN and RNN where each hidden layer contains a BN layer and Dropout layer, CNN only introduces a BN layer and Dropout layer before the output layer. This design choice is attributed to the effectiveness of MaxPooling layers 1 and 2 in preventing overfitting. These layers facilitate feature extraction after convolution, emphasizing key data and minimizing irrelevant noise. Table 7 outlines the details of the number of parameters per layer and the corresponding number of nodes of CNN.

Table 7. Number of parameters and nodes of CNN.

Layers	Neurons	Parameters	
		Binary	Multi-Class
1	256	13,313	15,112
	512	26,625	30,216
	768	39,937	45,320
3	256	19,521	19,976
	512	63,617	64,520
	768	146,945	148,744

3.1.4. LSTM

The architecture of LSTM is shown in Figure 3d. LSTM is a variant of RNN designed to better handle long sequence dependencies and overcome the vanishing gradient problem of traditional RNN. The number of parameters in each layer and the corresponding number of nodes are shown in Table 7. The architecture of CNN + RNN is shown in Figure 3e. In this architecture, there are two architectures: one with one convolutional layer and one recurrent layer, and one with three convolutional layers and three recurrent layers. The number of parameters in each layer and the corresponding number of nodes are shown in Table 8.

Table 8. Number of parameters and nodes of LSTM.

Layers	Neurons	Parameters	
		Binary	Multi-Class
1	256	311,553	313,352
	512	1,147,393	1,150,984
	768	2,507,521	2,512,904
3	256	173,121	173,576
	512	354,433	619,528
	768	1,364,225	1,366,024

3.1.5. CNN + RNN

The architecture of CNN + RNN is shown in Figure 3e. In this architecture, there are two architectures: one with one convolutional layer and one recurrent layer, and one with three convolutional layers and three recurrent layers. The number of parameters in each layer and the corresponding number of nodes are shown in Table 9.

Table 9. Number of parameters and nodes of CNN + RNN.

Layers	Neurons	Parameters	
		Binary	Multi-Class
1	256	78,849	133,160
	512	288,769	365,864
	768	629,761	729,640
3	256	44,097	86,568
	512	161,921	215,336
	768	343,553	397,864

3.1.6. CNN + LSTM

The architecture of CNN + RNN is shown in Figure 3f. In this architecture, there are two architectures: one with one convolutional layer and one recurrent layer, and one with three convolutional layers and three recurrent layers. The number of parameters in each layer and the corresponding number of nodes are shown in Table 10.

Table 10. Number of parameters and nodes of CNN + LSTM.

Layers	Neurons	Parameters	
		Binary	Multi-Class
1	256	420,041	428,840
	512	1,346,849	1,350,440
	768	2,790,945	2,796,328
3	256	246,625	247,080
	512	756,641	757,544
	768	1,479,713	1,481,512

3.2. *Transformer*

The architecture of the Transformer used in this paper is shown in Figure 4, and the detailed parameters are shown in Table 11. The main architecture of Transformer includes an encoder and a decoder, but for binary and multivariate classification tasks involving a single output sequence, the decoder is unnecessary. Therefore, only encoders [7] are used in our architecture.

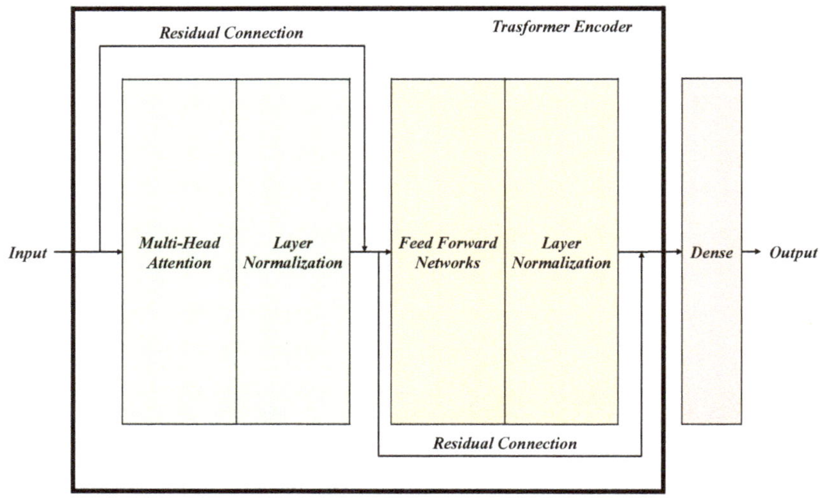

Figure 4. Transformer encoder architecture diagram.

Table 11. Number of parameters of Transformer.

Dense Dimension (FFN)	Number of Heads	Number of Layers (Encoder)	Parameters	
			Binary	Multi-Class
256	1	1	32,733	33,062
128			20,829	21,158
512			56,541	56,870
1024			104,157	104,486
2048			199,389	199,718
	2		41,335	41,664
	4		58,539	58,868
	8		94,947	93,276
		2	41,381	41,710
		4	58,677	59,006
		8	94,269	93,598

Additionally, two structures can be omitted for classification purposes. First, word embedding, which converts language vocabulary into a vector space for deep learning analysis, is unnecessary for our model. The material we are classifying is already in numeric form and converted to integers, thus eliminating the need for word embeddings. Secondly, positional encoding (Positional Encoding) used to determine the relative and absolute positions of tokens in sentences is not needed for our dataset. The length and composition of similar "sentences" in our data are fixed, making this structure not necessary [5].

3.2.1. Self Attention

The most important structures in Transformer are the self-attention mechanism and the multi-head attention mechanism. The schematic diagram of finding one of the outputs b_1 is shown in Figure 5.

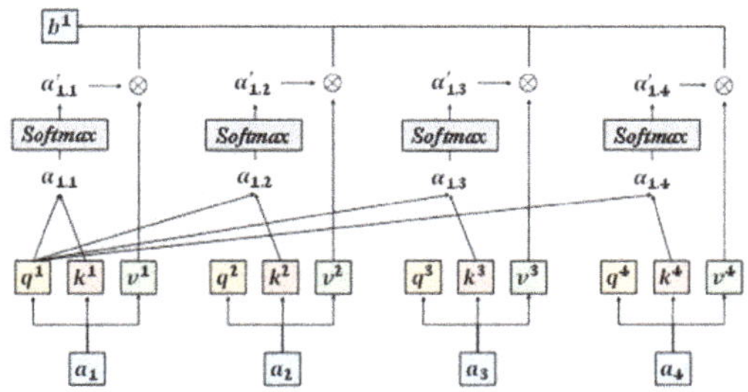

Figure 5. The schematic diagram of finding one of the outputs b_1.

First, we assume that the input is a sequence of four vectors a_1, a_2, a_3, a_4, and then multiply these four vectors by three transformation matrices W^Q, W^K and W^V to get each q^i, k^i and v^i corresponding to each input vector, that is:

$$q^i = W^Q a^i \tag{1}$$

$$k^i = W^k a^i \tag{2}$$

$$v^i = W^v a^i \tag{3}$$

where $i = 1, 2, 3, 4$.

After getting these three elements, we can start attention, as shown in Figure 5. Here, we take the output b_1 as an example.

First, we perform Scaled Dot Product on q^1 with k^1, k^2, k^3 and k^4, and we can get $\alpha_{1,1}$, $\alpha_{1,2}$, $\alpha_{1,3}$ and $\alpha_{1,4}$.

Then, we perform Softmax on $\alpha_{1,1}$, $\alpha_{1,2}$, $\alpha_{1,3}$ and $\alpha_{1,4}$, we can get $\alpha'_{1,1}$, $\alpha'_{1,2}$, $\alpha'_{1,3}$ and $\alpha'_{1,4}$, and then $\alpha'_{1,1}$, $\alpha'_{1,2}$.

$$\alpha_{1,1} = q^1 \cdot k^1 \tag{4}$$

$$\alpha_{1,2} = q^1 \cdot k^2 \tag{5}$$

$$\alpha_{1,3} = q^1 \cdot k^3 \tag{6}$$

$$\alpha_{1,4} = q^1 \cdot k^4 \tag{7}$$

$\alpha'_{1,3}$ and $\alpha'_{1,4}$ are multiplied by v^1, v^2, v^3 and v^4, respectively, and finally the four results are added to obtain the output b_1, that is:

$$b_1 = \sum_{i=1}^{4} \alpha'_{1,i} v^i = \sum_{i=1}^{4} Softmax(\alpha_{1,i}) v^i \tag{8}$$

As for b_2, b_3 and b_4, we can refer to Formula (8) and express it as the following formula:

$$b_2 = \sum_{i=1}^{4} \alpha'_{2,i} v^i \tag{9}$$

$$b_3 = \sum_{i=1}^{4} \alpha'_{3,i} v^i \tag{10}$$

$$b_4 = \sum_{i=1}^{4} \alpha'_{4,i} v^i \tag{11}$$

3.2.2. Multi-Head Attention

There is an advanced version of self-attention called the multi-head attention mechanism. In the previous chapter, the input was multiplied only once by the transformation matrices W^Q, W^K, and W^v, and then its corresponding q , k , and v values.

In the multi-head attention mechanism, taking two inputs a_1 and a_2 as an example, q, k, and v will be multiplied again by a transformation matrix. Assuming there are two attention heads, two types of q, k, and v will be obtained, respectively. As shown in Figure 6a, the first attention head $q^{1,1}$ will perform an attention calculation with $k^{1,1}$, then it will perform Softmax, and then it will multiply by $v^{1,1}$. Next, $q^{1,1}$ will be calculated with $k^{2,1}$ for attention, then Softmax, and finally multiplied by $v^{2,1}$. Finally, adding the previous two results gives $b^{1,1}$, that is:

$$b^{1,1} = \sum_{i=1}^{n} Softmax\left(q^{1,1} \cdot k^{n,1}\right) v^{n,1} \quad (12)$$

where n is 2, which is the number of heads.

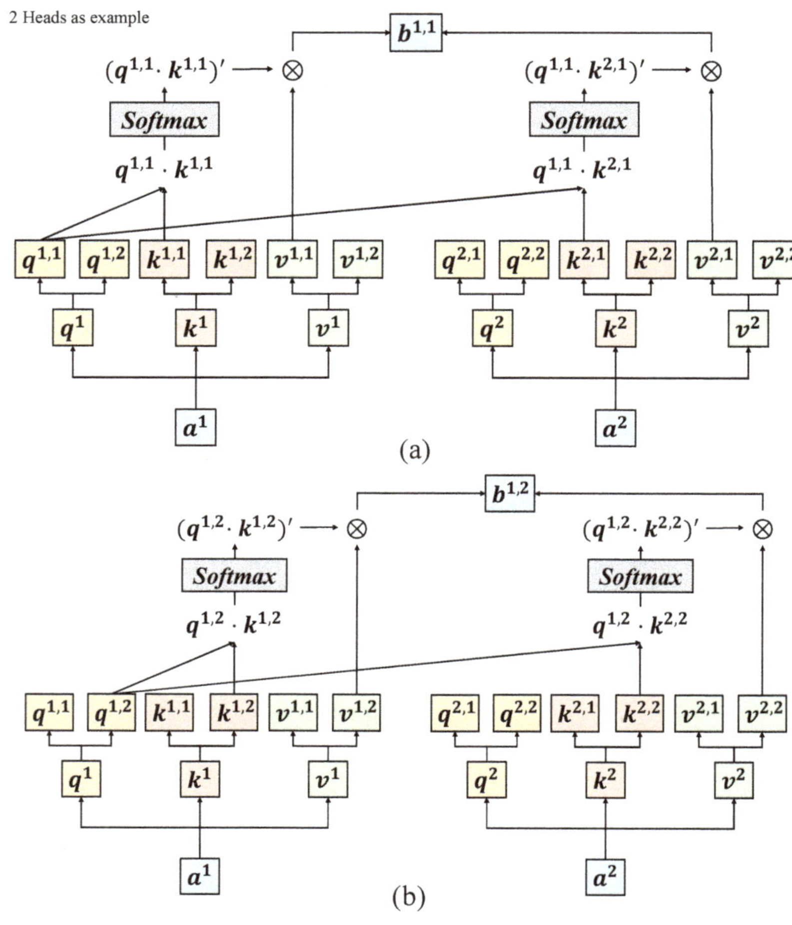

Figure 6. *Cont.*

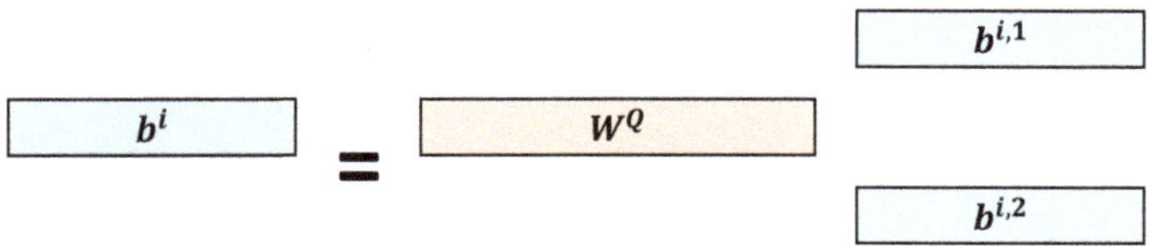

(c)

Figure 6. (**a**) The schematic diagram of finding one of the output $b^{1,1}$; (**b**) the schematic diagram of finding one of the output $b^{1,2}$; and (**c**) the schematic diagram of adding two results.

Then, as shown in Figure 6b, the second attention head $q^{1,2}$ will perform an attention calculation with $k^{1,2}$, then it will perform Softmax, and finally it will multiply by $v^{1,2}$. Then, $q^{1,2}$ performs an attention calculation with $k^{2,2}$, then it performs Softmax, and finally it multiplies $v^{2,2}$. Finally, adding the previous two results gives $b^{1,2}$, that is:

$$b^{1,2} = \sum_{i=1}^{n} Softmax\left(q^{1,2} \cdot k^{n,1}\right) v^{n,1} \tag{13}$$

Finally, these two outputs are concatenated and multiplied by an output transformation matrix W^{O} to obtain the final output b^{1}, as shown in Figure 6c.

3.2.3. Feed Forward Network

In our architecture, the main classification task is performed in a feed forward network. The feed forward network lies behind the multi-head attention mechanism and consists of two fully connected layers. The activation function of the first layer is Relu, and no activation function is used in the second layer.

3.2.4. Layer Normalization

Layer Normalization is a technique that normalizes each input feature independently, aiming to eliminate scale differences between different features and maintain output stability. Layer normalization helps control the output of each layer to keep it within a smaller range, helping to prevent gradient explosion. Sometimes, it can accelerate the convergence of the model and improve the training speed. Compared with Batch Normalization, Layer Normalization does not need to consider batch information.

3.2.5. Residual Connection

In neural networks, complex features are learned by stacking multiple layers. However, as the number of network layers increases, the gradient may gradually decrease, making the training process difficult. The idea of residual connections is to introduce skip connections, allowing the network to directly skip one or more layers and add the input signal to the output signal. In this way, even in deep networks, the information of the original input signal can still be propagated directly to deeper layers, thus helping to alleviate the vanishing gradient problem.

4. Experimental Results

4.1. Experimental Environment

The equipment specifications and environment settings used in this article are shown in Table 12. Since simply using tensorflow will cause the training speed to be too slow; this article chooses to use tensorflow-gpu to run our model to speed up the training. The hyperparameters of the six neural network models are shown in Table 13. Due to the large size of the dataset, we increased the batch size to 1024.

Table 12. Number of parameters of Transformer.

Project	Properties
OS	Windows 11
CPU	Intel® Core™ i7-13700 Processor
GPU	NVIDA Geforce RTX 4080
Memory	128 GB
Disk	1TB SSD
Python	3.7.16
NVIDIA CUDA	11.3.1
Framework	Tensorflow-gpu 2.5 & 2.6

Table 13. Number of parameters of Transformer.

Hyperparameter	Value
Batch Size	1024
Epochs	10
Learning Rate	0.001
Dropout	0.1

4.2. Experimental Metrics

We employ four metrics to evaluate the model's predictions of the number of accurate and inaccurate outcomes. These metrics are as follows: (1) True Positives (TPs), which represent the number of correctly classified benign samples; (2) False Positives (FPs), which represent the number of attack samples that are incorrectly predicted to be benign; (3) True Negatives (TNs), which represent the correct number of classified attack samples; and (4) False Negatives (FNs), indicating the number of benign samples that are incorrectly predicted as attacks. These four metrics produce four evaluation metrics: accuracy, precision, recall, and F1-Score. Accuracy measures the proportion of correctly classified samples. Precision measures the accuracy of predicting benign samples, while recall measures the accuracy of identifying benign samples. The F1-Score is an indicator of the classification model's performance and is the harmonic mean of precision and recall. The formulas for these metrics are summarized below:

$$Accuracy = \frac{TP + TN}{TP + TN + FP + FN} \tag{14}$$

$$Precision = \frac{TP}{TP + FP} \tag{15}$$

$$Recall = \frac{TP}{TP + FN} \tag{16}$$

$$F1 - Score = 2 \times \frac{Precision \times Recall}{Precision + Recall} \tag{17}$$

4.3. Experimental Result

The accuracy results of DNN are shown in Table 14, and the evaluation results of DNN are shown in Table 15.

Table 14. The accuracy results of DNN.

Layers	Neurons	Accuracy (%)	
		Binary	Multi-Class
1	256	99.48	97.35
	512	99.47	97.73
	768	99.53	99.13
3	256	99.56	99.16
	512	99.56	99.23
	768	99.56	99.36

Table 15. The evaluation results of DNN.

Layer	Node	Precision (%)		Recall (%)		F1-Score (%)	
		Binary	Multi-Class	Binary	Multi-Class	Binary	Multi-Class
1	256	99.51	97.35	99.48	97.35	99.49	97.30
	512	99.51	97.74	99.48	97.73	99.49	97.66
	768	99.49	99.12	99.47	99.13	99.48	99.10
3	256	99.54	99.17	99.53	99.16	99.54	99.12
	512	99.57	99.24	99.56	99.23	99.56	99.18
	768	99.57	99.35	99.56	99.36	99.57	99.32

The accuracy results of RNN are shown in Table 16, and the evaluation results of RNN are shown in Table 17.

Table 16. The accuracy results of RNN.

Layers	Neurons	Accuracy (%)	
		Binary	Multi-Class
1	256	99.49	99.21
	512	99.49	99.22
	768	99.48	99.24
3	256	99.53	99.26
	512	99.50	99.27
	768	99.50	99.28

Table 17. The evaluation results of RNN.

Layer	Node	Precision (%)		Recall (%)		F1-Score (%)	
		Binary	Multi-Class	Binary	Multi-Class	Binary	Multi-Class
1	256	99.51	99.21	99.49	99.21	99.50	99.17
	512	99.50	99.23	99.49	99.22	99.49	99.19
	768	99.51	99.23	99.48	99.24	99.49	99.21
3	256	99.54	99.26	99.53	99.26	99.53	99.21
	512	99.50	99.27	99.50	99.27	99.50	99.24
	768	99.52	99.28	99.50	99.28	99.51	99.23

The accuracy results of CNN are shown in Table 18, and the evaluation results of CNN are shown in Table 19.

Table 18. The evaluation results of CNN.

Layer	Node	Precision (%)		Recall (%)		F1-Score (%)	
		Binary	Multi-Class	Binary	Multi-Class	Binary	Multi-Class
1	256	99.51	99.21	99.49	99.21	99.50	99.17
	512	99.50	99.23	99.49	99.22	99.49	99.19
	768	99.51	99.23	99.48	99.24	99.49	99.21
3	256	99.54	99.26	99.53	99.26	99.53	99.21
	512	99.50	99.27	99.50	99.27	99.50	99.24
	768	99.52	99.28	99.50	99.28	99.51	99.23

Table 19. The evaluation results of CNN.

Layer	Node	Precision (%)		Recall (%)		F1-Score (%)	
		Binary	Multi-Class	Binary	Multi-Class	Binary	Multi-Class
1	256	99.30	96.11	99.27	96.06	99.28	95.93
	512	99.29	97.83	99.27	97.73	99.28	97.64
	768	99.31	91.95	99.24	90.91	99.27	89.88
3	256	99.50	99.18	99.48	99.19	99.48	99.15
	512	99.51	99.21	99.48	99.23	99.49	99.1
	768	99.52	99.23	99.48	99.25	99.50	99.21

The accuracy results of LSTM are shown in Table 20, and the evaluation results of LSTMare shown in Table 21.

Table 20. The accuracy results of LSTM.

Layers	Neurons	Accuracy (%)	
		Binary	Multi-Class
1	256	99.51	99.28
	512	99.51	99.28
	768	99.50	99.28
3	256	99.54	99.32
	512	99.54	99.21
	768	99.52	99.34

Table 21. The evaluation results of LSTM.

Layer	Node	Precision (%)		Recall (%)		F1-Score (%)	
		Binary	Multi-Class	Binary	Multi-Class	Binary	Multi-Class
1	256	99.52	99.27	99.51	99.28	99.51	99.24
	512	99.53	99.28	99.51	99.28	99.52	99.25
	768	99.53	99.28	99.50	99.28	99.51	99.24
3	256	99.55	99.31	99.54	99.32	99.54	99.28
	512	99.55	99.31	99.54	99.31	99.54	99.28
	768	99.54	99.32	99.54	99.34	99.52	99.31

The accuracy results of CNN + RNN are shown in Table 22, and its evaluation results are shown in Table 23.

Table 22. The accuracy results of CNN + RNN.

Layers	Neurons	Accuracy (%)	
		Binary	Multi-Class
1	256	99.37	99.15
	512	99.29	99.19
	768	99.45	99.11
3	256	99.46	99.16
	512	99.42	99.07
	768	99.15	99.03

Table 23. The evaluation results of CNN + RNN.

Layer	Node	Precision (%)		Recall (%)		F1-Score (%)	
		Binary	Multi-Class	Binary	Multi-Class	Binary	Multi-Class
1	256	99.44	99.15	99.37	99.15	99.39	99.10
	512	99.36	99.19	99.29	99.19	99.32	99.15
	768	99.48	99.12	99.45	99.11	99.47	99.04
3	256	99.48	99.15	99.46	99.16	99.47	99.12
	512	99.43	99.07	99.42	99.07	99.43	99.00
	768	99.23	99.02	99.15	99.03	99.18	98.98

The accuracy results of CNN + LSTM are shown in Table 24, and its evaluation results are shown in Table 25.

Table 24. The accuracy results of CNN + LSTM.

Layers	Neurons	Accuracy (%)	
		Binary	Multi-Class
1	256	99.56	99.33
	512	99.46	98.70
	768	99.55	99.34
3	256	99.53	99.31
	512	99.49	99.26
	768	99.48	99.26

Table 25. The evaluation results of CNN + LSTM.

Layer	Node	Precision (%)		Recall (%)		F1-Score (%)	
		Binary	Multi-Class	Binary	Multi-Class	Binary	Multi-Class
1	256	99.57	99.31	99.56	99.33	99.56	99.30
	512	9.57	98.70	99.56	98.70	99.56	98.66
	768	99.57	99.33	99.55	99.34	99.56	99.31
3	256	99.55	99.29	99.53	99.31	99.54	99.28
	512	99.49	99.25	99.49	99.26	99.49	99.22
	768	99.48	99.25	99.48	99.26	99.48	99.22

The accuracy results of Transformer are shown in Table 26 and its evaluation results are shown in Tables 27 and 28.

Table 26. The accuracy results of Transformer.

Dense Dimension (FFN)	Number of Heads	Number of Layers (Encoder)	Accuracy (%)	
			Binary	Multi-Class
256	1	1	99.51	99.12
128			99.50	97.54
512			99.51	99.40
1024			99.51	99.36
2048			99.52	99.21
	2		99.50	99.19
	4		99.50	98.96
	8		99.51	99.32
		2	99.50	99.34
		4	99.49	99.23
		8	99.48	99.24

Table 27. The precision of Transformer.

Dense Dimension (FFN)	Number of Heads	Number of Layers (Encoder)	Binary	Multi-Class
256	1	1	99.52	94.03
128			99.53	98.72
512			99.52	99.27
1024			99.54	99.31
2048			99.54	99.33
	2		99.53	98.88
	4		99.52	99.23
	8		99.53	95.03
		2	99.53	99.25
		4	99.52	99.32
		8	99.49	99.11

Table 28. The recall of Transformer.

Dense Dimension (FFN)	Number of Heads	Number of Layers (Encoder)	Binary	Multi-Class
256	1	1	99.50	93.68
128			99.51	98.72
512			99.51	99.27
1024			99.52	99.43
2048			99.52	99.33
	2		99.50	98.88
	4		99.50	94.94
	8		99.51	98.88
		2	99.50	99.24
		4	99.49	99.30
		8	99.48	99.11

4.4. Accuracy Figure

In this subsection, we show the comparison between the validation and training accuracy in every model. In Figures 7–13, we provide the most complex case for each model (DNN, RNN, CNN, LSTM, CNN + RNN, CNN + LSTM, Transformer, etc.). As shown in Figures 7–13, there is no overfitting.

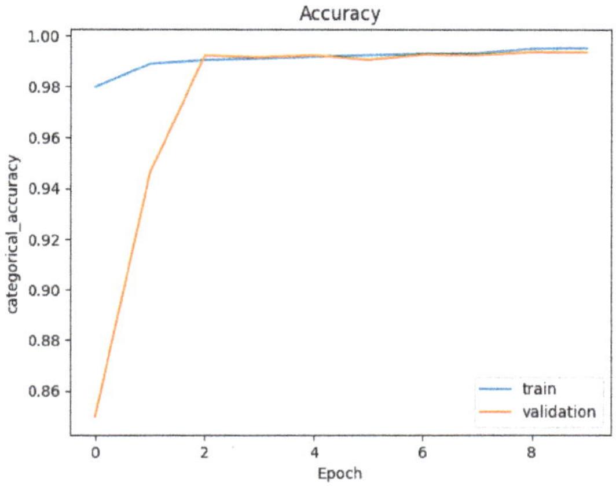

Figure 7. Accuracy figure of DNN with (layer = 3, Node = 768, multi-class).

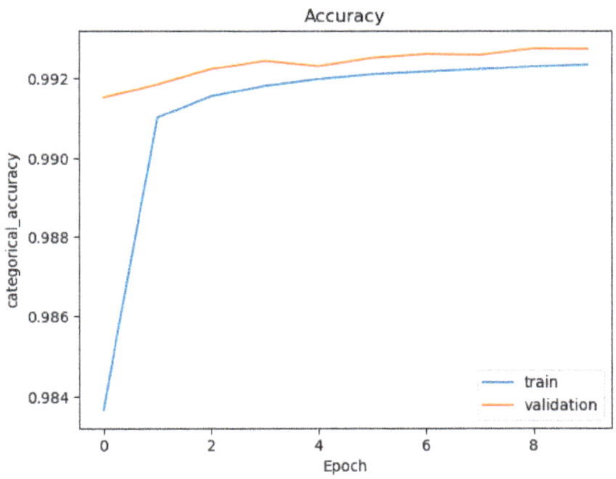

Figure 8. Accuracy figure of RNN (with layer = 3, node = 768, multi-class classification).

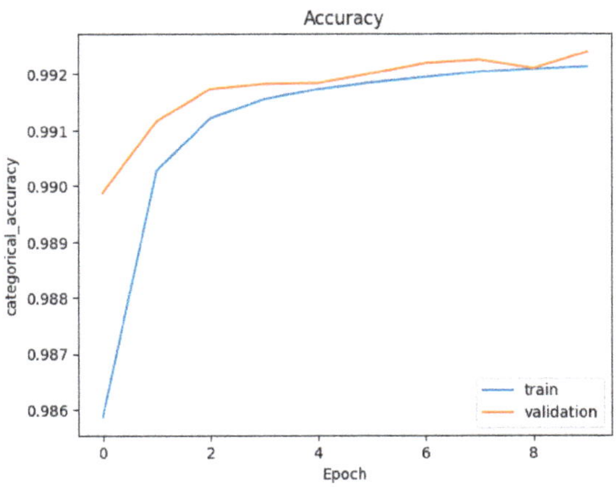

Figure 9. Accuracy figure of CNN (with layer = 3, node = 768, multi-class classification).

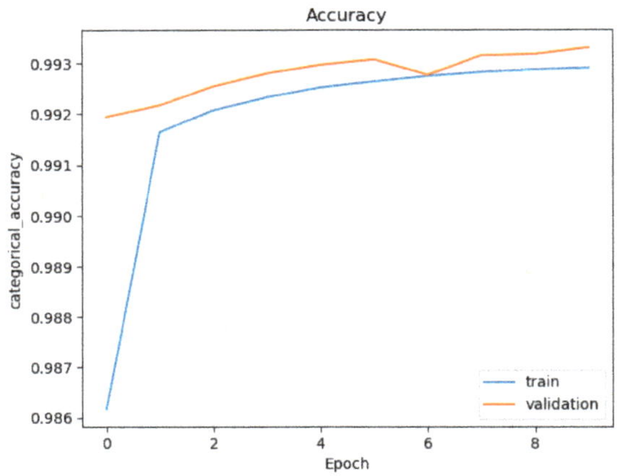

Figure 10. Accuracy figure of LSTM (with layer = 3, node = 768, multi-class classification).

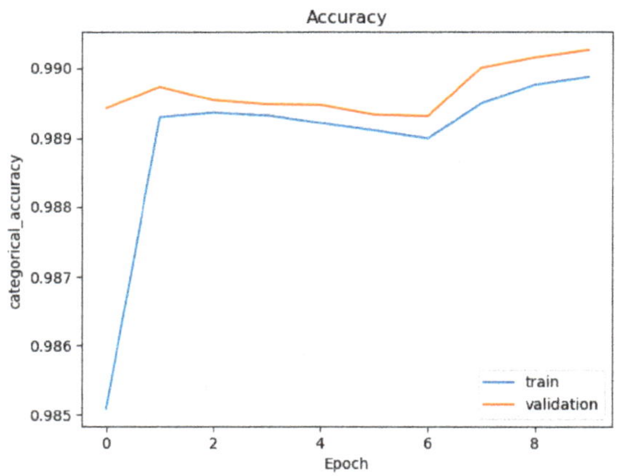

Figure 11. Accuracy figure of CNN + RNN (with layer = 3, node = 768, multi-class classification).

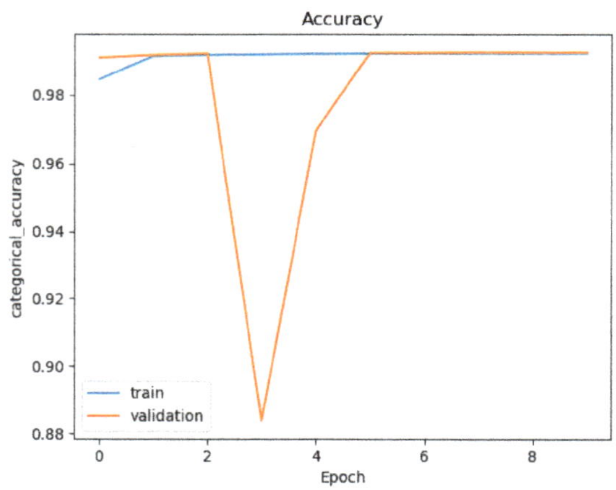

Figure 12. Accuracy figure of CNN + LSTM (with layer = 3, node = 768, multi-class classification).

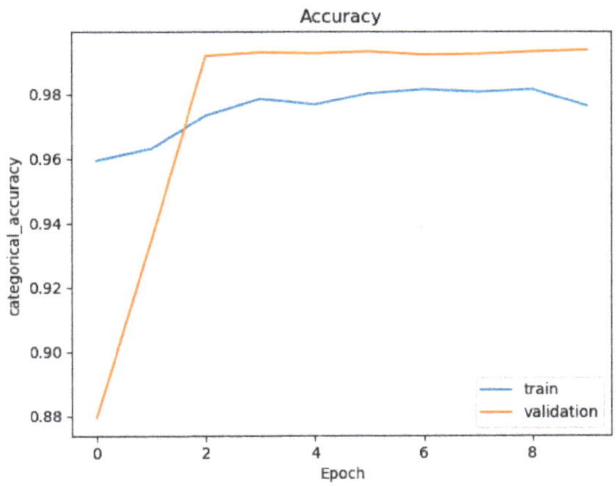

Figure 13. Accuracy figure of Transformer (with Dense Dimension = 2048, Number of Heads = 1, Number of Layers = 1, multi-class classification).

4.5. Time Consumption

The time consumption of each model is show in Table 29.

Table 29. Time consumption of each model (per sample).

Model	Binary Testing Time (μs)	Multi-Class Testing Time (μs)
DNN	3.8	3.8
RNN	7	7
CNN	12.3	12.3
LSTM	8	8
CNN + RNN	15	15
CNN + LSTM	18	18
Transformer	5	5

4.6. Confusion Matrices

In this subsection, we show the confusion matrix in every model. In Tables 30–36 we provide the most complex case for each model (DNN, RNN, CNN, LSTM, CNN + RNN, CNN + LSTM, Transformer, etc.).

Table 30. Confusion matrix figure of DNN (with layer = 3, node = 768, multi-class classification).

Actual		Benign Traffic	DDos	Dos	Recon	Web-Based	Brute Force	Spoofing	Mirai
	Benign Traffic	1,073,132	87	287	8001	30	3	16,647	8
	DDos	47	83,980,302	2712	1338	0	0	12	149
	Dos	22	18,808	8,071,716	79	0	0	34	7915
	Recon	82,758	5445	105	220,880	1550	138	43,664	15
	Web-Based	5367	0	7	3462	3193	12	12,787	1
	Brute Force	2508	0	2	1938	15	3749	4852	0
	Spoofing	56,557	132	141	13,208	91	945	415,405	25
	Mirai	9	13,504	289	1175	0	0	18	2,619,129

Table 31. Confusion matrix figure of RNN (with layer = 3, node = 768, multi-class classification).

Actual									
	Benign Traffic	1,057,073	7	4	17,204	40	1	23,866	0
	DDos	51	83,980,261	2463	1198	0	0	96	491
	Dos	26	7272	8,083,199	32	0	0	46	163
	Recon	83,296	1312	37	236,622	196	9	33,083	10
	Web-Based	8200	0	0	5175	2746	0	8708	0
	Brute Force	4089	0	0	3834	29	2298	2812	2
	Spoofing	108,726	24	7	24,986	220	14	352,524	3
	Mirai	18	350	56	11	0	0	33	2,633,656
		Benign Traffic	DDos	Dos	Recon	Web-Based	Brute Force	Spoofing	Mirai
		Predicted							

Table 32. Confusion matrix figure of CNN (with layer = 3, node = 768, multi-class classification).

Actual									
	Benign Traffic	1,034,444	14	7	22,362	127	47	41,192	2
	DDos	83	83,979,984	3238	764	0	0	63	428
	Dos	36	6228	8,084,368	20	0	0	37	49
	Recon	78,798	2093	40	236,729	790	161	35,930	24
	Web-Based	6077	1	2	5485	2960	7	10,297	0
	Brute Force	3564	0	0	3584	78	2401	3437	0
	Spoofing	101,541	23	4	24,349	880	98	359,605	4
	Mirai	5	380	63	6	0	0	16	2,633,654
		Benign Traffic	DDos	Dos	Recon	Web-Based	Brute Force	Spoofing	Mirai
		Predicted							

Table 33. Confusion matrix figure of LSTM (with layer = 3, node = 768, multi-class classification).

Actual									
	Benign Traffic	1,049,179	16	3	17,245	244	34	31,472	2
	DDos	46	83,980,598	2405	1335	2	0	47	136
	Dos	24	6531	8,084,054	28	1	0	37	63
	Recon	68,011	723	29	247,281	1212	179	37,128	2
	Web-Based	5230	1	0	4826	5520	16	9235	1
	Brute Force	3258	1	0	3384	142	2864	3415	0
	Spoofing	88,611	29	30	21,880	1797	170	373,965	22
	Mirai	11	865	38	19	0	0	25	2,633,166
		Benign Traffic	DDos	Dos	Recon	Web-Based	Brute Force	Spoofing	Mirai
		Predicted							

Table 34. Confusion matrix figure of CNN + RNN (with layer = 3, node = 768, multi-class classification).

Actual	Benign Traffic	1,043,235	67	3	20,089	81	2	34,715	3
	DDos	108	83,962,688	160,078	3626	0	2	290	1768
	Dos	42	29,673	8,058,272	1521	3	0	47	1180
	Recon	95,693	4048	638	217,211	55	14	36,490	416
	Web-Based	7995	7	0	5812	1501	0	9513	1
	Brute Force	4772	1	0	3641	5	1904	2741	0
	Spoofing	131,007	95	0	27,761	203	0	327,415	23
	Mirai	29	10,576	1292	1130	0	2	161	2,620,934
		Benign Traffic	DDos	Dos	Recon	Web-Based	Brute Force	Spoofing	Mirai
		Predicted							

Table 35. Confusion matrix figure of CNN + LSTM (with layer = 3, node = 768, multi-class classification).

Actual	Benign Traffic	1,042,720	31	6	25,929	367	26	29,116	0
	DDos	33	83,980,794	2611	778	0	3	83	258
	Dos	15	6435	8,084,207	10	1	0	30	40
	Recon	66,965	1731	27	251,565	1386	155	32,689	47
	Web-Based	4273	6	1	6214	5465	10	8410	0
	Brute Force	3036	1	0	3710	177	2740	3400	0
	Spoofing	93,724	109	28	26,392	2532	77	363,638	4
	Mirai	7	368	31	70	0	0	103	2,633,545
		Benign Traffic	DDos	Dos	Recon	Web-Based	Brute Force	Spoofing	Mirai
		Predicted							

Table 36. Confusion matrix figure of Transformer (with layer = 3, node = 768, multi-class classification).

Actual	Benign Traffic	1,050,021	1264	1	23,943	61	11	22,828	66
	DDos	13	83,975,357	2031	3208	1	0	688	3262
	Dos	46	25,250	8,064,500	498	0	0	60	384
	Recon	59,531	2309	2	257,601	28	7	35,007	80
	Web-Based	5513	23	0	4960	7361	0	6971	1
	Brute Force	3300	6	0	2589	2	2318	4848	1
	Spoofing	68,286	613	0	23,988	379	333	392,815	90
	Mirai	3	7796	79	212	0	0	262	2,625,772
		Benign Traffic	DDos	Dos	Recon	Web-Based	Brute Force	Spoofing	Mirai
		Predicted							

5. Conclusions

This research is based on the CIC-IoT-2023 dataset and conducts an in-depth discussion and analysis of IoT network intrusion detection. We apply deep learning methods to improve the detection performance of abnormal behaviors and intrusions. Compared with other papers, we further use the Transformer model and further use multi-class classification. The experimental results show that in binary classification, DNN and CNN + LSTM have the highest accuracy, while in multi-class classification, the Transformer model has the highest accuracy. This proves the potential application value of deep learning methods in IoT network intrusion detection. In the future, the dataset can be reconstructed and balanced to avoid the unpredictable situation of minority category attacks, so that these 34 categories can be directly used for classification to improve the generalization ability of the model and remove some features that have no impact on model classification to improve classification efficiency.

The method used in this study brings new possibilities to the field of IoT network intrusion detection. It is hoped that the results of this study can provide a valuable reference for the development of the field of IoT security.

Author Contributions: Conceptualization, S.-M.T. and Y.-C.W.; methodology, S.-M.T. and Y.-C.W.; software and data curation, Y.-Q.W.; funding acquisition, S.-M.T. All authors have read and agreed to the published version of the manuscript.

Funding: This research was funded by National Science and Technology Council, Taiwan grant number NSTC 112-2221-E-027-079-MY2.

Data Availability Statement: The data can be shared up on request. The data are not publicly available due to privacy restrictions.

Conflicts of Interest: The authors declare no conflict of interest.

References

1. Abbas, S.; Al Hejaili, A.; Sampedro, G.A.; Abisado, M.A.; Almadhor, A.M.; Shahzad, T.; Ouahada, K. A novel federated edge learning approach for detecting cyberattacks in IoT infrastructures. *IEEE Access* **2023**, *11*, 112189–112198. [CrossRef]
2. Asharf, J.; Moustafa, N.; Khurshid, H.; Debie, E.; Haider, W.; Wahab, A. A review of intrusion detection systems using machine and deep learning in Internet of Things: Challenges solutions and future directions. *Electronics* **2020**, *9*, 1177. [CrossRef]
3. Dadkhah, S.; Mahdikhani, H.; Danso, P.K.; Zohourian, A.; Truong, K.A.; Ghorbani, A.A. Towards the development of a realistic multidimensional IoT pofiling dataset. In Proceedings of the 2022 19th Annual International Conference on Privacy, Security & Trust (PST), Fredericton, NB, Canada, 22–24 August 2022; pp. 1–11.
4. Talpur, A.; Gurusamy, M. Machine learning for security in vehicular networks: A comprehensive survey. *IEEE Commun. Surv. Tutor.* **2022**, *24*, 346–379. [CrossRef]
5. Li, Q.F.; Liu, Y.Q.; Niu, T.; Wang, X.M. Improved Resnet Model Based on Positive Traffic Flow for IoT Anomalous Traffic Detection. *Electronics* **2023**, *12*, 3830. [CrossRef]
6. Wang, Y.C.; Yng, Y.C.; Chen, H.X.; Tseng, S.M. Network anomaly intrusion detection based on deep learning approach. *Sensors* **2023**, *23*, 2171. [CrossRef] [PubMed]
7. Ahmed, S.W.; Kientz, F.; Kashef, R. A modified transformer neural network (MTNN) for robust intrusion detection in IoT networks. In Proceedings of the 2023 International Telecommunications Conference (ITC-Egypt), Alexandria, Egypt, 18–20 July 2023; pp. 663–668.
8. Mezina, A.; Burget, R.; Travieso-González, C.M. Network Anomaly Detection with Temporal Convolutional Network and U-Net model. *IEEE Access* **2021**, *9*, 143608–143622. [CrossRef]
9. He, M.S.; Wang, X.J.; Wei, P.; Yang, L.; Teng, Y.L.; Lyu, R.J. Reinforcement learning meets network intrusion detection: A transferable and adaptable framework for anomaly behavior identification. *IEEE Trans. Netw. Serv. Manag.* **2024**, *21*, 2477–2492. [CrossRef]
10. Jony, A.I.; Arnob, A.K.B. A long short-term memory based approach for detecting cyber attacks in IoT using CIC-IoT2023 dataset. *J. Edge Comput.* **2024**, *3*, 28–42. [CrossRef]
11. Jaradat, A.S.; Nasayreh, A.; Al-Na'amneh, Q.; Gharaibeh, H.; Al Mamlook, R.E. Genetic optimization techniques for enhancing web attacks classification in machine learning. In Proceedings of the IEEE International Conference on 11 Dependable 2023, Autonomic & Secure Computing, Abu Dhabi, United Arab Emirates, 14–17 November 2023; pp. 0130–0136.
12. Guo, G.; Pan, X.; Liu, H.; Li, F.; Pei, L.; Hu, K. An IoT intrusion detection system based on TON IoT network dataset. In Proceedings of the 2023 IEEE 13th Annual Computing and Communication Workshop and Conference (CCWC), Las Vegas, NV, USA, 8–11 March 2023; pp. 0333–0338.

13. Neto, E.C.P.; Dadkhah, S.; Ferreira, R.; Zohourian, A.; Lu, R.; Ghorbani, A.A. CICIoT2023: A real-time dataset and benchmark for large-scale attacks in IoT environment. *Sensors* **2023**, *23*, 5941. [CrossRef]
14. Shtayat, M.M.; Hasan, M.K.; Sulaiman, R.; Islam, S.; Khan, A.U.R. An explainable ensemble deep learning approach for intrusion detection in industrial Internet of Things. *IEEE Access* **2023**, *11*, 115047–115061. [CrossRef]
15. Vaswani, A.; Shazeer, N.; Parmar, N.; Uszkoreit, J.; Jones, L.; Gomez, A.N.; Kaiser, L.; Polosukhin, I. Attention is all you need. In *Advances in Neural Information Processing Systems*; MIT Press: Cambridge, MA, USA, 2023; Volume 30.
16. Haque, S.; El-Moussa, F.; Komninos, N.; Muttukrishnan, R. A systematic review of data-driven attack detection trends in IoT. *Sensors* **2023**, *23*, 7191. [CrossRef] [PubMed]
17. Le, T.T.H.; Wardhani, R.W.; Putranto, D.S.C.; Jo, U.; Kim, H. Toward enhanced attack detection and explanation in intrusion detection system-based IoT environment data. *IEEE Access* **2023**, *11*, 131661–131676. [CrossRef]

future internet

MDPI

Article

Implementation of Lightweight Machine Learning-Based Intrusion Detection System on IoT Devices of Smart Homes

Abbas Javed [1], Amna Ehtsham [1], Muhammad Jawad [1,2], Muhammad Naeem Awais [1], Ayyaz-ul-Haq Qureshi [3,*] and Hadi Larijani [4]

1 Department of Electrical and Computer Engineering, COMSATS University Islamabad, Lahore Campus, Punjab 54000, Pakistan; abbasjaved@cuilahore.edu.pk (A.J.); amna.ehtsham@gmail.com (A.E.); mjawad@cuilahore.edu.pk (M.J.); naeem.awais@cuilahore.edu.pk (M.N.A.)

2 Hitachi Energy Research, Pawia 7, 31-154 Kraków, Poland

3 Department of Cyber Security and Networks, School of Computing, Engineering and Built Environment, Glasgow Caledonian University, Glasgow G4 0BA, UK

4 SMART Technology Research Centre, Department of Cyber Security and Networks, School of Computing, Engineering and Built Environment, Glasgow Caledonian University, Glasgow G4 0BA, UK; h.larijani@gcu.ac.uk

* Correspondence: aqu2@gcu.ac.uk

Abstract: Smart home devices, also known as IoT devices, provide significant convenience; however, they also present opportunities for attackers to jeopardize homeowners' security and privacy. Securing these IoT devices is a formidable challenge because of their limited computational resources. Machine learning-based intrusion detection systems (IDSs) have been implemented on the edge and the cloud; however, IDSs have not been embedded in IoT devices. To address this, we propose a novel machine learning-based two-layered IDS for smart home IoT devices, enhancing accuracy and computational efficiency. The first layer of the proposed IDS is deployed on a microcontroller-based smart thermostat, which uploads the data to a website hosted on a cloud server. The second layer of the IDS is deployed on the cloud side for classification of attacks. The proposed IDS can detect the threats with an accuracy of 99.50% at cloud level (multiclassification). For real-time testing, we implemented the Raspberry Pi 4-based adversary to generate a dataset for man-in-the-middle (MITM) and denial of service (DoS) attacks on smart thermostats. The results show that the XGBoost-based IDS detects MITM and DoS attacks in 3.51 ms on a smart thermostat with an accuracy of 97.59%.

Keywords: intrusion detection system; embedded machine learning; TinyML; internet of things; machine learning; cloud computing; edge machine learning

1. Introduction

Despite the impact of COVID-19, the number of Internet of Things (IoT) devices grew by 9% as observed in a 2021 report [1]. It is estimated that the number of IoT devices will surpass 27 billion by 2025 [1]. The reason behind this boom can be attributed to the easy availability of internet connectivity and low-cost sensors. While these devices have made our lives easier, they have also created a window of opportunity for hackers to exploit privacy. Some hacked systems, such as medical devices, can even be life-threatening. Smart home devices, when hacked, can also compromise the privacy of users. Every layer of the IoT, including the application, network, middleware, and sensing layer, is susceptible to attacks [2]. Intrusion detection systems (IDSs) designed for IoT systems aim to detect and respond to these threats in real time, ensuring the security and integrity of the IoT ecosystem. Nowadays, the use of IoT devices in our homes is increasingly geared towards creating a more comfortable living environment. These smart home devices communicate with one another using Zigbee, Bluetooth, and WiFi, and connect to the cloud via internet access (typically through a WiFi router) [3]. They are usually controlled remotely through cloud services and mobile apps. However, this remote accessibility of IoT devices in smart homes presents numerous opportunities for attackers, especially considering that most occupants have limited knowledge of security measures [4]. Securing such devices proves challenging and complex due to their limited storage and computational power.

Several machine learning and deep learning algorithms have been studied for intrusion detection [5–9]. All the aforementioned papers discuss a centralized approach. A few researchers also presented distributed approaches for intrusion detection in IoT applications [10–13].

Researchers utilized fog computing in [13–16] for implementing IDSs in fog but employed desktop PCs for the implementation. Similarly, in [17], the authors employed Raspberry Pi for binary class IDS implementation on a fog node. Raspberry Pi-based edge devices were also used for IDS implementation in [18,19]. In [20], the authors utilized Google Edge TPU and Raspberry Pi for IDS implementation on the edge, while in [21], the authors developed an IDS for mobile edge computing (MEC), but the proposed technique was tested on a desktop computer. Due to limited resources, the authors implemented a binary class IDS on an edge device [20,21].

The researchers used edge devices (Raspberry Pi/Desktop PCs/gateways), fog, and the cloud for implementing the IDS due to the availability of network traffic analyzers, such as Wireshark (https://www.wireshark.org (accessed on 26 April 2024)) and tcpdump (https://www.tcpdump.org/(accessed on 26 April 2024)) but an ML-based IDS is not embedded in IoT devices. Due to limited processing power, the lightweight IP (lwIP) (https://github.com/espressif/esp-lwip(accessed on 26 April 2024)) library for ESP32 (https://www.espressif.com/en/products/socs/esp32(accessed on 26 April 2024)) has restricted access to network features. Consequently, implementing an IDS on a microcontroller-based device without using network traffic analyzer software is an exceedingly challenging task. In this paper, we have implemented a real-world scenario in which we employed a smart thermostat using ESP32, an HTTP page on a cloud server (http://16.170.215.67/display (accessed on 26 April 2024)), and a Raspberry Pi-based adversary node for generating denial of service (DoS) and man-in-the-middle (MITM) attacks to collect a dataset called the intrusion detection in smart homes (IDSH) dataset [22]. The dataset is collected by using lwip and socket library for an ESP32 microcontroller. An ML-based binary class IDS is embedded in a smart thermostat using TinyML [23], which is responsible for monitoring room temperature and controlling HVAC systems. Additionally, this smart thermostat connects to WiFi and uploads air temperature and humidity data to a hosted web page on a cloud-based web services server, where an ML-based multiclass IDS is also deployed. To enhance the security of the microcontroller-based smart thermostat, we propose deploying a lightweight IDS based on XGBoost. Considering that IoT devices in smart homes connect to WiFi routers, they become susceptible to various security risks, including DoS, DDoS, MITM, ransomware, and scanning attacks. The main research objective of this research article is to develop an IDS for IoT devices (a smart thermostat in our case) of smart homes which are directly communicating with web servers through WiFi access points and additional hardware (Raspberry Pi-based edge device) is not available. Therefore, in this work, we proposed a two-layered ML-based IDS which can protect the smart thermostat by embedding an IDS in the smart thermostat and can also protect the cloud by implementing the IDS on the cloud.

The main contributions of this paper are as follows:

- A novel bi-directional computationally efficient ML-based decentralized multiclass IDS is proposed for the deployment on IoT devices and the cloud.
- An embedded XGBoost-based IDS for real-time binary classification of attacks in smart thermostats using TinyML is proposed. Moreover, a thorough comparison is made for ANN-, XGBoost-, RF-, and DT-based IDS implementation on low-cost microcontroller-based IoT devices for binary classification. The algorithms are compared in terms of accuracy, inference time, and storage requirement.

- A computationally efficient XGBoost IDS is implemented on the cloud for monitoring the incoming traffic from IoT devices and external attacks. The XGBoost IDS is implemented for the identification of DoS, DDoS, MITM, port scanning, injection, backdoor, XSS, and ransomware attacks. Moreover, a detailed comparison of different ML algorithms is made for IDS implementation on the cloud side in terms of accuracy, F1-score, precision, recall, inference time, and computational complexity.
- To conduct real-time testing and validation of the IDS deployed on a smart thermostat, we developed a Raspberry Pi-based adversary specifically designed to generate DoS and MITM attacks on the smart thermostat. We collected a new dataset called the intrusion detection in smart homes (IDSH) dataset [22] comprising 4144 samples, encompassing normal activities, DoS attacks, and MITM attacks on the smart thermostat.

The rest of the paper is organized as follows: Section 2 presents the literature review on centralized and decentralized IDS. In Section 3, the proposed methodology is explained. Section 4 discusses the results along with a comparative analysis. The paper is concluded in Section 5 along with future research directions.

2. Related Work

An IoT system is vulnerable to different types of attacks [2]. These attacks are explained in detail in [24] and include password cracking attacks, ransomware, port scanning, MITM attacks, DoS/DDoS attacks, backdoors, injection attacks, and XSS attacks. A password cracking attack is launched against a device to guess its password using a commonly available set of passwords online. A ransomware attack is launched to lock a device's data and demand money in exchange for the data. A port scanning attack is used to check which port on a device is open to launch an attack against that port. An MITM attack is used to intercept traffic between any two nodes in the network. A DoS/DDoS attack is used to occupy bandwidth in a network. For example, a device or a set of devices is directed toward a single server to send false queries, making the server unresponsive to the actual queries. A backdoor attack is launched to use/hack devices without anyone knowing. A hacker who launches a backdoor attack has full access to the device. Injection/XSS attacks are launched against web pages to alter their data.

Recently, in [25], the authors calculated the energy consumption of running DT-, RF-, and ANN-based ML models for intrusion detection in IoT devices using the TinyML library. However, the energy consumption is based on theoretical calculations, and the ML models were not tested for real-world intrusion detection systems. The authors in [26] developed an IoT device dataset by generating a botnet attack on a smart health service testbed. The dataset is labeled as normal and attack traffic. The authors utilized Wireshark for collecting the dataset. The results show that the accuracy of an RF-based IDS on the collected dataset is 99.98%.

In [9], the TON_IoT dataset [27] is used to train multiple ML algorithms for intrusion detection in intelligent transportation systems, where the XGBoost algorithm outperforms other ML algorithms with an accuracy of 99.92%. In [28], the authors developed an enhanced anomaly-based intrusion detection method (EIDM) for classifying 15 attacks with an accuracy of 95%. The first application of random neural networks (RNNs) for IDSs was proposed in our previous work [29] in which an RNN with an artificial bee colony algorithm is used for binary classification of intrusion detection in the cloud. In [30], the authors developed an IDS using the hybrid deep learning model. The proposed technique achieved 96% accuracy, but it incurred a high computational burden. In [31], a five-stack ResNet was used as a deep learning method, trained on two different datasets: N-BaIoT and the power system dataset.

The authors in [32] proposed to implement ensemble ML model selection on the cloud and IDS implementation on fog for real-time prediction to reduce the attack detection time. In [33], a distributed IDS approach is presented. Attacks were classified as normal or attack at the fog node. If identified as an attack, further classification occurs at the cloud node. The DNN-KNN algorithm showcased accuracies of 99.77% and 99.85% on NSL-KDD and CICIDS2017, respectively. In [34], a fog computing-based distributed IDS approach is introduced. Data are analyzed for attacks at the fog node, and if detected, relevant information is stored in the cloud server for subsequent action. In [16], an anomaly-based IDS is moved to fog nodes, and the Distributed Smart Space Orchestration System (DS2OS) dataset is used to train different ML algorithms. RF showed an accuracy of 99.99%. A distributed IDS using fog computing is designed in [35] to detect DDoS attacks in the memory pool of a blockchain-enabled IoT network. The performance of the proposed IDS is evaluated using machine learning algorithms (RF and XGBoost) and evaluation metrics on an actual IoT-based BoT-IoT dataset containing various recent botnet attacks.

In [19], the authors presented Passban, an intelligent IDS for edge devices. The IDS was deployed on an IoT gateway developed with Raspberry Pi 3. Passban successfully detected HTTP and SSH brute force, port scanning, and SYN flood attacks. Another IDS, named IoT-KEEPER, is proposed in [18], capable of detecting MITM, DoS, and scanning attacks at the IoT gateway. The authors tested IoT-KEEPER's performance on Raspberry Pi 3.

In [36], an IDS is introduced to secure edge IoT devices, operating in two phases. In the first phase, features are extracted and then these features are trained using the DNN algorithm. This system presents an accuracy of 99.23% and an F1-score of 99.27%. In [37], an edge-of-things computing-based intrusion detection mechanism is presented. The best accuracy achieved by this network is 88.4%.

The literature review above has discussed both centralized and decentralized approaches deployed on the edge, fog, and cloud sides. To effectively implement an IDS on the edge and fog sides, it needs to be both accurate and computationally efficient in promptly detecting attacks. Successfully detecting intrusions on the edge/fog side of an IoT network could proactively save cloud resources from further proliferation. Additionally, detailed studies on IDSs for IoT devices, developed with microcontrollers having limited computation resources, are lacking. There has been no study evaluating the feasibility of embedding an IDS on both IoT devices and the cloud side.

3. Materials and Methods

This research investigated a multilayered approach to classify intrusions that an IoT network might face. The goal is to distribute the load between the cloud and edge sides of the IoT network for intrusion classification. After load balancing, the TON_IoT dataset [27] was divided according to attacks on the edge and cloud sides of the IoT network. Multiple ML algorithms were then trained on the dataset to select the one that shows the best results. In this work, we considered an application of a smart thermostat that uploads temperature, humidity levels, and air conditioner status to a webpage hosted on the Amazon Web Service (AWS) cloud server. The proposed technique involves a two-layered IDS, which begins intrusion detection at the device level. The first layer of the IDS is deployed on a low-cost ESP32 microcontroller-based smart thermostat controller for binary classification. This IDS on the smart thermostat detects DoS, MITM, ransomware, and scanning attacks.

The second layer of the IDS is deployed on the cloud side to classify DoS, DDoS, brute force, injection, XSS, ransomware, port scanning, MITM, and backdoor attacks. The architecture of the proposed distributed approach is shown in Figure 1. The approach is evaluated in real time by implementing the adversary node using Raspberry Pi 4 (manufactured by the Raspberry Pi Foundation, Cambridge, United Kingdom.) with Kali Linux OS (version: 2023.3) The IDS implementation on the smart thermostat is evaluated in real time by generating attacks from the adversary node targeted at the smart thermostat.

For real-time testing of the IDS on the smart thermostat, DoS and MITM attacks are generated to disrupt the communication between the smart thermostat and the AWS cloud server.

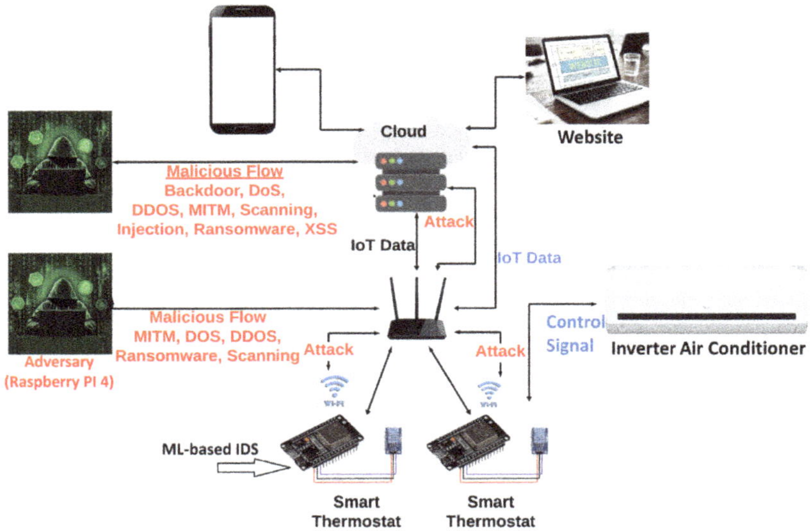

Figure 1. System architecture for distributed IDS.

3.1. Threat Model

In this work, an adversary seeks to disrupt, intercept, and manipulate the communication between the smart thermostat and the cloud. The adversary considered in this work has no knowledge of the ML-based IDS deployed on the smart thermostat.

3.1.1. Targeted Model

The smart thermostat monitors the temperature and humidity of the building and uploads the indoor environment data to the cloud. The user can send the control signal of the inverter air conditioner from the website to the smart thermostat. The bi-directional communication between the smart thermostat and the cloud is established through WiFi.

3.1.2. Adversarial Capabilities

The adversary possesses the capability to enable various attack as shown in Figure 1. Being connected to the same hotspot as the smart thermostat allows the adversary to intercept and disrupt communication between the thermostat and the cloud. The adversary is proficient in launching the following attacks: DoS, MITM, scanning, and ransomware.

3.1.3. Adversary Goals

The primary objective of the adversary is to intercept the communication between the smart thermostat and the cloud. The adversary goals are as follows:

- Executing DoS attacks to overwhelm the smart thermostat or cloud server, rendering them unresponsive.
- Intercepting and tampering with the data transmission between the smart thermostat and the cloud through MITM attacks.
- Attempting to exploit vulnerabilities in the smart thermostat or cloud infrastructure via scanning or injection attacks.
- Potentially deploying ransomware to encrypt data or compromise the operation of the smart thermostat or cloud server.

3.2. Training Dataset for IDS

3.2.1. TON_IoT Dataset

This is a heterogeneous dataset specifically captured for intrusion detection in IoT applications totaling 461,043 instances. The edge layer of the testbed comprises sensors, weather stations, smart TVs, gateways, and Virtual Machines (VMs) managing the network. The fog layer includes client and vulnerable VMs, along with offensive Kali systems. Additionally, the fog layer hosts a middleware server that manages seven IoT sensors and their message queuing telemetry transport (MQTT) services using the Node-RED tool. The cloud layer encompasses servers simulating communication with the cloud, a vulnerable website for attack simulations, and an MQTT broker. This testbed covers various attack categories, including port scanning, DoS/DDoS, ransomware, backdoor, data injection, cross-site scripting, brute force, and man-in-the-middle attacks. A total of 45 features are extracted from this testbed.

The main points considered for selection of the dataset are as follows:

- Testbed architecture;
- Number of features;
- Number of attacks simulated.

The MQTT IoT dataset simulates only data of sensors that are communicating over MQTT and there are only four attack categories covered [38]. The Bot-IoT dataset focuses more on the network and there are a fewer number of attacks covered [39]. In the TON_IoT dataset, the testbed is heterogeneous and mimics the behavior of the edge, fog, and cloud side very well. Moreover, this testbed includes seven IoT sensors, and it covers a wide range of attacks that proved helpful while doing load balancing for the distributed approach for the IDS.

3.2.2. Load Balancing

The cloud has enough computational resources, and any complex deep learning algorithm can be trained and deployed on the cloud; therefore, it is decided to deploy a classifier that classifies DoS, DDoS, brute force, injection/XSS attacks, ransomware, port scanning, and backdoor attacks.

On the other hand, DoS/DDoS, MITM, ransomware, scanning, and backdoor can affect the smart thermostat, so a classifier deployed in the smart thermostat will protect it from potential attacks. For this reason, the datasets for MITM, DoS, and Normal traffic are converted into binary class problems.

3.2.3. Data Preprocessing

The TON_IoT dataset is selected to be used in our research. However, the dataset needed preprocessing to be further used for classification. We employed feature scaling to normalize all input features. We used the standard minmax function for data normalization that converts all data points of the column in the range of [0,1] or [−1,1] depending on all positive data entries or those having negative values. Moreover, the output variable include string parameters that must be converted into an integer array to be further used in the ML algorithms. Therefore, label encoding is used for the output.

3.2.4. Feature Selection and Feature Extraction

In this work, we utilized chi-square [40] for feature selection (FS) and Principal Component Analysis (PCA) for feature extraction (FE) [41] in order to reduce the features. The features selected by chi-square are shown in Table 1. PCA transforms original features into new, uncorrelated features (principal components) that capture the variance in data. The first few principal components usually capture most of the variance, allowing for effective dimensionality reduction while preserving the data's essential structure. In this work, we tested PCA for FE using 10, 15, and 25 components.

Table 1. Selected features.

No. of Features	Selected Features
10	src_port, dst_port, src_bytes, dst_bytes, missed_bytes, src_ip_bytes, dst_ip_bytes, dns_query, dns_qclass, http_response_body_len,
15	src_port, dst_port, service, duration, src_bytes, dst_bytes, missed_bytes, src_pkts, src_ip_bytes, dst_pkts, dst_ip_bytes, dns_query, dns_qclass, dns_qtype, http_response_body_len
25	src_port, dst_port, proto, service, duration, src_bytes, dst_bytes, conn_state, missed_bytes, src_pkts, src_ip_bytes, dst_pkts, dst_ip_bytes, dns_query, dns_qclass, dns_qtype, dns_rcode, dns_AA, dns_RD, dns_RA, dns_rejected, http_request_body_len, http_response_body_len, http_status_code, http_user_agent,

3.3. Implementation of Machine Learning-Based Intrusion Detection System on Cloud

Different ML algorithms are implemented to check their performance on the cloud side of an IoT network. First, the data are preprocessed and divided into training, testing, and validation datasets. Then, five different ML algorithms are trained on the data. After training, the algorithms are tested on the test dataset. In this work, we implemented the XGBoost-, LSTM-, Conv1d-, RF-, and MLP-based IDSs for deployment on the cloud.

3.4. Implementation of Adversary for Real-Time Testing and IDSH Dataset Collection

The ToN_IoT dataset contains thermostat data, including temperature, thermostat status, timestamp, date, label, and type. However, this dataset is not generalized and may not be suitable for smart home applications operating in different environmental conditions. In addition to sensor data, every data packet sent through a network by an IoT device contains additional information, such as connectivity and network protocols. This provides raw information about the internal and external activity of these IoT devices, complementing sensor data. In this study, we used network features, such as connection activity, statistical activity, and DNS activity, to train the IDS deployed on IoT devices.

For IDS implementation on the IoT devices in our smart home, specifically, the smart thermostat, we generated our own dataset named the IDSH dataset, available on Kaggle [22]. This dataset combines sensor data, thermostat status, and network features (i.e., connection activity and statistical activity) for MITM, DoS, and normal traffic.

The smart thermostat is designed to monitor the indoor temperature and humidity of the room and control the air conditioner by sending ON/OFF signals. The temperature and humidity are measured by the thermostat using a DHT22 sensor. These measurements are sent to a web application via an HTTP POST request, which receives the data and displays the indoor temperature on the webpage. Additionally, the user can control the air conditioner remotely through the web application by sending ON/OFF commands.

In this work for testing the accuracy of an IDS deployed on a smart thermostat, the adversary is implemented with Kali Linux scripts running on Raspberry Pi 4. The attacker node generates the MITM, and DoS attacks on the smart thermostat communicating with the cloud server for data uploading and control signal input. The attacker node carried out MITM using Address Resolution Protocol (ARP) spoofing and DoS attacks on the smart thermostat by flooding them with the high volume of traffic and requests. The smart thermostat does not have access to packet analyzer tools like Wireshark and tcpdump for extracting network features. Therefore, we utilized the Esp32 lwIP library and socket library to extract real-time network parameters. The block diagram of the smart thermostat for collecting the dataset is shown in Figure 2. The parameters of the dataset collected at each step are shown in Figure 2.

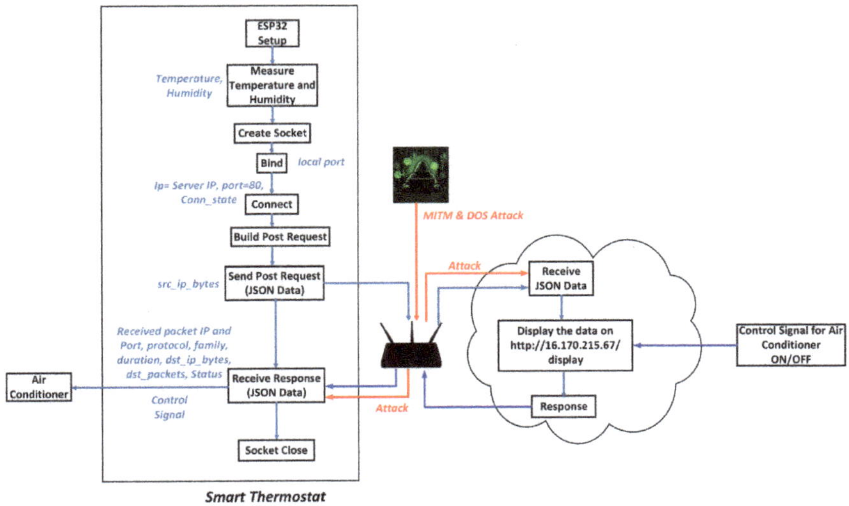

Figure 2. Dataset collection on smart thermostat.

The steps involved in dataset collection are as follows:

1. Setup the microcontroller by including header files for the lightweight IP and socket (`lwip/socket.h`).
2. Create, bind, and connect the server using the server IP and port.
3. Build a POST request and send the POST request to the web server.
4. The web server receives the POST request, displays the data, and responds to the smart thermostat with the status of the air conditioner (i.e., ON/OFF).
5. The smart thermostat receives the response and collects the features of the collected dataset as shown in Table 2.

For MITM and DoS attacks, the adversary generates an MITM attack using the `arpspoof` command and a DoS attack using `hping3`. During the attack, we collected the dataset from the smart thermostat by following steps 1–5. We collected an IDSH dataset comprising 4144 samples, encompassing instances of normal traffic, DoS attacks, and MITM attacks. Among these, 2762 samples correspond to normal traffic, 292 samples are of DoS attacks, and 1090 samples represent MITM attacks. In this work, we used ID 21 (Label) as the target for binary classification, while for multiclass classification, ID 22 (Type) could be used as the target. We used IDs 3 and 5-20 as input features, excluding the timestamp (ID 1), source IP (ID 2), and destination IP (ID 4) from the input features to avoid overfitting.

Table 2. Description of IDSH dataset.

ID	Feature	Type	Description
1	timestamp	Time	Timestamp of connection
2	source_ip	String	Source IP address
3	source_port	Number	Source ports which originate endpoint's TCP/UDP ports
4	destination_ip	String	Destination IP address
5	dst_port	Number	Destination ports which respond to endpoint's TCP/UDP ports
6	protocol	String	Transport layer protocols of flow connections

Table 2. *Cont.*

ID	Feature	Type	Description
7	Family	String	Address family
8	Service	String	Dynamically detected protocols, such as DNS, HTTP, and SSL
9	Duration	Time	The difference in the time between the packet being sent from the source and receiving the response from the cloud server
10	source_bytes	Number	Source bytes which originate from the source
11	destination_bytes	Number	Destination bytes which are responses from the destination
12	conn_state	String	Various connection states, such as S0 (connection without replay), S1 (connection established), and REJ (connection attempt rejected)
13	missed_bytes	Number	Number of missing bytes in content gaps
14	source_packets	Number	Number of original packets which is estimated from source systems
15	src_ip_bytes	Number	Number of original IP bytes which is the total length of IP header field of source systems
16	destination_packets	Number	Number of destination packets which is estimated from destination systems
17	dst_ip_bytes	Number	Number of destination IP bytes which is the total length of IP header field of destination systems
18	Temperature	String	Room temperature (°C) of the Zone
19	Humidity	String	Humidity (%) of the Zone.
20	Status	String	Status of air conditioner (ON/OFF).
21	Label	Number	Tag Normal traffic as 0 and attack as 1.
22	Type	String	Tag attack categories as Normal, DoS, and MITM.

3.5. Implementation of Machine Learning-Based Intrusion Detection System on Smart Thermostat (IoT Device)

As a feasibility study for the implementation of an IDS on a smart thermostat, two models of the IDS are trained using the TON_IoT dataset. The IDS is first trained with connection activity, statistical activity, and DNS activity features. The second model is trained with connection activity and statistical activity. To avoid overfitting, the source and destination IP addresses and timestamps are removed from the training and testing dataset.

Four different ML algorithms, XGBoost, DT, RF, and ANN, are deployed on the microcontroller (ESP32)-based smart thermostat for binary classification of attacks. The ML-based IDS is deployed on a microcontroller using the TinyML [23] library.

4. Results

This section covers a discussion of various ML algorithms used for implementing an IDS on the cloud, followed by the presentation of ML-based IDS results on IoT devices (smart thermostat). Additionally, this section provides details on the implementation of ML algorithms on a microcontroller using the TinyML library [23]. Various ML models are trained to be deployed on the cloud side of an IoT network with and without FS techniques. The TON_IoT dataset is used to train the XGBoost, LSTM, Conv1d, MLP, and RF algorithms and their results are discussed in this section. For implementation on a smart thermostat (edge device), XGBoost is compared with DT, RF, and ANN in terms of accuracy, storage requirement, and computational delay. The highlighted values, in bold in the tables, denote the models with superior performance. Finally, the accuracy of the IDS is also evaluated for MITM and DoS attacks on the smart thermostat generated by the adversary.

4.1. Machine Learning-Based IDS on the Cloud without FS Method

The LSTM, Conv1d, XGBoost, RF, and MLP algorithms are trained to classify nine types of attacks on the cloud side of an IoT network. The TON_IoT dataset is divided into train, test, and validation datasets. The training dataset is 60% of the total dataset, and the test and validation datasets are each 20% of the total dataset.

4.1.1. LSTM-Based IDS on Cloud without FS Method

We studied different LSTM models with varying numbers of layers and neurons to find the optimal LSTM model for deployment on the cloud side of an IoT network for an IDS. The details of the LSTM model are shown in Table 3. To determine the optimal learning rate for training, Model1 and Model2 are trained using learning rates of 0.1, 0.01, and 0.001 with 50, 80, and 100 epochs. The results indicate that the best learning rate for training the LSTM model is 0.001. Therefore, Model3 and Model4 are trained using a learning rate of 0.001 with 50 epochs. The training and testing results of Model1–Model4 are shown in Table 3. The results show that Model 1, trained with a learning rate of 0.001 and 50 epochs, gives the detection accuracy of 94.2%.

Table 3. Test results of the LSTM and Conv1d models for IDS implementation on cloud.

ML Models	Models	Configuration Details	Epochs	Learning Rate	Accuracy	Precision	Recall	F1-Score
LSTM	Model1	Layers = 2, Layer1,2 = 100 neurons	50	0.001	94.2%	0.83	0.82	0.82
LSTM	Model2	Layers = 2, Layer1 = 120 neurons, Layer2 = 100 neurons	50	0.001	94.01%	0.83	0.83	0.83
LSTM	Model3	Layers = 2, Layer1 = 180 neurons, Layer2 = 140 neurons	50	0.001	94.02%	0.84	0.82	0.82
LSTM	Model4	Layers = 3, Layer1 = 180 neurons, Layer2 = 140 neurons, Layer3 = 100 neurons	50	0.001	93.87%	0.84	0.80	0.81
Conv1d	Model1	Layers = 2, Kernel size = 3, Filters = 64,32	50	0.001	79.8%	0.59	0.59	0.57
Conv1d	Model2	Layers = 3, Kernel size = 3, Filters = 64, 32 , Layer3 = 100 neurons	50	0.001	73%	0.41	0.41	0.40
Conv1d	Model3	Layers = 1, Kernel size = 3, Filters = 32	50	0.001	76.5%	0.59	0.49	0.50
Conv1d	Model4	Layers = 1, Kernel size = 5, Filters = 32	50	0.001	79%	0.48	0.52	0.45
Conv1d	Model5	Layers = 1, Kernel size = 5, Filters = 64	50	0.001	80%	0.55	0.53	0.515
Conv1d	Model6	Layers = 1, Kernel size = 7, Filters = 64	50	0.001	83.28%	0.65	0.60	0.59

4.1.2. Conv1d-Based IDS on Cloud without FS Method

We studied different models of Conv1d for IDS implementation on the cloud. The Conv1d results are reported for different models after changing their number of layers, filters, and kernel sizes. All models are trained for 50 epochs with a learning rate of 0.001, after observing the best results with this learning rate. The details of the models are mentioned in Table 3. The testing and training results of Conv1D for IDS implementation on the cloud are shown in Table 3. The results show that the single-layered Model6, with a kernel size of 7 and 64 filters, outperformed the other models, achieving an accuracy of 83.28%, a precision of 0.65, a recall of 0.60, and an F1-score of 0.59. However, this accuracy of 83.28% is not sufficient for the implementation of IDS due to the low precision, F1-score, and recall.

4.1.3. Random Forest-Based IDS Implementation on Cloud without FS Methods

The random forest model is trained on the TON_IoT dataset with 50, 100, 150, and 200 estimators. The testing results of the RF model are shown in Table 4. The results show that there is a nominal difference in the performance of different RF models. It is observed that Model2 showed the best results with a testing accuracy of 99.4%, precision of 0.95, recall of 0.97, and F1-score of 0.96.

Table 4. Test results of RF, XGBoost, and MLP models evaluated for IDS implementation on cloud.

ML Models	Models	No. of Estimators/Neurons	Accuracy	Precision	Recall	F1-Score
RF	Model1	50	99.40%	0.95	0.97	0.96
RF	Model2	100	99.30%	0.95	0.97	0.96
RF	Model3	150	99.38%	0.95	0.97	0.96
RF	Model4	200	99.41%	0.95	0.97	0.96
XGBoost	Model1	50	99.46%	0.96	0.97	0.96
XGBoost	Model2	100	99.49%	0.96	0.97	0.96
XGBoost	**Model3**	**150**	**99.50%**	**0.96**	**0.97**	**0.97**
XGBoost	Model4	200	99.50%	0.96	0.97	0.97
MLP	Model1	50	93.40%	0.83	0.80	0.80
MLP	Model2	100	93.70%	0.83	0.81	0.80
MLP	Model3	150	93.90%	0.84	0.81	0.82
MLP	Model4	200	93.87%	0.84	0.81	0.82

4.1.4. XGBoost-Based IDS Implementation on Cloud without FS Methods

The XGBoost model is trained on the TON_IoT dataset with 50, 100, 150, and 200 estimators. The testing results of the XGBoost-based IDS are shown in Table 4. The results show that there is a nominal difference in the performance of the XGBoost model for 50, 100, 150, and 200 estimators. It is observed that the XGBoost model with 150 estimators showed the best results with a testing accuracy of 99.50%, precision of 0.96, recall of 0.97, and F1-score of 0.97.

4.1.5. MLP-Based IDS Implementation on Cloud without FS Methods

Four models of MLP are tested for IDS implementation on the cloud without using FS techniques. Model1 had 50 neurons in the hidden layer, Model2 had 150 neurons in the hidden layer, Model3 had 250 neurons in the hidden layer, and Model4 had 400 neurons in the hidden layer. The results of the MLP models are described in Table 4. The results indicate that MLP Model3 outperformed the other MLP models with an accuracy of 93.90%, a precision of 0.84, a recall of 0.81, and an F1-score of 0.82.

4.1.6. Comparison of Machine Learning-Based IDS on the Cloud without Using FS Techniques

We deployed and compared the LSTM, Conv1d, RF, MLP, and XGBoost algorithms for IDS implementation on the cloud. From the results, it is evident that XGBoost presented the best results with a detection accuracy of 99.50%. After XGBoost, the second-best results are presented by the RF algorithm with a detection accuracy of 99.4% on attacks. The third-best results are presented by the LSTM algorithm with a detection accuracy of 94.2% followed by MLP with 93.9%. Overall XGBoost and RF are suitable for the implementation of an IDS in terms of accuracy, and Conv1d is not feasible for the implementation of an IDS on the cloud.

4.2. *Machine Learning-Based IDS on the Cloud with FS Methods*

The FS techniques are applied to improve the accuracy of the IDS. Chi-square and PCA techniques are used for FS on the best models of XGBoost, LSTM, RF, and MLP.

4.2.1. LSTM-Based IDS on the Cloud with FS/FE Methods

The performances of LSTM with 25, 15, and 10 features are presented in Table 5. The testing accuracies with PCA are 94.07%, 94.4%, and 94.4% for 25, 15, and 10 extracted features, respectively. In contrast, the chi-square demonstrates testing accuracies of 94.25%, 94.5%, and 94% for 25, 15, and 10 selected features, respectively. The results reveal that with the chi-square FS technique, the accuracy of LSTM improved using 15 features compared to not employing any FS technique.

Table 5. Test results of LSTM-, RF-, MLP-, XGBoost-based IDSs with FS methods.

ML Model	FS Technique	No. of Features	Accuracy	Precision	Recall	F1-Score
LSTM	PCA	25	94.07%	0.82	0.84	0.83
LSTM	Chi-square	25	94.25%	0.84	0.84	0.84
LSTM	PCA	15	94.4%	0.84	0.83	0.83
LSTM	Chi-square	15	94.5%	0.84	0.83	0.83
LSTM	PCA	10	94.4%	0.84	0.84	0.84
LSTM	Chi-square	10	94.0%	0.84	0.82	0.83
RF	PCA	25	97.50%	0.92	0.91	0.91
RF	Chi-square	25	96.50%	0.90	0.87	0.88
RF	PCA	15	94.64%	0.85	0.84	0.84
RF	Chi-square	15	94.40%	0.84	0.84	0.84
RF	PCA	10	94.44%	0.84	0.84	0.84
RF	Chi-square	10	94.53%	0.85	0.82	0.85
MLP	PCA	25	93.90%	0.84	0.82	0.82
MLP	Chi-square	25	93.88%	0.84	0.81	0.81
MLP	PCA	15	94.00%	0.84	0.82	0.83
MLP	Chi-square	15	93.83%	0.83	0.80	0.80
MLP	PCA	10	93.99%	0.84	0.81	0.82
MLP	Chi-square	10	92.99%	0.82	0.81	0.81
XGBoost	PCA	25	97.67%	0.98	0.98	0.98
XGBoost	**Chi-square**	**25**	**98.35%**	**0.98**	**0.98**	**0.98**
XGBoost	PCA	15	95.58%	0.96	0.96	0.96
XGBoost	Chi-square	15	98.13%	0.98	0.98	0.98
XGBoost	PCA	10	95.55%	0.96	0.96	0.96
XGBoost	Chi-square	10	95.69%	0.96	0.96	0.96

4.2.2. RF-Based IDS on the Cloud with FS Methods

PCA and chi-square are deployed on the RF algorithm to record the results. The testing accuracies of the RF algorithm on PCA are 97.5%, 94.64%, and 94.44% for 25, 15, and 10 features, respectively. On chi-square, the accuracies for 25, 15, and 10 selected features are 96.5%, 94.4%, and 94.53%, respectively. The detailed results are presented in Table 5.

4.2.3. MLP-Based IDS Implementation on the Cloud with FS Methods

PCA and chi-square are deployed on the MLP algorithm, and their results are recorded for 25, 15, and 10 features, respectively. On PCA, MLP testing accuracies are 93.9%, 94.0%, and 93.99% for 25, 15, and 10 extracted features, respectively. On chi-square, MLP testing accuracies are 93.88%, 93.83%, and 92.99% for 25, 15, and 10 features, respectively. The results are presented in Table 5.

4.2.4. XGBoost-Based IDS Implementation on the Cloud with FS Methods

The testing results of XGBoost trained with 10, 15, and 25 features selected/extracted by chi-square and PCA are shown in Table 5. The accuracy of XGBoost with 25 features computed by PCA is 97.67%, while for features selected with chi-square, it is 98.35%. Similarly, for 15 features computed by PCA, the accuracy is 95.58%, while with chi-square, the accuracy is 98.13%. Finally, with 10 features computed by PCA, the accuracy is 95.55%, and with chi-square, the accuracy is 95.69%. In terms of accuracy, XGBoost trained with 25 features selected by chi-square achieved the highest accuracy of 98.35%.

4.2.5. Comparison of XGBOOST-, LSTM-, RF-, and MLP-Based IDS on the Cloud with FS Techniques

FS involves choosing a subset of the most informative features from the original set while reducing dimensionality. It aims to retain the semantic interpretability of the selected features. In contrast, FE transforms the original features into a new low-dimensional space using mathematical projection. Although it effectively reduces dimensionality, the extracted features lose their intuitive meanings.

For an IDS, FS allows the creation of a lightweight and efficient IDS by carefully selecting relevant original features. On the other hand, FE techniques provide a valuable way to transform and distill the essence of the original feature set, reducing overall data dimensionality while preserving critical information. Both FS and FE are essential tools for enhancing the cybersecurity posture of IoT ecosystems, ensuring effective threat detection tailored to the limitations and intricacies of IoT devices and networks.

Two FS/FE techniques, i.e., PCA and chi-square, are applied to the XGBoost-, LSTM-, RF-, and MLP-based IDSs. The results for LSTM showed that chi-square performed best with 15 out of 40 selected features, achieving a detection accuracy of 94.5%. With RF, PCA proved to be the most effective technique, resulting in a detection accuracy of 97.5% using 25 features. Similarly, for MLP, PCA resulted in the best detection accuracy of 94% with 15 features. XGBoost trained with features selected by chi-square gave the best results. With 25 features, the accuracy is 98.35%, while with 15 features the accuracy is 98.13%. The results above indicate that the highest training accuracy attained with the FS/FE technique is 98.35%, whereas without using FS/FE, it reaches 99.5%. While reducing features might reduce prediction time for an IDS, prioritizing accuracy remains crucial for effective IDS implementation, even if it means retaining a higher number of features. Therefore, the XGBoost-based IDS without FS/FE outperformed the other ML-based IDSs evaluated in this study.

We compared the inference times of the FS and FE techniques. We analyzed the inference times of the XGBoost models trained with both FS and FE as shown in Table 6. The simulations are carried out on Intel(R) Core(TM) i5-8250U CPU with 8GB RAM. The inference time of XGBoost without FS/FE is 0.6631 milliseconds. The chi-square method (FS) showed a higher inference time compared to the PCA method (FE). Overall, the inference time with FS/FE was more than double that of the XGBoost model without them.

While FS/FE reduced the inference time of XGBoost compared to no FS, real-time testing considers the combined time of both FS/FE and XGBoost inference. Importantly, FS is a one-time calculation performed during training. In the testing phase, directly selecting the top features from the high-dimensional data for dimensionality reduction can be a preferred choice. However, applying FS to real-time captured packets incurs a higher time cost than XGBoost inference itself.

Our discussions and results align with the detailed research presented in [42,43]. For time-critical attacks like DoS/DDoS and MitM, a low inference time is crucial for the IDS. Therefore, we deployed the XGBoost model (estimator = 150) without FS/FE due to its superior accuracy and faster inference time.

Table 6. PCA vs chi-square for multiclassification using XGBoost—inference time in milliseconds.

No. of Features	PCA	XGBoost + PCA	Chi-Square	XGBoost + Chi-Square
10	1.1547	1.7944	1.3518	1.9761
15	1.2732	1.8900	1.4709	2.0856
25	1.2629	1.8813	1.6112	2.2363

4.3. Machine Learning-Based IDS Implementation on IoT Device

An ML-based IDS has been embedded in a microcontroller-based smart thermostat, a low-power and cost-efficient IoT device functioning as an HTTP client to upload building temperature and humidity data to the AWS cloud server via WiFi technology. The RF-, XGBoost-, DT-, and ANN-based IDSs are embedded in the smart thermostat to determine their feasibility in terms of accuracy, storage requirements, and inference time. The TinyML library is used to embed the trained IDS on the microcontroller. The trained models of RF, XGBoost, ANN, and DT are embedded in the smart thermostat to classify the network traffic as attack or normal. Low-power IoT devices are vulnerable to various security threats due to their limited resources. Consequently, these devices may be exploited for backdoor, DoS/DDoS, MITM, scanning, and ransomware attacks. Given the restricted access of low-cost IoT devices to network traffic features, researchers opted to deploy an IDS on a Raspberry Pi-based edge device, leveraging tools like tcpdump and Wireshark for extracting network features. This study focuses on implementing the primary defense layer on the microcontroller-based IoT device (smart thermostat), which lacks packet analyzer tools. An ML-based IDS is specifically designed for the binary classification of attacks. The IDS classified backdoor, scanning, DDoS, MITM, and ransomware as attacks (i.e., 1), while normal traffic was classified as 0.

4.3.1. ML-Based IDS Implementation on Smart Thermostat Using Connection, Statistical, and DNS Activity Features of TON_IoT Dataset

In this work, ANN, RF, XGBoost, and DT are tested as ways of implementing the binary classifier IDS. The TON_IoT dataset is used for training the IDS at the edge device. The dataset is split into 70% training and 30% testing data. The 10-fold cross-validation has been applied during training to ensure the generalization of the ML model. Due to limited computational and storage resources at the edge device, we trained the IDS with 25 features (i.e., connection activity, statistical activity, and DNS activity). The ML-based IDS is evaluated in terms of accuracy, precision, recall, F1-score, false positive rate (FPR), and false negative rate (FNR). The testing results of the binary classification of the XGBoost-, RF-, DT-, and ANN-based IDSs are shown in Table 7. These results indicate that the RF-based IDS (100 estimators, depth = 8) outperformed the other RF models. Additionally, the DT model with a depth of 18 achieved an accuracy of 99.85%. Regarding ANN, experiments were conducted with 50, 100, 150, and 200 neurons, revealing that all ANN models performed best at 100 epochs. Among these, the three-layered ANN model exhibited the highest accuracy of 98.93%. XGBoost outperformed the other ML models and achieved the highest accuracy of 99.92%.

The implementation results are shown in Table 7. The table shows the testing accuracy, program storage, and inference time average of 30 packets. DT outperformed RF, XGBoost, and ANN in terms of inference time, being capable of classifying network traffic as normal/attack in 5.09 μs with 99.05% accuracy. The DT-based IDS (depth = 8) consumed 65.94% of program memory of the IoT device. The DT model with a depth of 20 achieved the best accuracy of 99.85% and the inference time for classifying network traffic is 11.36 μs. The precision, recall, and F1-score for this model are 0.99, while the program storage required for this model is 66.73%. In terms of accuracy, FNR, FPR, and XGBoost with 100 estimators outperformed RF, ANN, and DT with an accuracy of 99.92%, FPR of 0.04%, and FNR of 0.23%, but the inference time is 3002.78 μs. The best accuracy achieved by the RF-based IDS is 98.89% with 100 estimators. The FNR for this model is

1.28% and the FPR is 1.06%. It is not feasible to implement the RF model with 200 estimators since the required memory is not available on an ESP32-based edge device. The ANN model-based IDS is also studied in this work. Two-layered and three-layered ANN models are used for the IDS. The best accuracy achieved with the ANN model (Layer 1 = 96, Layer 2 = 64, Layer 3 = 32) is 98.93%.

Table 7. IDS implementation on microcontroller-based IoT device using ToN_IoT dataset (connection, statistical, and DNS activity features).

ML Model (No. of Estimators)	Accuracy	Precision	Recall	F1-Score	FNR	FPR	Computation Time μs (Average)	Program Storage
XGBoost (Estimator = 50, Depth = 8)	99.91%	0.99	0.99	0.99	0.23%	0.04%	1840.70	80.92%
XGBoost (Estimator = 100, Depth = 8)	**99.92%**	**0.99**	**0.99**	**0.99**	**0.23%**	**0.04%**	**3002.78**	**82.71%**
XGBoost (Estimator = 150, Depth = 8)	99.92%	0.99	0.99	0.99	0.23%	0.04%	3514.39	83.34%
XGBoost (Estimator = 200, Depth = 8)	99.91%	0.99	0.99	0.99	0.25%	0.04%	4100.54	83.86%
RF (Estimator = 50, Depth = 8)	98.67%	0.95	0.98	0.97	1.34%	1.32%	628.62	72.76%
RF (Estimator = 100, Depth = 8)	98.89%	0.96	0.98	0.97	1.28%	1.06%	1565.01	79.0%
RF (Estimator = 150, Depth = 8)	98.72%	0.95	0.98	0.97	1.28%	1.28%	2679.09	85.12%
RF (Estimator = 200, Depth = 8)	98.71%	0.95	0.98	0.97	1.28%	1.29%	–	Memory overflow
DT (Depth = 6)	97.94%	0.92	0.99	0.95	1.01%	2.34%	6.05	65.83%
DT (Depth = 8)	99.05%	0.98	0.97	0.97	2.37%	0.56%	5.09	65.94%
DT (Depth = 10)	99.53%	0.98	0.99	0.99	0.92%	0.34%	6.96	66.13%
DT (Depth = 12)	99.69%	0.99	0.99	0.99	0.54%	0.25%	8.82	66.40%
DT (Depth = 14)	99.78%	0.99	0.99	0.99	0.45%	0.15%	9.90	66.56%
DT (Depth = 16)	99.84%	0.99	0.99	0.99	0.37%	0.10%	11.61	66.68%
DT (Depth = 18)	99.85%	0.99	0.99	0.99	0.34%	0.10%	11.82	66.72%
DT (Depth = 20)	99.85%	0.99	0.99	0.99	0.31%	0.10%	11.36	66.73%
ANN (Layer 1 = 32, Layer 2 = 16)	98.62%	0.97	0.96	0.97	3.31%	0.65%	131.98	75%
ANN (Layer 1 = 64, Layer 2 = 32)	98.98%	0.97	0.97	0.97	2.59%	0.58%	296.12	76.15%
ANN (Layer 1 = 64, Layer 2 = 32, Layer 3 = 16)	98.92%	0.97	0.97	0.97	2.74%	0.62%	350.16	76.34%
ANN (Layer 1 = 96, Layer 2 = 64, Layer 3 = 32)	98.93%	0.97	0.97	0.97	2.41%	0.70%	3088.97	78.32%

Due to the limited storage and computational power of the microcontroller-based edge device, our objective is to identify an IDS that can deliver accurate results within a shorter time frame. The XGBoost-based IDS has proven superior to DT, RF, and ANN in terms of accuracy, FNR, and FPR. The highest accuracy achieved by the XGBoost-based IDS is 99.92%, but it requires 3002.78 μs for threat detection. In contrast, XGBoost's performance is only 0.07% better than DT, yet DT completes computations in 11.36 μs. Considering DT's significantly quicker detection time compared to XGBoost, it could be the preferred choice for implementing the IDS on edge devices. However, the accuracy of the IDS is crucial. Therefore, XGBoost should be preferred for the implementation of the IDS.

4.3.2. ML-Based IDS Implementation on Smart Thermostat Using Connection and Statistical Activity Features

Considering the limited access to the lwIP library and the nature of our application, only connection activity and statistical activity network features are considered. To avoid overfitting, we excluded timestamp, source and destination IP addresses. The input features that can be extracted on the Esp32-based smart thermostat are source port, destination port, proto, service, duration, source bytes, destination bytes, connection state, missed bytes, source packets, source IP header bytes, destination packets, and destination IP header bytes. Based on these 13 features, the XGBoost, RF, DT, and ANN models are trained for binary classification and the results are shown in Table 8. The results show that XGBoost with the depth of 8 and 100 estimators outperformed DT, RF, and ANN in terms of accuracy, FPR, and FNR, while DT with a depth of 5 is the fastest in terms of inference time. The best results of XGBoost, DT, RF, and ANN are summarized in Figure 3. XGBoost (100 estimators, depth = 8), DT depth = 5), RF (150 estimators, depth = 8), and ANN are compared in terms of accuracy, program memory, inference time, FPR, and FNR. The F1-score, recall, precision, and accuracy are summarized in the subfigure titled Accuracy(%). Although the inference time of DT is 3.2 µs, the FPR and FNR of DT are 0.60% and 0.72%, respectively, compared to XGBoost, which has an FPR and FNR of 0.30% and 0.06%, respectively. Since the required program memory is available in the microcontroller of the smart thermostat, XGBoost is the preferred choice for implementing an IDS with 13 features due to its superior performance.

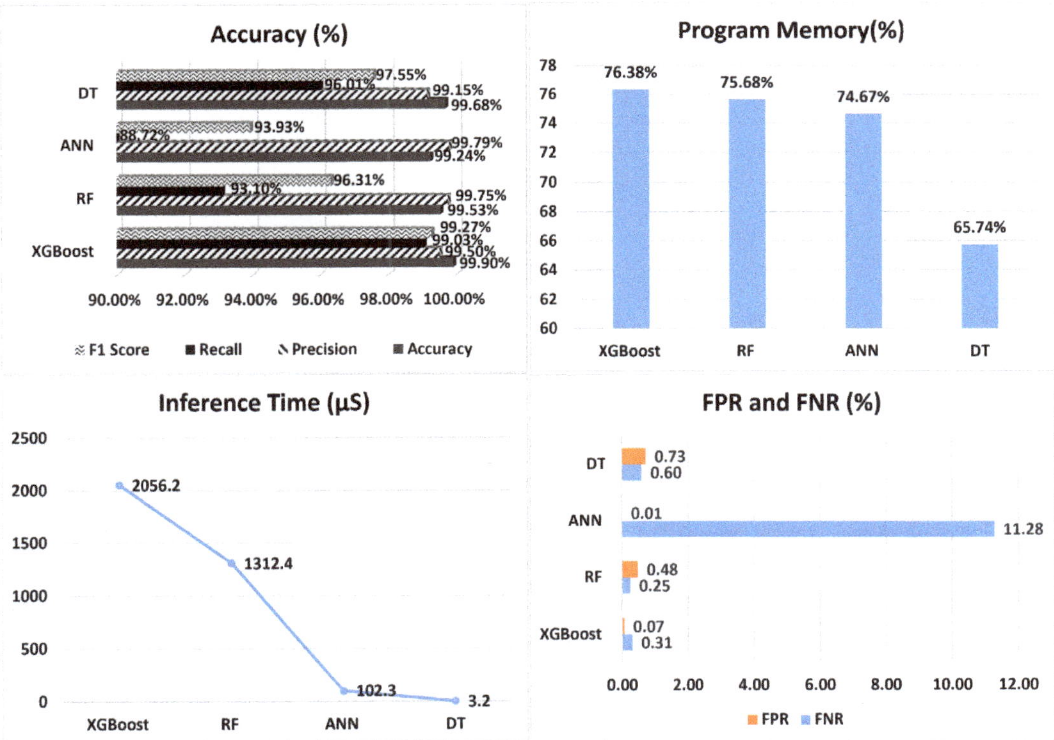

Figure 3. Comparison of XGBoost-, RF-, DT-, and ANN-based IDS implementation on smart thermostat using Ton_IoT dataset.

Table 8. IDS implementation on edge using connection and statistical activity features of TON_IoT dataset.

ML Model (No. of Estimators)	Accuracy	Precision	Recall	F1-Score	FNR	FPR	Computation Time μs (Average)	Program Storage
XGBoost (Estimator = 50, Depth = 8)	99.92%	0.99	0.99	0.99	0.35%	0.05%	1223.4	75.0%
XGBoost (Estimator = 100, Depth = 8)	**99.91%**	**0.99**	**0.99**	**0.99**	**0.30%**	**0.06%**	**2056.2**	**76.38%**
XGBoost (Estimator = 150, Depth = 8)	99.92%	0.99	0.99	0.99	0.30%	0.06%	2480	76.8%
XGBoost (Estimator = 200, Depth = 8)	99.92%	0.99	0.99	0.99	0.30%	0.06%	2936.7	77.32%
RF (Estimator = 50, Depth = 8)	99.52%	0.99	0.92	0.96	0.25%	0.49%	407.9	70.57%
RF (Estimator = 100, Depth = 8)	99.52%	0.99	0.93	0.96	0.25%	0.48%	1312.4	75.68%
RF (Estimator = 150, Depth = 8)	99.53%	0.99	0.93	0.96	0.25%	0.47%	2729.7	80.39%
RF (Estimator = 200, Depth = 8)	99.52%	0.99	0.93	0.96	0.25%	0.48%	3584.2	85.08%
DT (Depth = 5)	99.68%	0.99	0.96	0.97	0.60%	0.72%	3.2	65.74%
DT (Depth = 10)	99.59%	0.99	0.94	0.96	0.79%	0.38%	8.4	65.96%
DT (Depth = 15)	99.58%	0.99	0.94	0.96	0.93%	0.38%	12	66.23%
DT (Depth = 20)	99.59%	0.99	0.94	0.96	0.84%	0.30%	11.4	66.34%
ANN (Layer 1 = 32, Layer 2 = 16)	99.24%	0.99	0.88	0.93	11.28%	0.01%	102.3	74.67%
ANN (Layer 1 = 64, Layer 2 = 32)	99.23%	0.99	0.88	0.97	11.09%	0.01%	242.8	75.87%
ANN (Layer 1 = 64, Layer 2 = 32, Layer 3 = 16)	99.17%	0.98	0.89	0.93	10.78%	0.12%	478.2	76.01%
ANN (Layer 1 = 96, Layer 2 = 64, Layer 3 = 32)	99.22%	0.99	0.89	0.93	10.83%	0.06%	3986.2	76.15%

4.4. Real-Time Testing of IDS on Smart Thermostat

The smart thermostat uploads the data on the AWS cloud server (http://16.170.215.67/display). The smart home application provides users with remote access to turn ON/OFF the HVAC through the webpage. This bidirectional communication is vulnerable to DoS and MITM attacks. Using our smart thermostat dataset, we trained XGBoost, DT, RF, and ANN for IDS implementation on the smart thermostat. The testing results of the IDS implemented with XGBoost, RF, DT, and ANN are shown in Table 9. The IDS implemented with XGBoost (depth = 8, estimator = 100) achieved the highest accuracy of 97.66%. The best accuracy achieved with RF (depth is 8, estimators = 20) is 95.33%, with DT (with a depth of 15) it is 96.54%, and with ANN it is 93.41% as shown in Figure 4. The accuracy, F1-score, recall, and precision are summarized under the subfigure titled Accuracy (%), whereas the comparison of program memory requirements, inference time, FPR, and FNR are also shown in Figure 4. The results clearly show that although the inference time of XGBoost is high and it requires more program memory, it outperformed DT, ANN, and RF in terms of accuracy, F1-score, recall, precision, FPR, and FNR.

Table 9. IDS implementation on smart thermostat using IDSH dataset.

ML Model (No. of Estimators)	Accuracy	Precision	Recall	F1-Score	FNR	FPR	Computation Time µs (Average)	Program Storage
XGBoost (Estimator = 50, Depth = 8)	**97.59%**	**0.97**	**0.97**	**0.97**	**2.76%**	**2.24%**	**1502.3**	**77.0%**
XGBoost (Estimator = 100, Depth = 8)	97.66%	0.97	0.97	0.97	2.76%	2.12%	3515.9	84.01%
XGBoost (Estimator = 150, Depth = 8)	97.50%	0.97	0.97	0.97	3.26%	2.12%	Memory Out of Bound	-
XGBoost (Estimator = 200, Depth = 8)	97.58%	0.97	0.97	0.97	3.01%	2.12%	Memory Out of Bound	-
RF (Estimator = 50, Depth = 8)	95.17%	0.93	0.96	0.94	1.19%	2.48%	439	69.53%
RF (Estimator = 100, Depth = 8)	95.17%	0.93	0.96	0.94	1.00%	6.61%	1357.6	73.46%
RF (Estimator = 150, Depth = 8)	95.25%	0.93	0.96	0.95	1.00%	6.50%	2331.4	77.29%
RF (Estimator = 200, Depth = 8)	95.33%	0.93	0.96	0.95	1.00%	6.38%	3314.4	80.96%
DT (Depth = 5)	90.59%	0.88	0.90	0.89	8.54%	9.81%	3.7	66.54%
DT (Depth = 10)	94.61%	0.93	0.94	0.94	4.77%	5.67%	6.2	66.61%
DT (Depth = 15)	96.54%	0.96	0.96	0.96	5.77%	2.36%	7.3	66.71%
DT (Depth = 20)	96.38%	0.96	0.95	0.96	6.03%	2.48%	8.0	66.78%
ANN (Layer 1 =32, Layer 2 = 16)	92.76%	0.85	0.93	0.89	6.28%	7.68%	117.5	78.02%
ANN (Layer 1 = 64, Layer 2 = 32)	91.23%	0.80	0.97	0.87	3.01%	11.46%	286.6	76.11%
ANN (Layer 1 = 64, Layer 2 = 32, Layer 3 = 16)	92.92%	0.84	0.95	0.89	4.77%	8.15%	313.9	75.92%
ANN (Layer 1 = 96, Layer 2 = 64, Layer 3 = 32)	93.41%	0.85	0.96	0.90	3.26%	8.15%	2498.1	75.28%

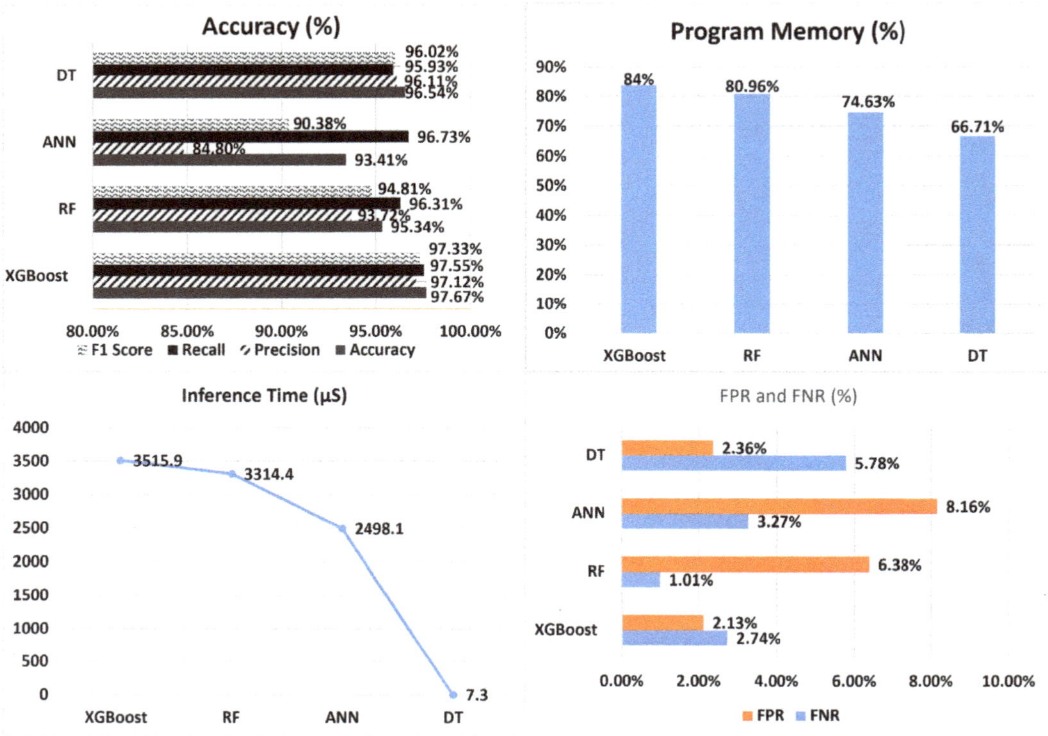

Figure 4. Comparison of XGBoost-, RF-, DT-, and ANN-based IDS implementation on smart thermostat using IDSH dataset.

4.5. Discussion

In this study, the IDS is deployed on a smart thermostat built with the ESP32 microcontroller. The microcontroller boasts 440 KB of ROM and 520 KB of SRAM for program memory and instructions, respectively.

We conducted an initial feasibility test by implementing the IDS, incorporating connection activity, statistical activity, and DNS activity features. Utilizing XGBoost, the IDS consumed 82.71% of program memory and required 3002.78 µs to compute the output. Conversely, the IDS implemented with RF consumed 79.0% of program memory and took 1565.01 µs for computation. Similarly, the IDS implemented with ANN utilized 76.15% of program memory and took 296.12 µs for computation. Notably, DT outperformed XGBoost, ANN, and RF in terms of program memory and inference time, consuming just 66.73% of program memory and requiring only 11.37 µs for computation.

We also implemented the IDS using connection and statistical activity features. The most efficient XGBoost model utilized 76.38% of program storage and took 2056.2 µs for computation. Following closely in accuracy, the DT model consumed 65.74% of program memory with an inference time of only 3.2 µs. In contrast, RF consumed 75.68% of program memory with an inference time of 1312.4 µs. The ANN model, ranking fourth in accuracy, consumed 75.87% of program memory with an inference time of 242.8 µs.

Furthermore, we implemented the IDS with the IDSH dataset, which combines sensor and network datasets. The highest accuracy achieved by XGBoost (estimator = 100, depth = 8) is 97.66% but with an inference time of 3515.9 µs, whereas with XGBoost (estimator = 50, depth = 8), the IDS consumed 77.0% of program memory with an inference time of 1502.3 µs. The RF model consumed 80.96% of program memory with an inference time of 3314.4 µs, while the DT model consumed 66.78% of program memory with an inference time of 8.0 microseconds. The ANN model consumed 75.28% of program memory with an inference time of 2498.1 µs. It is noteworthy that for the IDSH dataset, the XGBoost models with estimators of 150 and above encountered memory constraints preventing their implementation on the smart thermostat.

DT operates on a simpler model, making decisions based on if–else rules at each node, which requires less computation time compared to the matrix multiplications and activity functions utilized in XGBOOST, ANN, and RF. As a result, the inference time of DT is less than that of XGBOOST, ANN, and RF. However, XGBoost captures complex relations in the data and handles non-linear patterns more effectively. Moreover, it possesses the capability to consider both past and future covariates present in the input data. The internal feature of hyperparameter tuning further contributes to its higher accuracy, making XGBoost's accuracy superior.

Table 9 and Figure 4 present the results of the IDS deployed on the smart thermostat device using our IDSH dataset. The trained ML models were embedded in the ESP32 microcontroller-based smart thermostat, and the inference time was calculated after generating attacks from our Raspberry Pi-based attacker node. Based on these results, we determined that the inference time of XGBoost exceeds that of DT. However, given that the building dynamics are slow and a delay of a few milliseconds in HVAC control input will not significantly impact the indoor environment, we prioritize accuracy. Therefore, for the smart thermostat, the XGBoost (estimator = 50, depth = 8)-based IDS is embedded in the smart thermostat for intrusion detection.

5. Conclusions and Future Work

In this work, a two-layered ML-based IDS is proposed. The proposed IDS is trained to be deployed on IoT devices and the cloud side of an IoT network to detect threats as soon as possible. The first layer of the IDS is embedded in the microcontroller-based smart thermostat using TinyML for binary classification. DDoS, MITM, ransomware, scanning, and backdoor attacks are detected on IoT devices. These attacks are labeled as an attack class for binary classification. The results show that the decision tree (DT)-based IDS can detect the attacks with 99.85% accuracy in 11.36 µs. The smart thermostat is also tested against real attacks (DoS, MITM) generated by the Raspberry Pi-based attacker node, and the accuracy of XGBoost is 97.59%. The dataset is comprised of 4144 samples, which were collected in this work.

The second layer of the IDS is deployed on the cloud, and five ML algorithms, namely LSTM, RF, MLP, Conv1d, and XGBoost, are trained to detect attacks such as DoS, DDoS, port scanning, MITM, XSS/injection, brute force, backdoor, and ransomware. The XGBoost algorithm showed the best results on the cloud with a detection accuracy of 99.5%, followed by RF, which showed the second-best results on the TON_IoT dataset with a detection accuracy of 99.4%. Two FS techniques, chi-square and PCA, are also employed on algorithms trained on the cloud side of the IoT network, but they did not significantly improve detection accuracy. The best results are obtained with chi-square, which showed 98.35% accuracy with XGBoost, while the best accuracy achieved with PCA is 97.67% with XGBoost. The IDS on the cloud detects incoming traffic and, if it is classified as normal, uploads it to the webpage.

Based on the experimental results, it is found that the DT-based IDS outperformed ANN, RF, and XGBoost in terms of inference time and memory requirements, while the XGBoost-based IDS outperformed the other ML models in terms of accuracy, precision, recall, f1 score, FPR, and FNR. For an IDS, accuracy is crucial. Therefore, prioritizing accuracy over inference time, XGBoost is the preferred choice for IDS implementation on the cloud and smart thermostat due to its superior performance in terms of accuracy. The XGBoost-based IDS is deployed on the cloud, and prediction results are also shared on the website along with the smart thermostat data. For the future prospects of this work, the presented two-layered IDS will be tested for additional attacks, and we will extend the number of samples in our smart home dataset. Due to limited resources and the restricted access of the lwIP library to network parameters, we managed to retrieve only a limited set of network parameters on the microcontroller. In the future, we will work on extracting additional network parameters at the IoT device.

Author Contributions: All authors contributed extensively to the work presented in this paper. Conceptualization, A.J., A.-u.-H.Q., and H.L; methodology, A.J., A.E., M.J. and M.N.A.; software, A.J., A.E. and M.J.; validation, A.J., A.E., M.J., M.N.A., A.-u.-H.Q. and H.L.; formal analysis, A.J., H.L., M.N.A., M.J. and A.-u.-H.Q.; investigation, A.J., M.N.A., H.L. and A.-u.-H.Q.; resources, A.J., A.E. and A.-u.-H.Q.; data curation, A.J., A.E., M.N.A., H.L. and M.J.; writing—original draft preparation, A.J., A.E., M.J. and A.-u.-H.Q.; writing—review and editing, A.J., A.E., M.J., M.N.A., H.L. and A.-u.-H.Q.; visualization, A.J., M.N.A. and A.-u.-H.Q.; supervision, A.J. and A.-u.-H.Q.; project administration, A.J. and A.-u.-H.Q.; funding acquisition, A.J. and A.-u.-H.Q. All authors have read and agreed to the published version of the manuscript.

Funding: The APC was funded by Department of Cyber Security and Networks, School of Computing, Engineering and Built Environment, Glasgow Caledonian University, UK

Data Availability Statement: https://www.kaggle.com/datasets/bc7c97914edab17a5821f5b27f465904bad79132f07cfcefc83e9669daeb3f98(accessed on 26 April 2024.) Shorturl http://surl.li/psyjo (accessed on 26 April 2024.)

Conflicts of Interest: The authors declare no conflicts of interest.

References

1. IoT.Business.News. Number of Connected IOT Devices Growing 9% to 12.3 Billion Globally, Cellular IOT Now Surpassing 2 Billion. Available online: https://iotbusinessnews.com/2021/09/23/13465-number-of-connected-iot-devices-growing-9-to-12-3-billion-globally-cellular-iot-now-surpassing-2-billion/ (accessed on 24 January 2024).
2. Hassija, V.; Chamola, V.; Saxena, V.; Jain, D.; Goyal, P.; Sikdar, B. A survey on IoT security: Application areas, security threats, and solution architectures. *IEEE Access* **2019**, *7*, 82721–82743. [CrossRef]
3. Singh, S.; Ra, I.H.; Meng, W.; Kaur, M.; Cho, G.H. SH-BlockCC: A secure and efficient Internet of things smart home architecture based on cloud computing and blockchain technology. *Int. J. Distrib. Sens. Netw.* **2019**, *15*, 1550147719844159. [CrossRef]
4. Sohail, S.; Fan, Z.; Gu, X.; Sabrina, F. Multi-tiered Artificial Neural Networks model for intrusion detection in smart homes. *Intell. Syst. Appl.* **2022**, *16*, 200152. [CrossRef]
5. Ferrag, M.A.; Maglaras, L.; Ahmim, A.; Derdour, M.; Janicke, H. Rdtids: Rules and decision tree-based intrusion detection system for internet-of-things networks. *Future Internet* **2020**, *12*, 44. [CrossRef]
6. Mighan, S.N.; Kahani, M. A novel scalable intrusion detection system based on deep learning. *Int. J. Inf. Secur.* **2021**, *20*, 387–403. [CrossRef]
7. Ahmed, S.; Khan, Z.A.; Mohsin, S.M.; Latif, S.; Aslam, S.; Mujlid, H.; Adil, M.; Najam, Z. Effective and efficient DDoS attack detection using deep learning algorithm, multi-layer perceptron. *Future Internet* **2023**, *15*, 76. [CrossRef]
8. Zhong, M.; Zhou, Y.; Chen, G. Sequential model based intrusion detection system for IoT servers using deep learning methods. *Sensors* **2021**, *21*, 1113. [CrossRef]
9. Gad, A.R.; Nashat, A.A.; Barkat, T.M. Intrusion detection system using machine learning for vehicular ad hoc networks based on ToN-IoT dataset. *IEEE Access* **2021**, *9*, 142206–142217. [CrossRef]
10. Meidan, Y.; Avraham, D.; Libhaber, H.; Shabtai, A. CADeSH: Collaborative anomaly detection for smart homes. *IEEE Internet Things J.* **2022**, *10*, 8514–8532. [CrossRef]
11. Shi, L.; Wu, L.; Guan, Z. Three-layer hybrid intrusion detection model for smart home malicious attacks. *Comput. Electr. Eng.* **2021**, *96*, 107536. [CrossRef]
12. Thakur, S.; Chakraborty, A.; De, R.; Kumar, N.; Sarkar, R. Intrusion detection in cyber-physical systems using a generic and domain specific deep autoencoder model. *Comput. Electr. Eng.* **2021**, *91*, 107044. [CrossRef]
13. Rahman, M.A.; Asyhari, A.T.; Leong, L.; Satrya, G.; Tao, M.H.; Zolkipli, M. Scalable machine learning-based intrusion detection system for IoT-enabled smart cities. *Sustain. Cities Soc.* **2020**, *61*, 102324. [CrossRef]
14. Reddy, D.K.K.; Behera, H.S.; Nayak, J.; Naik, B.; Ghosh, U.; Sharma, P.K. Exact greedy algorithm based split finding approach for intrusion detection in fog-enabled IoT environment. *J. Inf. Secur. Appl.* **2021**, *60*, 102866. [CrossRef]
15. Labiod, Y.; Amara Korba, A.; Ghoualmi, N. Fog computing-based intrusion detection architecture to protect iot networks. *Wirel. Pers. Commun.* **2022**, *125*, 231–259. [CrossRef]
16. Kumar, P.; Gupta, G.P.; Tripathi, R. Design of anomaly-based intrusion detection system using fog computing for IoT network. *Autom. Control Comput. Sci.* **2021**, *55*, 137–147. [CrossRef]
17. Pacheco, J.; Benitez, V.H.; Felix-Herran, L.C.; Satam, P. Artificial neural networks-based intrusion detection system for internet of things fog nodes. *IEEE Access* **2020**, *8*, 73907–73918. [CrossRef]

18. Hafeez, I.; Antikainen, M.; Ding, A.Y.; Tarkoma, S. IoT-KEEPER: Detecting malicious IoT network activity using online traffic analysis at the edge. *IEEE Trans. Netw. Serv. Manag.* **2020**, *17*, 45–59. [CrossRef]
19. Eskandari, M.; Janjua, Z.H.; Vecchio, M.; Antonelli, F. Passban IDS: An Intelligent Anomaly-Based Intrusion Detection System for IoT Edge Devices. *IEEE Internet Things J.* **2020**, *7*, 6882–6897. . [CrossRef]
20. Hosseininoorbin, S.; Layeghy, S.; Sarhan, M.; Jurdak, R.; Portmann, M. Exploring edge TPU for network intrusion detection in IoT. *J. Parallel Distrib. Comput.* **2023**, *179*, 104712. [CrossRef]
21. Bangui, H.; Buhnova, B. Lightweight intrusion detection for edge computing networks using deep forest and bio-inspired algorithms. *Comput. Electr. Eng.* **2022**, *100*, 107901. . [CrossRef]
22. Javed, A. Intrusion Detection in Smart Homes (IDSH) Dataset. Available online: https://www.kaggle.com/datasets/bc7c97914edab17a5821f5b27f465904bad79132f07cfcefc83e9669daeb3f98 (accessed on 24 January 2024).
23. TensorFlow Lite TinyML for ESP32. Available online: https://eloquentarduino.com/posts/tensorflow-lite-tinyml-esp32 (accessed on 30 March 2024).
24. Suresh, P.; Daniel, J.V.; Parthasarathy, V.; Aswathy, R. A state of the art review on the Internet of Things (IoT) history, technology and fields of deployment. In Proceedings of the 2014 International Conference on Science Engineering and Management Research (ICSEMR), Chennai, India, 27–29 November 2014; pp. 1–8.
25. Tekin, N.; Acar, A.; Aris, A.; Uluagac, A.S.; Gungor, V.C. Energy consumption of on-device machine learning models for IoT intrusion detection. *Internet Things* **2023**, *21*, 100670. [CrossRef]
26. Koirala, A.; Bista, R.; Ferreira, J.C. Enhancing IoT device security through network attack data analysis using machine learning algorithms. *Future Internet* **2023**, *15*, 210. [CrossRef]
27. The TON_IoT Datasets: UNSW Research. Available online: https://research.unsw.edu.au/projects/toniot-datasets (accessed on 30 April 2024).
28. Elnakib, O.; Shaaban, E.; Mahmoud, M.; Emara, K. EIDM: Deep learning model for IoT intrusion detection systems. *J. Supercomput.* **2023**, *79*, 13241–13261. [CrossRef]
29. Qureshi, A.U.H.; Larijani, H.; Mtetwa, N.; Javed, A.; Ahmad, J. RNN-ABC: A new swarm optimization based technique for anomaly detection. *Computers* **2019**, *8*, 59. [CrossRef]
30. Sahu, A.K.; Sharma, S.; Tanveer, M.; Raja, R. Internet of Things attack detection using hybrid Deep Learning Model. *Comput. Commun.* **2021**, *176*, 146–154. [CrossRef]
31. Alotaibi, B.; Alotaibi, M. A stacked deep learning approach for IoT cyberattack detection. *J. Sens.* **2020**, *2020*, 8828591. [CrossRef]
32. Tomer, V.; Sharma, S. Detecting iot attacks using an ensemble machine learning model. *Future Internet* **2022**, *14*, 102. [CrossRef]
33. De Souza, C.A.; Westphall, C.B.; Machado, R.B.; Sobral, J.B.M.; dos Santos Vieira, G. Hybrid approach to intrusion detection in fog-based IoT environments. *Comput. Netw.* **2020**, *180*, 107417. [CrossRef]
34. Kumar, P.; Gupta, G.P.; Tripathi, R. A distributed ensemble design based intrusion detection system using fog computing to protect the internet of things networks. *J. Ambient. Intell. Humaniz. Comput.* **2021**, *12*, 9555–9572. [CrossRef]
35. Kumar, R.; Kumar, P.; Tripathi, R.; Gupta, G.P.; Garg, S.; Hassan, M.M. A distributed intrusion detection system to detect DDoS attacks in blockchain-enabled IoT network. *J. Parallel Distrib. Comput.* **2022**, *164*, 55–68. [CrossRef]
36. Nasir, M.; Javed, A.R.; Tariq, M.A.; Asim, M.; Baker, T. Feature engineering and deep learning-based intrusion detection framework for securing edge IoT. *J. Supercomput.* **2022**, *78*, 8852–8866. [CrossRef]
37. Almogren, A.S. Intrusion detection in Edge-of-Things computing. *J. Parallel Distrib. Comput.* **2020**, *137*, 259–265. [CrossRef]
38. Hindy, H.; Bayne, E.; Bures, M.; Atkinson, R.; Tachtatzis, C.; Bellekens, X. Machine learning based IoT intrusion detection system: An MQTT case study (MQTT-IoT-IDS2020 dataset). In *Selected Papers from the 12th International Networking Conference: INC 2020*; Springer: Berlin/Heidelberg, Germany, 2021; pp. 73–84.
39. Koroniotis, N.; Moustafa, N.; Sitnikova, E.; Turnbull, B. Towards the development of realistic botnet dataset in the internet of things for network forensic analytics: Bot-iot dataset. *Future Gener. Comput. Syst.* **2019**, *100*, 779–796. [CrossRef]
40. Pearson, K.X. On the criterion that a given system of deviations from the probable in the case of a correlated system of variables is such that it can be reasonably supposed to have arisen from random sampling. *London Edinburgh Dublin Philos. Mag. J. Sci.* **1900**, *50*, 157–175. [CrossRef]
41. Hotelling, H. Analysis of a complex of statistical variables into principal components. *J. Educ. Psychol.* **1933**, *24*, 417. [CrossRef]
42. Li, J.; Othman, M.S.; Chen, H.; Yusuf, L.M. Optimizing IoT intrusion detection system: Feature selection versus feature extraction in machine learning. *J. Big Data* **2024**, *11*, 36. [CrossRef]
43. Ngo, V.D.; Vuong, T.C.; Van Luong, T.; Tran, H. Machine learning-based intrusion detection: Feature selection versus feature extraction. *Clust. Comput.* **2023**, *27*, 2365–2379. [CrossRef]

future internet

Article

A Survey on Energy-Aware Security Mechanisms for the Internet of Things

Peixiong He [1], Yi Zhou [2,*] and Xiao Qin [1,*]

1 Department of Computer Science and Software Engineering, Auburn University, Auburn, AL 36849, USA; pzh0029@auburn.edu
2 TSYS School of Computer Science, Columbus State University, Columbus, GA 31907, USA
* Correspondence: zhou_yi@columbusstate.edu (Y.Z.); xqin@auburn.edu (X.Q.)

Abstract: The Internet of Things (IoT) employs sensors and the Internet for information exchange, enabling intelligent identification, monitoring, and management, which has deeply impacted various sectors such as power, medical care, and security, transforming social activities and lifestyles. Regrettably, IoT systems suffer from two main challenges, namely sustainability and security. Hence, pondering how to enhance sustainable and energy-efficient practices for IoT systems to mitigate risks becomes a worthwhile endeavor. To address this issue, we conduct a survey of energy-aware security mechanisms in the Internet of Things. Specifically, we examine the challenges that IoT is facing in terms of energy efficiency and security, and we inspect current energy-saving and privacy-preserving technologies for IoT systems. Moreover, we delineate a vision for the future of IoT, emphasizing energy-aware security mechanisms. Finally, we outline the challenges encountered in achieving energy-aware security mechanisms, as well as the direction of future research. Motivated by this study, we envision advancements in the IoT that not only harness the benefits of science and technology but also enhance the security and safety of our data.

Keywords: Internet of Things; energy saving; security

1. Introduction

With the beginning of the industrial 4.0 era, human production and life have entered a completely new period—and the Internet of Things (IoT) interconnects numerous sensing devices through the Internet and improves industrial productivity by providing innovative technological facilities and intelligent services and applications [1]. During this period, IoT devices are capable of self-programming as well as collaborating among themselves, and the devices can accomplish computation, decision making, and control of data without access to cloud computing [2]. The proliferation of IoT has changed the way individuals interact with the world and leading-edge technology. From the smallest smartwatch to the rise of autonomous vehicles, from smart homes to the development of smart cities, the IoT has been playing a role in advancing the technology and civilization of human society [3]. The IoT technology has significant economic and environmental impacts thanks to the billions of connected devices communicating over the Internet using various types of sensors [4,5]. These connected devices imply large amounts of energy consumption and data management.

1.1. Motivation

Our research underpinnings are inspired by two motivations: (1) the importance of energy efficiency and (2) the critical issues of security and protection. Figure 1 illustrates the co-citation network of publications and their citation relationships for the period of 2019–2024. Among them, the topics of IoT, security, and energy are closely related. In order to provide a comprehensive survey and promote potential research in the area of an energy-efficient and secured IoT, we systematically present existing work on the energy-aware IoT in terms of the way in which the IoT consumes energy and the available energy-saving technologies. Then, we sort the current challenges and future research directions for achieving high energy efficiency in the IoT. Finally, we combine existing technologies for an energy-efficient and secure IoT, and we conclude that seamlessly integrating energy-efficient computing and security is one of the future megatrends of the IoT.

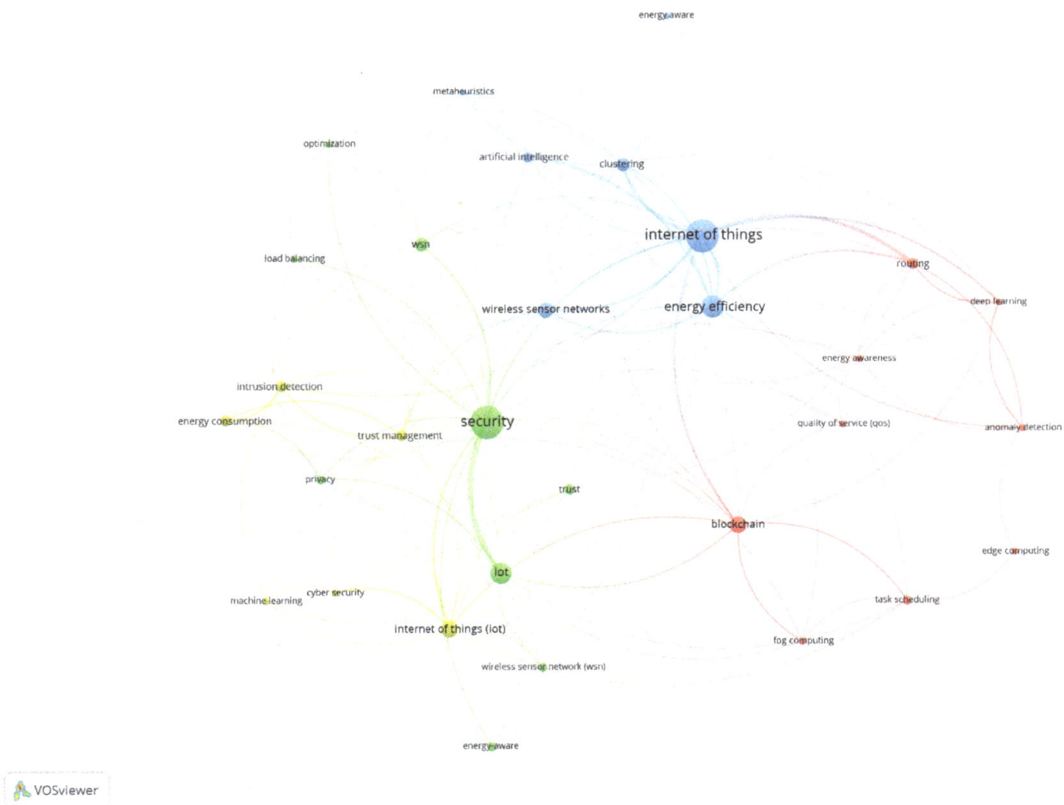

Figure 1. Visualization of the co-citation network of 'IoT', 'energy', and 'security' publications. Reference relationship from 2019–2024.

1.2. Importance of Energy Efficiency

More often than not, IoT devices are deployed remotely or in mobile environments—and the use of batteries to power IoT terminals has become the dominant paradigm today. While the use of batteries to power IoT terminals provides flexibility and independence for the devices, it also presents a number of challenges and drawbacks. First, the battery life limits the long-term operational capability of the device. After all, the battery life is limited, and with the passage of time, the battery capacity will gradually decrease, and providing convenient installation also means that the battery needs to be replaced periodically to ensure the normal operation of the sensor network. Frequently changing batteries increases the difficulty and cost of operation and maintenance. This greatly limits the growth rate of the Internet of Things. Imagine that when billions or even tens of billions of sensors are battery-powered, the labor and material costs of maintenance will become an unpredictable economic burden. According to a prior study [6], the size of IoT nodes will be limited—and hundreds of billions of nodes may not be deployed if batteries have to be regularly replaced. This not only leads to huge maintenance expenses, but also has the potential to compromise at least 80% of the value of the IoT. Thus, battery replacement costs pose a significant challenge to the sustainability and economics of a large-scale IoT. Efforts to address this issue have focused on finding more durable and sustainable energy solutions, such as energy-harvesting technologies, long-life battery technologies, and wireless charging technologies, in order to reduce the pressure on battery maintenance costs.

Thanks to the advantages of lithium batteries such as a light weight and long life, they have now become the preferred power supply method for IoT sensors. However, with the increasing demand for batteries, the convenience brought by lithium batteries is accompanied by a series of problems. First, there are potentially toxic materials in lithium batteries, posing a serious threat to human health and the natural environment. Second, in order to produce lithium batteries, manufacturers need to mine large quantities of key raw materials such as lithium, cobalt, nickel, manganese, and graphite, a process that consumes large amounts of energy and water resources and often results in chemical pollution and geological damage to the local environment. In addition, batteries can accidentally release cobalt and copper during production and disposal, posing a direct risk to human health [7]. Therefore, despite the significant advantages of lithium batteries in providing energy, the benefits and drawbacks must be carefully weighed in the quest for a more environmentally friendly and sustainable energy sources.

In fact, most of the traditional sensors use batteries as the main energy supply method [8], which is obviously a huge consumption of human and material resources. Sensors, as an irreplaceable part of the Internet of Things, have a limited battery life to power them, and in order to guarantee the proper functioning of the sensor network, all batteries need to be replaced periodically to ensure that the sensors continue to operate properly. The battery life depends on factors such as the power consumption of the sensor, its operating frequency, and the parameters it measures. Hence, maintenance personnel need to check the status of the batteries—and periodic replacement prevents sensors from stopping working due to energy depletion. This manual maintenance inevitably involves cost and labor resources, and in some cases may result in temporary sensor failures until the batteries are replaced. In areas that are difficult to reach or require frequent monitoring, such a maintenance becomes more complex and expensive. Even worse, frequent battery replacement undermines the core value of connected sensors, and one of the main reasons that organizations deploy IoT sensors is that these devices can help them automate monitoring. If these sensors themselves continue to require regular human maintenance to ensure their proper functioning, then implementing automated monitoring makes far less sense.

1.3. Importance of Security Protection

IoT devices are widely used in industries such as healthcare, manufacturing, transportation, and smart homes because of the IoT's ability to provide features like intelligence, automation, and real-time monitoring to increase efficiency [9], reduce costs, and enhance the quality of life. However, it is these very same advantages that also make IoT devices a major target for hackers, because IoT devices—being deployed on a large scale—cover a wide range of applications. This nature gives attackers ample opportunities to locate potential targets, so it is of paramount importance to implement cyber security solutions to safeguard these devices.

Similarly, data security is at the core of information security. In today's world of increasingly advanced intelligence, data-faking techniques based on smart science pose a huge challenge to information security. This challenge is demanding because healthcare devices may contain the sensitive medical data of patients, manufacturing devices may store production processes and trade secrets, and transportation and smart home devices may involve the personal information of users. If an attacker obtains this critical information, and conducts theft, extortion, or other malicious activities leading to the violation of personal privacy, or in more serious cases, even the leakage of confidential information, then offering strong data security is important to securely protect the user information.

IoT devices play an important role in critical infrastructures, such as medical devices, transportation-control systems, and manufacturing processes. Attackers may cause service disruptions through malicious operations [10], which can have a significant impact on society and the economy. The security of the Internet of Things is more of a precursor to the protection of critical infrastructure, which is directly related to the infrastructure of the economic operation, social order, and public interest, and has a significant impact on the information system, including communications, electric power, water conservancy, transportation, finance, energy, and municipal and other areas of the various networks, as well as information infrastructures and important information systems. Once a critical information infrastructure is damaged, loses its functions, or has a data leakage, it may seriously jeopardize national security, economic operations, and the social order, and even cause widespread social panic. Therefore, safeguarding the security of IoT infrastructures is a top priority for national security and social stability.

1.4. Contributions

This study of energy-aware security mechanisms provides an effective solution to the conflict between the security and energy efficiency of IoT devices. Compared with existing research, we comprehensively examine multiple dimensions such as hardware, software, network, and data management, summarize the main contributions of the current research results in terms of the two key themes of energy efficiency and security, and provide an in-depth analysis of the presence of potential problems. It also provides new perspectives and ideas for subsequent research on energy-aware security mechanisms, which will help promote the sustainable development of IoT technologies. This survey will help future researchers apply energy-aware security mechanisms in real IoT systems.

1.5. Organization

The remainder of this paper is organized as follows, see Figure 2. In Section 2, we introduce several energy consumption factors in the IoT, challenges in realizing IoT energy efficiency, existing IoT energy-saving technologies, and emerging trends and future directions in energy-efficient computing for the IoT. In Section 3, we discuss the evolving IoT threats, analyze the defense layer of IoT security from multiple dimensions, and reflect on the challenges and future directions of IoT security. Next, in Section 4, we take a look at energy-aware security mechanisms in the IoT, and summarize ways of making the energy-security trade-offs in the IoT, the challenges of implementing energy-aware security mechanisms, and the approaches to achieving energy-aware security. We elaborate on case studies and examples of energy-aware security mechanisms, as well as discuss their directions and related open research questions. Finally, the last section presents concluding remarks.

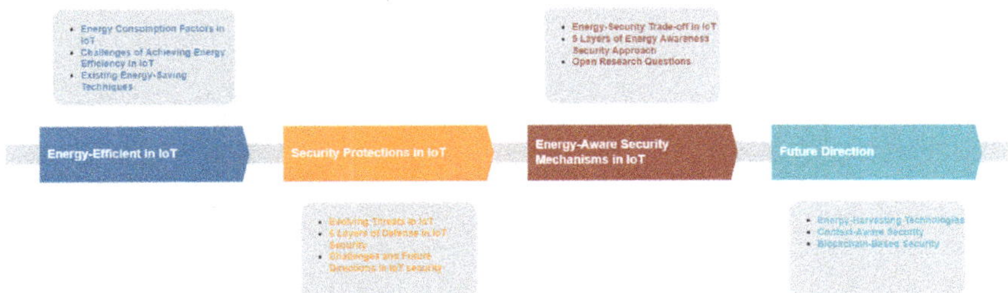

Figure 2. The graphical abstract of this paper.

2. Energy-Efficient IoT

2.1. Energy Consumption Factors in the IoT

We will now delve into the energy consumption factors in the IoT (see Figure 3), which are categorized as follows:

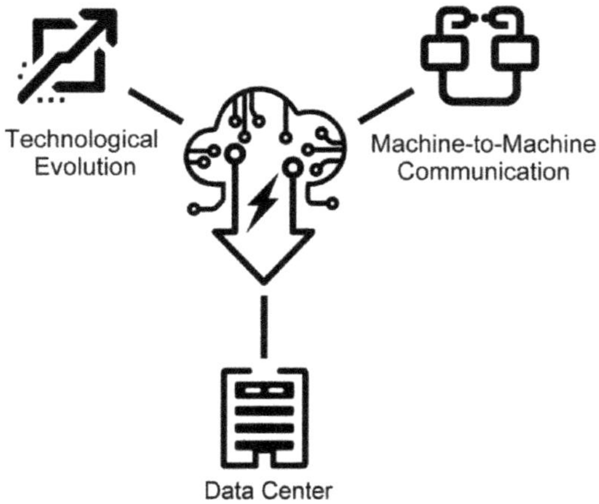

Figure 3. Energy-consumption factors in IoT systems.

2.1.1. Data Centers

IoT devices, equipped with sensors, cameras, and other components, generate a large amount of data collected from their environments [11], which is then transferred to data centers, becoming a critical source of input for servers, storage devices, and cooling systems. Such a process ultimately poses a huge strain on existing infrastructure, including cloud data centers [12]. Consequently, data centers must constantly undergo upgrades and expansions to meet the increasing demand for servers, storage devices, and cooling systems. Unfortunately, the constant upgrades not only lead to a high energy consumption in data centers but also cause additional environmental and economic costs. To address this issue, rethinking how to achieve higher energy efficiency and mitigate the over-reliance on power resources in data centers becomes indispensable.

2.1.2. Machine-to-Machine (M2M) Communication

Communication protocols in the IoT, such as short-range LAN communications, cellular networks, and satellite communications, ensure the real-time data transmission between devices. However, these communication protocols also pose various energy-management challenges. For example, communication operations, signal transmission, and network maintenance all place significant demands on power resources. WiFi or Bluetooth technologies used in LAN communications, as well as cellular networks and satellite communications on a wider scale, require stable communication connectivity, which places tremendous demands on power resources. This power demand phenomenon becomes more severe in machine-to-machine (M2M) communication scenarios, where 'smart devices' communicate with each other autonomously and make collaborative decisions without human intervention [13]. Even worse, since these devices are battery-powered and often require constant and uninterrupted connections, frequent charging becomes inevitable, thereby leading to increased energy costs. Therefore, carefully managing the charging cycles of devices is essential to maintaining reliable yet high-speed data transmission while minimizing power consumption.

2.1.3. Technological Evolution

The rapid development of IoT technology makes device renewal and iteration inevitable. As technology continues to advance, replacing old devices with new ones results in excessive e-waste. In addition to the potential environmental threat posed by the e-waste generated by equipment obsolescence, the disposal process also induces energy resource demands [14]. Meanwhile, producing, configuring, and deploying new-generation equipment also leads to transitional energy waste. Though it is an inevitable part when embracing new technologies, we need to provide energy-efficient strategies during device-renewal processes.

A variety of strategies can be utilized to effectively reduce energy consumption in the IoT. For instance, optimizing data-processing algorithms can reduce the burden on data centers, thereby reducing energy consumption. Energy-efficient communication technologies can help slash the amount of power support required for communications. The use of renewable energy in the manufacturing and operation of IoT devices can decrease the reliance on non-renewable energy sources, thereby enhancing overall energy sustainability. In addition, sustainable update strategies for devices are conductive to mitigating energy demands caused by device renewal. Moreover, energy-efficient hardware and software technologies can be introduced to further enhance the energy efficiency of IoT devices and thus reduce energy costs. Lastly, holistic approaches can be leveraged to enhance IoT energy efficiency and achieve the goal of sustainable development.

2.2. Challenges of Achieving Energy Efficiency in the IoT

In this part of the study, we discuss the challenges of realizing energy efficiency in the IoT as follows:

2.2.1. Resource Constraints

Resource constraints, such as processing power, memory capacity, and communication bandwidth are major challenges to achieving energy efficiency in the IoT domain. IoT devices are often equipped with processors with limited computing power (industrial sensors or sensor nodes, RFID tags, etc.) [15], making it difficult to perform complex tasks. For example, the limited memory capacity of these devices restricts the amount of data they can store and process, which has implications for energy efficiency. This challenge is particularly critical in application scenarios that require IoT devices to process large amounts of data in real-time [16]. Similarly, IoT applications, like smart cities, environmental monitoring, and health monitoring, require quick data processing to provide real-time feedback and decision support. However, due to the limitations of processing power, these devices often need to offload complex data analysis tasks to cloud- or edge-computing platforms. This not only increases the data transmission latency and energy consumption but also raises concerns about data privacy and security.

2.2.2. Heterogeneity

The heterogeneity of the IoT poses multiple obstacles to achieving energy efficiency. IoT environments typically consist of a wide variety of devices, technologies, platforms, and protocols [17]. Although this heterogeneity provides configuration flexibility for various applications, it also brings about issues such as integration complexity, interoperability, management, and security. For example, IoT systems are normally comprised of different types of devices like sensors, smart cameras, air pollution monitors, communication protocols, and others [18]; as a result, these devices differ broadly in design and functionality, energy consumption, and battery life. Such differences make it complicated to implement a generic energy-saving strategy.

2.2.3. Dynamic Atmospheres

IoT devices are often deployed in dynamic environments, where their operating conditions and network statuses are constantly changing [19]. This dynamism significantly influences the effectiveness of energy management strategies: first, IoT devices transmitting data rely on networks, the quality and availability of which fluctuate depending on the location, time, and other factors. Second, high network latency or low bandwidth environments may compel devices to make multiple attempts to transmit data, thereby increasing energy consumption [20]. Third, an IoT device may switch its operating state, such as transitioning from a low-power mode to a high-power mode, according to current operational requirements [21]. Therefore, it is obvious that adjusting the states of IoT devices in a timely manner while meeting performance requirements becomes increasingly challenging.

2.3. Existing Energy-Saving Techniques

Energy-saving technologies for the IoT are defined from five main perspectives: hardware, software, network protocols, data management, and machine learning. See Figure 4.

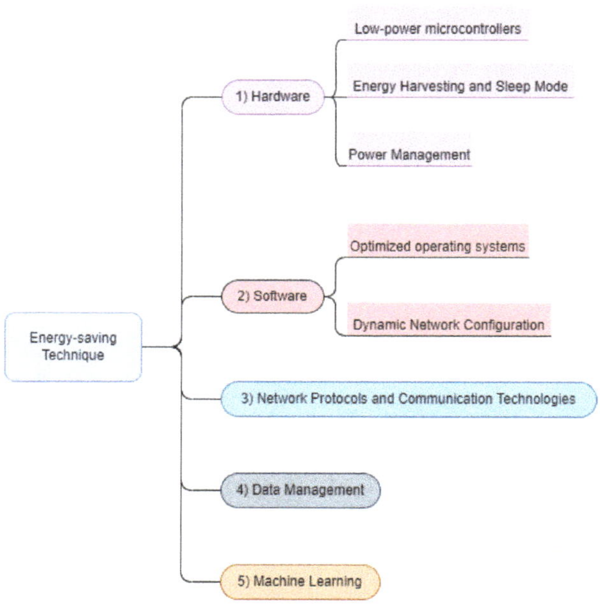

Figure 4. Existing energy-saving techniques.

2.3.1. Hardware Energy-Saving Techniques

- *Low-power microcontrollers.* Low-power microcontrollers in IoT systems considerably extend the battery life, making them ideal for applications that require long runtimes. Due to the fact that sensor nodes are often battery-powered in reality, lowering the energy consumption not only extends battery life but also reduces battery replacement needs, which in turn slashes the risk of environmental contamination when discarding old batteries [22]. Additionally, energy savings yielded by low-power microcontrollers help cut back the demand for power resources.
- *Energy Harvesting and Sleep Mode.* Energy harvesting technologies refer to the processes that capture and convert external energy sources into electrical energy. There exists a broad spectrum of external energy sources, including solar, mechanical, thermal, wind, water, radio frequency, etc. For example, solar energy-harvesting technologies strive to leverage solar cells to convert light energy into electrical energy, whereas radio-frequency energy-harvesting technologies harness radio frequency signals to perform electrical energy conversion. On the other hand, the development of sleep-mode technologies becomes essential to achieve long-term self-sustainability for IoT applications [23]. Taking a sensor node as an example, if there is no need for it to

sense its target environment for a certain period of time, it can transition to sleep mode for energy-saving purposes. Likewise, its sensors can be transitioned to sleep mode if its battery power drops below a critical threshold. The transitions can be performed dynamically based on multiple factors such as the sensors' battery status and information quality. In short, energy-harvesting and sleep mode technologies help extend devices' life and enhance the energy utilization of IoT systems [24].

- *Power Management.* Advanced power-management techniques, such as power-curtailment strategies and dynamic voltage and frequency scaling (DVFS), can effectively diminish power consumption. Power-curtailment strategies (e.g., power-gating techniques) focus on reducing the static power consumption of digital circuits. The power consumption of digital circuits consists of two main contributors: dynamic power consumption and static power consumption. Dynamic power consumption refers to the power consumed when the circuit is switched, while static power consumption is primarily due to the leakage current of the transistors, which consumes power even when the circuit is not performing any operation [25]. The power-gating technique inserts control switches between different parts of a circuit such that the power supply to a block of circuitry will be cut off when the block has no task to perform, thereby reducing the power consumption of digital circuits [26]. As for DVFS, it is a commonly used strategy that dynamically adjusts the power voltage and clock frequency of processors. In particular, in underload conditions, DVFS lowers a processor's voltage and frequency to reduce the power consumption. Conversely, in overload conditions, DVFS increases the processor's voltage and frequency to provide necessary computing power [27]. This technique is especially critical for battery-powered mobile devices because it enables IoT devices to achieve the best performance-to-energy ratio under various workload conditions, thereby prolonging their service time. In brief, power-management techniques fine-tune the power supply to IoT systems, reducing the overall power consumption of IoT devices and extending the battery life of battery-powered devices.

2.3.2. Software Energy-Saving Techniques

- *Optimized operating systems.* IoT devices often utilize specifically designed lightweight operating systems (e.g., Contiki and TinyOS) to enhance the operation efficiency and reduce system overhead [28], satisfying the needs of resource-constrained environments. For instance, an optimized operating system can intelligently switch an IoT device between sleep and active modes to reduce the power consumption when it sits in an idle state for a certain period, thereby effectively improving the energy efficiency of the device.
- *Dynamic Network Configuration.* Dynamic network configuration can improve the energy efficiency of IoT devices through communication optimization [29]. It allows IoT devices to make adjustments according to changing network conditions, such as the signal strength, network load, and interference. Such adaptability enables IoT devices to operate with minimal energy consumption under various conditions. For example, reducing the frequency of data transmission when a network signal is weak can reduce the power consumption. This example signifies that a dynamic network configuration not only lowers the energy consumption but also mitigates network congestion.

2.3.3. Network Protocols and Communication Technologies

Communication technologies, such as low-power WiFi, Bluetooth low energy (LE) [30], and low-power wide area network (LPWAN) [31], were developed to minimize energy consumption, making them ideal for IoT applications that require a long battery life. WiFi HaLow [32], one of the low-power WiFi versions, constructed based on the IEEE 802.11ah standard [33] features high data transmission efficiency so as to diminish power consumption. Bluetooth LE, characterized by short communication intervals and quick connection establishment, reduces the power consumption while maintaining stable communication. LPWAN technology, allowing long-distance communication (several kilometers), reduces the need for multiple relays or access points, making it suitable for long-range and low-data rate scenarios.

2.3.4. Data-Management Technology

Data aggregation refers to the process of combining multiple data sources or sensors into a single unified data set. Data aggregation lessens the power consumption required for communication by reducing the amount of data transmitted. In-network processing, on the other hand, strives to reduce the energy consumption by processing data at the edge of a network, with only the necessary information or processing results being sent to the cloud.

2.3.5. Optimizing Machine Learning

Machine learning algorithms can dynamically adjust equipment power settings and forecast equipment failures, based on real-time conditions and historical information, thereby harvesting energy savings. For example, by intervening before the occurrence of equipment problems and preventing equipment from running in an inefficient or lossy state, the use of machine learning algorithms can yield energy savings. Likewise, machine learning is capable of fine-tuning the equipment runtime and task scheduling, aligning the energy consumption closely with the real demand.

2.4. Emerging Trends and Future Directions

The new trends and future directions for the energy-aware IoT involve a number of areas, including energy harvesting, artificial intelligence, and regional blockchains.

2.4.1. Energy Harvesting

New materials and technologies: recently, energy-harvesting technologies, such as flexible solar cells, thermal energy-harvesting materials, and vibration-based technologies have emerged [34]. Tiny energy sources in the environment, such as differences in light and temperature, are harnessed by flexible nanogenerators and thermal energy converters to generate electricity. Meanwhile, device vibration or motion is utilized by vibration-based energy-harvesting technologies to generate electricity for wireless sensors and wearable devices.

2.4.2. Artificial Intelligence

Machine learning and artificial intelligence show promise for optimizing the resource allocation and data collection in IoT systems. Edge computing and edge AI can make local real-time decision making feasible for IoT devices and thus reduce their reliance on cloud services, thereby lowering the power consumption for communications and cloud computing. AI-powered data analysis can also facilitate optimizing energy management such that IoT devices can operate intelligently and efficiently.

2.4.3. Blockchain

Blockchain technology is demonstrating great potential in pursuing a sustainable future [35]. This is mainly attributed to its trait of decentralized, secure, and transparent data-management mechanisms. Blockchain technology, through its real-time monitoring capabilities, creates ample opportunities to implement appropriate energy-saving measures. In particular, the combination of edge computing, which processes data closer to data sources to reduce the data transmission time and latency, with the goal of reducing energy consumption, ensures security and transparency. Advances in these emerging areas will stimulate continued innovation in energy-efficient IoT technologies, making IoT systems smart, sustainable, and secure.

3. Security Protections in IoT Environments

Along with the rapid development of the IoT industry, IoT attacks—such as privacy leakage, illegal invasion, and local network damage—become frequent. It is expected that with the further expansion of the scale of the IoT, the destructive power of attacking the IoT will be further expanded, and the IoT security issues are increasingly becoming a concern of the society. The following is a more detailed discussion of cyber-threats to IoT devices. In Section 3.1, we will discuss a variety of cyber-threats that target IoT devices. Next, we will elaborate on layers of defense in IoT security in Section 3.2.

3.1. Evolving Threats in the IoT

We start this part with the introduction of denial of services. Then, we articulate IoT security issues such as data breaches and physical manipulation. Finally, we discuss three vulnerabilities of IoT devices.

3.1.1. Denial of Service Attacks (DoS)

A Denial of Service (DoS) attack (see Figure 5) is a cyber attack that makes a website or service unavailable by overwhelming the system with an enormous amount of requests from multiple sources [36]. A Distributed Denial of Service (DDoS) attack [37] is a special type of DoS attacks that utilizes a network of compromised devices, called a botnet, to send attack requests. Such swift DoS and DDoS attacks are difficult to defend against and therefore, their consequences are highly destructive. In DDoS attacks, web servers are flooded with a large number of requests for replies to the message, consuming network bandwidth or system resources, resulting in overloaded networks or systems where normal services stop providing [38]. DDoS manifests itself in two main forms, namely flow-of-traffic attacks [39] and resource-exhaustion attacks [40].

- *Flow-of-Traffic Attacks.* Under this type of attacks, the network bandwidth is blocked by a large number of malicious packets that overwhelm legitimate traffic. These attacks aim to exhaust the network's capacity to handle data, effectively denying service to legitimate users.
- *Resource-Exhaustion Attacks.* The focal point of these attacks is the server itself, which receives a multitude of attack packets that deplete memory or CPU resources. Such attacks aim to prevent servers from processing legitimate requests, leading to a denial of service.

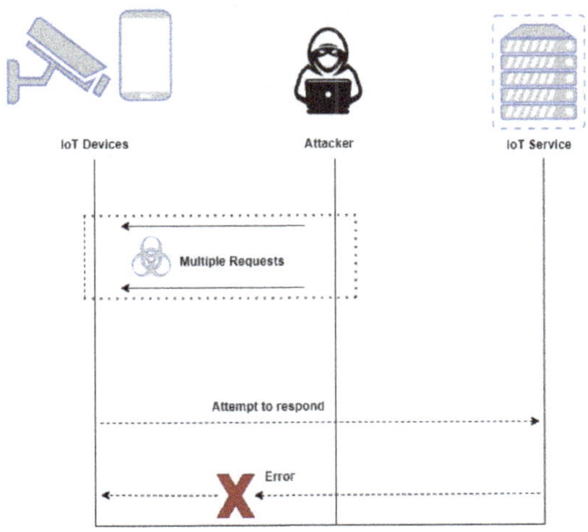

Figure 5. Denial of service attack in IoT systems.

3.1.2. Botnets, Data Breaches, and Physical Manipulation

Attackers often infect and control thousands, if not millions, of computers to form a large *botnet* that is capable of launching DDoS attacks, large-scale spam campaigns, or other types of cyberattacks. Data breaches in DDoS are security incidents that involve both the exposure of confidential or sensitive information and the disruption of the availability or performance of a website or service [41]. When attackers use malware to infect IoT devices, the attackers do more than just adding the device to a botnet. For example, cyberattackers can access device data and steal sensitive information stored in it, and the attackers also use IoT to obtain credentials from device firmware. Using these credentials, the attackers access corporate networks or other systems storing sensitive data. In this way, an attack on these devices could turn into a full-blown data breach.

Attacks mainly targeting sensing devices may result in the leakage of sensitive information or malicious tracking. Since IoT devices are deployed in distributed remote environments, hackers are able to access and tamper with the physical layer, obtain sensitive information, and interrupt services furnished by IoT devices. Because IoT devices are used in most IoT applications such as smart homes and smart healthcare, it is crucial to protect them from IoT attacks. In cases of product failure or any kind of cyberattacks on these devices, the device systems and the life of users will be seriously affected.

3.1.3. Unique Vulnerabilities of IoT Devices

Now let us analyze the unique vulnerabilities of IoT devices from the following three perspectives, namely weak authentication [42], insecure communication protocols [43], and outdated firmware [44].

- *Weak Authentication.* Weak authentication in IoT devices, like unchangeable default passwords, opens doors for attackers to seize control of entire networks.
- *Insecure Communication Protocols.* Insecure communication protocols, similar to weak authentication, leave users vulnerable to data theft and manipulation attacks by acting as open doors for hackers, especially on public WiFi networks.
- *Outdated Firmware.* Outdated firmware and limited update capabilities in IoT devices create easy openings for hackers, leaving networks vulnerable to known software attacks.

Authentication technology is the most direct and cutting-edge line of defense in network security, and is an important means of preventing illegal invasion and virus damage. Many IoT devices have weak authentication mechanisms [45], such as default passwords or simple passwords, and users rarely change these passwords, thereby making IoT systems vulnerable to unauthorized accesses. Weak credentials, coupled with limited authentication methods, create opportunities for attackers to compromise devices and gain control of IoT networks.

As with weak authentication by default, insecure communication protocols allow hackers to intercept traffic or perform network "snooping" to easily view sensitive data traveling over the networks. This issue makes systems and devices vulnerable to man-in-the-middle (MITM) attacks [46], and one of the most common methods of MITM attacks is through public WiFi, which often has insecure communication protocols allowing an attacker to gain access to information from any devices connected to the network. The attacker can even lure the user to a fake server that has been set up in advance so as to conduct illegal activities such as fraud against the user.

IoT devices often have limited computing resources, and may lack appropriate mechanisms for regular firmware updates and security patches. As a result, these devices often run on outdated and vulnerable versions of software. Hackers actively exploit known vulnerabilities in outdated firmware to gain unauthorized access to, or control of, IoT devices. The lack of a streamlined process for providing timely updates and patches to IoT devices poses a significant challenge, as it exposes devices and networks to attacks that could be prevented.

3.2. Layers of Defense in IoT Security

A multilayered approach to ensuring the security of IoT devices and systems is a comprehensive challenge. Due to the large number of IoT front-end devices dispersed in unattended environments, the devices are highly susceptible to attacks and exploitation, resulting in the inability of core business systems to operate normally.

The IoT security requirements are mainly reflected in the following three layers of IoT systems.

- *Device Layer.* This layers contains a massive amount of sensors and control devices—such as sensors and control devices—deployed on sites.
- *Communication Layer.* The second layer provides a variety of communication protocols coupled with interfaces to realize functions such as data collection, device control, and system maintenance.
- *Application Layer.* This layer is comprised of a cloud platform performing the comprehensive configuration, operation and management of IoT terminals like smart grids and telemedicine.

In what follows, we discuss today's defense strategies for the IoT three-layer architecture from five aspects: device (see Section 3.3), network (see Section 3.4), software (see Section 3.5), application (see Section 3.6), and management (see Section 3.7). Figure 6 provides an overview of common threats in the IoT and corresponding defenses.

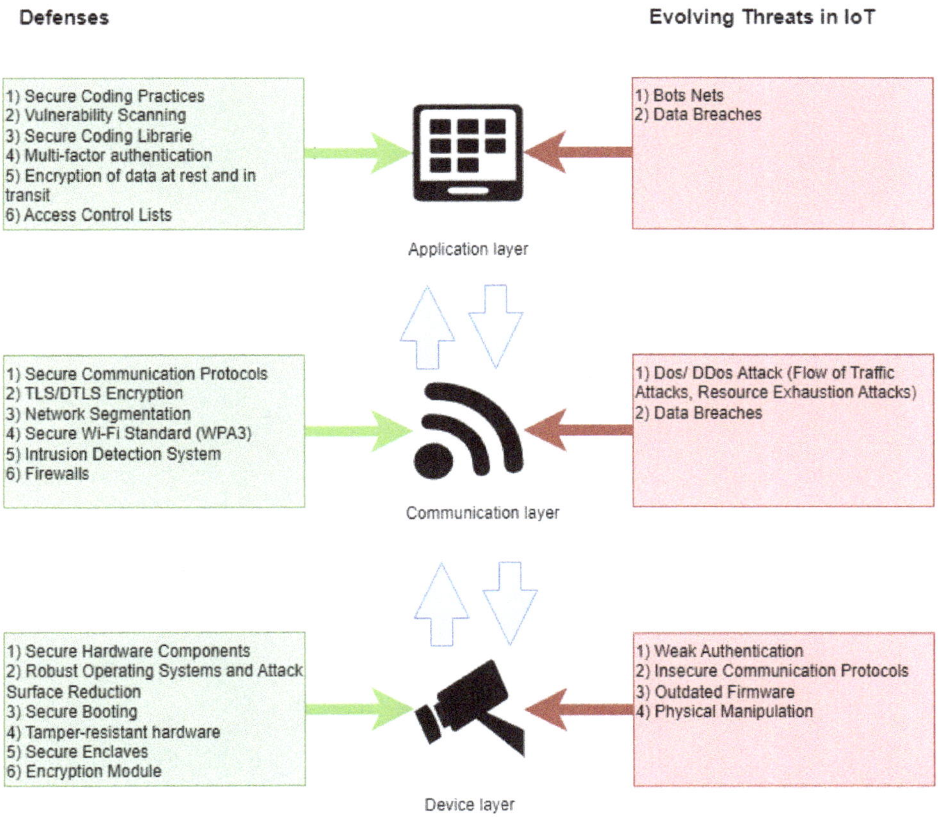

Figure 6. Common threats in the IoT with corresponding defenses.

3.3. Defense at the Device Layer

3.3.1. Secure Hardware Components

The selection of secure hardware components is critical to the overall security of IoT devices [47]. Microcontrollers are the core components of embedded systems, and microcontrollers specifically designed to enhance security can be selected to improve the security of a device. Similarly, hardware security modules [48] (*HSMs*) are widely used in scenarios in which IoT devices are protected by securely managing, processing, and the storing of cryptographic keys and digital certificates. HSMs are widely used in venues (e.g., such as financial services, data protection, and enterprise security) where security is highly desired. HSMs offer robust protection for encryption keys by utilizing dedicated secure cryptographic processors. These processors can be housed within plug-in cards (SAM/SIM cards) or external devices connected directly to computers or web servers. The key discrepancy of HSMs lies in their tamper-resistant design: this often includes a physically secure enclosure that automatically deletes stored keys upon unauthorized physical access, preventing key disclosure. In essence, HSMs offer a secure environment for the entire lifecycle of an encryption key, safeguarding IoT systems from various threats.

3.3.2. Robust Operating Systems and Attack Surface Reduction

In IoT environments, adopting an operating system with strong security and minimizing the attack surface is a key strategy for protecting devices from threats. It is wise to elect an operating system designed specifically for IoT security, and examples for OSs optimized for IoT devices include FreeRTOS, RIOT OS, and Zephyr [49]. These operating systems are usually designed to be lightweight and include only the necessary functional modules to reduce the potential attack surface. More importantly, unnecessary system services and applications, especially those that may listen to network ports or provide remote access capabilities, are disabled or removed from the operating systems. In these scenarios, system processes and applications are running with elevated privileges to mitigate the risks of being maliciously exploited.

3.3.3. Secure Booting

Secure booting is critical to prevent attackers from compromising operational IoT programs [50], because any malicious code inserted into a device could make that device part of a botnet. For example, an attacker may implant a local device with a file containing malware. If the device is not protected by a secure boot, the malicious code will execute on the next reboot to compromise the device. With the secure boot process, security checks during reboots identify unauthorized executables, prevent any threats from running, and enable the associated protections.

3.3.4. Tamper-Resistant Hardware

Choosing hardware devices equipped with built-in detection capabilities [51] makes it possible to recognize and respond to any form of physical tampering attempts. This strategy is a precaution that is especially important for IoT devices storing sensitive information or that control critical infrastructure, which, if tampered with, could pose a serious threat to personal privacy or public safety.

3.3.5. Secure Enclaves

Secure enclaves use specialized hardware controls used to securely isolate data and instructions at the CPU level [52]. Such an isolation is furnished by strong cryptography that verifies the authenticity of the enclave while offering privacy and integrity of the enclave code and the sensitive data being processed.

3.3.6. Encryption Module

Encryption modules at the hardware level are a technology specifically designed to realize data encryption and decryption operations on physical devices. These modules implement encryption algorithms through hardware rather than software, enhancing both security and performance. A good example is the trusted platform module, or TPM [53]—a hardware encryption module that is widely deployed in computing devices. A TPM can securely store encryption keys, digital certificates, and other sensitive data. Through these features, the TPM is capable of delivering strong hardware-level security services. Hardware-level security mechanisms provide a higher level of protection than software encryption because the hardware-level mechanisms are more difficult to compromise by remote hackers or software vulnerabilities. By integrating TPMs during the design and manufacturing phases of a device, users and organizations can establish a strong security foundation in IoT environments.

3.4. Defense at the Network Level

3.4.1. Secure Communication Protocols

Network security is an important aspect of end-to-end IoT security. As devices communicate with one another and with assorted cloud services, it is critical to ensure the secure transmission of data and prevent unauthorized access. This protection can be achieved by using secure communication protocols, such as datagram transport layer security (DTLS), to furnish secure communication among IoT devices [54].

In the network layer security, encrypted communication is seen as the cornerstone of securing data transmission [54]. This is achieved through the use of strong encryption algorithms such as transport layer security (TLS) or a secure sockets layer (SSL) [55] for secure website accesses (HTTPS) [56], and other network services that require a secure channel [57]. The network-level defense aims to ensure that data are not intercepted or tampered with during transmission and that mutual authentication is implemented between the client and server.

Although the TLS and DTLS protocols share the same goal of securing data in transit, they are each applicable to different network protocols and scenarios. TLS—a standard encryption protocol dedicated to providing communication security—is primarily used on TCP (transmission control protocol) [58] connections to offer security protection for the communication between web browsers and servers, e-mail, instant messaging, and other services. DTLS is a variant of TLS designed for the UDP (user datagram protocol). Since the UDP is a connectionless protocol, it is mainly used in applications that require high-speed transmission and low latency such as video conferencing. DTLS facilitates TLS-like security in these situations, including encryption, authentication, and data integrity protection.

3.4.2. Network Segmentation

Network segmentation is an effective means of improving network security [59]. Users may apply virtual local area networks (VLANs) [60], IP address ranges, and combinations to divide the network into smaller local networks. This strategy allows users to forge multiple security zones and represent different segments controlled by firewalls. Network segmentation reduces overall system risks, and facilitates rapid response and recovery by assuring that the data and resources in each segment are visible and accessible only to authorized users in the current segment.

3.4.3. Intrusion-Detection/Prevention Systems (IDS/IPS)

Evidence demonstrates that intrusion-detection systems (IDS) and intrusion-prevention systems (IPS) are essential for detecting and responding to network attacks [61]. An IDS is a technology used in network security to detect and identify suspicious activity [62]. When suspicious behavior or activity that violates security policies are detected, the IDS generates and sends an alert to administrators or to an integrated security information and event management (SIEM) system [63].

There are two main types of IDSs, namely network intrusion-detection systems (NIDSs) and host intrusion-detection systems (HIDSs) [64]. NIDSs are mainly deployed at network boundaries or data-center entrances to monitor all the network traffic passing through and detect potential malicious activities or violations, whereas HIDSs are installed on specific hosts or servers to monitor the system logs, file system changes, and detect attacks or abnormal behaviors.

Firewalls—the first line of defense against compromise—shield IoT devices from unauthorized access and malicious traffic, and by configuring the firewall, system administrators can limit the ports and services that are accessible, allowing only the necessary communications to effectively reduce the attack surface. For example, Cisco's enterprise firewall solutions empower organizations with advanced network security, including intrusion prevention and unified communications protection, safeguarding critical data and ensuring seamless communication [65].

3.4.4. Secure WiFi Standard (WPA3)

Adopting the latest WiFi security standards, such as WPA3, helps in bolstering the security of WiFi networks. WPA3 introduces the simultaneous authentication of equals (SAE) algorithm, which replaces the pre-shared key (PSK) authentication used in WPA2 [66]. SAE enhances the password security and improves resistance to brute-force breaking attacks, especially against dictionary attacks. In addition, WPA3 utilizes a higher level of encryption and provides a 192-bit encryption key, whereas WPA2 only supports a 128-bit encryption key. WPA3 is suitable for the government, financial, and medical industries that require high data security. Additionally, WPA3 provides perfect forward secrecy, ensuring that even if a long-term key is compromised, previous communication data remain secure: an attacker cannot access past communications by decrypting captured packets.

3.5. Defense at the Software Level

Software-level defense is an efficient approach to building robust and secure IoT systems. Continuous attention to security throughout the software development lifecycle and the adoption of appropriate defenses are key to ensuring that the software remains secure in the face of evolving threats. In what follows, we articulate the defense at the software level from the perspectives of secure coding practices (see Section 3.5.1), vulnerability management (see Section 3.5.2), and access control and data storage (see Section 3.5.3).

3.5.1. Secure Coding Practices

Secure coding practices are a critical part of the software-development process designed to guide developers on how to write more secure code [67]. These practices are designed to reduce the vulnerability of software and systems to security breaches, thereby protecting applications from attacks. Examples include using strong hash functions like Argon2, bcrypt, or PBKDF2 [68] to store user passwords, and employing salt to further enhance security.

Common security threats and vulnerabilities that can be protected by secure coding practices include memory security and buffer overflows. This method requires developers to use safe functions when coding, avoiding functions such as *strcpy()* and *sprintf()* that are known to cause problems [69].

Regularly reviewing code [70] is the process of checking source code to pinpoint and eliminate vulnerabilities or errors that are likely to compromise security in software. The code-reviewing process ensures that the implemented code meets the security standards and complies with the industry regulations. This practice not only helps to enhance the code quality and performance but also prevents potential attacks by hackers.

Using secure coding libraries coupled with software frameworks with embedded security is an effective way to improve the quality and security of code during software development (see Figure 7). These libraries provide a collection of rigorously vetted and tested code modules that enable developers to avert insecure code practices. Common secure coding libraries and frameworks that prevent security vulnerabilities include OWASP ESAPI, Spring Security, and Microsoft SDL. Figure 7 lists a set of example secure coding libraries, frameworks, and patches, which are devised to help software developers to implement security features throughout the development lifecycle [71].

Classes	Names	Types	Description
Cryptography	OpenSSL	Library	Provide cryptographic functions: TLS/SSL, X.509 certificates.
	BoringSSL	Library	It is smaller, faster, and more secure than OpenSSL.
	NaCl	Library	Offer a small set of well-vetted cryptographic primitives.
Web Security	OWASP AntiSamy	Library	Prevent XSS attacks by sanitizing user input.
	OWASP ESAPI	Library	Provides input validation, output encoding, and session management.
	Spring Security	Framework	Offer security features: authentication, authorization, and session management.
System Security	SELinux	MAC System	Allow administrators to define fine-grained security policies.
	AppArmor	MAC System	Allow administrators to define fine-grained security policies.
	Grsecurity	Patches	Security patches for the Linux kernel to be resistant to attacks.

Figure 7. A list of sample secure coding libraries, frameworks, and patches, which enable developers to build robust and secure IoT systems.

3.5.2. Vulnerability Management

Vulnerability management is a necessary measure to secure software [72]. Vulnerability management allows for an effective update policy to ensure that the device's firmware and software are kept up to date, reducing the risk of known vulnerabilities. For example, security patches are pushed to devices through a remote update mechanism after the product's release.

Regular vulnerability scanning helps to find and fix potential vulnerabilities in software [73]. Network application layers are regularly scanned for vulnerabilities, and any discovered vulnerabilities are fixed in a timely manner to optimize the security of the IoT device.

3.5.3. Access Control and Data Storage

Strict access controls in the facility limit software and system access. The risk of unauthorized access can be avoided by implementing the principle of least privilege, user authentication, and authorization. For example, IoT systems assign user-specific access permissions based on their roles, ensuring individuals access only to job-relevant information.

Strong data-storage practices, including encryption, access control, and regular backups, safeguard sensitive information, preventing breaches and minimizing the risk of theft, leaks, and associated consequences. An example is the use full-disk encryption like BitLocker [74] to encrypt the contents of the entire hard drive. For the complete security of IoT systems equipped with data storage, users should leverage robust encryption options like MySQL's AES function and SQL Server's transparent data encryption [75].

3.6. Defense at the Application Level

We will now shed light on the security practices and defenses at the application level, which facilitates the secure authentication of user identity and protects the secure transmission of sensitive data. By combining multi-factor authentication (see Section 3.6.1), data encryption (see Section 3.6.2), and access control (see Section 3.6.4), more robust and secure IoT applications can be built.

3.6.1. Secure User Authentication

The first line of defense at the application level is, of course, the use of secure user authentication. Applying strong password policies, multi-factor authentication, and the like can ensure that only authorized users are allowed to access applications, thus safeguarding IoT devices from malware infections and other security threats. In doing so, systems verify that only authorized users are allowed to access specific data or IoT device functions. This authentication technique prevents unauthorized access and operations and improves system security.

To improve security, an increasing number of IoT systems adopt multi-factor authentication, or MFA [76]—a mechanism that combines passwords, biometrics, and other authentication methods. This security approach greatly enhance the level of security, making it difficult for intruders to gain access through simple password guessing or stealing.

3.6.2. Data Security APIs

By using secure application program interfaces (APIs), it is possible to make data transfers between applications safe and secure. Data security APIs enable data signatures and integrity checks to confirm that data have not been tampered with during the storage or transmission phases [77]. IoT systems can verify data integrity by the virtue of hash functions and digital signatures, guaranteeing the systems' authenticity and reliability.

Figure 8 tabulates a list of popular data security APIs along with their descriptions and security features.

APIs	Description	Authentication and Access Control	Enterprise Grade	Monitor	Data Security
Amazon Cognito	User authentication, authorization, and management	✓			
Auth0	Passwordless authentication and social logins	✓			
Azure Active Directory	Cloud-based identity and access management	✓	✓		
Fortanix Data Security Fabric	Encrypted key management service, access control	✓			✓
Google Cloud Identity Platform	Cloud-based identity and access management	✓	✓		
IBM Guardium Data Encryption	Data encryption and access control for databases	✓	✓		✓
McAfee Data Loss Prevention	Data loss prevention and endpoint security		✓	✓	
Okta	Secure user access management	✓	✓		
OneLogin	Identity and access management (IAM) solution	✓	✓		
Palo Alto Networks Prisma Cloud	Protect data in cloud environments, detect and prevent data breaches			✓	✓

Figure 8. A list of sample data security APIs and their security features.

3.6.3. Encryption of Data at Rest and in Transit

Encryption of data at rest and in transit are two important concepts in data security that can be implemented at the application level. Data-at-rest encryption refers to the encryption of data stored on a device or server so as to protect the data from unauthorized access [78]. This type of encryption prevents data breaches even if IoT devices are stolen or data are illegally accessed.

Data-in-transit encryption refers to the process of encrypting data when the data are being transmitted over a network, or "in transit", between two IoT systems [79]. Encryption of data in transit is a fundamental way of protecting sensitive information from interception and eavesdropping attacks in IoT environments.

3.6.4. Access Control Lists

Access control lists (ALCs) define at the device level which users or systems are authorized to access a particular IoT device [80]. This scheme-preconditioned access control ensures that device operations and data access are limited to authorized individuals, thus reducing the chance of malicious accesses by adversaries.

Role-based access control, or RBAC, is a flexible access-control model that assigns appropriate privileges to users anchored on their roles [81]. With the RBAC model in place, sensitive data and device features are only available to any roles that need the information. This highly centralized privilege control effectively alleviates the risk of data leakage and unauthorized accesses. Even if a user's credentials are compromised, a threat actor can only gain access to resources allowed by that user's role, thereby mitigating security risks.

3.7. *Defense at the Management Level*

A wide range of security practices and defenses at the management level assure that IoT devices and systems maintain a high level of security throughout the lifecycle. Evolving security threats can be effectively addressed through timely configurations (see Section 3.7.1), firmware updates (see Section 3.7.2), patch management (see Section 3.7.3), and effective incident responses (see Section 3.7.4).

3.7.1. Secure Supply and Configuration

Secure supply and configuration play a crucial role as they directly affect the security and reliability of IoT devices and their data. Devices with secure provisioning should have authentication as a feature, which ensures that each device can be uniquely identified and its identity can be verified [82]. This is important for establishing secure communication between devices. In addition, the corresponding security provisioning can configure the necessary minimum privileges for the devices and the applications running on them to reduce the attack surface. There are also configurations for firewalls, intrusion-detection systems.

3.7.2. Firmware Updates

Firmware updates are the most directly useful for patching known security vulnerabilities [83]. As software vulnerabilities continue to be discovered on IoT devices, regular firmware updates can patch these vulnerabilities in a timely manner. In addition to patching vulnerabilities, firmware updates also introduce new security features and enhancements, such as improved encryption algorithms, stronger authentication mechanisms, and enhanced data protection. These updates strengthen the device's resistance in the face of unknown attacks.

Given firmware updates, the device is able to verify that the firmware was released from a trusted source. This advantage prevents malware or firmware from being injected by untrusted third parties, thereby avoiding the risk of the device being infected with malicious code [84]. Firmware updates are completed using encryption (typically public/private key encryption). When a device receives a firmware update, it verifies the signature using the publisher's public key. This process ensures that the firmware has not been tampered with during transmission, thus protecting the integrity of the firmware update.

3.7.3. Patch Management

One of the main roles of patch management is to patch security vulnerabilities in a timely manner to prevent attackers from exploiting them for unauthorized access or malicious attacks. Additionally, regular patch management can ensure that the software and firmware running on the IoT system are kept up to date, ensuring the overall stability of the IoT system [85].

Patch management systems furnish a systematic approach to offering timely updates and maintenance of device firmware and software: the management systems automatically identify and apply security patches to fix known vulnerabilities [86]. This automated process minimizes the likelihood of human error and ensures that vulnerabilities are swiftly patched before being widely exploited, thus protecting IoT devices and networks from attacks.

3.7.4. Incident Response

Incident-response mechanisms help to quickly detect and respond to security threats, and through real-time monitoring and alerting systems, security teams can detect threats at an early stage and take swift action to mitigate damage [87]. Moreover, the security team can analyze the security incident and propose follow-up improvement measures, such as fixing vulnerabilities, improving security policies and processes, and strengthening defenses to prevent similar incidents from happening again.

Incident response plans require a pre-defined set of processes and procedures designed to guide the response of security personnel when faced with a security incident. These plans are key to ensuring a quick and effective response to security threats, minimizing damage and restoring normal operations [88]. Additionally, a high-security incident response plan categorizes and prioritizes detected events to ensure that high-priority events are responded to quickly, which can greatly minimize the negative impact of security events on the IoT environment, while promoting the organization's ability to adapt to and resist future threats.

3.7.5. Security Configuration Protocols

The use of secure configuration protocols helps ensure that devices are initialized and configured with optimal security settings. By defining and enforcing security configuration standards, the exposure of devices to threats caused by configuration errors can be reduced [89]. The Arms Security Configuration Protocol ensures that only authorized users and devices have access to the network and data by implementing strong authentication and authorization mechanisms and secure communication protocols such as SSL/TLS.

3.8. Challenges and Future Directions in IoT Security

3.8.1. Challenges

The security challenges of the IoT are indeed multifaceted, especially due to its wide range of application scenarios and diverse device types. Some of these challenges include resource constraints, device heterogeneity, and a lack of standardization. Meanwhile, in the face of these challenges, future research directions present many promising areas, including lightweight encryption, AI-driven security, blockchain-based security, and privacy-preserving technologies.

- *Resource Constraints.* Many IoT devices have limited processing power, memory, and communication bandwidth, which limits the possibility of implementing robust security measures on these devices. Therefore, designing security solutions that adapt to resource-constrained environments is a challenge.
- *Heterogeneity of Devices.* There are various types of devices in the IoT that may have different operating systems, processor architectures, and communication protocols. Harmonizing security standards and mechanisms for these heterogeneous devices is a complex task.
- *Lack of Standardization.* The lack of unified IoT security standards and specifications makes it more difficult to develop comprehensive security policies and implementation strategies. The lack of standardization may lead device manufacturers and service providers to take different approaches to security.

3.8.2. Future Directions

The following research and innovation to be undertaken as future directions will overcome the aforementioned challenges to IoT security, and lay the foundation for a robust and trusted IoT ecosystem.

- *Lightweight Encryption.* Lightweight encryption algorithms for resource-constrained devices are a key future direction for IoT security. These algorithms need to secure data while minimizing the impact on device performance to improve the overall security of the IoT system [90]. Efficient and lightweight authentication is also one of the future directions of security research, which is important because verifying the identity of the user prevents sensitive data leakage and improves the performance of IoT networks.
- *Artificial Intelligence-Driven Security.* Traditional encryption methods are often utilized to address security and privacy issues in IoT networks; however, the nature of IoT nodes makes it impossible for existing methods to support the architecture of an entire complex and large IoT network, in part due to resource constraints and the large amount of real-time data generated by IoT devices. One may apply machine learning

and deep learning solutions to IoT devices and networks, aiming to optimize the overall security of the system by learning statistical information collected from sensors. For instance, IoT systems may adopt deep learning to train a model that automatically identifies malicious behaviors to improve the self-protection performance.

- *Blockchain-based Security.* Blockchain technology provides decentralized and tamper-proof data management, which is suitable for security and tamper-proof requirements in the IoT. Thus, the blockchain ensures trust between devices and provides traceable data records that help prevent data tampering and malicious access and can effectively protect customers from data privacy breaches [91].
- *Privacy-Protection Technologies.* IoT devices provide personalized services by collecting and analyzing user data, which poses the risk of privacy leakage. Therefore, the future development of IoT security will inevitably focus more on privacy-protection techniques.

4. Energy-Aware Security Mechanisms in IoT

With the rapid growth of IoT systems, sensitive data protection and secure operation in IoT systems become essential to guard against potential cyber-threats. Another challenge requiring special attention is energy efficiency in resource-limited IoT devices and networks. In this regard, the notion of energy-aware security not only cuts back energy consumption but also supplies an effective means for maintaining security in resource-constrained IoT environments.

4.1. Energy–Security Trade-off in the IoT

There is an intrinsic conflict between security and energy efficiency in resource-constrained IoT systems. Traditional security approaches usually require intensive computation and communication, including complex cryptographic algorithms, key management, and authentication processes, which conflict with the energy efficiency of IoT devices. High energy-consuming operations desire frequent battery replacements, which is a non-negligible factor for jeopardizing the battery life of IoT devices. As IoT devices are widely deployed, this issue will exacerbate the high energy consumption of IoT devices, harming network infrastructure. Therefore, taking into account factors of energy consumption and device lifetime becomes indispensable when designing sustainable yet secure IoT systems.

4.2. Challenges of Implementing Energy-Aware Security

The implementation of energy-aware security in IoT systems is facing several challenges. First, resource constraints have emerged as a primary concern. For example, security algorithms running on IoT devices must be energy-efficient, since IoT devices typically are equipped with relatively limited computing power and storage capacity. Second, the heterogeneity discussed above poses a challenge to applying targeted security policies to an entire IoT system consisting of various devices of different functionality. Third, environmental dynamics and uncertainty compel IoT devices to operate in unpredictable and harsh environments, which require security mechanisms to be capable of securing devices under diverse conditions. Fourth, modern IoT systems must feature real-time monitoring and response, as well as quick adaption to cope with evolving cyber-threats. Therefore, gaining in-depth insights into these challenges for implementing energy-aware security mechanisms in IoT systems is desired to provide guidelines for further growth.

4.3. Approaches to Energy-Aware Security

The design principle of energy-aware security aims to minimize power consumption while ensuring system security for IoT systems. We outline the implementation of energy-aware security from five perspectives: hardware, network, software, application, and management. Figure 9 list an overview of the approaches we provide to future energy-aware security mechanisms.

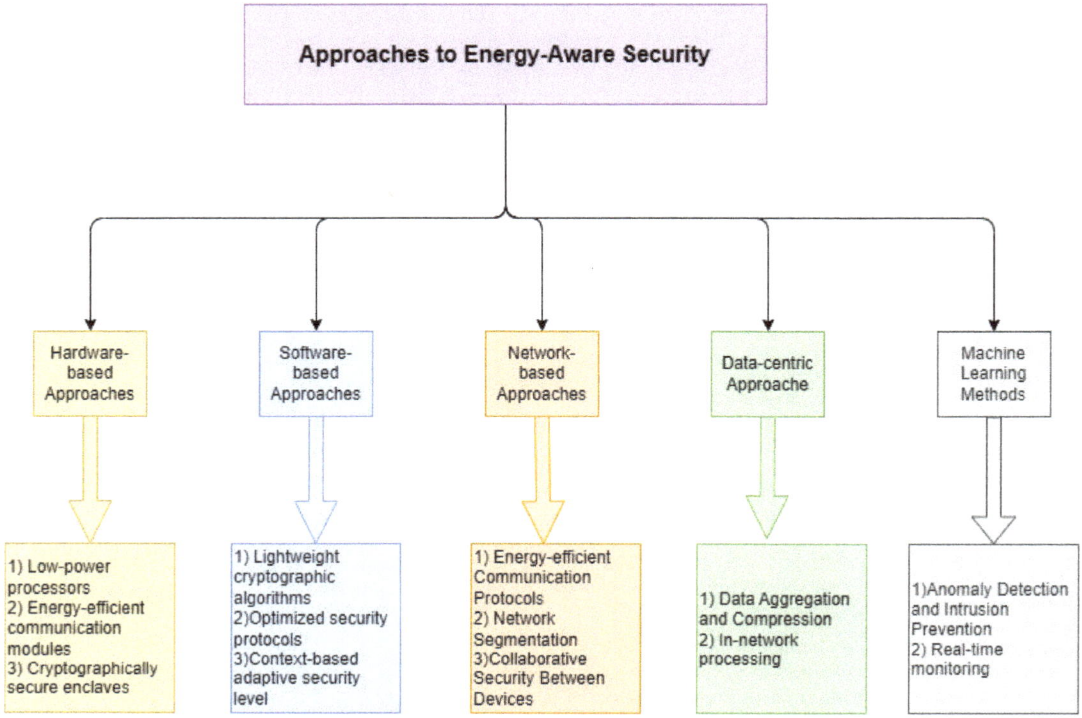

Figure 9. An overview of approaches to energy-aware security.

4.3.1. Hardware-Based Approaches

- *Low-power processors.* Low-power processor design aims to reduce the power consumption at an acceptable cost of performance degradation [92], which is widely used in mobile devices, as well as wearable and embedded systems. With low-power processors in place, devices gain longer battery life and better energy efficiency.
- *Energy-efficient communication modules.* Energy-efficient communication modules aim to reduce the power consumption of security operations, thereby ensuring security while achieving overall energy efficiency [93].
- *Cryptographically secure enclaves.* Cryptographically secure enclaves allow encryption and decryption operations to be executed efficiently at the hardware level. Applications executing in a secure enclave can reduce the demand for repetitive security checks and data encryption operations, thereby diminishing the power consumption.

4.3.2. Software-Based Approaches

- *Lightweight cryptographic algorithms.* Lightweight encryption algorithms are designed to utilize fewer computational resources when performing encryption and decryption operations to lower power consumption. This is extremely important for battery-powered devices, as these devices can perform security operations with a reduced amount of time and a lower energy consumption [94].
- *Optimized security protocols.* Optimized security protocols that require less computation can diminish the power consumption when performing security-related tasks. For example, security protocols for specific low-power communication standards, such as Bluetooth low-energy (BLE) security, can ensure secure communication with minimal energy consumption [95].
- *Context-based adaptive security levels.* Encryption algorithms that adaptively adjust the strength according to security requirements and energy availability are conducive

to achieving energy efficiency [96]. Specifically, When network conditions are stable or the data transmitted are non-sensitive, energy-efficient communication methods will be adopted. Conversely, when sensitive data need to be transmitted, secure but energy-intensive protocols will be utilized. Likewise, lower-strength encryption will be utilized in low-risk environments to conserve energy, whereas strong encryption algorithms will be adopted in high-risk environments to ensure data protection.

4.3.3. Network-Based Approaches

- *Energy-efficient Communication Protocols.* Energy-efficient communication protocols reduce packet sizes during data transmission to cut back on energy consumption. These protocols leverage effective data compression algorithms to diminish the number of communications. In addition, energy-efficient communication protocols harness optimized security mechanisms, such as lightweight encryption algorithms and efficient key management systems, for low-power environments.
- *Network Segmentation.* Network segmentation refers to monitoring and maintaining each segment independently in terms of security assurance. This security simplification facilitates reducing computational and communication activities, which in turn lowers power consumption.
- *Collaborative Security Between Devices.* Collaborative security mechanisms remove unnecessary security checks and response activities via information sharing and the collaborative analysis between devices, thereby conserving energy. Devices can also share security-processing tasks, such as distributed intrusion detection, to eliminate the burden on individual devices and thus remove power consumption.

4.3.4. Data-Centric Approaches

- *Data Aggregation and Compression.* This allows for data-processing tasks to be performed locally, thereby reducing data transmission, data leakage risks, network congestion, and power consumption.
- *In-network processing.* In-network processing reduces the amount of data transmitted to processing nodes over a network and thus conserves energy consumed for the communication between nodes.

4.3.5. Machine Learning Methods

- *Anomaly Detection and Intrusion Prevention.* Supervised learning algorithms can be used to identify types of attacks with high accuracy, whereas unsupervised learning algorithms are able to detect unknown, untagged attacks and anomalous behaviors. Pierpaolo et al. [97] demonstrated the outstanding effectiveness of machine learning (ML) models in identifying attacks, particularly in the realm of anomaly detection (binary classification) and anomaly classification (multi-class issues).
- *Real-Time Monitoring.* Based on historical energy usage data, ML models can be trained to identify patterns of energy wastage to facilitate designing energy-aware security policies. Additionally, ML models deployed on IoT devices can monitor incoming data streams to detect security threats in real-time while minimizing power consumption. For example, in IoT systems powered by federated learning algorithms, raw data are kept locally, with only model parameters transmitted to a central server or other devices (see Figure 10). By keeping sensitive data on local devices, federated learning reduces the risk of data leakage or unauthorized access, as well as the energy required to transfer large amounts of data [98].

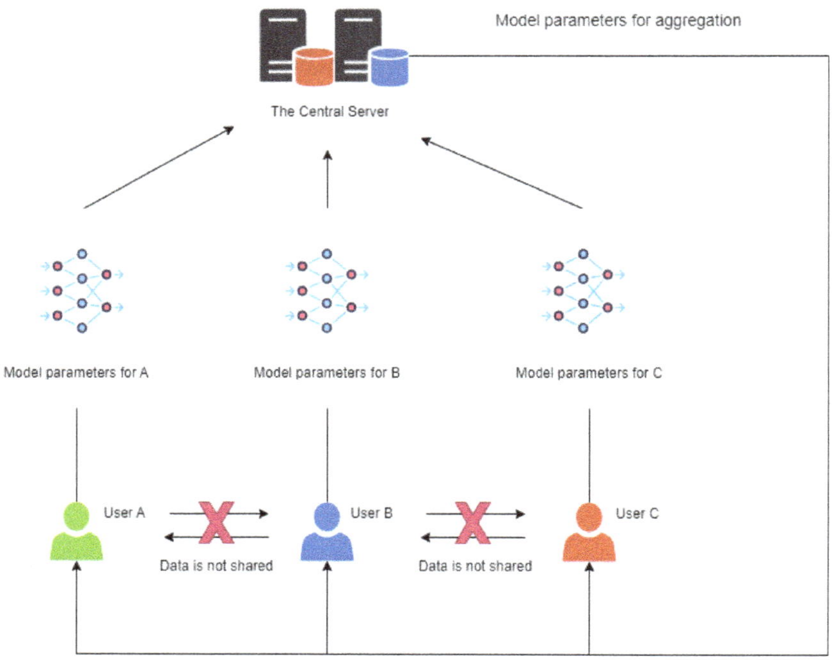

Figure 10. The structure of federated learning.

4.4. Case Studies

Bluetooth low-energy (BLE) technology finds extensive application in wearable devices. For example, Fitbit's wearable health tracker employs lightweight encryption to safeguard the transmission of user data, utilizing low-power Bluetooth (BLE) technology for synchronizing data with smartphones. Sports watches offer high-precision GPS tracking while maximizing battery usage through dynamic adjustments to the GPS frequency and the use of energy-efficient secure communication protocols.

Lightweight encryption algorithms are widely used in smart home devices, especially in resource-constrained devices, to strike a balance between security and energy efficiency. For example, the Advanced Encryption Standard (AES) is a symmetric block cipher scheme used to protect sensitive data [99], which is broadly employed in smart door locks. A smart door lock automatically enters sleep mode when the door is closed, and it wakes up only upon receiving a legitimate unlock command [100]. SimpliSafe, one of the most popular home security systems on the market today, employs secure TLS and elliptic curve encryption to protect video transmissions. Its cameras reduce power consumption by entering a low-energy standby state when no motion is detected [101].

Industrial sensors reshape the "sensing system" in Industry 4.0; improving the energy efficiency and security capabilities of sensing systems greatly stimulates IoT systems to progress toward the goal of energy-aware security. Intelligent industrial sensing has the capability to analyze, evaluate, and even adaptively learn to perform complex tasks, including image recognition, feature detection, and multi-dimensional detection. For example, Ching-ping et al. [102] proposed a sensor interface device crucial for sensor data acquisition in industrial wireless sensor networks (WSNs). This device utilizes a complex programmable logic device (CPLD) as the core controller application. CPLDs as the core controller greatly streamline the design of peripheral circuits and reduce the current consumption. Moreover, by adhering to the IEEE 1451.2 Smart Sensor Interface Specification standard [102], it ensures the secure and efficient acquisition of data from a variety of sensors, which is crucial for maintaining safety and promoting energy efficiency in industrial automation processes.

4.5. Future Directions and Open Research Questions

We delineate future research directions and open research questions in IoT energy-sensing security as the following emerging trends and promising areas (see Figure 11).

Figure 11. The future of energy-aware security in the IoT.

4.5.1. Energy-Harvesting Technologies

Given the necessity for future IoT devices to be more sustainable, energy-harvesting technologies will be a pivotal area of focus. Energy-harvesting technology is an environmentally friendly and innovative solution that extends the working life of sensors and, in some scenarios, can even completely replace traditional battery-powered methods. By optimizing the energy consumption and reducing the network maintenance costs, energy-harvesting technology offers both economic benefits and practical advantages [23]. Researchers will investigate methods to harness energy sources in the environment, such as solar, wind, and thermal energy, to deliver long-term stable power to devices. Emerging energy-harvesting materials, efficient conversion technologies, and strategies for integration with IoT devices to reduce the dependence on conventional batteries will also garner increased research attention.

4.5.2. Context-Aware Security

In the constantly changing environment of the IoT, context-aware security policies address the changing threats and challenges by utilizing contextual information about the surrounding environment to make security decisions [103]. Dynamic and smarter security measures should be proposed in response to dynamic changes in device states, environmental conditions, and threat levels. Sensors are the bridge for IoT devices to interact with the external environment, such as temperature, humidity, light, and motion, which can be used to collect context-awareness information. This involves assessing the context around the device in real-time through sensing technologies (e.g., image recognition, sensor data) and adapting security policies accordingly. For example, this includes increasing the level of security in high-risk environments while reducing power consumption in low-risk environments.

4.5.3. Blockchain-Based Security

Implementing secure and tamper-proof data-management systems with a minimal energy overhead will facilitate future breakthroughs in IoT security through the utilization of blockchain technology. The decentralized nature of the blockchain and its distributed ledger will offer enhanced data protection, particularly concerning secure data transfer and authentication among IoT devices [104].

4.5.4. Standardization and Interoperability

With the growing number of IoT devices, standardization and interoperability become increasingly crucial. E-learning in particular illustrates the predictability of this perspective: as IoT wearable devices such as smartwatches are widely used in education, it will be essential to establish strict security and privacy standards to ensure that all relevant devices and programs adhere to these privacy guidelines. In addition, the interoperability of IoT systems is demonstrated through the use of intelligent whiteboards and virtual reality (VR) technologies that enhance the interactivity of the learning experience and emphasize the value of seamless integration across devices and platforms [105]. Future research will concentrate on creating common frameworks and protocols to guarantee the efficient resource utilization across various IoT systems. This involves aligning security standards, communication protocols, and interoperability standards among devices to streamline complexity across the IoT ecosystem and enhance the system's overall security. These emerging trends will offer innovative solutions for energy-aware security in the IoT and propel the entire field toward greater intelligence, sustainability, and security.

Open research questions encompass balancing the costs and benefits of energy-harvesting technologies, addressing security challenges in dynamically changing environmental contexts, and striking a balance between flexibility and consistency in the standardization process. Exploring these questions will pave the way for future research directions, advancing the development of IoT energy-sensing security.

5. Concluding Remarks

5.1. Conclusions

While commonly used IoT applications enhance efficiency, automation, and convenience across various domains of life and industry, the future direction and current challenges in the IoT remain unclear. To this end, in this survey, we examined two critical factors—security and energy efficiency—affecting the utilization of the IoT. We explored the challenges that the IoT is encountering in these two domains. We scrutinized current solutions and technologies aimed at addressing these challenges. Moreover, we outlined a vision for the future of the IoT, emphasizing energy-aware security mechanisms. More specifically, we elaborated on the challenges encountered in realizing energy-aware security mechanisms, as well as the motivations and directions of future research.

Inspired by our vision of energy-aware security mechanisms, we aspire for advancements in the IoT to offer us the benefits of science and technology, while enhancing the security and safety of our data.

5.2. Limitations and Future Work

Although this paper provides a comprehensive overview and analysis of the application of security techniques in Internet of Things (IoT) systems, it must be acknowledged that there are some limitations. First, given the breadth and complexity of the IoT security domain, we have yet to be able to fully explore other essential specialized security techniques such as key management, information flow, and security audit. These techniques play an important role in protecting information systems from unauthorized access and data leakage. At the current stage, our review does not visually compare and evaluate the performance of existing methods in terms of energy-saving efficiency and safety by means of mathematical statistics, and we aspire that future studies will analyze and assess the proposed safety and energy-saving techniques in more depth, including but not limited to experimental validation and performance testing. In addition, the diverse application scenarios of the IoT imply that new energy-efficient technologies and strategies will continue to emerge, and we will continue to focus on emerging energy-efficient technologies and further explore the dynamic relationship between energy efficiency and security, in particular, we will aim to propose a framework on how to achieve higher energy efficiency without sacrificing security.

Author Contributions: Conceptualization—P.H., Y.Z. and X.Q.; writing original draft preparation—P.H.; original idea, review and editing—Y.Z. and X.Q. All authors have read and agreed to the published version of the manuscript.

Funding: Xiao Qin's work is supported by the National Aeronautics and Space Administration (Grant 80NSSC20M0044), the National Highway Traffic Safety Administration (Grant 451861-19158), the U.S. National Science Foundation (Grants IIS-1618669 and OAC-1642133), and Wright Media, LLC (Grant 240250).

Data Availability Statement: Data are contained within the article.

Conflicts of Interest: The authors declare no conflicts of interest.

References

1. Malik, P.K.; Sharma, R.; Singh, R.; Gehlot, A.; Satapathy, S.C.; Alnumay, W.S.; Pelusi, D.; Ghosh, U.; Nayak, J. Industrial Internet of Things and its applications in industry 4.0: State of the art. *Comput. Commun.* **2021**, *166*, 125–139. [CrossRef]
2. Yousefpour, A.; Fung, C.; Nguyen, T.; Kadiyala, K.; Jalali, F.; Niakanlahiji, A.; Kong, J.; Jue, J.P. All one needs to know about fog computing and related edge computing paradigms: A complete survey. *J. Syst. Archit.* **2019**, *98*, 289–330. [CrossRef]
3. Miller, M. *The Internet of Things: How Smart TVs, Smart Cars, Smart Homes, and Smart Cities Are Changing the World*; Pearson Education: London, UK, 2015.
4. Memić, B.; Džubur, A.H.; Avdagić-Golub, E. Green IoT: Sustainability environment and technologies. *Sci. Eng. Technol.* **2022**, *2*, 24–29. [CrossRef]
5. Georgakopoulos, D.; Jayaraman, P.P. Internet of things: From internet scale sensing to smart services. *Computing* **2016**, *98*, 1041–1058. [CrossRef]
6. Harrop, P. *Battery Elimination in Electronics and Electrical Engineering 2018–2028*; IDTechEx: Cambridge, UK, 2017.
7. Mrozik, W.; Rajaeifar, M.A.; Heidrich, O.; Christensen, P. Environmental impacts, pollution sources and pathways of spent lithium-ion batteries. *Energy Environ. Sci.* **2021**, *14*, 6099–6121. [CrossRef]
8. Raj, A.; Steingart, D. Power sources for the internet of things. *J. Electrochem. Soc.* **2018**, *165*, B3130. [CrossRef]
9. Tien, J.M. Internet of things, real-time decision making, and artificial intelligence. *Ann. Data Sci.* **2017**, *4*, 149–178. [CrossRef]
10. Stellios, I.; Kotzanikolaou, P.; Psarakis, M.; Alcaraz, C.; Lopez, J. A Survey of IoT-Enabled Cyberattacks: Assessing Attack Paths to Critical Infrastructures and Services. *IEEE Commun. Surv. Tutor.* **2018**, *20*, 3453–3495. [CrossRef]
11. Puschmann, D.; Barnaghi, P.; Tafazolli, R. Adaptive Clustering for Dynamic IoT Data Streams. *IEEE Internet Things J.* **2017**, *4*, 64–74. [CrossRef]
12. Ullah, R.; Ahmed, S.H.; Kim, B.S. Information-centric networking with edge computing for IoT: Research challenges and future directions. *IEEE Access* **2018**, *6*, 73465–73488. [CrossRef]
13. Chen, M.; Wan, J.; Li, F. Machine-to-machine communications: Architectures, standards and applications. *Ksii Trans. Internet Inf. Syst.* **2012**, *6*, 480–497. [CrossRef]
14. Gaidajis, G.; Angelakoglou, K.; Aktsoglou, D. E-waste: Environmental problems and current management. *J. Eng. Sci. Technol. Rev.* **2010**, *3*, 193–199. [CrossRef]
15. McKay, K.; Bassham, L.; Sönmez Turan, M.; Mouha, N. *Report on Lightweight Cryptography*; Technical Report; National Institute of Standards and Technology: Gaithersburg, MD, USA, 2016.
16. Lee, I.; Lee, K. The Internet of Things (IoT): Applications, investments, and challenges for enterprises. *Bus. Horiz.* **2015**, *58*, 431–440. [CrossRef]
17. Qiu, T.; Chen, N.; Li, K.; Atiquzzaman, M.; Zhao, W. How can heterogeneous internet of things build our future: A survey. *IEEE Commun. Surv. Tutor.* **2018**, *20*, 2011–2027. [CrossRef]
18. Al-Masri, E.; Kalyanam, K.R.; Batts, J.; Kim, J.; Singh, S.; Vo, T.; Yan, C. Investigating messaging protocols for the Internet of Things (IoT). *IEEE Access* **2020**, *8*, 94880–94911. [CrossRef]
19. Erdinc, O.; Vural, B.; Uzunoglu, M. A dynamic lithium-ion battery model considering the effects of temperature and capacity fading. In Proceedings of the 2009 International Conference on Clean Electrical Power 2009, Capri, Italy, 9–11 June 2009; IEEE: New York, NY, USA, 2009; pp. 383–386.
20. Azari, A.; Stefanović, Č.; Popovski, P.; Cavdar, C. On the Latency-Energy Performance of NB-IoT Systems in Providing Wide-Area IoT Connectivity. *IEEE Trans. Green Commun. Netw.* **2020**, *4*, 57–68. [CrossRef]
21. Al-Janabi, T.A.; Al-Raweshidy, H.S. An Energy Efficient Hybrid MAC Protocol With Dynamic Sleep-Based Scheduling for High Density IoT Networks. *IEEE Internet Things J.* **2019**, *6*, 2273–2287. [CrossRef]
22. Chulde, C.H.; Cantero, J.P. Internet of Things implementation with nodes based on low-power microcontroller MSP430. In Proceedings of the 2017 International Conference on Information Systems and Computer Science (INCISCOS), Quito, Ecuador, 23–25 November 2017; IEEE: New York, NY, USA, 2017; pp. 33–40.

23. Sanislav, T.; Mois, G.D.; Zeadally, S.; Folea, S.C. Energy harvesting techniques for internet of things (IoT). *IEEE Access* **2021**, *9*, 39530–39549. [CrossRef]
24. Kaur, N.; Sood, S.K. An Energy-Efficient Architecture for the Internet of Things (IoT). *IEEE Syst. J.* **2017**, *11*, 796–805. [CrossRef]
25. Kim, N.; Austin, T.; Baauw, D.; Mudge, T.; Flautner, K.; Hu, J.; Irwin, M.; Kandemir, M.; Narayanan, V. Leakage current: Moore's law meets static power. *Computer* **2003**, *36*, 68–75. [CrossRef]
26. Jiang, H.; Marek-Sadowska, M.; Nassif, S. Benefits and costs of power-gating technique. In Proceedings of the 2005 International Conference on Computer Design, San Jose, CA, USA, 2–5 October 2005; IEEE: New York, NY, USA, 2005; pp. 559–566. [CrossRef]
27. Zhuo, C.; Luo, S.; Gan, H.; Hu, J.; Shi, Z. Noise-Aware DVFS for Efficient Transitions on Battery-Powered IoT Devices. *IEEE Trans. Comput.-Aided Des. Integr. Circuits Syst.* **2020**, *39*, 1498–1510. [CrossRef]
28. Dunkels, A.; Gronvall, B.; Voigt, T. Contiki—A lightweight and flexible operating system for tiny networked sensors. In Proceedings of the 29th Annual IEEE International Conference on Local Computer Networks, Tampa, FL, USA, 16–18 November 2004; IEEE: New York, NY, USA, 2004; pp. 455–462. [CrossRef]
29. Santana, T.V.; Galindo-Serrano, A.; Sayrac, B.; López, S.M. Dynamic network configuration: Hotspot identification for Virtual Small Cells. In Proceedings of the 2016 International Symposium on Wireless Communication Systems (ISWCS), Poznan, Poland, 20–23 September 2016; IEEE: New York, NY, USA, 2016; pp. 49–53. [CrossRef]
30. Gomez, C.; Oller, J.; Paradells, J. Overview and evaluation of bluetooth low energy: An emerging low-power wireless technology. *Sensors* **2012**, *12*, 11734–11753. [CrossRef]
31. Mekki, K.; Bajic, E.; Chaxel, F.; Meyer, F. A comparative study of LPWAN technologies for large-scale IoT deployment. *ICT Express* **2019**, *5*, 1–7. [CrossRef]
32. Qiao, L.; Zheng, Z.; Cui, W.; Wang, L. A survey on WiFi HaLow technology for Internet of Things. In Proceedings of the 2018 2nd IEEE Conference on Energy Internet and Energy System Integration (EI2), Beijing, China, 20–22 October 2018; IEEE: New York, NY, USA, 2018; pp. 1–5.
33. Adame, T.; Bel, A.; Bellalta, B.; Barcelo, J.; Oliver, M. IEEE 802.11AH: The WiFi approach for M2M communications. *IEEE Wirel. Commun.* **2014**, *21*, 144–152. [CrossRef]
34. Gambier, P.; Anton, S.; Kong, N.; Erturk, A.; Inman, D. Piezoelectric, solar and thermal energy harvesting for hybrid low-power generator systems with thin-film batteries. *Meas. Sci. Technol.* **2011**, *23*, 015101. [CrossRef]
35. Wu, J.; Tran, N.K. Application of blockchain technology in sustainable energy systems: An overview. *Sustainability* **2018**, *10*, 3067. [CrossRef]
36. Wood, A.D.; Stankovic, J.A. Denial of service in sensor networks. *Computer* **2002**, *35*, 54–62. [CrossRef]
37. Osanaiye, O.; Choo, K.K.R.; Dlodlo, M. Distributed denial of service (DDoS) resilience in cloud: Review and conceptual cloud DDoS mitigation framework. *J. Netw. Comput. Appl.* **2016**, *67*, 147–165. [CrossRef]
38. Zargar, S.T.; Joshi, J.; Tipper, D. A survey of defense mechanisms against distributed denial of service (DDoS) flooding attacks. *IEEE Commun. Surv. Tutor.* **2013**, *15*, 2046–2069. [CrossRef]
39. Sacramento, L.; Medeiros, I.; Bota, J.; Correia, M. Flowhacker: Detecting unknown network attacks in big traffic data using network flows. In Proceedings of the 2018 17th IEEE International Conference on Trust, Security and Privacy in Computing Additionally, Communications/12th IEEE International Conference on Big Data Science and Engineering (TrustCom/BigDataSE), New York, NY, USA, 1–3 August 2018; IEEE: New York, NY, USA, 2018; pp. 567–572.
40. Groza, B.; Minea, M. Formal modelling and automatic detection of resource exhaustion attacks. In Proceedings of the 6th ACM Symposium on Information, Computer and Communications Security, Hong Kong, China, 22–24 March 2011; Association for Computing Machinery: New York, NY, USA, 2011; pp. 326–333.
41. Mansfield-Devine, S. The evolution of DDoS. *Comput. Fraud Secur.* **2014**, *2014*, 15–20. [CrossRef]
42. Janes, B.; Crawford, H.; OConnor, T. Never ending story: Authentication and access control design flaws in shared IoT devices. In Proceedings of the 2020 IEEE Security and Privacy Workshops (SPW), San Francisco, CA, USA, 21 May 2020; IEEE: New York, NY, USA, 2020; pp. 104–109.
43. Bagga, M.; Thakral, P.; Bagga, T. A Study on IoT: Model, Communication Protocols, Security Hazards & Countermeasures. In Proceedings of the 2018 Fifth International Conference on Parallel, Distributed and Grid Computing (PDGC), Solan, India, 20–22 December 2018; IEEE: New York, NY, USA, 2018; pp. 591–598.
44. Bakhshi, T.; Ghita, B.; Kuzminykh, I. A Review of IoT Firmware Vulnerabilities and Auditing Techniques. *Sensors* **2024**, *24*, 708. [CrossRef] [PubMed]
45. Albalawi, A.; Almrshed, A.; Badhib, A.; Alshehri, S. A Survey on Authentication Techniques for the Internet of Things. In Proceedings of the 2019 International Conference on Computer and Information Sciences (ICCIS), Sakaka, Saudi Arabia, 3–4 April 2019; IEEE: New York, NY, USA, 2019; pp. 1–5. [CrossRef]
46. Shivraj, V.; Rajan, M.; Singh, M.; Balamuralidhar, P. One time password authentication scheme based on elliptic curves for Internet of Things (IoT). In Proceedings of the 2015 5th National Symposium on Information Technology: Towards New Smart World (NSITNSW), Riyadh, Saudi Arabia, 17–19 February 2015; IEEE: New York, NY, USA, 2015; pp. 1–6.
47. Sidhu, S.; Mohd, B.J.; Hayajneh, T. Hardware security in IoT devices with emphasis on hardware trojans. *J. Sens. Actuator Netw.* **2019**, *8*, 42. [CrossRef]
48. Mavrovouniotis, S.; Ganley, M. Hardware security modules. In *Secure Smart Embedded Devices, Platforms and Applications*; Springer: Berlin/Heidelberg, Germany, 2013; pp. 383–405.

49. Raymundo Belleza, R.; de Freitas Pignaton, E. Performance study of real-time operating systems for internet of things devices. *IET Softw.* **2018**, *12*, 176–182. [CrossRef]
50. Liu, Y.; Briones, J.; Zhou, R.; Magotra, N. Study of secure boot with a FPGA-based IoT device. In Proceedings of the 2017 IEEE 60th International Midwest Symposium on Circuits and Systems (MWSCAS), Boston, MA, USA, 6–9 August 2017; IEEE: New York, NY, USA, 2017; pp. 1053–1056.
51. Simon, T.; Batina, L.; Daemen, J.; Grosso, V.; Massolino, P.M.C.; Papagiannopoulos, K.; Regazzoni, F.; Samwel, N. Friet: An authenticated encryption scheme with built-in fault detection. In Proceedings of the Annual International Conference on the Theory and Applications of Cryptographic Techniques 2020, Zagreb, Croatia, 10–14 May 2020; Springer: Berlin/Heidelberg, Germany, 2020; pp. 581–611.
52. Zhao, S.; Zhang, Q.; Qin, Y.; Feng, W.; Feng, D. Sectee: A software-based approach to secure enclave architecture using tee. In Proceedings of the 2019 ACM SIGSAC Conference on Computer and Communications Security, London, UK, 11–15 November 2019; Association for Computing Machinery: New York, NY, USA, 2019; pp. 1723–1740.
53. Arthur, W.; Challener, D.; Goldman, K. *A Practical Guide to TPM 2.0: Using the New Trusted Platform Module in the New Age of Security*; Springer Nature: Berlin, Germany, 2015.
54. Al Fardan, N.J.; Paterson, K.G. Lucky Thirteen: Breaking the TLS and DTLS Record Protocols. In Proceedings of the 2013 IEEE Symposium on Security and Privacy, Berkeley, CA, USA, 19–22 May 2013; IEEE: New York, NY, USA, 2013; pp. 526–540. [CrossRef]
55. Freier, A.; Karlton, P.; Kocher, P. The Secure Sockets Layer (SSL) Protocol Version 3.0. Technical Report. 2011. Available online: https://www.rfc-editor.org/rfc/rfc6101.html (accessed on 1 March 2024).
56. Durumeric, Z.; Kasten, J.; Bailey, M.; Halderman, J.A. Analysis of the HTTPS certificate ecosystem. In Proceedings of the 2013 Conference on Internet Measurement Conference, Barcelona, Spain, 23–25 October 2013; Association for Computing Machinery: New York, NY, USA, 2013; pp. 291–304.
57. Sicari, S.; Rizzardi, A.; Grieco, L.A.; Coen-Porisini, A. Security, privacy and trust in Internet of Things: The road ahead. *Comput. Netw.* **2015**, *76*, 146–164. [CrossRef]
58. Tian, Y.; Xu, K.; Ansari, N. TCP in wireless environments: Problems and solutions. *IEEE Commun. Mag.* **2005**, *43*, S27–S32. [CrossRef]
59. Al-Fuqaha, A.; Guizani, M.; Mohammadi, M.; Aledhari, M.; Ayyash, M. Internet of things: A survey on enabling technologies, protocols, and applications. *IEEE Commun. Surv. Tutor.* **2015**, *17*, 2347–2376. [CrossRef]
60. Shif, L.; Wang, F.; Lung, C.H. Improvement of security and scalability for IoT network using SD-VPN. In Proceedings of the NOMS 2018—2018 IEEE/IFIP Network Operations and Management Symposium, Taipei, Taiwan, 23–27 April 2018; IEEE: New York, NY, USA, 2018; pp. 1–5. [CrossRef]
61. Butun, I.; Morgera, S.D.; Sankar, R. A Survey of Intrusion Detection Systems in Wireless Sensor Networks. *IEEE Commun. Surv. Tutor.* **2014**, *16*, 266–282. [CrossRef]
62. Liao, H.J.; Richard Lin, C.H.; Lin, Y.C.; Tung, K.Y. Intrusion detection system: A comprehensive review. *J. Netw. Comput. Appl.* **2013**, *36*, 16–24. [CrossRef]
63. Bhatt, S.; Manadhata, P.K.; Zomlot, L. The Operational Role of Security Information and Event Management Systems. *IEEE Secur. Priv.* **2014**, *12*, 35–41. [CrossRef]
64. Samrin, R.; Vasumathi, D. Review on anomaly based network intrusion detection system. In Proceedings of the 2017 International Conference on Electrical, Electronics, Communication, Computer, and Optimization Techniques (ICEECCOT), Mysuru, India, 15–16 December 2017; IEEE: New York, NY, USA, 2017; pp. 141–147. [CrossRef]
65. Frahim, J.; Santos, O.; Ossipov, A. *Cisco ASA: All-in-One Firewall, IPS, and VPN Adaptive Security Appliance*; Pearson Education: London, UK, 2014.
66. Kwon, S.; Choi, H.K. Evolution of WiFi Protected Access: Security Challenges. *IEEE Consum. Electron. Mag.* **2021**, *10*, 74–81. [CrossRef]
67. Meng, N.; Nagy, S.; Yao, D.; Zhuang, W.; Argoty, G.A. Secure coding practices in java: Challenges and vulnerabilities. In Proceedings of the 40th International Conference on Software Engineering, Gothenburg, Sweden, 27 May–3 June 2018; Association for Computing Machinery: New York, NY, USA, 2018; pp. 372–383.
68. Hatzivasilis, G. Password-hashing status. *Cryptography 2017, 1*; Molecular Diversity Preservation International (MDPI): Basel, Switzerland, 2017; p. 10.
69. Smirnov, A.; Chiueh, T.C. Automatic patch generation for buffer overflow attacks. In Proceedings of the Third International Symposium on Information Assurance and Security, Manchester, UK, 29–31 August 2007; IEEE: New York, NY, USA, 2007; pp. 165–170.
70. Meneely, A.; Tejeda, A.C.R.; Spates, B.; Trudeau, S.; Neuberger, D.; Whitlock, K.; Ketant, C.; Davis, K. An empirical investigation of socio-technical code review metrics and security vulnerabilities. In Proceedings of the 6th International Workshop on Social Software Engineering, Hong Kong, China, 17 November 2014; Association for Computing Machinery: New York, NY, USA, 2014; pp. 37–44.
71. Fonseca, J.; Vieira, M. A survey on secure software development lifecycles. In *Software Development Techniques for Constructive Information Systems Design*; IGI Global: Hershey, PA, USA, 2013; pp. 57–73.

72. Schumacher, M. *Security Engineering with Patterns: Origins, Theoretical Models, and New Applications*; Springer Science & Business Media: Berlin, Germany, 2003; Volume 2754.
73. Schagen, N.; Koning, K.; Bos, H.; Giuffrida, C. Towards automated vulnerability scanning of network servers. In Proceedings of the 11th European Workshop on Systems Security, Porto, Portugal, 23–26 April 2018; Association for Computing Machinery: New York, NY, USA, 2018; pp. 1–6.
74. Casey, E.; Stellatos, G.J. The impact of full disk encryption on digital forensics. *ACM SIGOPS Oper. Syst. Rev.* **2008**, *42*, 93–98. [CrossRef]
75. Shmueli, E.; Vaisenberg, R.; Gudes, E.; Elovici, Y. Implementing a database encryption solution, design and implementation issues. *Comput. Secur.* **2014**, *44*, 33–50. [CrossRef]
76. Ometov, A.; Petrov, V.; Bezzateev, S.; Andreev, S.; Koucheryavy, Y.; Gerla, M. Challenges of multi-factor authentication for securing advanced IoT applications. *IEEE Netw.* **2019**, *33*, 82–88. [CrossRef]
77. Siriwardena, P. *Advanced API Security*; Apress: New York, NY, USA, 2014.
78. Sidorov, V.; Ng, W.K. Transparent data encryption for data-in-use and data-at-rest in a cloud-based database-as-a-service solution. In Proceedings of the 2015 IEEE World Congress on Services, New York, NY, USA, 27 June–2 July 2015; IEEE: New York, NY, USA, 2015; pp. 221–228.
79. Ghouse, M.; Nene, M.J.; Vembuselvi, C. Data leakage prevention for data in transit using artificial intelligence and encryption techniques. In Proceedings of the 2019 International Conference on Advances in Computing, Communication and Control (ICAC3), Mumbai, India, 20–21 December 2019; IEEE: New York, NY, USA, 2019; pp. 1–6.
80. He, W.; Golla, M.; Padhi, R.; Ofek, J.; Dürmuth, M.; Fernandes, E.; Ur, B. Rethinking Access Control and Authentication for the Home Internet of Things ({{{{{IoT}}}}}). In Proceedings of the 27th USENIX Security Symposium (USENIX Security 18), Baltimore, MD, USA, 15–17 August 2018; USENIX Association: Berkeley, CA, USA, 2018; pp. 255–272.
81. Sandhu, R.S. Role-based access control. In *Advances in Computers*; Elsevier: Amsterdam, The Netherlands, 1998; Volume 46, pp. 237–286.
82. Mao, B.; Kawamoto, Y.; Liu, J.; Kato, N. Harvesting and threat aware security configuration strategy for IEEE 802.15. 4 based IoT networks. *IEEE Commun. Lett.* **2019**, *23*, 2130–2134. [CrossRef]
83. Xie, W.; Jiang, Y.; Tang, Y.; Ding, N.; Gao, Y. Vulnerability detection in iot firmware: A survey. In Proceedings of the 2017 IEEE 23rd International Conference on Parallel and Distributed Systems (ICPADS), Shenzhen, China, 15–17 December 2017; IEEE: New York, NY, USA, 2017; pp. 769–772.
84. Nilsson, D.K.; Larson, U.E. Secure firmware updates over the air in intelligent vehicles. In Proceedings of the ICC Workshops-2008 IEEE International Conference on Communications Workshops, Beijing, China, 19–23 May 2008; IEEE: New York, NY, USA, 2008; pp. 380–384.
85. Mugarza, I.; Flores, J.L.; Montero, J.L. Security issues and software updates management in the industrial internet of things (iiot) era. *Sensors* **2020**, *20*, 7160. [CrossRef]
86. Okhravi, H.; Nicol, D. Evaluation of patch management strategies. *Int. J. Comput. Intell. Theory Pract.* **2008**, *3*, 109–117.
87. Schlette, D.; Caselli, M.; Pernul, G. A comparative study on cyber threat intelligence: The security incident response perspective. *IEEE Commun. Surv. Tutor.* **2021**, *23*, 2525–2556. [CrossRef]
88. Shinde, N.; Kulkarni, P. Cyber incident response and planning: A flexible approach. *Comput. Fraud Secur.* **2021**, *2021*, 14–19. [CrossRef]
89. Neisse, R.; Steri, G.; Baldini, G. Enforcement of security policy rules for the internet of things. In Proceedings of the 2014 IEEE 10th International Conference on Wireless and Mobile Computing, Networking and Communications (WiMob), Larnaca, Cyprus, 8–10 October 2014; IEEE: New York, NY, USA, 2014; pp. 165–172.
90. Usman, M.; Ahmed, I.; Aslam, M.I.; Khan, S.; Shah, U.A. SIT: A lightweight encryption algorithm for secure internet of things. *arXiv* **2017**, arXiv:1704.08688.
91. Monrat, A.A.; Schelén, O.; Andersson, K. A survey of blockchain from the perspectives of applications, challenges, and opportunities. *IEEE Access* **2019**, *7*, 117134–117151. [CrossRef]
92. Ekanayake, V.; Kelly IV, C.; Manohar, R. An ultra low-power processor for sensor networks. In Proceedings of the 11th International Conference on Architectural Support for Programming Languages and Operating Systems, Boston, MA, USA, 7–13 October 2004; Association for Computing Machinery: New York, NY, USA, 2004; pp. 27–36.
93. Li, T.; Zhang, J.; Obaidat, M.S.; Lin, C.; Lin, Y.; Shen, Y.; Ma, J. Energy-efficient and secure communication toward UAV networks. *IEEE Internet Things J.* **2021**, *9*, 10061–10076. [CrossRef]
94. Thakor, V.A.; Razzaque, M.A.; Khandaker, M.R. Lightweight cryptography algorithms for resource-constrained IoT devices: A review, comparison and research opportunities. *IEEE Access* **2021**, *9*, 28177–28193. [CrossRef]
95. Potlapally, N.R.; Ravi, S.; Raghunathan, A.; Jha, N.K. A study of the energy consumption characteristics of cryptographic algorithms and security protocols. *IEEE Trans. Mob. Comput.* **2005**, *5*, 128–143. [CrossRef]
96. Nawrocki, P.; Sniezynski, B.; Kolodziej, J.; Szynkiewicz, P. Adaptive context-aware energy optimization for services on mobile devices with use of machine learning considering security aspects. In Proceedings of the 2020 20th IEEE/ACM International Symposium on Cluster, Cloud and Internet Computing (CCGRID), Melbourne, VIC, Australia, 11–14 May 2020; IEEE: New York, NY, USA, 2020; pp. 708–717. [CrossRef]

97. Dini, P.; Elhanashi, A.; Begni, A.; Saponara, S.; Zheng, Q.; Gasmi, K. Overview on Intrusion Detection Systems Design Exploiting Machine Learning for Networking Cybersecurity. *Appl. Sci.* **2023**, *13*, 7507. [CrossRef]
98. McMahan, B.; Moore, E.; Ramage, D.; Hampson, S.; y Arcas, B.A. Communication-efficient learning of deep networks from decentralized data. In Proceedings of the Artificial Intelligence and Statistics, Fort Lauderdale, FL, USA, 20–22 April 2017; pp. 1273–1282.
99. Sultan, I.; Mir, B.J.; Banday, M.T. Analysis and Optimization of Advanced Encryption Standard for the Internet of Things. In Proceedings of the 2020 7th International Conference on Signal Processing and Integrated Networks (SPIN), Noida, India, 27–28 February 2020; IEEE: New York, NY, USA, 2020; pp. 571–575.
100. Ahtsham, M.; Yan, H.Y.; Ali, U. IoT based door lock surveillance system using cryptographic algorithms. In Proceedings of the 2019 IEEE 16th International Conference on Networking, Sensing and Control (ICNSC), Banff, AB, Canada, 9–11 May 2019; IEEE: New York, NY, USA, 2019; pp. 448–453.
101. Hutchinson, S.; Stanković, M.; Ho, S.; Houshmand, S.; Karabiyik, U. Investigating the Privacy and Security of the SimpliSafe Security System on Android and iOS. *J. Cybersecur. Priv.* **2023**, *3*, 145–165. [CrossRef]
102. Chi, Q.; Yan, H.; Zhang, C.; Pang, Z.; Da Xu, L. A reconfigurable smart sensor interface for industrial WSN in IoT environment. *IEEE Trans. Ind. Inform.* **2014**, *10*, 1417–1425.
103. Ramos, J.L.H.; Bernabe, J.B.; Skarmeta, A.F. Managing context information for adaptive security in IoT environments. In Proceedings of the 2015 IEEE 29th International Conference on Advanced Information Networking and Applications Workshops, Gwangiu, Republic of Korea, 24–27 March 2015; IEEE: New York, NY, USA, 2015; pp. 676–681.
104. Ferrag, M.A.; Shu, L. The performance evaluation of blockchain-based security and privacy systems for the Internet of Things: A tutorial. *IEEE Internet Things J.* **2021**, *8*, 17236–17260. [CrossRef]
105. Bakhouyi, A.; Dehbi, R.; Talea, M.; Hajoui, O. Evolution of standardization and interoperability on E-learning systems: An overview. In Proceedings of the 2017 16th International Conference on Information Technology Based Higher Education and Training (ITHET), Ohrid, Macedonia, 10–12 July 2017; IEEE: New York, NY, USA, 2017; pp. 1–8. [CrossRef]

future internet

MDPI

Article

Smart Grid Security: A PUF-Based Authentication and Key Agreement Protocol

Nasour Bagheri [1,†], Ygal Bendavid [2,*,†], Masoumeh Safkhani [3,†] and Samad Rostampour [4,†]

1 Electrical Engineering Department, Shahid Rajaee Teacher Training University (SRTTU), Tehran 16788-15811, Iran; nbagheri@sru.ac.ir
2 AOTI Department, School of Management, Université du Québec à Montréal (UQAM), Montreal, QC H2X 1L7, Canada
3 Computer Engineering Department, Shahid Rajaee Teacher Training University (SRTTU), Tehran 16788-15811, Iran; safkhani@sru.ac.ir
4 Computer Science Department, Vanier College, Montreal, QC H4L3X9, Canada; rostamps@vaniercollege.qc.ca
* Correspondence: bendavid.ygal@uqam.ca
† These authors contributed equally to this work.

Abstract: A smart grid is an electricity network that uses advanced technologies to facilitate the exchange of information and electricity between utility companies and customers. Although most of the technologies involved in such grids have reached maturity, smart meters—as connected devices—introduce new security challenges. To overcome this significant obstacle to grid modernization, safeguarding privacy has emerged as a paramount concern. In this paper, we begin by evaluating the security levels of recently proposed authentication methods for smart meters. Subsequently, we introduce an enhanced protocol named PPSG, designed for smart grids, which incorporates physical unclonable functions (PUF) and an elliptic curve cryptography (ECC) module to address the vulnerabilities identified in previous approaches. Our security analysis, utilizing a real-or-random (RoR) model, demonstrates that PPSG effectively mitigates the weaknesses found in prior methods. To assess the practicality of PPSG, we conduct simulations using an Arduino UNO board, measuring computation, communication, and energy costs. Our results, including a processing time of 153 ms, a communication cost of 1376 bits, and an energy consumption of 13.468 mJ, align with the requirements of resource-constrained devices within smart grids.

Keywords: smart grid; smart meter; authentication; Internet of Things; security; elliptic curve cryptography

1. Introduction

As COP28 concluded in the UAE to accelerate climate action and gradually transition to a decarbonized energy system, the evolution and modernization of existing grids with new technologies are positioned as key enablers to this increasingly urgent transition [1]. Aging power infrastructures are being modernized to meet growing demand for electricity and efficiently distribute both traditional and renewable energy while also meeting the environmental imperative to reduce greenhouse gas emissions and ensure sustainable growth. In this context, along with other low-less carbon technologies (e.g., nuclear power, thermal and hydro-energy, solar photovoltaic power, and wind energy), utilities are responding to this challenge by investing in smart grids (SG) to ensure a safe and reliable supply of electricity.

Smart grids are electricity networks that use digital technologies, sensors, and software to better match the supply and demand of electricity in real time while minimizing costs and maintaining the stability and reliability of the grid [2]. This network integrates advanced metering devices, information and communication technologies (ICT), demand response mechanisms, and real-time control systems. This shift towards smart grids is part of a broader trend observed in the electricity sector, integrating with remote sensing, cloud computing, and the Internet of Things (IoT). Within this context, IoT technologies are instrumental in transforming the sector from a centralized to a distributed, smart, and integrated energy system [3]. Indeed, in the age of digital transformation, IoT-enabled smart grids empower utilities to sense, analyze, control, and optimize their grids and explore new revenue streams by building innovative business models.

Among the components shaping this transformation in the electricity sector, grid sensors such as smart meters (SMs) not only monitor and transmit electricity consumption data to utility offices but also eliminate the need for manual meter readings. Indeed, SMs, as connected devices, automatically communicate with gateways such as neighborhood area networks (NANs) or other base stations using various communication technologies, such as LoraWAN, cellular, or satellite. SMs capture the date and time of electricity consumption, allowing the implementation of effective energy management systems. For instance, dynamic pricing strategies, where utilities charge higher rates during peak demand periods, enable consumers and businesses to manage their energy consumption remotely, shifting it to off-peak hours when costs are lower. Additionally, smart meters enhance utility services by detecting tampering and theft, offering faster responses to meter failures and power outages. The interest in efficient and accurate metering solutions is reflected by the smart meters market size (gas, water, and electricity), which surpassed USD 22 billion in 2021 and is expected to grow at a CAGR of 13 percent between 2022 and 2028. [4]. Electricity metering has the largest share of this market, with over 60 percent of the global market value [5].

While SMs play a vital role in efficient energy management, their intricate design introduces new security challenges. The ability of smart meters to communicate with nearby IoT devices raises concerns about grid resilience in the face of potential disruptions leading to increased operational costs loss of productivity and loss of sales as well as [6] user security and privacy. Hackers could potentially access personal data and exploit the system for financial gains. Consequently, ensuring privacy has become a top priority in the realm of smart metering.

From a professional perspective, one recent benchmark study from IANS and Artico cited in VentureBeat found that utilities spent an average of 8% of their IT budgets on cybersecurity in 2022, highlighting the importance of this critical domain [7].

From an academic perspective, in recent years, extensive research has been conducted to secure the infrastructure of smart grids. In a review of cyber attacks and defense mechanisms for improving security in smart grid energy systems, Ghiasi et al. point out the expanding use of multiple sensors, controllers, meters, and wireless networks to control and transmit data, suggesting that the issues caused by cyber attacks on these heterogeneous types of infrastructures should receive more attention. They also call for researchers to keep pace with different methods of detecting cyber attacks and develop up-to-date countermeasures—among which they suggest updating or creating new protocols to prevent the access of attackers to the grid [8]. Similarly, Kamrul Hasan et al. conducted a review on cyber-physical and cyber-security systems in smart grid. The authors focus on the increased complexity of managing the security aspects of the grids due to the challenging combination of communication technology, standards, protocols, and applications. To reduce security threats and increase the system's reliability, they also propose to look at security requirements from a defense life cycle (pre-attack, under attack, and post-attack) where, at each phase, different techniques can be used [9].

To address these concerns, the community of researchers proposes various cybersecurity protocols. However, many existing designs suffer from security vulnerabilities. In this paper, we propose a new protocol for smart metering systems to address issues found in existing protocols and enhance the efficiency of smart grids.

1.1. Our Contributions

This paper has two main contributions, as follows:

1. We contribute to the literature on smart meter security by proposing a new protocol based on PUFs and ECC for smart grids named PPSG.
2. We provide an in-depth security analysis (with a real-or-random model) for the proposed protocol and also the communication and communication overheads analysis (with an Arduino UNO R3 board) to show that it is among the lightest protocols, compared to the recent related proposals.

1.2. Paper Organization

In the rest of the paper, first, we analyze the existing protocols in Section 2; in Section 3, the required preliminaries are provided. Next, we propose PPSG as a secure protocol in Section 4. The security evaluation of PPSG is detailed in Section 5, and the comprehensive cost analysis is provided in Section 6. The concluding remarks and summary of the paper can be found in Section 7.

2. Related Work

In this section, some recent protocols are described. In Table 1, every protocol is evaluated considering communication overhead, time-consuming processes, encryption techniques, and vulnerability. The assessment is represented by triangles (▼ for low and ▲ for high). A check mark (✓) indicates a documented successful attack, whereas a multiplication symbol (×) signifies an attack not yet published. Interest in the subject is reflected in the number of publications, which have increased exponentially over the last decade, particularly in the field of cyber security, which remains a major concern [10]. Recently substantial efforts have been directed towards establishing a reliable and secure communication infrastructure for smart metering. For example, Kumar et al. introduced the LAKA system, a lightweight authentication and key agreement scheme, aimed at ensuring an acceptable level of security and integrity in smart energy networks [11]. To ensure the confidentiality of messages, LAKA incorporates both hash functions and an ECC module. Moreover, it employs a message authentication code (MAC) function to maintain message integrity. This integration of multiple functions contributes to the heightened complexity of the smart meter (SM). Furthermore, as observed by Baghestani et al. [12], this protocol exhibits susceptibility to traceability attacks.

Kumar et al. introduced ECCAuth, a recent authentication protocol for smart grid applications that relies on ECC cryptography [13]. According to the authors, ECCAuth's primary objective is to establish a secure connection between a smart grid (SG) device and a utility center (UC), ensuring user privacy and the confidentiality of data. Nevertheless, ECCAuth, while maintaining acceptable communication costs, exhibits time-consuming authentication procedures and computational operations. Furthermore, ECCAuth's vulnerability has been exposed by Yu et al., who identified security weaknesses, including session key disclosure, stolen devices, and masquerade, attacks [14]. In response, they proposed a new lightweight protocol that incorporates XOR and hash functions to rectify these shortcomings. Wu et al. also suggested an ECC-based authentication protocol [15]. Although it secures message confidentiality through an ECC module and data encryption, the protocol's functionality falls short of an acceptable level. Notably, it exhibits high communication and computation overhead, leading to extended authentication processing times. Garg et al. recently introduced another authentication protocol for SMs based on the ECC method [16]. Despite their claim of robustness against diverse attacks and reasonable computational expenses, our assessment highlights susceptibility to traceability and impersonation attacks. Additionally, the authors inaccurately calculated and underestimated computational costs.

By utilizing the ECC technique, He et al. [17], Abbasinezhad-Mood [18], and PALK [19] also proposed some protocols, aiming to establish a secure infrastructure. However, they face efficiency challenges, which will be discussed in detail in Section 6.

Tanveer et al. introduced an innovative access control protocol for smart grids, known as RACP-SG [20]. This protocol utilizes lightweight-cryptography-based authenticated encryption with associative data (AEAD) techniques, hash functions, and elliptic curve cryptography (ECC) to successfully execute the authentication process. Moreover, RACP-SG enables mutual authentication between a service provider and an SM, allowing them to establish a session key during communication over the public channel.

Chaudhry et al. recently introduced a new ECC-based protocol called LAS-SG, emphasizing its lightweight nature to ensure satisfactory security and privacy levels [21]. Their approach involves optimizing communication by utilizing only two transferred messages, containing 192 bytes. Although the computation cost of LAS-SG is deemed acceptable, it remains higher than the protocol proposed in this paper.

PUF-based techniques present an intriguing approach utilized in smart metering and grid applications [22]. Numerous PUF-based protocols have been developed for SG/SM, such as the Gope and Sikdar scheme—a key agreement method with privacy-aware authentication protocol to improve security in these kinds of applications [23]. Recognizing the potential impact of cyber attacks on electrical networks, such as real-time decision-making in demand and supply management as well as data manipulation, they created a method to boost the confidentiality of communication channels between UCs and SMs, guaranteeing physical security. Nevertheless, Baeken et al. discovered weaknesses in this approach, suggesting that it does not fulfill all the necessary security criteria [24]. Moreover, the Gope–Sikdar protocol relies on a hash function as its main security measure, rendering it susceptible to key compromise impersonation attacks due to its symmetric nature. Additionally, their protocol includes XORing a temporal value with the secret key before transmitting it on the public channel (i.e., $np* = n_p \oplus K$), where K becomes the main source of authentication afterward This vulnerability exposes the protocol to known session-specific temporary information attacks, allowing various malicious actions, including impersonation and de-synchronization. Rostampour et al. introduced an authentication protocol, EPSG, for the smart grid in the IoT infrastructure [25]. This protocol, combining PUF functions and ECC encryption, establishes a secure environment, ensuring message confidentiality and integrity simultaneously. The authors conducted simulations of EPSG on an Arduino, assessing communication cost and energy consumption in a practical setting. Although EPSG's performance is acceptable, its ability to resist machine learning attacks is limited.

Mustapa et al. introduced a security scheme based on a ring oscillator physically unclonable function [26] to enhance information security in advanced metering infrastructures. Their primary goal was to create a robust and secure authentication approach for smart grid infrastructure. In the architecture named ROPUF, they created a secure connection between the utility center and the smart meter (SM) to transfer data. However, they did not provide details about the workings of this channel and how the SM utilizes it for communication. This channel imposes an additional burden on the SM, generating ciphertext, which was not factored into the protocol's computational cost. Moreover, the proposed protocol exhibited vulnerabilities to impersonation and tracing attacks when data exchanges occurred over a public channel. Furthermore, due to the absence of cryptographic primitives, the protocol was susceptible to advanced attacks, including insider attacks.

In a recent development, Harishma et al. presented a scheme to secure key exchange mutually [27]. Their scheme utilized advanced encryption techniques, such as identity-based encryption (IBE), SHA-2, and the advanced encryption standard (AES), with the possibility of employing ECC encryption and physically unclonable function (PUF) functions. The authors implemented and tested this scheme in a practical environment to provide experimental results. However, the scheme's use of identity-based encryption (IBE) for credential management raised concerns. Currently, the most efficient IBE schemes rely on bilinear pairings on elliptic curves, such as Weil or Tate pairings, while previously published non-pairing-based schemes tend to be inefficient in encryption, decryption, key generation, ciphertext size, or key size [28,29].

Considering that the scheme is designed for resource-constrained devices and involves various encryption methods in each authentication process, it exhibits high complexity and is time-consuming. As an illustration, the authenticated key-exchange protocol on the smart meter setup takes 525 ms for the meter and 360 ms for the server. Additionally, as highlighted in a study by Lounis [30], the protocol is vulnerable to spoofing attacks, where an attacker can impersonate the server and deceive the meter, compromising both the authentication and key-establishment claims of the protocol. Furthermore, the meter does not contribute to the protocol's freshness during the authentication phase, potentially allowing impersonation of the server using the GUMAP attack [31].

LAKE-BSG, a lightweight key exchange scheme empowered by blockchain, was devised by Badshah et al. specifically for smart grids [32]. Leveraging the inherent security of a blockchain system, the authors aimed to establish a secure authentication method for smart meters (SM) while safeguarding user privacy. The proposed technique boasts comparable transmission and computation costs to existing authentication protocols. Furthermore, the integration of blockchain technology is asserted to enhance security by ensuring data storage in a secure, decentralized, and immutable ledger.

Table 1. Comparison of related work.

Reference	Communication Cost	Time-Consuming	Method	Approved Attack
[11]	▲	▲	ECC	✓
[13]	▼	▲	ECC + MAC	✓
[15]	▲	▲	ECC	✓
[16]	▼	▲	ECC	✓
[17]	▲	▼	ECC	✓
[18]	▼	▼	ECC	✓
[19]	▲	▲	ECC	✓
[20]	▼	▼	ECC + AEAD	✓
[21]	▲	▼	ECC	×
[23]	▼	▼	PUF	✓
[25]	▼	▼	PUF	×
[26]	▲	▼	PUF	×
[27]	▼	▲	AES + IBE(ECC) + PUF	✓
[32]	▲	▼	Blockchain	×

3. System Model

The infrastructure of a smart metering system is illustrated in Figure 1. As shown, an SM, a NAN, and a certificate authority (CA) server are the key components, and the communication between the CA and other parties is established via a secure channel. On the other hand, the SM and the NAN are connected over a public channel, which can be the weak point of this structure. Through this paper, we use the list of notations listed in Table 2.

The proposed protocol adopts Canetti and Krawczyk's adversary model (CK-adversary model) [33], which is more robust than the commonly used Dolev–Yao (DY) adversary model [34] in many designs. In the DY-adversary model, the adversary possesses complete control over message transmission through a public channel. It can eavesdrop, delete, insert, or modify fake messages in different instances. Under the CK-adversary model, the adversary possesses all the powers of the DY model and more, enabling them to infiltrate session states and secret information, encompassing secret keys. Consequently, if these session states and secret details are exposed during a particular session, this revelation must not jeopardize the confidentiality of other involved parties, as emphasized in [35]. The CK-adversary model proves advantageous over the DY model, especially in contexts where forward secrecy is a vital protocol requirement.

Table 2. List of used notations.

Symbol	Description
P	Generator point of a large group G
q	A large prime number
N_i	ith IoT node
CA	A trusted server
ID_i	The unique identifier of N_i
d_{SM}	The ECC based private key of the smart meter (SM)
d_{NAN}	The ECC based private key of neighborhood area network gateway (NAN)
$Q_{SM/NAN}$	The ECC based public key of SM/NAN
$r_{SM/NAN}$	A random number generated by SM/NAN
$Auth_{SM/NAN}$	Authentication token generated by SM/NAN
$H(.)$	One-way hash function
$T_{SM/NAN}$	Timestamp of SM/NAN
$I_{SM/NAN}$	Identifier of SM/NAN
$a.P$	Multiplying a point P on the elliptic curve E by natural number (scalar) a, results another point on the curve
$\|\|$	Concatenation
ΔT	An acceptable threshold for time
SK	The shared session key between SM and NAN gateway
$\|X\|$	Cardinality of the set X

To thwart potential attacks stemming from the exposure of secret information, we presume that every smart meter (SM) is equipped with a robust Physical unclonable function ($PUF(.)$). This measure is essential considering the attacker's capability to compromise a SM and extract its confidential data. Given challenges $C \neq C'$, $PUF(C)$ and $PUF(C')$ are expected to be completely different. On the other hand, given the same challenge C to $PUF(.)$, it is expected to have the same response. However, different PUFs should return completely different responses for the same challenge with a high probability. It should be noted attempting to design such a PUF function is an active research area but out of the scope of this paper, although many proposed schemes are vulnerable to modeling attacks or machine learning attacks [36]. An example of such attempts is the proposed scheme by [37] Zalivaka et al., which is claimed to be reliable and secure against modeling attacks.

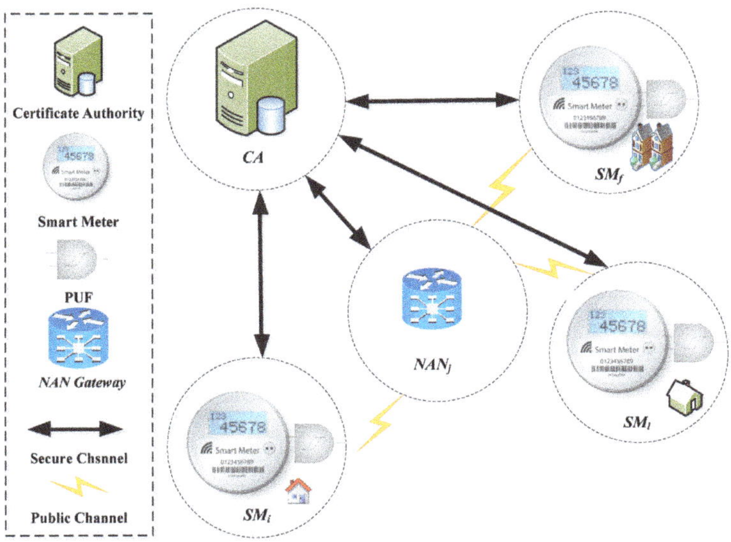

Figure 1. Infrastructure of a smart metering system.

We assume that the public information is stored in the smart metering infrastructure (SMI), which is accessible by all protocol parties (including the adversary), but its integrity is guaranteed and the adversary cannot modify its content.

4. Proposed Protocol (PPSG)

To overcome the security pitfalls of existing protocols, following our system model, we propose a secure protocol that is named PUF-based protocol for the smart grid—in the shortened form, PPSG. In the initialization phase, the CA selects and discloses the protocol's parameters publicly in the smart metering infrastructure (SMI). We take into consideration that each smart meter is outfitted with a $PUF(.)$. As a result, during this stage, the certificate authority (CA) discloses the system parameters, i.e., $\{q, P, h(.), E_q(c,d)\}$, and they are stored in the SMI.

The registration phase of the protocol is used for the SMs and the NAN gateways enrollment to the CA over a secure channel. In this phase, to register a SM, it generates an identity I_{SM} for itself and transmits it to the CA. It will be accepted by the CA if it is unique, i.e., has not been used by another SM already. When SM chooses a unique identity I_{SM}, the CA assigns it to the SM and generates a pair (d_{SM}, $Q_{SM} = d_{SM}.P$) as the SM's private and public keys, respectively. The CA then sends the token $< d_{SM}, Q_{SM} = d_{SM}.P >$ to the SM through a secure channel and deletes d_{SM} from its database. Once the message is received, the SM stores $(I_{SM}, sd_{SM} = PUF(I_{SM}) \oplus d_{SM}, Q_{SM})$ in its memory. To register a NAN gateway, the same process will be run, and it chooses its unique identifier I_{NAN} and the CA computes $< d_{NAN}, Q_{NAN} = d_{NAN}.P >$ as its private and public keys, respectively, and shares with the NAN. The set I_{SM}, Q_{SM} is also stored in the smart metering infrastructure (SMI), similarly (I_{NAN}, Q_{NAN}).

Assume that the ith SM, which is denoted by SM_i, wants to communicate with a nearby jth NAN gateway, which is denoted by NAN_j. The mutual authentication and key agreement phase of the protocol process is as follows, as also depicted in Figure 2:

1. The SM_i obtains I_{NAN} and Q_{NAN} from SMI, generates a random number $r_{SM} \in Z_q^*$ and the timestamp T_{SM}, computes $R1_{SM} = r_{SM}.Q_{SM}$, $R2_{SM} = r_{SM}.(PUF(I_{SM}) \oplus sd_{SM}).Q_{NAN}$, and $Auth1_{SM} = H(R2_{SM}, I_{SM}, T_{SM})$ and sends the message $M_1 =< (I_{SM}, Auth1_{SM}) \oplus R2_{SM}, R1_{SM}, T_{SM} >$ to the NAN.
2. Once the NAN_j received M_1, it validates T_{SM}, calculates $R2^*_{SM} = d_{NAN}.R1_{SM}$, and extracts I^*_{SM} and $Auth1^*_{SM}$. Next, it verifies whether $Auth1^*_{SM} \stackrel{?}{=} H(R2^*_{SM}, I^*_{SM}, T_{SM})$ to accept the login request. Assuming the request has been accepted, using I^*_{SM}, NAN_j obtains Q^*_{SM} from SMI, generates a random number $r_{NAN} \in Z_q^*$ and its timestamp T_{NAN} and computes $R1_{NAN} = r_{NAN}.Q_{NAN}$, $R2_{NAN} = r_{NAN}.R2^*_{SM}$ and $Auth_{NAN} = H(R2_{NAN}, I_{NAN} \oplus I_{SM}, T_{SM} \oplus T_{NAN})$, and sends the message $M_2 =< Auth_{NAN}, R1_{NAN}, T_{NAN} >$ to the SM_i.
3. Once the SM_i receives M_2, it validates T_{NAN}, calculates $R2^*_{NAN} = (PUF(I_{SM}) \oplus sd_{SM}).r_{sm}.R1_{NAN}$, and verifies whether $Auth_{NAN} \stackrel{?}{=} H(R2^*_{NAN}, I_{NAN} \oplus I_{SM}, T_{SM} \oplus T_{NAN})$ to authenticate the NAN_j. Next, it extracts its current timestamp T'_{SM} and computes the shared key $SK = H(I_{NAN} \| I_{SM} \| R2^*_{NAN} \| T'_{SM} \| T_{NAN})$ and $Auth2_{SM} = H(SK \| T'_{SM})$ and sends $M_3 =< Auth2_{SM}, T'_{SM} >$ to the NAN_j.
4. Once the NAN_j receives M_3, it verifies T'_{SM}, calculates $SK^* = H(I_{NAN} \| I^*_{SM} \| R2_{NAN} \| T'_{SM} \| T_{NAN})$, and verifies whether $Auth2_{SM} \stackrel{?}{=} H(SK^* \| T'_{SM})$ to authenticate the SM_i.
5. Once the legitimacy of both SM_i and NAN_j has been verified and they have been successfully authenticated, the mutual authentication and key agreement process concludes, and the shared key will be $SK = H(I_{NAN} \| I_{SM} \| r_{NAN}.r_{SM}.d_{SM}.d_{NAN}.P \| T'_{SM} \| T_{NAN})$.

SM_i $(I_{SM}, sd_{SM} = PUF(I_{SM}) \oplus d_{SM}, Q_{SM})$	NAN_j $< d_{NAN}, Q_{NAN} = d_{NAN}.P >$
Obtains I_{NAN} and Q_{NAN} from SMI, generates $r_{SM} \in Z_q^*$ and T_{SM}, computes $R1_{SM} = r_{SM}.Q_{SM}$, $R2_{SM} = r_{SM}.(PUF(I_{SM}) \oplus sd_{SM}).Q_{NAN}$ and $Auth1_{SM} = H(R2_{SM}, I_{SM}, T_{SM})$ $\xrightarrow{M_1=<(I_{SM}, Auth1_{SM}) \oplus R2_{SM}, R1_{SM}, T_{SM}>}$	
	Validates T_{SM}, calculates $R2^*_{SM} = d_{NAN}.R1_{SM}$ and extracts I^*_{SM} and $Auth1^*_{SM}$, verifies $Auth1^*_{SM} \stackrel{?}{=} H(R2^*_{SM}, I^*_{SM}, T_{SM})$ to accept the login request. Assuming the request has been accepted, using I^*_{SM}, NAN_j obtains Q^*_{SM} from SMI, generates $r_{NAN} \in Z_q^*$ and T_{NAN}, and computes $R1_{NAN} = r_{NAN}.Q_{NAN}$, $R2_{NAN} = r_{NAN}.R2^*_{SM}$ and $Auth_{NAN} = H(R2_{NAN}, I_{NAN} \oplus I_{SM}, T_{SM} \oplus T_{NAN})$ $\xleftarrow{M_2=<Auth_{NAN}, R1_{NAN}, T_{NAN}>}$.
Validates T_{NAN}, calculates $R2^*_{NAN} = (PUF(I_{SM}) \oplus sd_{SM}).r_{sm}.R1_{NAN}$, verifies $Auth_{NAN} \stackrel{?}{=} H(R2^*_{NAN}, I_{NAN} \oplus I_{SM}, T_{SM} \oplus T_{NAN})$ to authenticate the NAN_j, extracts T'_{SM}, and computes $SK = H(I_{NAN} \| I_{SM} \| R2^*_{NAN} \| T'_{SM} \| T_{NAN})$ and $Auth2_{SM} = H(SK \| T'_{SM})$ $\xrightarrow{M_3=<Auth2_{SM}, T'_{SM}>}$	
	Verifies T'_{SM}, calculates $SK^* = H(I_{NAN} \| I^*_{SM} \| R2_{NAN} \| T'_{SM} \| T_{NAN})$, and verifies $Auth2_{SM} \stackrel{?}{=} H(SK^* \| T'_{SM})$ to authenticate the SM_i $\xleftarrow{M_4=<Auth2_{SM}>}$.

Figure 2. Mutual authentication and key agreement phase of PPSG.

5. Security Analysis of PPSG

In this section, we embark on a comprehensive security evaluation of the proposed authentication and key agreement protocol for smart grid PPSG. The primary objective of this evaluation is to thoroughly assess the security aspects of PPSG from multiple perspectives.

To begin with, we employ a heuristic evaluation approach to scrutinize the security of PPSG. This method involves a systematic examination of the protocol's components, algorithms, and implementation details to identify any potential vulnerabilities or weaknesses. Through this heuristic analysis, we leverage our expertise and knowledge in the field to identify possible security risks and provide valuable insights into the overall security posture of PPSG.

Furthermore, we conduct a formal security evaluation of PPSG within the real-or-random model. By adopting this formal model, we can rigorously assess the security guarantees provided by the protocol.

In order to further validate and reinforce the security claims of PPSG, we employ an automated security protocol verification tool named Scyther [38]. This tool plays a crucial role in validating the security properties of the protocol by subjecting it to rigorous analysis. By utilizing Scyther's advanced algorithms and formal methods, we can exhaustively examine PPSG for any potential security flaws, design vulnerabilities, or weaknesses. The utilization of Scyther ensures a comprehensive assessment of the security of PPSG and offers additional confidence in its effectiveness.

By combining these three evaluation approaches—heuristic evaluation, formal analysis in the real-or-random model, and security validation using Scyther—we aim to provide a robust and multi-dimensional assessment of the security of the proposed PUF-based authentication and key agreement protocol for smart grid PPSG. This comprehensive evaluation approach enhances the reliability of our findings and strengthens the confidence in the security claims made for PPSG.

5.1. Heuristic Security Evaluation

In the PPSG protocol, the secret key of the smart meter, denoted as d_{SM}, is protected through the process of masking with the $PUF(.)$ function. As a result, if an adversary manages to compromise the smart meter, they are unable to directly extract the original secret key d_{SM}. Instead, the adversary can only obtain a modified version of the secret key, denoted as sd_{SM}, which is computed as the XOR operation between d_{SM} and the output of the $PUF(.)$ function applied to a unique identifier I_{SM} associated with the smart meter. Mathematically, this can be expressed as $sd_{SM} = d_{SM} \oplus PUF(I_{SM})$. Assuming that the employed $PUF(.)$ function is secure enough, the adversary faces significant difficulties in extracting the actual secret key d_{SM} or conducting related attacks, such as impersonation. The security of the PPSG protocol relies on the assumption that the $PUF(.)$ function effectively masks the secret key and prevents its direct extraction. By leveraging the security properties of the $PUF(.)$ function, the protocol ensures that even if the adversary compromises the smart meter, they cannot obtain the original secret key and are limited to accessing the modified version sd_{SM}.

Additionally, the session key used in the PPSG protocol is randomized using a combination of parameters: r_{NAN}, r_{SM}, d_{SM}, d_{NAN}, and P. The adversary, however, only has access to $r_{NAN} \cdot Q_{NAN}$ and $r_{SM} \cdot Q_{SM}$, where Q_{NAN} and Q_{SM} are the public keys corresponding to d_{NAN} and d_{SM}, respectively. This means that even if the adversary possesses knowledge of d_{NAN} and d_{SM}, they are unable to extract the session key without solving the elliptic curve discrete logarithm problem (ECDLP) or the elliptic curve computational Diffie–Hellman problem (EC-CDHP). Therefore, the proposed PPSG protocol provides forward secrecy, ensuring that even with compromised long-term secret keys, the adversary cannot retroactively derive the session key. In the proposed protocol, the integrity of the messages is guaranteed by the following equations:

$$\begin{aligned} Auth1_{SM} &= H(R2_{SM}, I_{SM}, T_{SM}) \\ Auth_{NAN} &= H(R2_{NAN}, I_{NAN} \oplus I_{SM}, T_{SM} \oplus T_{NAN}) \\ Auth2_{SM} &= H(SK \| T'_{SM}) \end{aligned}$$

where $SK = H(I_{NAN} \| I_{SM} \| R2^*_{NAN} \| T'_{SM} \| T_{NAN})$. Given that the timestamp has been used in all messages, the adversary cannot use these messages in a later session to apply a replay attack, thus demonstrating the security of PPSA against this attack.

In conclusion, the PPSG protocol strengthens the security of the smart grid system by masking the secret key using the $PUF(\cdot)$ function, preventing direct extraction. Furthermore, the randomized session key construction and the computational hardness of the ECDLP or EC-CDHP problems ensure forward secrecy, protecting the confidentiality of past sessions even in the presence of compromised long-term secret keys.

5.2. Formal Security Evaluation—RoR

Throughout the remaining part of this section, we conduct a comprehensive security evaluation of PPSG within the framework of the real-or-random (RoR) model. In this model, an initial random selection is made where a bit b is uniformly chosen; when $b = 0$, it represents the random world (RW), and when $b = 1$, it signifies the real world (target protocol). The adversary's objective is to accurately distinguish the value of b in this scenario. To do this, the adversary $\mathcal{A}$ can run the following query types [39]:

- Execute: it models a passive adversary $\mathcal{A}$, which eavesdrops transferred messages over public channel;
- Send: it models an active adversary on the public channel;
- Reveal (N_i): its output is the session key that is held by the instance N_i;
- Test (N_i): it returns the session key for instance N_i if $b = 1$ or a random value of the same size if $b = 0$.

Consider protocol $\mathcal{P}$, in which $\mathcal{A}$ is given access to the Execute , Send, Reveal (N_i) and Test (N_i) oracles, and outputs a guess bit b_0. The adversary wins the semantic security game in the RoR sense if $b_0 = b$ and its advantage to win this game, $Adv^{RoR}_{\mathcal{D},\mathcal{P}}(t, R)$, is defined as follows:

$$Adv^{RoR}_{\mathcal{D},\mathcal{P}}(t, R) \quad = \quad ((Pr(\mathcal{A} \rightarrow b_0 = 1 : b = 1) - (Pr(\mathcal{A} \rightarrow b_0 = 1 : b = 0)))$$

$\mathcal{P}$ offers RoR semantic security if:

$$Adv^{RoR}_{\mathcal{D},\mathcal{P}(t,R)} < \varepsilon(.)$$

with $\varepsilon(.)$ being some negligible function.

In this section, as outlined in [39], we conduct a formal assessment of PPSG's security within the RoR model. This evaluation involves gauging the adversary's advantage in differentiating PPSG from the random world (RW).

Theorem 1. *Let q_{exe}, q_{send}, q_{Reveal}, and q_{test}, respectively, represent the number of queries to* Execute, Send, Reveal, *and* Test *oracles on PPSG/RW, then:*

$$\begin{aligned} Adv^{RoR}_{\mathcal{D},PPSG}(t, q_{exe}; q_{send}; q_{Reveal}; q_{test}) \quad & - \\ Adv^{RoR}_{\mathcal{D},RW}(t, q_{exe}; q_{send}; q_{Reveal}; q_{test}) \quad & \leq \\ 3.q.\varepsilon_{ECC} + 4.q.\varepsilon_{H} + q.\varepsilon_{PUF} & \end{aligned}$$

In the given context, ε_{ECC} represents the utmost advantage an adversary can gain in solving ECDLP or EC-CDHP with each query. Additionally, ε_H signifies the maximum advantage in challenging the collision resistance property of $H(.)$, while ε_{PUF} denotes the maximum advantage in distinguishing the output of $PUF(.)$ from a random sequence. Here, q is calculated as the sum of q_{exe}, q_{send}, q_{Reveal}, and q_{test}.

Proof. Consider the scenario where SM_i and NAN_j engage in communication to establish a session key SK. Let $\mathcal{A}$ denote an adversary aiming to challenge the semantic security of PPSG within the real-or-random (RoR) model.

To establish the theorem, a game-based methodology is employed. This approach involves defining a sequence of games denoted as $\mathcal{G}$, initiating from the random world RW, and concluding in the real-world PPSG. Each game, represented as $\mathcal{G}_n$, introduces an event $Adv^{RoR-\mathcal{G}_n}_{\mathcal{D},\mathcal{P}}(t, R)$. This event signifies the adversary's advantage in accurately determining the hidden bit b involved in the Test queries. It should be noted the structure of the transferred messages is identical in RW and PPSG, including plain values such as timestamps; otherwise distinguishing them is trivial.

Game $\mathcal{G}_0$. It is corresponding to RW and $Adv^{RoR-\mathcal{G}0}_{\mathcal{D},RW}(t, R) = 0$.

Game $\mathcal{G}_1$. In this game, any instance follows the structure of the generated and transferred messages in PPSG, e.g., $(SK, R1_{SM}, \ldots)$. However, all computed messages, excluding timestamps, are selected completely randomly. It is clear $Adv^{RoR-\mathcal{G}0}_{\mathcal{D},RW}(t, R) - Adv^{RoR-\mathcal{G}1}_{\mathcal{D},RW}(t, R) = 0$.

Game $\mathcal{G}_2$. In this game, $Auth1_{SM} = H(R2_{SM}, I_{SM}, T_{SM})$, $Auth2_{SM} = H(SK \| T'_{SM})$, and $Auth_{NAN} = H(R2_{NAN}, I_{NAN} \oplus I_{SM}, T_{SM} \oplus T_{NAN})$. Given that $R2_{SM}$, $R2_{SM}$, and SK

are session-dependent random values, this modification has no impact on the adversary's advantage as long as $H(.)$ is not distinguishable from a random function. Hence:

$$Adv_{\mathcal{D},RW}^{RoR-\mathcal{G}_2}(t,R) \leq Adv_{\mathcal{D},RW}^{RoR-\mathcal{G}_1}(t,R) + 3.q.\varepsilon_H$$

where $q = q_{exe} + q_{send} + q_{test}$.

Game $\mathcal{G}_3$. In this game, $R1_{SM}$ and $R2_{NAN}$ are calculated using ECC point multiplication. Given that r_{SM} and r_{NAN} are fresh random numbers, the adversary's advantage to distinguish $\mathcal{G}_3$ from $\mathcal{G}_2$ is as follows:

$$Adv_{\mathcal{D},RW}^{RoR-\mathcal{G}_3}(t,R) \leq Adv_{\mathcal{D},RW}^{RoR-\mathcal{G}_2}(t,R) + 2.q.\varepsilon_{ECC}.$$

Game $\mathcal{G}_4$. In this game, as a part of the transferred messages, the values of $(I_{SM}, Auth1_{SM}) \oplus R2_{SM}$ is used in M_1, where $R2_{SM} = r_{SM}.(PUF(I_{SM}) \oplus sd_{SM}).Q_{NAN}$. It is clear this modification does not affect the adversary's advantage as long as it cannot solve ECDLP or EC-CDHP. Hence,

$$Adv_{\mathcal{D},RW}^{RoR-\mathcal{G}_4}(t,R) \leq Adv_{\mathcal{D},RW}^{RoR-\mathcal{G}_3}(t,R) + q.\varepsilon_{ECC}.$$

Game $\mathcal{G}_5$. In this game, I_{SM}, Q_{SM}, I_{NAN}, and Q_{NAN} are, respectively, replaced by their real values and are taken from SMI. However, all these parameters are already masked by ECC or $H(.)$ and we have considered the adversary's advantages of those masking in the previous games. Hence, this modification does not give a new advantage to $\mathcal{A}$, and $Adv_{\mathcal{D},RW}^{RoR-\mathcal{G}_5}(t,R) = Adv_{\mathcal{D},RW}^{RoR-\mathcal{G}_4}(t,R)$.

Game $\mathcal{G}_6$. This game is identical to $\mathcal{G}_5$, excluding that d_{SM} is computed as $PUF(I_{SM}) \oplus sd_{SM}$. Hence,

$$Adv_{\mathcal{D},RW}^{RoR-\mathcal{G}_6}(t,R) \leq Adv_{\mathcal{D},RW}^{RoR-\mathcal{G}_5}(t,R) + q.\varepsilon_{PUF}.$$

Game $\mathcal{G}_7$. In this game, the session key is computed using the hash function as $SK = H(I_{NAN}||I_{SM}||R2_{NAN}||T'_{SM}||T_{NAN})$. Given that the input value for SK_{ij} is randomized by nonce and the timestamps therefore,

$$Adv_{\mathcal{D},RW}^{RoR-\mathcal{G}_7}(t,R) \leq Adv_{\mathcal{D},RW}^{RoR-\mathcal{G}_6}(t,R) + q.\varepsilon_H.$$

It is clear that $\mathcal{G}_7$ represents the implementation of PPSG. Hence,

$$\begin{aligned} Adv_{\mathcal{D},PPSG}^{RoR}(t,R) - Adv_{\mathcal{D},RW}^{RoR}(t,R) &\leq \\ Adv_{\mathcal{D},RW}^{RoR-\mathcal{G}_7}(t,R) - Adv_{\mathcal{D},RW}^{RoR-\mathcal{G}_0}(t,R) &\leq \\ 3.q.\varepsilon_{ECC} + 4.q.\varepsilon_H + q.\varepsilon_{PUF} \end{aligned}$$

which completes the proof. □

5.3. Formal Security Validation—Scyther

In this section, we validate the security of the proposed protocol using the Scyther tool. Scyther is a powerful tool that is widely used for security analysis and verification of cryptographic protocols. One of the main advantages of Scyther is its ability to detect vulnerabilities in protocols that are not easily detected by other tools. It uses a formal language called SPDL (Scyther protocol description language) to specify the protocol being analyzed. SPDL allows Scyther to model the protocol's behavior and identify potential weaknesses or flaws in its design. Scyther makes several security claims, including the ability to detect all possible attacks on a protocol, provide a complete analysis of its security properties, and offer automated proof of security properties. Some of the specific security claims made by Scyther include:

- Alive: Scyther claims to be able to detect liveness violations, which occur when a protocol becomes stuck or deadlocked;

- Secret: Scyther claims to be able to detect confidentiality violations, which occur when an attacker gains unauthorized access to sensitive information;
- Weakagree: Scyther claims to be able to detect weaknesses in agreement protocols, which are used to establish shared secrets between parties;
- Niagree: Scyther claims to be able to detect non-injective agreement protocols, which can allow an attacker to impersonate one of the parties involved;
- Nisynch: Scyther claims to be able to detect non-injective synchronization protocols, which can allow an attacker to manipulate the order of messages between parties.

The security analysis results of the proposed protocol, i.e., PPSG, are depicted in Figure 3.

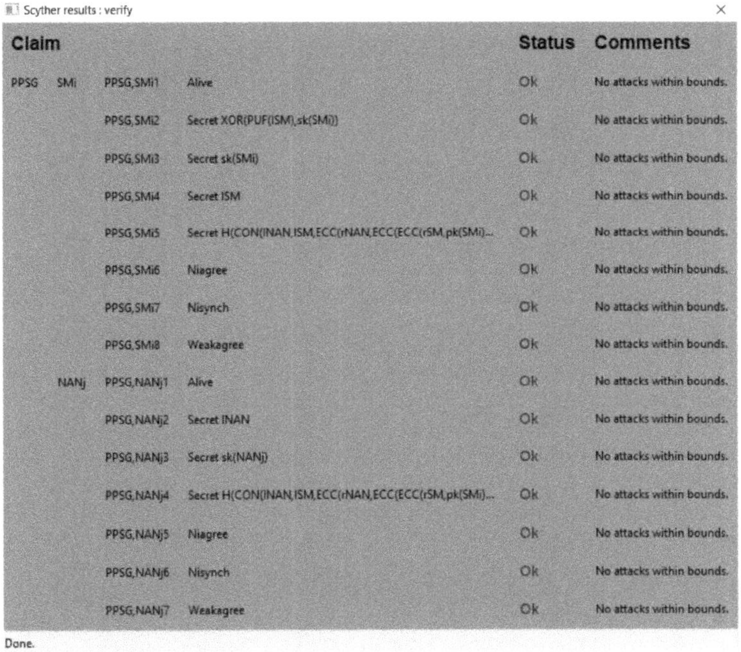

Figure 3. Security validation of PPSG using Scyther tool.

6. Cost Analysis

To set up our experiments and obtain practical results, we designed a simulation of a smart home network, as shown in Figure 4. This simulation included crucial components like a microcontroller, photoresistor sensor, humidity sensor, temperature sensor, and a relay for controlling AC power. To perform cryptographic operations on each smart meter client, we employed an Arduino UNO board. This board is equipped with an ATmega328P microcontroller boasting 32-kB flash memory, 2-kB SRAM, and operates at a clock speed of 16 MHz. It is worth mentioning that we verified the reliability of physical unclonable functions (PUF) in a similar microcontroller, as stated in [40].

In our evaluation, we examined the power-up values of SRAM in 20 microcontrollers, collected 100 times at room temperature. This assessment aimed to determine the quality of these values for implementing an SRAM PUF. The results were promising: the mean bias across all devices (indicating uniformity) stood at 48.38%, a figure remarkably close to the ideal 50%. Moreover, the intra-distance between different acquisitions (which measures reliability) was 97.58%, indicating strong consistency. Additionally, the inter-distance between distinct devices (indicative of uniqueness) was 38.62%, aligning well with findings in similar microcontroller studies documented in the existing literature. These results affirm the robustness of our experimental setup and validate the viability of our approach.

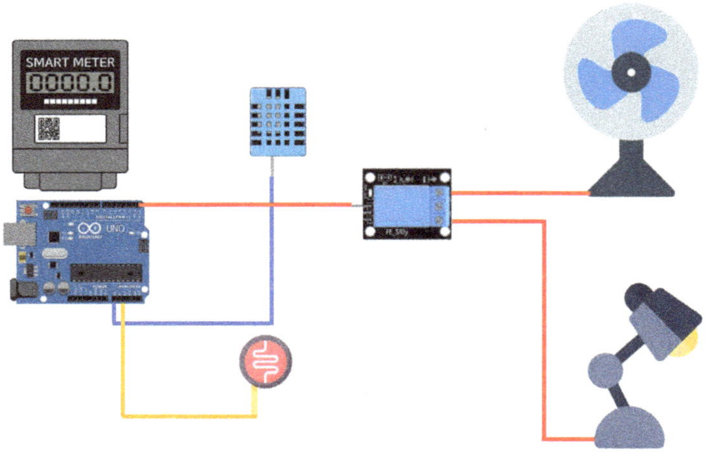

Figure 4. Simulation of a smart home system.

Using this setup, we achieved timings of approximately 21 ms for elliptic curve cryptography (T_{ECC}), 26 ms for double elliptic curve cryptography (T_{2ECC}), 6 ms for symmetric encryption (T_{SE}), 3 ms for SHA-256 hashing (T_h), and 3.7 ms for error syndrome calculation (T_{Es}). It is worth mentioning that SHA-256 might be replaced by SHA-3 based on system performance requirements or if SHA-256 is deemed insecure. We also considered the time of a PUF invocation (T_{PUFn}) as equal to T_h. This equivalence was established under the assumption of utilizing a key management module capable of generating multiple keys from a single root key. To ensure cryptographic separation between these derived keys, a secure key derivation function (KDF) utilizing cryptographic primitives like SHA-256 is employed. In a comparable research effort, functions $FE.GEN$ and $FE.REC$ utilize fuzzy extractors and helper data, among other algorithms. According to the information outlined in [23], the times for $T_{FE.REC}$ and $T_{FE.GEN}$ can be estimated as $30 \times T_{PUF}$ and $10 \times T_{PUF}$, respectively.

Garg et al. estimated the computational complexity of their protocol ([16] Section 5.2.1, Table 4) and claimed the computational complexity of the SM and the NAN are same and equal to $2.T_{em} + 4.T_H$. Based on this claim, they have shown that their protocol outperforms related protocols, e.g., [11,41]. However, after comparing Garg et al.'s protocol computational cost with PPSG, we understood that they underestimated the protocol's complexity.

By summing up all the ECC point-multiplication in the SM side, we come up with $3T_{em} + T_{2em}$ which is 150% more than the reported value by Garg et al. ([16], Section 5.2.1, Table 4), which was $2T_{em}$. The same argument can be expressed for the NAN gateway's computations. On the other hand, in PPSG, the SM's computations costs $3.T_{em} + 4.T_H + 2T_{PUF}$ and the NAN gateway's computations costs $3.T_{em} + 4.T_H$.

Table 3 displays a cost comparison between PPSG and other protocols discussed in Section 2. To compare communication overhead, we examined the bit lengths of various components: a timestamp, an identifier, a random number, a hash value, and an ECC point, which were set at 32, 64, 128, 160, and 320 bits, respectively. It is important to note that we used SHA-256 but truncated its output to 160 bits to address recent security vulnerabilities in SHA-1 [42]. Following these parameters, the communication overhead of PPSG includes $M1$ at 512 bits, $M2$ at 512 bits, $M3$ at 192 bits, and $M4$ at 160 bits, totaling 1376 bits.

Table 3. Cost comparison of the related protocols and PPSG.

Protocol	Computations	Time (ms)	Communications (Bit)	Energy (mJ)
[15]	$2 \times T_{2ECC} + 6 \times T_{ECC} + 11 \times T_h$	211	1600	18.568
[16]	$2 \times T_{2ECC} + 6 \times T_{ECC} + 8 \times T_h$	202	1344	17.776
[17]	$2 \times T_{2ECC} + 6 \times T_{ECC} + 5 \times T_h$	193	1632	16.984
[18]	$8 \times T_{ECC} + 10 \times T_h +$	198	1440	17.424
[19]	$8 \times T_{ECC} + 4 \times T_{Es} + 19 \times T_h$	240	2912	21.12
[20]	$8 \times T_h + T_{PUF} + T_{FE.REC} + 3 \times T_{ECC} + 4 \times T_{Es}$	198	1408	17.414
[21]	$10 \times T_h + 4 \times T_{SE} + 7 \times T_{ECC}$	205	1536	18.034
[23]	$11 \times T_h + T_{PUF} + T_{FE.GEN} + T_{FE.REC}$	156	896	13.728
[25]	$9 \times T_h + T_{PUF} + 6 \times T_{ECC}$	156	1408	13.728
[32]	$16 \times T_h + 1 \times T_{SE} + 3 \times T_{ECC} + T_{PUF} + 2 \times T_{FE.GEN}$	180	1664	15.835
PPSG	$8 \times T_h + 6 \times T_{ECC} + 1 \times T_{PUF}$	153	1376	13.468

In contrast, the study by [19] documented a communication cost of 1184 bits for identical parameters. However, our analysis uncovered a possible typographical error in their report, leading to an underestimation of the communication cost. This discrepancy might have originated from the mismatched bit lengths used for values calculated via symmetric encryption, a critical factor in accurate cost estimation. Examining the findings in Figure 5 (time and byte), our comprehensive evaluation clearly showcases PPSG's superiority, as it imposes significantly lower communication overhead compared to its counterparts. This discrepancy underscores the importance of precise calculations when assessing the efficiency of communication protocols.

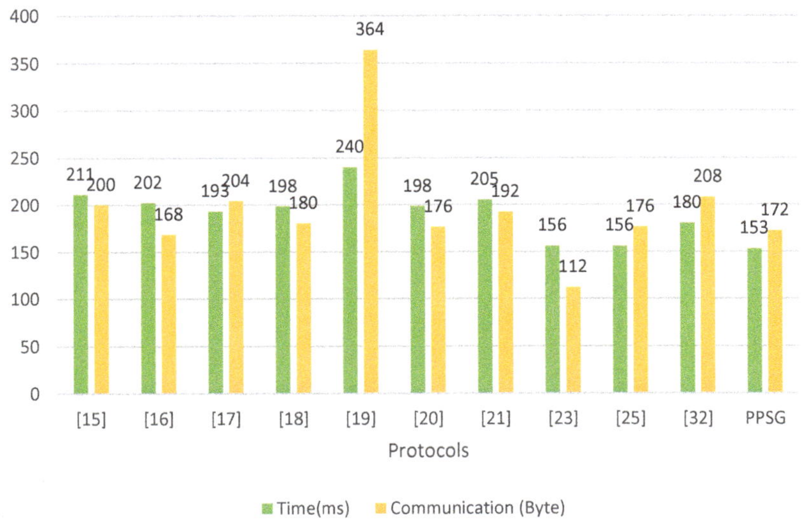

Figure 5. Computation and communication comparison of PPSG versus related protocols [15–21,23,25,32].

Regarding computational complexity, SM_i involves four hash function calls (T_h), three ECC scalar multiplications (T_{ECC}), and one PUF invocation (T_{PUF}) during its operation. On the other hand, NAN_j performs four hash function calls and three ECC scalar multiplications (T_{ECC}). Consequently, the total computational cost for the login and key agreement phase in PPSG amounts to $6 \times T_{ECC} + 1 \times T_{PUF} + 8 \times T_h$. As per our analysis, the key agreement session within PPSG demonstrates remarkable efficiency, completing in a mere 153 ms, establishing its position as the fastest protocol among those under comparison.

Energy consumption can be limited by the formula $Ec = V_{max}.I_{max}.T_c$, where Ec represents energy consumption, I_{max} stands for maximum consumed current, V_{max} represents the upper limit of working voltage, and Tc signifies the cumulative computational time essential for session key sharing. Based on the specifications outlined in the ATmega328P datasheet [43], the maximum operational power, denoted as $(V.I)$, for the ATmega328P stands at 14 mA × 5.5 V = 77 mW under active mode with a clock speed of 16 MHz. The energy measurement of PPSG on the Arduino board is depicted in Figure 6. In addition, the energy efficiency of PPSG was compared with other schemes, as illustrated in Figure 7. These findings reveal that the energy consumption for a PPSG session is notably lower compared to other schemes.

Figure 6. Energy measurement on an Arduino UNO board.

LAS-SG [21], operating as a lightweight protocol, involves the transmission of only two messages totaling 205 bits. The authentication process, taking 205 ms and consuming 18.034 mJ, indicates a resource-intensive nature compared to PPSG. Lake-BGS [32], designed for constrained smart meters (SMs), prioritizes lightweight functionality. However, being a blockchain-based protocol, it exhibits higher computation costs, with an authentication process requiring 180 ms—still more than PPSG. Consequently, with higher power consumption and overall, PPSG demonstrates superior performance.

In the comparison with [25], while both the proposed PPSG protocol and the one proposed by [25] incorporate PUF functions, PPSG outperforms it when considering computation and communication costs, resulting in lower energy consumption. This makes PPSG a more appropriate choice for smart meter security. In addressing the vulnerability of PUF functions to machine learning attacks, a novel aspect of PPSG remains in its combination of ECC and PUF. This integration safeguards transferred messages, offering an enhanced and more reliable technique compared to existing PUF-based solutions.

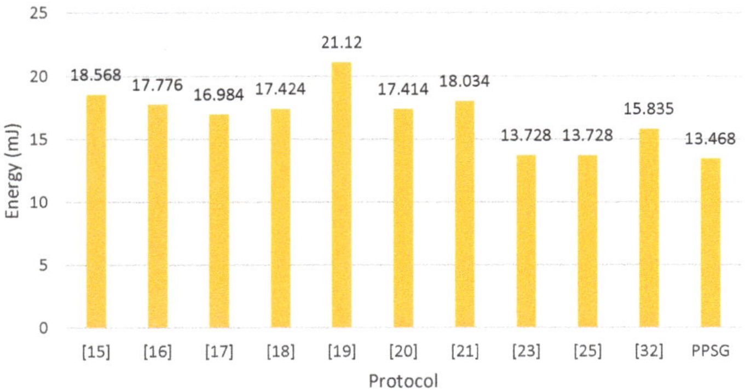

Figure 7. Energy consumption of PPSG versus related protocols [15–21,23,25,32].

7. Conclusions and Future Work

When considering the phases of grid modernization, key requirements such as data security, reliability, and accuracy are crucial for realizing the grid's full potential [44]. A breach in any of these aspects can jeopardize the entire system. This concern is even more critical in emerging new grids, such as water and gas grids, often fully working on battery, therefore operating in resource-limited environments with constraints on processing power, memory, and energy consumption.

Initially, we examined the security of various research protocols using different models, highlighting their vulnerabilities and potential solutions. Subsequently, to address these issues, we introduced a PUF-based protocol for smart grids (SG) named PPSG, utilizing PUF and ECC methods. Our formal security analysis of PPSG within the RoR model demonstrated that it offers robust security against adversaries constrained by polynomial time. Furthermore, our cost analysis revealed that PPSG stands out as one of the most lightweight protocols compared to recent related work.

To validate PPSG's performance in a real-world scenario, we simulated a smart meter and connected it to various electrical components representing smart home devices. The results showcased PPSG's superiority in terms of computation and communication costs, as well as energy consumption, making it a promising choice for smart grid applications.

Finally, although PUF-based protocols offer an interesting approach to SMs security they have certain limitations, such as vulnerability to machine learning attacks, environmental variability, and aging. In this paper, we aimed to tackle the issue of machine learning attacks by developing an efficient protocol in terms of energy use and computation speed. This area of research is a call for researchers to explore further options to overcome additional challenges. For instance, they could introduce features like temperature compensation to lessen the effect of environmental changes on PUF responses. Another approach could involve continuous monitoring to spot any alterations in PUF behavior over time. These strategies offer potential ways to enhance the overall performance of PUFs and contribute to enhancing the reliability, security, and longevity of PUF functions in smart meters.

Author Contributions: N.B., Y.B., M.S. and S.R. contributed equally to this work. All authors have read and agreed to the published version of the manuscript.

Funding: This research received no external funding.

Data Availability Statement: The data presented in this study are available in this article.

Acknowledgments: Masoumeh Safkhani was supported by Shahid Rajaee Teacher Training University under grant number 4899.

Conflicts of Interest: The authors declare no conflict of interest.

Reference

1. Agency, I.E. Electricity Grids and Secure Energy Transitions Report. 2023. Available online: https://www.iea.org/reports/electricity-grids-and-secure-energy-transitions (accessed on 25 December 2023).
2. What Are Smart Grids? Available online: https://www.iea.org/energy-system/electricity/smart-grids (accessed on 31 October 2023).
3. Hossein Motlagh, N.; Mohammadrezaei, M.; Hunt, J.; Zakeri, B. Internet of Things (IoT) and the Energy Sector. *Energies* **2020**, *13*, 494. [CrossRef]
4. Insights, G.M. Mart Meters Market—By Application (Residential, Commercial, Utility), By Technology (AMI, AMR), by Product (Smart Gas Meter). 2022. Available online: https://www.gminsights.com/industry-analysis/smart-metering-systems-market (accessed on 25 December 2023).
5. Analytics, I. Smart Meter Market Report 2019–2024. 2019. Available online: https://iot-analytics.com/product/smart-meter-market-report-2019-2024 (accessed on 25 December 2023).
6. Thomson, J.; Motyka, M.; Hardin, K.; Nagdeo, J. Electric Power Supply Chains: Achieving Security, Sustainability, and Resilience. 2022. Available online: https://www2.deloitte.com/us/en/insights/industry/power-and-utilities/supply-chain-resilience-electric-power-sector.html (accessed on 31 October 2023).
7. Columbus, L. Benchmarking Your Cybersecurity Budget in 2023. 2023. Available online: https://venturebeat.com/security/benchmarking-your-cybersecurity-budget-in-2023/ (accessed on 31 October 2023).
8. Ghiasi, M.; Niknam, T.; Wang, Z.; Mehrandezh, M.; Dehghani, M.; Ghadimi, N. A comprehensive review of cyber-attacks and defense mechanisms for improving security in smart grid energy systems: Past, present and future. *Electr. Power Syst. Res.* **2023**, *215*, 108975. [CrossRef]
9. Hasan, M.K.; Habib, A.A.; Shukur, Z.; Ibrahim, F.; Islam, S.; Razzaque, M.A. Review on cyber-physical and cyber-security system in smart grid: Standards, protocols, constraints, and recommendations. *J. Netw. Comput. Appl.* **2023**, *209*, 103540. [CrossRef]
10. Mazhar, T.; Irfan, H.M.; Khan, S.; Haq, I.; Ullah, I.; Iqbal, M.; Hamam, H. Analysis of Cyber Security Attacks and Its Solutions for the Smart Grid Using Machine Learning and Blockchain Methods. *Future Internet* **2023**, *15*, 83. [CrossRef]
11. Kumar, P.; Gurtov, A.; Sain, M.; Martin, A.; Ha, P.H. Lightweight authentication and key agreement for smart metering in smart energy networks. *IEEE Trans. Smart Grid* **2018**, *10*, 4349–4359. [CrossRef]
12. Baghestani, S.H.; Moazami, F.; Tahavori, M. Lightweight Authenticated Key Agreement for Smart Metering in Smart Grid. *IEEE Syst. J.* **2022**, *16*, 4983–4991. [CrossRef]
13. Kumar, N.; Aujla, G.S.; Das, A.K.; Conti, M. ECCAuth: A Secure Authentication Protocol for Demand Response Management in a Smart Grid System. *IEEE Trans. Ind. Inform.* **2019**, *15*, 6572–6582. [CrossRef]
14. Yu, S.; Park, K.; Lee, J.; Park, Y.; Park, Y.; Lee, S.; Chung, B. Privacy-preserving lightweight authentication protocol for demand response management in smart grid environment. *Appl. Sci.* **2020**, *10*, 1758. [CrossRef]
15. Wu, F.; Xu, L.; Li, X.; Kumari, S.; Karuppiah, M.; Obaidat, M. S. A lightweight and provably secure key agreement system for a smart grid with elliptic curve cryptography. *IEEE Syst. J.* **2018**, *13*, 2830–2838. [CrossRef]
16. Garg, S.; Kaur, K.; Kaddoum, G.; Rodrigues, J.J.P.C.; Guizani, M. Secure and Lightweight Authentication Scheme for Smart Metering Infrastructure in Smart Grid. *IEEE Trans. Ind. Inform.* **2020**, *16*, 3548–3557. [CrossRef]
17. He, D.; Wang, H.; Khan, M.K.; Wang, L. Lightweight anonymous key distribution scheme for smart grid using elliptic curve cryptography. *IET Commun.* **2016**, *10*, 1795–1802. [CrossRef]
18. Abbasinezhad-Mood, D.; Nikooghadam, M. An Anonymous ECC-Based Self-Certified Key Distribution Scheme for the Smart Grid. *IEEE Trans. Ind. Electron.* **2018**, *65*, 7996–8004. [CrossRef]
19. Khan, A.A.; Kumar, V.; Ahmad, M.; Rana, S.; Mishra, D. PALK: Password-based anonymous lightweight key agreement framework for smart grid Author links open overlay panel. *Int. J. Electr. Power Energy Syst.* **2020**, *121*, 106121. [CrossRef]
20. Tanveer, M.; Kumar, N.; Naushad, A.; Chaudhry, S.A. A robust access control protocol for the smart grid systems. *IEEE Internet Things J.* **2021**, *9*, 6855–6865. [CrossRef]
21. Chaudhry, S.A.; Yahya, K.; Garg, S.; Kaddoum, G.; Hassan, M.M.; Zikria, Y.B. LAS-SG: An elliptic curve-based lightweight authentication scheme for smart grid environments. *IEEE Trans. Ind. Inform.* **2022**, *19*, 1504–1511. [CrossRef]
22. Rincón, A.E.R.; Melo, W.S.; de Farias, C.M.; Carmo, L.F.R.C. Securing Smart Meters Through Physical Properties of Their Components. *IEEE Trans. Instrum. Meas.* **2021**, *70*, 1–11. [CrossRef]
23. Gope, P.; Sikdar, B. Privacy-aware authenticated key agreement scheme for secure smart grid communication. *IEEE Trans. Smart Grid* **2018**, *10*, 3953–3962. [CrossRef]
24. Braeken, A.; Kumar, P.; Martin, A. Efficient and provably secure key agreement for modern smart metering communications. *Energies* **2018**, *11*, 2662. [CrossRef]
25. Rostampour, S.; Bagheri, N.; Ghavami, B.; Bendavid, Y.; Kumari, S.; Martin, H.; Camara, C. Using a Privacy-Enhanced Authentication Process to Secure IoT-based Smart Grid Infrastructures. Available online: https://www.researchsquare.com/article/rs-2802756/v1 (accessed on 25 December 2023).
26. Mustapa, M.; Niamat, M.Y.; Nath, A.P.D.; Alam, M. Hardware-Oriented Authentication for Advanced Metering Infrastructure. *IEEE Trans. Smart Grid* **2018**, *9*, 1261–1270. [CrossRef]
27. Harishma, B.; Mathew, P.; Patranabis, S.; Chatterjee, U.; Agarwal, U.; Maheshwari, M.; Dey, S.; Mukhopadhyay, D. Safe is the New Smart: PUF-Based Authentication for Load Modification-Resistant Smart Meters. *IEEE Trans. Dependable Secur. Comput.* **2022**, *19*, 663–680. [CrossRef]

28. Liu, J.; Ke, L. New efficient identity based encryption without pairings. *J. Ambient. Intell. Humaniz. Comput.* **2019**, *10*, 1561–1570. [CrossRef]
29. Salimi, M. A New Efficient Identity-Based Encryption Without Pairing. *Cryptol. Eprint Arch.* **2021**, *10*, 1561–1570.
30. Lounis, K. PUF Security: Reviewing The Validity of Spoofing Attack Against Safe is the New Smart. Available online: https://eprint.iacr.org/2021/985 (accessed on 25 December 2023).
31. Safkhani, M.; Rostampour, S.; Bendavid, Y.; Sadeghi, S.; Bagheri, N. Improving RFID/IoT-based generalized ultra-lightweight mutual authentication protocols. *J. Inf. Secur. Appl.* **2022**, *67*, 103194. [CrossRef]
32. Badshah, A.; Waqas, M.; Abbas, G.; Muhammad, F.; Abbas, Z.H.; Vimal, S.; Bilal, M. LAKE-BSG: Lightweight authenticated key exchange scheme for blockchain-enabled smart grids. *Sustain. Energy Technol. Assess.* **2022**, *52*, 102248. [CrossRef]
33. Canetti, R.; Krawczyk, H. Universally Composable Notions of Key Exchange and Secure Channels. In *Lecture Notes in Computer Science, Proceedings of the Advances in Cryptology—EUROCRYPT 2002, International Conference on the Theory and Applications of Cryptographic Techniques, Amsterdam, The Netherlands, 28 April–2 May 2002*; Knudsen, L.R., Ed.; Springer: Berlin/Heidelberg, Germany, 2002; Volume 2332, pp. 337–351. [CrossRef]
34. Dolev, D.; Yao, A. On the security of public key protocols. *IEEE Trans. Inf. Theory* **1983**, *29*, 198–208. [CrossRef]
35. Jangirala, S.; Das, A.K.; Vasilakos, A.V. Designing secure lightweight blockchain-enabled RFID-based authentication protocol for supply chains in 5G mobile edge computing environment. *IEEE Trans. Ind. Inform.* **2019**, *16*, 7081–7093. [CrossRef]
36. Khalafalla, M.; Gebotys, C.H. PUFs Deep Attacks: Enhanced modeling attacks using deep learning techniques to break the security of double arbiter PUFs. In Proceedings of the Design, Automation & Test in Europe Conference & Exhibition, Florence, Italy, 25–29 March 2019; pp. 204–209.
37. Zalivaka, S.S.; Ivaniuk, A.A.; Chang, C. Reliable and Modeling Attack Resistant Authentication of Arbiter PUF in FPGA Implementation With Trinary Quadruple Response. *IEEE Trans. Inf. Forensics Secur.* **2019**, *14*, 1109–1123. [CrossRef]
38. Cremers, C.J.F. The Scyther Tool: Verification, Falsification, and Analysis of Security Protocols. In Proceedings of the Computer Aided Verification, Princeton, NJ, USA, 7–14 July 2008; Springer: Berlin/Heidelberg, Germany, 2008; pp. 414–418.
39. Abdalla, M.; Fouque, P.; Pointcheval, D. Password-Based Authenticated Key Exchange in the Three-Party Setting. In *Lecture Notes in Computer Science, Proceedings of the Public Key Cryptography—PKC 2005, 8th International Workshop on Theory and Practice in Public Key Cryptography, Les Diablerets, Switzerland, 23–26 January 2005*; Vaudenay, S., Ed.; Springer: Berlin/Heidelberg, Germany, 2005; Volume 3386, pp. 65–84.
40. Wang, R.; Selimis, G.; Maes, R.; Goossens, S. Long-term Continuous Assessment of SRAM PUF and Source of Random Numbers. In Proceedings of the 2020 Design, Automation & Test in Europe Conference & Exhibition (DATE), Grenoble, France, 9–13 March 2020; pp. 7–12. [CrossRef]
41. Tsai, J.; Lo, N. Secure Anonymous Key Distribution Scheme for Smart Grid. *IEEE Trans. Smart Grid* **2016**, *7*, 906–914. [CrossRef]
42. Leurent, G.; Peyrin, T. From Collisions to Chosen-Prefix Collisions Application to Full SHA-1. In *Lecture Notes in Computer Science, Proceedings of the Advances in Cryptology—EUROCRYPT 2019—38th Annual International Conference on the Theory and Applications of Cryptographic Techniques, Darmstadt, Germany, 19–23 May 2019*; Part III; Ishai, Y., Rijmen, V., Eds.; Springer: Berlin/Heidelberg, Germany, 2019; Volume 11478, pp. 527–555.
43. Atmel. 8-Bit AVR Microcontroller with 32K Bytes In-System Programmable Flash. Microchip. Available online: http://ww1.microchip.com/downloads/en/DeviceDoc/Atmel-7810-Automotive-Microcontrollers-ATmega328P_Datasheet.pdf (accessed on 10 June 2020).
44. Young, R.; McCue, J.; Grant, C. The Power Is On: How IoT Technology Is Driving Energy Innovation. 2016. Available online: https://www2.deloitte.com/us/en/insights/focus/internet-of-things/iot-in-electric-power-industry.html (accessed on 25 December 2023).

future internet MDPI

Review

IoT Firmware Emulation and Its Security Application in Fuzzing: A Critical Revisit

Wei Zhou [1,*], Shandian Shen [1] and Peng Liu [2,*]

[1] School of Cyber Science and Engineering, Huazhong University of Science and Technology, Wuhan 430074, China; shenshandian@hust.edu.cn
[2] College of Information Sciences and Technology, The Pennsylvania State University, University Park, PA 16802, USA
* Correspondence: weizhou_sec@hust.edu.cn (W.Z.); pliu@ist.psu.edu (P.L.)

Abstract: As IoT devices with microcontroller (MCU)-based firmware become more common in our lives, memory corruption vulnerabilities in their firmware are increasingly targeted by adversaries. Fuzzing is a powerful method for detecting these vulnerabilities, but it poses unique challenges when applied to IoT devices. Direct fuzzing on these devices is inefficient, and recent efforts have shifted towards creating emulation environments for dynamic firmware testing. However, unlike traditional software, firmware interactions with peripherals that are significantly more diverse presents new challenges for achieving scalable full-system emulation and effective fuzzing. This paper reviews 27 state-of-the-art works in MCU-based firmware emulation and its applications in fuzzing. Instead of classifying existing techniques based on their capabilities and features, we first identify the fundamental challenges faced by firmware emulation and fuzzing. We then revisit recent studies, organizing them according to the specific challenges they address, and discussing how each specific challenge is addressed. We compare the emulation fidelity and bug detection capabilities of various techniques to clearly demonstrate their strengths and weaknesses, aiding users in selecting or combining tools to meet their needs. Finally, we highlight the remaining technical gaps and point out important future research directions in firmware emulation and fuzzing.

Keywords: IoT devices; MCU; firmware; vulnerability detection; peripheral modeling; firmware emulation; fuzz testing; hardware-in-the-loop

1. Introduction

A microcontroller unit (MCU) is a compact computer on a single integrated circuit, containing one or more CPUs (processor cores), memory like flash, ROM, or RAM, and programmable peripherals. MCUs are widely used in constrained IoT devices due to their low power consumption, compact size, cost-effectiveness, and ability to integrate peripherals for specific tasks. A recent report [1] states that over half of constrained IoT devices use MCUs. However, due to resource constraints, on-chip MCUs lack the security mechanisms present in general computers like x64, x86, and ARM Cortex-A, as well as systems like Windows and Linux [2,3]. For instance, most microcontrollers (MCUs) lack a memory management unit (MMU), which translates virtual memory addresses to physical ones. As a result, firmware on MCUs typically cannot support task isolation or address space randomization protection. In addition, firmware on MCU-based devices, often written in memory-unsafe languages like C/C++, is prone to memory bugs. Due to market pressure and cost constraints, these devices are frequently released without thorough code auditing or security testing, leaving many vulnerabilities. Consequently, MCU-based devices are easily compromised, posing significant risks. The American Information Security Conference in April 2023 reported that over 50% of Distributed Denial of Service (DDoS) attacks stem from the growing number of compromised IoT devices [4].

The rise in vulnerabilities within MCU firmware has led researchers to adapt general software vulnerability detection techniques, particularly for fuzzing. Fuzzing has proven to be a highly effective tool for vulnerability detection over the past decade [5], uncovering thousands of security bugs in various software applications. However, directly applying fuzzing tests to MCU based devices is impractical for firmware due to the slow fuzzing speeds resulting from limited hardware resources. Researchers have attempted dynamic testing in emulated environments, but fuzzing firmware without the original device is difficult due to its tight integration with hardware interfaces (i.e., peripherals). Unlike traditional system-based programs that use well-defined I/O interfaces like POSIX APIs (e.g., `read(fd, buf, len)`), firmware must directly interact with peripheral registers and interfaces. For instance, while a Linux program reads input using `scanf` or `fread(buf, 1, size, fd)`, MCU firmware must first poll peripheral status registers (Line 3), read input from registers (Line 5), and check for errors (Line 6), as shown in Listing 1. The diverse configurations of peripherals across devices make universal emulation difficult. Consequently, there are still significant research gaps in developing automatic, high-fidelity firmware emulation environments and efficient fuzzing techniques.

Listing 1. Code snnippnet of external input reading from UART peripheral in a real-world MCU firmware.

```
1 uint8_t read(...) {
2     ...
3     while (!(USART1->SR & USART_SR_RXNE));
4     uint8_t data = USART1->DR;
5     if (USART1->SR & USART_SR_FE)  return -1;
6     else return data;
7 }
```

Our paper reviews MCU firmware emulation and its fuzzing applications, focusing on works from top international computer security conferences and journals over the past decade (2014–2024), including IEEE S&P, CCS, USENIX Security, NDSS, ACSAC, ASIA CCS, RAID, DSN, ESORICS, IEEE TIFS, and IEEE TDSC. Previous surveys only include works up to 2022 [6–8]. With recent advancements in embedded device emulation technology, especially from 2021 (as shown in Figure 1), it is crucial to revisit the state-of-the-art in MCU-based firmware emulation and its applications. Unlike previous surveys, such as those by Feng et al. [8], which summarize vulnerability detection methods across all firmware types, including Linux-based and MCU-based, on real devices and emulators, our study specifically targets MCU firmware emulation and its fuzzing applications. We deliberately exclude Linux-based firmware and real device fuzzing applications to focus on MCU firmware. This allows for a more detailed discussion of these tools and enables direct comparisons, as they share a common dataset. Moreover, while earlier works categorize studies based on technologies and applications, as seen in Fasano et al. [6] and Wright et al. [7], our approach begins by identifying the key features of MCU firmware to reveal the core challenges impacting emulation and fuzzing. We then reorganize the research on embedded device firmware emulators around these challenges, emphasizing how each study addresses them.

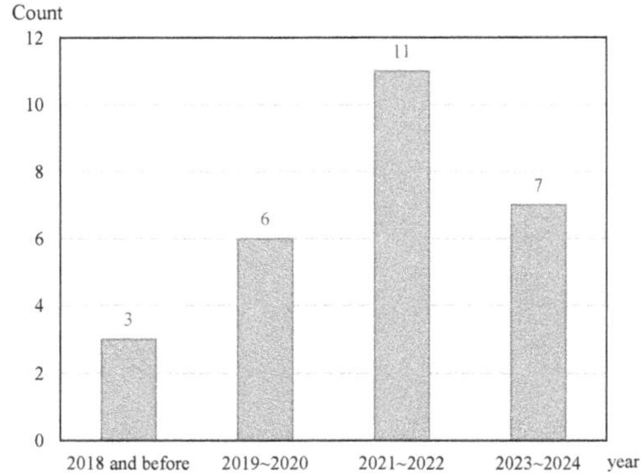

Figure 1. Number of papers related to MCU firmware emulators published in international conferences within 10 years.

The remainder of this article is structured as follows: Section 2 summarizes the software and hardware environment of MCU firmware, highlighting key differences from general software. Section 3 explores the challenges and requirements for full system emulation and enhanced fuzzing applications. Section 4 classifies recent work based on the challenges addressed, summarizing methods, advantages, and drawbacks. Section 5 compares the emulation fidelity and bug detection capabilities of existing approaches. Section 7 identifies technical gaps and suggests future research directions in firmware emulation and fuzzing. Finally, Section 8 concludes the article.

2. Feature of MCU Firmware

This section summarizes the background information of MCU firmware , highlighting three key features that differentiate it from general software as show in in Table 1.

Table 1. Comparison among MCU Firmware, General Purpose OS-based Firmware and General Software.

	Hardware Dependence	OS Type	Layer Boundaries	Driver Diversity	Driver Interfaces
General Software	Low	Few	Clear	Low	Standard
General-purpose OS Based Firmware	Less (Application) High (Driver)	Few	Clear	Moderate	Standard
MCU-based Firmware	High	Many	Blur	No	Custom

2.1. Embedded Firmware Classification and Microcontroller-Based Firmware

Firmware refers to all software on an embedded device, including drivers, systems, and applications. It can be categorized into three types based on the system types used [7].

- **General-purpose OS-based firmware.** This firmware uses adapted versions of traditional operating systems like Linux and Windows for embedded environments, maintaining most desktop functionalities. They rely on high-end CPU architectures like x86 and ARM Cortex-A, allowing general OS functions such as memory isolation of processes. These systems can only run on high-end CPU-based embedded devices like routers, with system and application components compiled separately.
- **Specialized Embedded OS-based firmware.** This category of systems employs specialized embedded operating systems, predominantly real-time operating systems (RTOS), which have lower computing power but higher real-time requirements. Exam-

ples of such RTOS include Zephyr, FreeRTOS, and RIoT. They are typically found in commercial IoT products like small drones. In these systems, the OS and applications are compiled into a unified binary.

- **Bare-metal firmware.** This category includes firmware without an OS abstraction (also called Bare-metal Firmware). The application code directly accesses hardware and is also statically linked into a single binary file, as seen in small sensors.

Due to limited computing and storage resources, only specialized embedded operating systems or bare-metal firmware can run on MCUs. In this paper, "MCU firmware or firmware" refers to this specialized embedded OS or bare-metal firmware.

2.2. Features of MCU Firmware

F1: Diverse hardware dependency environments. Unlike general software that interacts directly with users or external files, firmware relies on hardware peripherals for external interaction, making it tightly to these components. Figure 2 illustrates the hardware environment of a drone based on ARM Cortex-M4 MCU, showcasing various peripherals. These peripherals are categorized into on-chip (e.g., SPI, I2C, UART) and off-chip (e.g., WiFi, Button). Firmware accesses off-chip peripherals indirectly through on-chip peripherals. Firmware interacts with peripherals in four ways (highlighted with red lines):

① **Peripheral Registers R/W:** In most MCUs, such as ARM-based ones, peripheral hardware registers are memory-mapped (MMIO), allowing the processor to access them for status, configuration, and data queries. In a few MCUs, such as Intel 8051, these registers are accessed via port instructions.

② **IRQ:** Actively verifying peripheral registers reading values wastes CPU cycles when no events occur. Many MCUs support configuring peripherals to trigger interrupts for events like timer completions or new data arrivals, allowing firmware to handle them promptly in interrupt service routines (ISRs).

③ **DMA:** To enhance high-throughput data transfer, some MCUs offer Direct Memory Access (DMA), enabling peripherals to transfer data directly to and from main memory, bypassing peripheral register reading via processor for faster large data transfers.

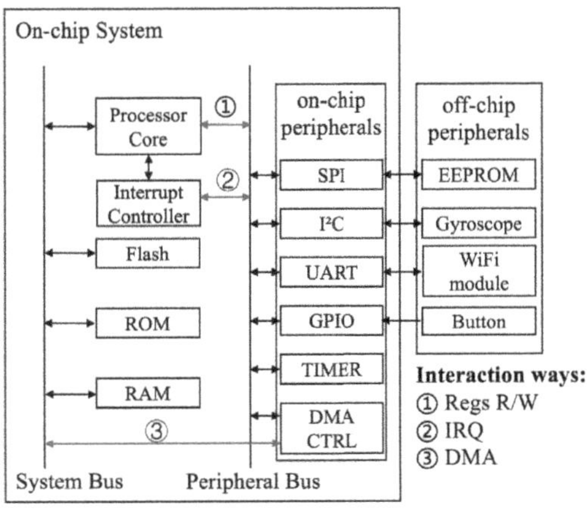

Figure 2. Hardware components of a drone based on ARM Cortex-M4 MCU.

Firmware functionality varies significantly across devices, such as drones and door locks, due to different peripheral controls and methods that can change at runtime. Consequently, peripheral usage by firmware is highly varied, involving numerous methods.

F2: Blurring of boundaries and interface among application, library, and driver code. As illustrated in Figure 3, in general, MCU firmware consists of three layers: the driver layer, the operating system layer, and the application layer. The application layer, developed by programmers, contains the device's functional logic. The system layer includes real-time operating systems like FreeRTOS, Zephyr, and MbedOS for task scheduling and control, along with protocol libraries for external interactions. The driver layer manages hardware peripherals, with most code provided by manufacturers through board support packages (BSP) or open-source hardware abstraction layers (HALs). However, unlike general OSs and software, the layer boundaries in firmware are often blurred, with many components being optional, as shown in Figure 3. For instance, FreeRTOS [9] allows library or application code to interact with hardware directly, bypassing system calls like bare-metal firmware. Moreover, driver code can invoke system calls, such as system queue operations, making it difficult to distinguish driver layers from other code layers.

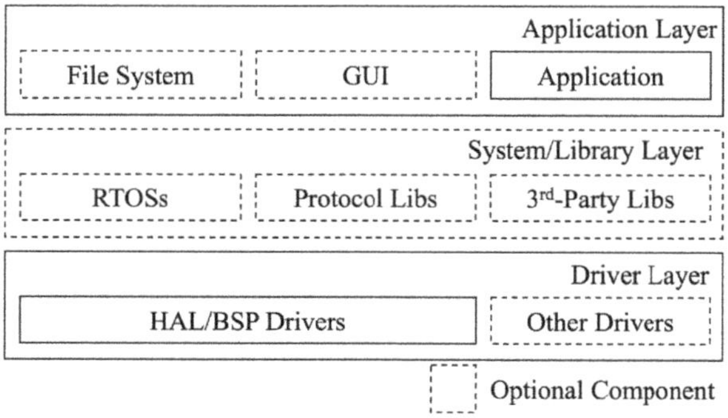

Figure 3. Common components and layers in MCU firmware.

F3: Fragmentation of MCU Firmware Ecosystem. MCU-based devices are tailored for specific tasks, such as sensors or drones, and their firmware is fragmented, unlike the dominant OSs like Linux or Windows. Over 20 IoT operating systems exist, each with its own compatible libraries, such as RT-Thread [10], which offers over 700 packages with multiple versions. Different MCU vendors provide their own HAL/BSP libraries, like STM32CubeMX [11], which are specific to their MCUs. These libraries often implement different driver interfaces for peripheral controls, leading to incompatibility across various HAL/BSP functions and OS drivers. Developers can also integrate third-party libraries or create custom driver code for unique peripherals, compounding to the fragmented software stack in the MCU firmware ecosystem.

3. Challenges Faced by Firmware Emulation and Its Application in Fuzzing

This section highlights the challenges and the ideal goal of firmware emulation and its application in fuzzing, focusing on three aspects of support for firmware emulation approaches. First, CPU emulation, including CPU registers and instruction set translation, is crucial for executing across various hardware architectures. Second, emulating peripheral interactions is challenging due to the diverse peripherals and lack of general system interfaces in MCU-based devices. Lastly, since firmware emulation aims for dynamic testing, it must support fuzzing tests.

3.1. CPU Emulation Support

Although MCU devices use diverse CPU architectures, the number is typically limited to fewer than ten, such as ARM, MIPS, and RISC-V. Tools like *QEMU* [12] and *Unicorn* [13] already support a wide range of commonly used embedded architectures. However, devices used in specialized fields like industrial or automotive applications, such as ECUs, may employ esoteric or custom architecture-specific instructions. Therefore, to emulate MCU firmware, support for any given CPU architecture is necessary.

3.2. Peripheral Interaction Emulation Support

As mentioned in Section 2, while CPU emulation can be manually achieved, the diverse configurations of individual devices make manual support for hundreds or thousands of peripherals impractical. For instance, *QEMU* supports only a few peripherals for fewer than ten MCU versions. Although *QEMU* lists the STM32F405 MCU, it actually supports only six on-chip peripherals, like UART and SPI, out of more than 20 available. Moreover, *QEMU* does not fully support peripheral configurations and interactions; for example, it supports SPI only via peripheral register read/write, lacking interrupt and DMA support. Initially, research like *Avatar* [14] proposed a hardware-in-the-loop solution that emulates only the CPU and forwards peripheral access to real hardware. However, this method suffers from performance issues, as peripheral operations on MCUs are much slower than virtual memory operations on servers (MCU CPU frequency is in the hundreds of MHz, compared to x64 CPUs operating over GHz) and cannot be used for parallel testing. Peripheral emulation should ideally be automatic, have high applicability (capable of emulating any MCU peripheral functions), and offer high fidelity (replicating the control and data flow of a real device without actual hardware).

3.3. Fuzzing Application Enhancement

Fuzzing refers to an automated software testing technique that providing invalid, unexpected, or random data as inputs to a computer program to test whether the program perform as expected, which has been widely used in vulnerability detections. In general software fuzzing, the process includes input generation, delivery, execution, feedback collection, and feedback-guided input mutation. It is divided into a front-end (input generation and mutation) and a back-end (execution environment and feedback). In firmware fuzzing within an emulation environment (see Figure 4), the emulator serves as the back-end, facilitating (1) test case reception, (2) emulated execution, (3) feedback collection, and (4) crash detection. The emulated execution environment relies on CPU and peripheral emulation. Inputs should be delivered when the firmware reads data from peripherals, as fuzzing aims to uncover software bugs, which are more exploitable than hardware bugs. Unlike general software with defined data I/O interfaces (as discussed in F2 and F3 in Section 2), identifying external input/output interfaces in black-box firmware is challenging. For feedback, fuzzers mainly use code coverage, requiring the emulator to support instruction emulation at the basic block level and collect path and basic block feedback [15]. For bug detection, general fuzzers detect bugs by using existing security mechanisms within the target system or an integrated sanitizer. The sanitizer identifies bugs by detecting undefined or suspicious behavior through instrumentation code inserted by the compiler at runtime. However, MCU firmware, often using RTOS or bare-metal resources, lacks these mechanisms and source code for instrumentation, leading to undetected memory corruptions, also known as "silent" bugs [16]. Therefore, the emulator needs to support more fine-grained memory monitoring for bug detection. An ideal fuzzing application on an emulator should have low false-positive and -negative rates for bug detection and testing at high speed.

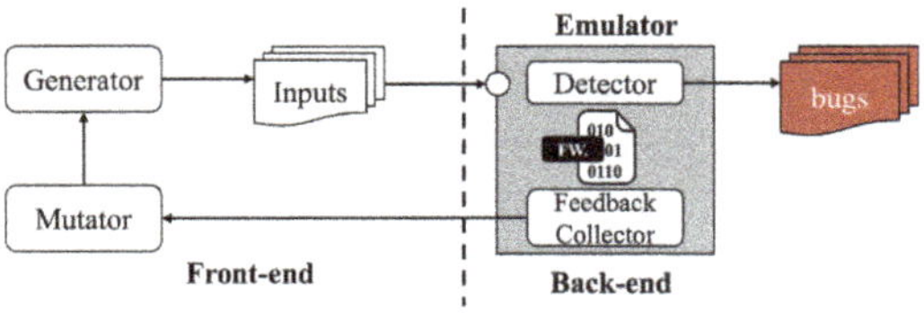

Figure 4. Firmware fuzzing in an emulated environment.

4. State-of-the-Art Firmware Emulation and Its Application in Fuzzing

In this section, we summarize and reorganize the tools from all the research included in Figure 1, categorizing them by the main challenges they address. As shown in Figure 5, since CPU emulation is a fundamental component of firmware emulation, the following works all depend on CPU emulation tools. Tools built on the same platform are generally compatible, as demonstrated by the compatibility between *Fuzzware* and *Halucinator*.

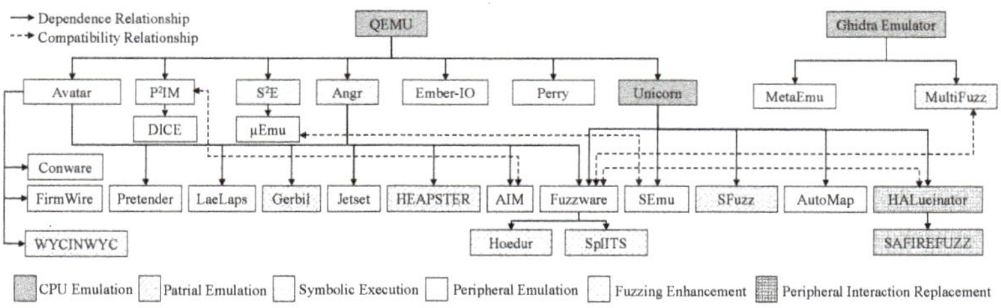

Figure 5. Dependence and compatibility among firmware emulators (the single-arrow line denotes dependence, showing one tool is built upon or enhanced by another; the dotted double-arrow line denotes compatibility, connecting tools that can be used together directly).

4.1. Solution to CPU Emulation Support

General binary emulators like *Simics* [17], *QEMU* [12], and *Unicorn* [13] support most common CPU architectures. *QEMU* and *Unicorn* also offer memory mapping and peripheral forwarding, making them popular for full-system emulation with peripheral interaction emulation tools. However, these emulators struggle with unknown CPU architectures, requiring significant manual effort to add new ones within their Intermediate Representation (IR) frameworks. The *Ghidra* Emulator [18], developed by the NSA, supports more instruction set architectures than *QEMU* and allows users to add new ones using SLEIGH language definitions. For instance, *MetaEmu* [19] addresses the challenge of uncommon processor architectures in automotive firmware through the *Ghidra* Emulator.

In addition, *SAFIREFUZZ* [20] pinpoint instruction translation as a key factor slows down emulation. Instead of translating instructions for a general processor, it executes firmware on more powerful hardware within the same instruction set family. By using high-level peripheral function replacement and dynamic binary rewriting, it replaces peripheral interactions and filters ARM Cortex-M specific instructions, allowing ARM Cortex-M firmware to run on ARM Cortex-A servers without CPU emulation.

4.2. Solutions to Peripheral Interaction Support

Aside from the hardware-in-the-loop solutions, three approaches have been proposed for handling diverse peripheral interaction in an emulated environment as summarized in Table 2.

4.2.1. High-Level Peripheral Interaction Replacement

For Linux-based firmware, researchers can hook the Linux system call interface and redirect it to driver function replacements for full-system emulations, as seen in *Firmadyne* [21], *FirmAE* [22], and *ECMO* [23]. Inspired by this, although MCU-based firmware lacks a standard system call interface and has diverse OS kernels, researchers found that hardware abstraction layer (HAL) interface functions are more common. They proposed intercepting firmware calls to the HAL and replacing them with emulator functions, as performed by *HALucinator* [24]. However, this approach requires a library matching tool to identify HAL functions in the firmware and manual creation of replacement functions, limiting its applicability and increasing labor costs.

4.2.2. Peripheral Interaction Modeling

To emulate diverse peripheral hardware with minimal manual effort, existing research proposes various automatic peripheral interaction modeling methods.

Hardware Record-based method. *Pretender* [25] enhances hardware-in-the-loop solutions for full-system emulation by recording real hardware feedback and using machine learning to create peripheral emulation models. However, *Pretender* still needs the same hardware as the firmware, which is often hard to access for practical firmware analysis. Similarly, *Conware* [26] relies on hardware peripheral operation logs to build peripheral models.

Human Heuristic-based method. P^2IM [27] introduces the first hardware-independent automated method for creating peripheral emulation models. It infers peripheral register types from firmware peripheral access patterns and establishes feedback models based on these types. While effective for simple interactions, its reliance on human assumptions limits its success with complex peripherals. *DICE* [28] uses a similar approach by modeling DMA access patterns to automate DMA emulation models, supporting firmware emulation with DMA-based peripherals. However, it is also constrained by human assumptions, making it unsuitable for complex devices like Ethernet and USB DMA. *FirmWire* [29] offers human-crafted peripheral models for baseband firmware.

Symbolic Constraints-based method. Peripheral modeling using symbolic contrarians is a common approach in current emulation solutions to address the limitations of human heuristics-based approach. *Laelaps* [30] uses symbolic execution to handle unknown peripheral reads by returning symbolic values and exploring program paths. However, it requires continuous symbolic execution, leading to high overhead. To address this, *μEmu* [31] automatically determines execution paths by analyzing execution states. It uses symbolic execution to learn path constraints on valid execution state and create a peripheral feedback knowledge base, which is used during dynamic execution, eliminating the need for continuous symbolic execution and reducing overhead. *Jetset* [32] employs a search strategy with incremental control flow graphs to guide symbolic execution for firmware execution, similar to *μEmu*. *Fuzzware* [33] pinpoints models based on single or few path constraints for overly restricting reachable paths. It uses symbolic execution to generate broad peripheral feedback constraints, allowing more mutations during fuzz testing to explore additional paths. This increases code coverage compared to previous models but also results in more false positives than real hardware. Note that continuous symbolic execution for peripheral input can lead to path explosion and high overhead, so current solutions use local symbolic execution within functions handling peripheral input without exploring all paths.

Fuzzing Feedback-based method. *Ember-IO* [34] introduces a feedback peripheral access method using a fuzz testing feedback scheme. Instead of generating complete peripheral models, it generates all hardware inputs through fuzz testing, caching only those values that achieve higher code coverage to accelerate execution. This method increases code coverage quickly but also results in more false positives and negatives.

External Information-based method. In 2022, Zhou et al. [35] noted that previous methods for generating peripheral models relied solely on firmware, which lacks complete peripheral logic, such as interrupt timing. This limitation leads to false positives in firmware-oriented peripheral modeling. To enhance the accuracy of peripheral emulation models without hardware reliance, they introduced *SEmu*. *SEmu* uses natural language processing (NLP) to learn peripheral behavior from hardware manuals, converting this information into structured conditional-action rules. By executing and linking these rules during runtime, *SEmu* dynamically creates a peripheral model for each accessed peripheral, achieving nearly 100% consistency with real hardware at the basic block level for simple peripherals. Similarly, *Perry* [36] develops high-fidelity peripheral emulator models using external open-source peripheral drivers.

4.2.3. Partial Emulation

For research on specific vulnerabilities or code snippets in firmware where full system emulation is not required, researchers [37–39] propose slicing the code snippet without peripheral interactions. For instance, *HEAPSTER* [37] focuses on detecting heap vulnerabilities within firmware by emulating only a limited number of functions related to heap operations.

Table 2. Summary of peripheral interaction emulation solution.

<table>
<tr><th colspan="2">Method</th><th>Years</th><th>Tools</th><th>Fidelity *</th><th>Automation</th></tr>
<tr><td colspan="2" rowspan="2">Hardware-in-the-loop</td><td>2014</td><td>Avatar [40]</td><td>High</td><td>Low</td></tr>
<tr><td>2022</td><td>AutoMap [41]</td><td>High</td><td>Low</td></tr>
<tr><td colspan="2" rowspan="2">High-level Replacement</td><td>2020</td><td>HALucinator [24]</td><td>Moderate</td><td>Low</td></tr>
<tr><td>2023</td><td>SAFIREFUZZ [20]</td><td>Moderate</td><td>Low</td></tr>
<tr><td rowspan="14">Peripheral Modeling</td><td rowspan="6">Symbolic Constraints-based</td><td>2020</td><td>Laelaps [30]</td><td>Moderate</td><td>Low</td></tr>
<tr><td>2021</td><td>μEmu [31]</td><td>Moderate</td><td>Moderate</td></tr>
<tr><td>2021</td><td>Jetset [32]</td><td>Moderate</td><td>Moderate</td></tr>
<tr><td>2022</td><td>Fuzzware [33]</td><td>Moderate</td><td>High</td></tr>
<tr><td>2022</td><td>MetaEmu [19]</td><td>Low</td><td>Low</td></tr>
<tr><td>2024</td><td>AIM [42]</td><td>Moderate</td><td>Moderate</td></tr>
<tr><td rowspan="2">Hardware Record-based</td><td>2019</td><td>Pretender [25]</td><td>Moderate</td><td>Moderate</td></tr>
<tr><td>2021</td><td>Conware [26]</td><td>Moderate</td><td>Moderate</td></tr>
<tr><td rowspan="3">Human Heuristic-based</td><td>2020</td><td>P²IM [27]</td><td>Moderate</td><td>Moderate</td></tr>
<tr><td>2021</td><td>DICE [28]</td><td>Moderate</td><td>Moderate</td></tr>
<tr><td>2022</td><td>FirmWire [29]</td><td>Moderate</td><td>Low</td></tr>
<tr><td>Fuzzing Feedback-based</td><td>2023</td><td>Ember-IO [34]</td><td>Moderate</td><td>High</td></tr>
<tr><td>Manual-based</td><td>2022</td><td>SEmu [35]</td><td>High</td><td>Low</td></tr>
<tr><td>Driver-based</td><td>2024</td><td>Perry [36]</td><td>High</td><td>Low</td></tr>
<tr><td colspan="2" rowspan="3">Partial Emulation</td><td>2019</td><td>Gerbil [38]</td><td>Low</td><td>Low</td></tr>
<tr><td>2022</td><td>HEAPSTER [37]</td><td>Moderate</td><td>Low</td></tr>
<tr><td>2022</td><td>SFuzz [39]</td><td>Low</td><td>Low</td></tr>
</table>

*: The fidelity level combines execution and data/memory fidelity, as shown in Figure 6.

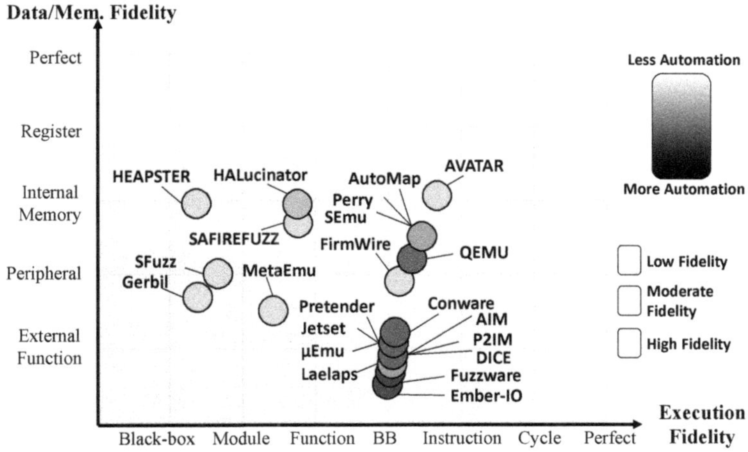

Figure 6. Fidelity of firmware emulators.

4.3. Solutions to Fuzzing Application Enhancement

Recent advancements in peripheral emulation technology have led researchers to redesign the general fuzzing technology to better accommodate real-world firmware-specific features including coverage feedback, input generation and mutation, and crash detection as summarized in Table 3.

Coverage Feedback. As mentioned in Section 2, peripheral interrupts can actively trigger ISR functions causing uncertain bursts in firmware execution. The exact point where the interrupt occurs is usually not crucial, but switching execution to the ISR at different points can create many meaningless new edges for edge-based coverage feedback fuzzers. To address this, *Ember-IO* [34] remaps edge-coverage feedback to separate edges in ISRs from normal execution, eliminating invalid edges from unpredictable interrupts. *MultiFuzz* directly uses basic block coverage to avoid these issues. Additionally, firmware often performs multi-byte magic string checks for command processing in protocols. *SplITS* [43] introduces feedback mechanisms for input-to-state mapping and seed retention for targeted replacement mutations, efficiently handling multi-byte comparisons.

Input Generation and Mutation. Since real-world firmware typically not only uses single peripheral but multiple peripherals at the same time, as shown in the drone in Figure 2. However, existing fuzzers for general applications typically offer only a single flat input. Thus, *Hoedur* [44] and *MultiFuzz* [45] enhanced general fuzzing techniques, especially for input generation and mutation, to address the multi-stream nature of firmware inputs from various peripherals.

Bug Detection. Firmware often contains "silent" bugs that do not cause device crashes. While typical firmware fuzzing applications use basic crash detection, they often miss these silent memory corruptions. To address this, *µSBS* [46] statically instruments binaries to make memory corruptions observable. However, static binary rewriting for firmware is challenging and lacks accuracy, making these solutions suitable only for simple bare-metal firmware.

Table 3. Summary of fuzzing application enhancement solution.

Firmware Feature	Enhanced Component	Years	Tools
Random Peripheral Interrupt	Coverage Feedback	2023	*Ember-IO* [34]
Multi-stream Input	Input Generation & Mutation	2023	*Hoedur* [44]
Magic Value Check		2023	*SplITS* [43]
Multi-stream Input		2024	*MultiFuzz* [45]
Silent Bug	Bug Detection	2018	*WYCINWYC* [16]
		2020	*μSBS* [46]

5. Emulation Fidelity

Emulation fidelity is vital for firmware emulation, affecting its accuracy and applicability in security applications. We qualitatively classify and compare fidelity among firmware emulators, following the approach by Wright et al. [7]. This involves two dimensions: *execution fidelity*, which measures control flow similarity to real hardware, and *data/memory fidelity*, which assesses data consistency in the MCU device (memory and registers) and data output to device peripherals compared to real hardware. Figure 6 summarizes the fidelity distribution of these emulators and their degree of automation.

5.1. Execution Fidelity

Execution fidelity can be categorized into black-box, module-level, function-level, basic-block, instruction-level, cycle-level, and perfect. As illustrated in Figure 5, firmware emulators use *QEMU* [12], *Unicorn* [13], and *Ghidra* [18] for instruction set translation. They convert instructions from a target set to a host set at the basic block level, using an intermediate representation (IR) for translation. This approach provides execution fidelity at most the basic block and instruction levels, even without considering peripheral emulation. Consequently, no firmware emulator can achieve cycle-level fidelity, which accurately replicates the CPU instruction cycle as real hardware does, or perfect fidelity, where the emulator's internal execution mirrors that of the actual machine.

Avatar achieves the highest execution fidelity by forwarding all peripheral access to real hardware. Full system emulation solutions emulate all peripherals to execute entire firmware code, thus their execution fidelity relies on the accuracy of peripheral modeling. Solutions like *AutoMap*, *SEmu* and *Perry*, employ real hardware, hardware descriptions, or driver source code to construct individual models for each peripheral, offering higher fidelity compared to *QEMU*'s manually crafted peripheral emulation. Firmware-specific modeling solutions such as *Jetset*, *P^2IM*, and *Fuzzware*, while more automated, depend on general assumptions without detailed hardware information, leading to lower fidelity. *Conware*, which does not model peripherals but instead uses fuzzing input, results in even lower fidelity. Partial emulation solutions such as *SFuzz*, *Gerbil*, and *HEAPSTER* support only specific firmware functions, achieving module-level execution fidelity. For instance, *HEAPSTER* concentrates on heap operations using heuristic methods, with many functions returning constraint-solved values without actual execution. High-level function replacement solutions fall in the middle; they bypass all peripheral emulation by hooking and replacing the original driver function with a manually crafted function on the host. This approach misses the execution of peripheral-related instructions, thereby ensuring function-level execution consistency. Generally, firmware emulation based solely on the firmware itself tends to have lower execution fidelity. Achieving higher fidelity necessitates additional hardware information and the development of specific peripheral models for various peripherals.

5.2. Data/Memory Fidelity

Data/memory fidelity ordered from coarsest to finest granularity are as follows:

- **External Function:** Data output from firmware in an emulator leads to similar functions as real hardware.
- **Peripheral:** Data output from an emulator matches that of real hardware.
- **Internal Memory:** Data in the memory for running firmware in an emulator is consistent with real hardware.
- **Register:** Data in memory and registers for running firmware in an emulator is consistent with real hardware.
- **Perfect:** All data input, output, and memory space in the emulator matches real hardware at all times, which is virtually unobtainable.

Avatar interacts with real peripherals, ensuring high data memory fidelity. However, due to basic block translation, it handles peripheral interrupts only between blocks, not simultaneously with triggers, maintaining internal memory fidelity. In full system emulation, data fidelity relies on peripheral modeling methods. Solutions like *SEmu*, which use external info for individual peripheral modeling, offer higher fidelity than general firmware-specific models like P^2IM and *Fuzzware*. In partial emulation, fidelity depends on the consistency of emulated module functions. For example, while *HEAPSTER* only emulates heap-related functions, resulting in low execution fidelity, it excludes peripheral data and maintains memory consistency with real hardware. *FirmWire*'s function replacement and peripheral emulation specific to baseband firmware also achieve high fidelity but with less automation. Similarly, high-level replacement solutions using functional replacement functions can achieve higher data consistency than peripheral emulation solutions. As shown in Figure 6, higher execution fidelity enhances data and memory fidelity in full system emulation. In addition, partial emulations or HAL replacement solutions bypass driver code and involve fewer peripheral operations, resulting in data and memory consistency that closely resembles the real device.

Fidelity VS Automation: To achieve higher-fidelity peripheral modeling, simply analyzing firmware itself for general peripheral modeling is insufficient. Specific modeling for different peripherals requires hardware information. Extracting this information directly from the device can lead to hardware dependence issues, while obtaining it from hardware reference manuals or driver code is complex and error-prone. This complexity demands more human effort and reduces automation in high-fidelity modeling, as shown in Figure 6. In contrast, when focusing on a specific application domain, achieving high-fidelity peripheral emulation may not be essential. For instance, HAL-based solutions, as discussed in [24], can be utilized for testing application code exclusively. However, these solutions necessitate the manual implementation of replacement functions. Similarly, partial emulation can be employed to identify bugs that are less pertinent to peripheral operations, such as specific heap-related issues [37], which demand higher-fidelity emulation solely in memory. Nonetheless, the removal of peripheral-dependent code often requires manual intervention, which can impede automation due to indistinct boundaries and custom interfaces, as elaborated in Section 2. In summary, high-fidelity firmware emulation results in reduced automation, as illustrated in Figure 6 and Table 2.

6. Bug Detection Capability of Emulator's Fuzzing Application

Given that the main use of current firmware emulators is fuzzing, this section further compares and discusses their bug detection capabilities in fuzzing applications. We focus on emulators whose main purpose is fuzzing and which have been tested for at least 24 h over multiple targets. Emulators not primarily used for fuzzing, such *Gerbil* [38], *HEAPSTER* [37], and *AIM* [42], are excluded. Similarly, *Conware* [26] and *Avatar* [14], which perform short-time and single-target fuzzing without a dedicated fuzzing process adoption, are also out of scope, as are *Pretender* [25], *Laelaps* [30], and *Jetset* [32]. In our study, we evaluate emulators that satisfy our predefined criteria by comparing their relative false-positive and false-negative rates. This comparison utilizes results derived from fuzzing experiments conducted on shared datasets. Specifically, we employ real-world firmware samples from *P²IM* [27], which have been tested across all the tools under consideration. For instance, the *Fuzzware* tool research paper reports a higher false-positive rate, and subsequent studies confirm this using *P²IM* samples. In contrast, *SEmu* tests the same dataset with no false positives, indicating a low false-positive rate. Meanwhile, *MultiFuzz* claims to find more bugs and achieve higher coverage on the same dataset as *Fuzzware*, suggesting a lower false-negative rate. The results are summarized in Table 4. Table 4 also outlines their fuzzing strategies, including the main functions in front-end and back-end components.

6.1. False Positives

False positives in firmware fuzzing with emulators often result from low-fidelity peripheral emulation, leading to increased manual effort for bug reproduction and confirmation.

Low fidelity in peripheral emulation increases false positives. For instance, feeding fuzzing test cases to peripheral hardware responses can lead to false crashes. Tools like *Fuzzware* and *Ember-IO* might trigger peripheral interrupts before peripheral initialization and even feed fuzzing test cases to hardware-generated MMIO registers reading, such as SRs, causing uninitialized function pointers in interrupt service routines (ISRs) to lead to false crashes. In comparison, fine-grained peripheral models, which incorporated additional hardware information like *SEmu* and *Perry*, have relatively low false-positive rates. Similarly, *FirmWire* and *MetaEmu*, designed for specific applications, rely on manual configuration and tailored test constraints, resulting in fewer false positives. The accuracy of fuzzing enhancements relies on the fidelity of their emulators.

6.2. False Negatives

False negatives in firmware fuzzing can have serious consequences, particularly for security-sensitive devices in applications such as automotive, healthcare, and industry. False negatives can be caused by two reasons: limited code coverage and bug detection capabilities. Greater coverage means more parts of the firmware have been tested, which typically results in fewer false negatives, and the ability to detect more types of bugs in less time also reduces false negatives.

Coverage relies on both emulation capability and fuzzing strategies. If peripheral emulation fails, the firmware may stall, resulting in limited coverage. Improving emulation fidelity can increase coverage and reduce false negatives. Lower fidelity emulation can increase error handling coverage in firmware, but it may mislead fuzzing mutations to focus more on error handling rather than normal operations. For fuzzing strategies, many fuzzing applications rely on general-purpose fuzzers like AFL [47], AFL++ [48], or libafl [49]. Many fuzzing applications use general-purpose fuzzers such as AFL [47], AFL++ [48], and libafl [49]. To achieve higher coverage, recent research [34,43–45] has enhanced general fuzzing technologies for real firmware targets by improving input generation, mutation, and coverage feedback. For instance, *Hoedur* enhances libfuzzer [50] by handling multiple peripheral input streams and applying mutation techniques specific to firmware, such as recognizing peripheral input types and performing cross-input stream mutations, resulting in higher coverage than previous methods.

Table 4. Comparison of firmware emulation's fuzzing applications in bug finding capability.

Tools	Mutation and Generation	Input Interface/Constraints	Coverage Feedback	Bug Detection	FP	FN
HALucinator [24]	AFL	Specified Func./None	Edge	Basic Mem. Error+ Heap-checking	Moderate-low	Moderate
SAFIREFUZZ [20]	LibAFL	Specified Func./None	Non-colliding Edge	Basic Mem. Error	Moderate-low	Moderate
P^2IM [27]	AFL	Identified Data IO/None	Edge	Basic Mem. Error	Moderate-high	Moderate
μEmu [31]	AFL	Identified Data IO/None	Edge	Basic Mem. Error	Moderate	Moderate
DICE [28]	AFL	Identified Data IO/None	Edge	Basic Mem. Error	Moderate	Moderate
Ember-IO [34]	AFL/AFL++	MMIO/Fuzz Cache	Functionally Equivalent Edge	Basic Mem. Error	High	Moderate
Fuzzware [33]	AFL/AFL++	MMIO/Modeling	Edge	Basic Mem. Error	Moderate-high	Moderate
SEmu [35]	AFL/AFL++	Identified Data IO/None	Edge	Basic Mem. Error	Moderate-low	Moderate
Perry [36]	AFL	Specified Func./None	Edge	Basic Mem. Error	Moderate-low	Moderate
Hoedur [44]	LibFuzzer + Δ	MMIO/Multi-Stream +Modeling	Functionally Equivalent Edge	Basic Mem. Error	Emulator Depended	Moderate-low
SplITS [43]	AFL + I2S	MMIO/Multi-Stream +Modeling	Edge + Comparison +Len.	Basic Mem. Error		Moderate-low
MultiFuzz [45]	AFL + I2S+ Len Extension	Specified Func./None	Block	Basic Mem. Error		Moderate-low
μSBS [46]	Fuzzer front-end Depended			Memory Sanitizer *		Moderate-low
SFuzz [39]	AFL++	Specified Func./None	Edge	Basic Mem. Error	Moderate	Moderate
FirmWire [29]	AFL++	Specified Func./Protocol	Edge + Per-task	Basic Mem. Error	Moderate-low	Moderate-low
MetaEmu [19]	LibAFL	Specified Function/None	Edge	Basic Mem. Error	Moderate-low	Moderate
AutoMap [41]	AFL	Identified Data IO/None	Edge	Basic Mem. Error	Moderate-low	Moderate-high

Δ: Len Extension + Cross-value + Cross-stream + Type-awareness. *: includes Null Pointer Dereference, Stack/Heap-based buffer overflow, format string, and double free detection.

Most firmware fuzzers includes basic memory error detection targeting memory segment permission violations, such as buffer overflows or access to unmapped memory. While studies suggest more detailed memory error detection and diverse bug identification, these solutions often come with high overhead or require source code, which is not feasible for real-world firmware [16]. Additionally, they are often specific to simple bare-metal firmware, making them unsuitable for complex firmware like *μSBS* [46].

7. Discussion and Future Research

In this section, we explore current approaches for improved usage and propose directions for future research, as outlined in Figure 7.

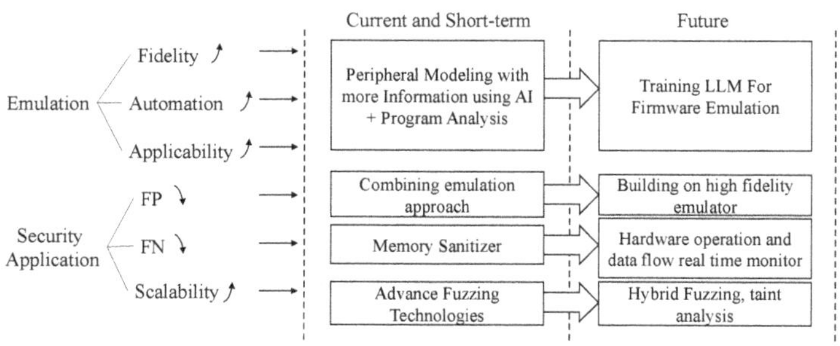

Figure 7. Roadmap for future research directions.

7.1. Selection and Combination of Different Emulation Approaches

With the rise of firmware emulation approaches, various solutions offer distinct advantages for different peripherals and application scenarios, affecting their performance and stability across test sets. Selecting or combining emulators to test target firmware can achieve higher fidelity and efficiency. For instance, while "hardware-in-the-loop" solutions have hardware dependence, it provides a realistic debugging environment through real hardware connections to accomplish high-fidelity emulation. If developers test a device with an unknown peripheral that current tools cannot emulate, they can forward this peripheral to the real hardware while keeping other peripherals in emulation. This approach facilitates testing the device efficiently compared to complete "hardware-in-the-loop" solutions.

HALucinator bypasses peripheral emulation by replacing high-level hardware abstraction layer (HAL) functions with host implementations. However, building a comprehensive database requires HAL source codes from major MCU vendors, limiting support for SoCs with proprietary SDKs. Combining HAL replacement with peripheral modeling approach could create an advanced firmware emulator with higher execution and data fidelity at the same time. Developers can use *HALucinator* to match HAL functions and hook them to host implementations, while peripheral modeling tools can emulate unknown peripherals during runtime.

For applications like baseband or automotive, specialized firmware emulators such as *FirmWire* and *MetaEmu* are preferable over general ones, as they offer more features tailored to these specific uses.

7.2. Basic Information Recovery for Emulation

Most current firmware emulators require developers to configure basic memory layout, start address, and other firmware information, assuming this can be found in the MCU hardware manual or in formats like ELF files with symbol tables. However, firmware dumped from real-world devices is often a pure binary without any information, even the MCU model. Unlike general software binaries, basic information such as memory loading address, entry address, and other definitions vary with different MCU models. For accurate firmware dynamic emulation, knowledge of this information is essential. The absence of this basic information significantly limits the practicality of current academic dynamic analysis tools for real firmware and incurs much manual effort to identify these information before running the tools. Combining statistical analysis techniques, such as determining base addresses through fixed static global variable address analysis, was performed in [51]. The automation of the extraction and construction of a comprehensive firmware information knowledge base is a key technical challenge for firmware emulators.

7.3. Automated High-Fidelity Emulation for Complex and Custom Peripherals

Firmware in safety-critical applications demands high-fidelity emulation for fuzzing, as even minor errors can have severe consequences. For instance, small mistakes in ADAS firmware can result in traffic accidents, and deviations in medical IoT device firmware could endanger lives. However, devices in automotive and industrial sectors often use complex or custom peripherals that current emulators cannot accurately replicate. For example, there is no existing tool that can automatically model complex peripherals like USB or WiFi with precision. As a result, firmware analysis for these devices relies heavily on statistical analysis or custom emulation models, requiring significant manual effort. Automating the accurate generation of complex peripheral emulation models without real hardware is a major technical challenge.

Advancements in AI technology offer new opportunities for achieving high-fidelity peripheral emulation more automatically. For instance, *Conware* converts logs of real peripheral interactions (such as interrupts, reads, and writes) into directed acyclic graphs (DAGs) and uses a novel graph-transformation technique to generate high-fidelity peripheral models. Advanced Reinforcement Learning [52] can also be applied to continually learn from recorded logs, enhancing peripheral modeling. Similarly, `SEmu` utilizes NLP to automatically generate peripheral models from hardware manuals, improving fidelity for complex peripherals. The development of large language models like GPT-4, which have shown greater capability than traditional NLP [53], may further enhance peripheral modeling by learning from hardware manuals. With the advancement of LLMs, we can train specialized models for firmware emulation using extensive firmware datasets, hardware manuals, and open-source MCU software stacks in future.

7.4. More and Effective Security Application Support

Currently, advanced fuzzing techniques like hybrid fuzzing [54], directed fuzzing [55], and stateful fuzzing [56], along with dynamic bug detectors such as *MSan* [57] and *UBSan* [58], are not widely adopted for firmware targets. This is primarily due to two reasons: first, the black-box nature of binaries makes instrumentation and context inference, such as state variables, challenging for directed, stateful fuzzing and sanitizers. Second, although symbolic execution has been integrated into emulation environments, it is mainly used for peripheral modeling rather than continuous hybrid fuzzing like *QSYM* [54]. This limitation arises from the need to modify machine code for improved symbolic execution performance, which is tightly coupled with host architecture. The diverse and distinct nature of firmware architectures presents challenges for such applications. To advance fuzzing technology, future efforts should combine it with statistical analysis for better information inference and focus on instrumenting intermediate representations rather than directly on binary code to support diverse CPU architectures.

Firmware emulation security applications are mainly limited to fuzz testing due to low data and memory fidelity. As emulation fidelity improves, more security analysis technologies, such as taint analysis for detecting vulnerabilities like command injections, can be applied to firmware targets. Additionally, MCU devices are used in security-sensitive environments. Compliance checks with hardware operations are crucial, as errors that do not affect control or data flow can still cause serious issues, such as failing to engage brakes in an ASDS.

8. Conclusions

The increasing security vulnerabilities in microcontroller unit (MCU)-based devices have heightened the focus on vulnerability detection in MCU firmware. Current research emphasizes testing firmware in emulated environments to achieve higher levels of automation and efficiency, as well as to extract more internal information for identifying a broader range of security issues. Our paper revisits the latest MCU firmware emulation approaches, focusing on its key features and identifying core challenges in CPU emulation, peripheral emulation, and fuzzing application enhancement. We categorize existing emulators based on fidelity and bug detection capabilities to help users choose the right tools. Although advancements have been made, current emulators still face challenges in balancing fidelity, automation, and adaptability, indicating room for improvement. We also explore future research opportunities and how emerging technologies, such as LLM, can address these challenges. We posit that the integration of binary analysis with advanced AI technologies will significantly enhance the automation, fidelity, and applicability of firmware emulation and expanding security applications, making it a prominent area of interest in the near future.

Funding: Peng Liu was funded by National Science Foundation under grant number CNS-2019340, ECCS-2140175, the Department of Energy Office of Cybersecurity, Energy Security, and Emergency Response (DOE CESER) under grant number RC-40125b-2023. Wei Zhou and Shandian Shen were funded by the National Natural Science Foundation of China under grant number 62202188.

Conflicts of Interest: The authors declare no conflicts of interest.

References

1. Foundation, E. IoT and Embedded Survey Report 2024. Available online: https://outreach.eclipse.foundation/iot-embedded-developer-survey-2024 (accessed on 21 December 2024).
2. Abbasi, A.; Wetzels, J.; Holz, T.; Etalle, S. Challenges in designing exploit mitigations for deeply embedded systems. In Proceedings of the 2019 IEEE European Symposium on Security and Privacy (EuroS&P), Stockholm, Sweden, 17–19 June 2019; pp. 31–46.
3. Zhou, W.; Jiang, Z.; Guan, L. Understanding MPU Usage in Microcontroller-based Systems in the Wild. In Proceedings of the Workshop on Binary Analysis Research (BAR) 2023, San Diego, CA, USA, 3 March 2023.
4. NSFoCus. Insight RSA 2023: Botnet Threat Situation Observation. Available online: http://blog.nsfocus.net/rsa-2023insight2/ (accessed on 19 November 2024).
5. Godefroid, P. Fuzzing: Hack, art, and science. *Commun. ACM* **2020**, *63*, 70–76. [CrossRef]
6. Fasano, A.; Ballo, T.; Muench, M.; Leek, T.; Bulekov, A.; Dolan-Gavitt, B.; Egele, M.; Francillon, A.; Lu, L.; Gregory, N.; et al. Sok: Enabling security analyses of embedded systems via rehosting. In Proceedings of the 2021 ACM Asia Conference on Computer and Communications Security (CCS), Online, Hong Kong, 7–11 June 2021; pp. 687–701.
7. Wright, C.; Moeglein, W.A.; Bagchi, S.; Kulkarni, M.; Clements, A.A. Challenges in firmware re-hosting, emulation, and analysis. *ACM Comput. Surv. (CSUR)* **2021**, *54*, 1–36. [CrossRef]
8. Feng, X.; Zhu, X.; Han, Q.L.; Zhou, W.; Wen, S.; Xiang, Y. Detecting vulnerability on IoT device firmware: A survey. *IEEE/CAA J. Autom. Sin.* **2022**, *10*, 25–41. [CrossRef]
9. FreeRTOS. FreeRTOS LTS libraries. Available online: https://www.freertos.org/Documentation/03-Libraries/01-Library-overview/03-LTS-libraries/01-LTS-libraries (accessed on 21 December 2024).

10. RT-Thread. RT-Thread Packages. Available online: https://packages.rt-thread.org/ (accessed on 21 December 2024).
11. STMicroelectronics. STM32Cube Initialization Code Generator. Available online: https://www.st.com/en/development-tools/stm32cubemx.html (accessed on 21 December 2024).
12. Bellard, F. QEMU, a fast and portable dynamic translator. In Proceedings of the USENIX Annual Technical Conference, FREENIX Track, Anaheim, CA, USA, 10–15 April 2005; pp. 41–46.
13. Quynh, N.A.; Vu, D.H. Unicorn: Next Generation CPU Emulator Framework. Available online: https://www.blackhat.com/docs/us-15/materials/us-15-Nguyen-Unicorn-Next-Generation-CPU-Emulator-Framework.pdf (accessed on 21 December 2024).
14. Muench, M.; Nisi, D.; Francillon, A.; Balzarotti, D. Avatar 2: A multi-target orchestration platform. In Proceedings of the Workshop on Binary Analysis Research (BAR) 2018, San Diego, CA, USA, 18 February 2018; pp. 1–11.
15. Kargén, U.; Shahmehri, N. Speeding up bug finding using focused fuzzing. In Proceedings of the 13th International Conference on Availability, Reliability and Security (ARES) 2018, Hamburg, Germany, 27–30 August 2018; pp. 1–10.
16. Muench, M.; Stijohann, J.; Kargl, F.; Francillon, A.; Balzarotti, D. What You Corrupt Is Not What You Crash: Challenges in Fuzzing Embedded Devices. In Proceedings of the 25th Annual Network and Distributed System Security Symposium (NDSS) 2018, San Diego, CA, USA, 18–21 February 2018.
17. Magnusson, P.S.; Christensson, M.; Eskilson, J.; Forsgren, D.; Hallberg, G.; Hogberg, J.; Larsson, F.; Moestedt, A.; Werner, B. Simics: A full system simulation platform. *Computer* **2002**, *35*, 50–58. [CrossRef]
18. Agency, N.S. NSA's Research Directorat Ghidra. Available online: https://ghidra-sre.org/ (accessed on 19 November 2024).
19. Chen, Z.; Thomas, S.L.; Garcia, F.D. Metaemu: An architecture agnostic rehosting framework for automotive firmware. In Proceedings of the 2022 ACM SIGSAC Conference on Computer and Communications Security (CCS), Los Angeles, CA, USA, 7–11 November 2022; pp. 515–529.
20. Seidel, L.; Maier, D.C.; Muench, M. Forming Faster Firmware Fuzzers. In the Proceedings of the 32nd USENIX Security Symposium, Anaheim, CA, USA, 9–11 August 2023; pp. 2903–2920.
21. Chen, D.D.; Woo, M.; Brumley, D.; Egele, M. Towards automated dynamic analysis for linux-based embedded firmware. 23rd Annual Network and Distributed System Security Symposium (NDSS) 2016, San Diego, California, USA, 21- 24 February 2016; Volume 1, p. 1.
22. Kim, M.; Kim, D.; Kim, E.; Kim, S.; Jang, Y.; Kim, Y. Firmae: Towards large-scale emulation of iot firmware for dynamic analysis. In Proceedings of the 36th Annual Computer Security Applications Conference (ACSAC) 2020, Online/Austin, TX, USA, 7–11 December 2020; pp. 733–745.
23. Jiang, M.; Ma, L.; Zhou, Y.; Liu, Q.; Zhang, C.; Wang, Z.; Luo, X.; Wu, L.; Ren, K. ECMO: Peripheral transplantation to Rehost embedded Linux kernels. In Proceedings of the 2021 ACM SIGSAC Conference on Computer and Communications Security (CCS), Online, Republic of Korea, 15–19 November 2021; pp. 734–748.
24. Clements, A.A.; Gustafson, E.; Scharnowski, T.; Grosen, P.; Fritz, D.; Kruegel, C.; Vigna, G.; Bagchi, S.; Payer, M. HALucinator: Firmware re-hosting through abstraction layer emulation. In Proceedings of the 29th USENIX Security Symposium, Online, 12–14 August 2020; pp. 1201–1218.
25. Gustafson, E.; Muench, M.; Spensky, C.; Redini, N.; Machiry, A.; Fratantonio, Y.; Balzarotti, D.; Francillon, A.; Choe, Y.R.; Kruegel, C.; et al. Toward the analysis of embedded firmware through automated re-hosting. In Proceedings of the 22nd International Symposium on Research in Attacks, Intrusions and Defenses (RAID) 2019, Chaoyang District, Beijing, China, 23–25 September 2019; pp. 135–150.
26. Spensky, C.; Machiry, A.; Redini, N.; Unger, C.; Foster, G.; Blasband, E.; Okhravi, H.; Kruegel, C.; Vigna, G. Conware: Automated modeling of hardware peripherals. In Proceedings of the 2021 ACM Asia Conference on Computer and Communications Security (AsiaCCS), Online, Hong Kong, 7–11 June 2021; pp. 95–109.
27. Feng, B.; Mera, A.; Lu, L. P^2IM: Scalable and hardware-independent firmware testing via automatic peripheral interface modeling. In Proceedings of the 29th USENIX Security Symposium, Online, 12–14 August 2020; pp. 1237–1254.
28. Mera, A.; Feng, B.; Lu, L.; Kirda, E. DICE: Automatic emulation of DMA input channels for dynamic firmware analysis. In Proceedings of the 2021 IEEE Symposium on Security and Privacy (SP), San Francisco, CA, USA, 24–27 May 2021; pp. 1938–1954.
29. Hernandez, G.; Muench, M.; Maier, D.; Milburn, A.; Park, S.; Scharnowski, T.; Tucker, T.; Traynor, P.; Butler, K. FIRMWIRE: Transparent dynamic analysis for cellular baseband firmware. In Proceedings of the Network and Distributed Systems Security Symposium (NDSS) 2022, San Diego, CA, USA, 24–28 April 2022.
30. Cao, C.; Guan, L.; Ming, J.; Liu, P. Device-agnostic firmware execution is possible: A concolic execution approach for peripheral emulation. In Proceedings of the 36th Annual Computer Security Applications Conference (ACSAC) 2020, Austin, TA, USA, 7–11 December 2020; pp. 746–759.
31. Zhou, W.; Guan, L.; Liu, P.; Zhang, Y. Automatic firmware emulation through invalidity-guided knowledge inference. In Proceedings of the 30th USENIX Security Symposium, Online, 11–13 August 2021; pp. 2007–2024.

32. Johnson, E.; Bland, M.; Zhu, Y.; Mason, J.; Checkoway, S.; Savage, S.; Levchenko, K. Jetset: Targeted firmware rehosting for embedded systems. In Proceedings of the 30th USENIX Security Symposium, Online, 11–13 August 2021; pp. 321–338.
33. Scharnowski, T.; Bars, N.; Schloegel, M.; Gustafson, E.; Muench, M.; Vigna, G.; Kruegel, C.; Holz, T.; Abbasi, A. Fuzzware: Using precise MMIO modeling for effective firmware fuzzing. In Proceedings of the 31st USENIX Security Symposium, Boston, MA, USA, 10–12 August 2022; pp. 1239–1256.
34. Farrelly, G.; Chesser, M.; Ranasinghe, D.C. Ember-IO: Effective firmware fuzzing with model-free memory mapped IO. In Proceedings of the 2023 ACM Asia Conference on Computer and Communications Security (AsiaCCS), Melbourne, VIC, Australia, 10–14 July 2023; pp. 401–414.
35. Zhou, W.; Zhang, L.; Guan, L.; Liu, P.; Zhang, Y. What your firmware tells you is not how you should emulate it: A specification-guided approach for firmware emulation. In Proceedings of the 2022 ACM SIGSAC Conference on Computer and Communications Security (CCS), Los Angeles, CA, USA, 7–11 November 2022; pp. 3269–3283.
36. Lei, C.; Ling, Z.; Zhang, Y.; Yang, Y.; Luo, J.; Fu, X. A Friend's Eye is A Good Mirror: Synthesizing MCU Peripheral Models from Peripheral Drivers. In Proceedings of the 33rd USENIX Security Symposium, Philadelphia, PA, USA, 14–16 August 2024; pp. 7085–7102.
37. Gritti, F.; Pagani, F.; Grishchenko, I.; Dresel, L.; Redini, N.; Kruegel, C.; Vigna, G. Heapster: Analyzing the security of dynamic allocators for monolithic firmware images. In Proceedings of the 2022 IEEE Symposium on Security and Privacy (SP), San Francisco, CA, USA, 22–26 May 2022; pp. 1082–1099.
38. Yao, Y.; Zhou, W.; Jia, Y.; Zhu, L.; Liu, P.; Zhang, Y. Identifying privilege separation vulnerabilities in IoT firmware with symbolic execution. In Proceedings of the 24th European Symposium on Research in Computer Security (ESORICS) 2019, Luxembourg, 23–27 September 2019; pp. 638–657.
39. Chen, L.; Cai, Q.; Ma, Z.; Wang, Y.; Hu, H.; Shen, M.; Liu, Y.; Guo, S.; Duan, H.; Jiang, K.; et al. Sfuzz: Slice-based fuzzing for real-time operating systems. In Proceedings of the 2022 ACM SIGSAC Conference on Computer and Communications Security (CCS), Los Angeles, CA, USA, 7–11 November 2022; pp. 485–498.
40. Zaddach, J.; Bruno, L.; Francillon, A.; Balzarotti, D.; et al. AVATAR: A Framework to Support Dynamic Security Analysis of Embedded Systems' Firmwares. In Proceedings of the 21st Annual Network and Distributed System Security Symposium (NDSS) 2014, San Diego, CA, USA, 23–26 February 2014; Volume 14, pp. 1–16.
41. Won, J.Y.; Wen, H.; Lin, Z. What You See is Not What You Get: Revealing Hidden Memory Mapping for Peripheral Modeling. In Proceedings of the 25th International Symposium on Research in Attacks, Intrusions and Defenses (RAID) 2022, Limassol, Cyprus, 26–28 October 2022; pp. 200–213.
42. Feng, B.; Luo, M.; Liu, C.; Lu, L.; Kirda, E. AIM: Automatic Interrupt Modeling for Dynamic Firmware Analysis. *IEEE Trans. Dependable Secur. Comput.* **2023**, *21*, 3866–3882. [CrossRef]
43. Farrelly, G.; Quirk, P.; Kanhere, S.S.; Camtepe, S.; Ranasinghe, D.C. SplITS: Split Input-to-State Mapping for Effective Firmware Fuzzing. In Proceedings of 28th European Symposium on Research in Computer Security (ESORICS) 2023, The Hague, The Netherlands, 25–29 September 2023; pp. 290–310.
44. Scharnowski, T.; Wörner, S.; Buchmann, F.; Bars, N.; Schloegel, M.; Holz, T. Hoedur: Embedded Firmware Fuzzing using Multi-Stream Inputs. In Proceedings of the 32nd USENIX Security Symposium, Anaheim, CA, USA, 9–11 August 2023.
45. Chesser, M.; Nepal, S.; Ranasinghe, D.C. MultiFuzz: A Multi-Stream Fuzzer For Testing Monolithic Firmware. In Proceedings of the 33rd USENIX Security Symposium, Philadelphia, PA, USA, 14–16 August 2024; pp. 5359–5376.
46. Salehi, M.; Hughes, D.; Crispo, B. μSBS: Static Binary Sanitization of Bare-metal Embedded Devices for Fault Observability. In Proceedings of the 23rd International Symposium on Research in Attacks, Intrusions and Defenses (RAID) 2020, San Sebastian, Spain, 14–15 October 2020; pp. 381–395.
47. Zalewski, M. American Fuzzy Lop. Available online: http://lcamtuf.coredump.cx/afl/ (accessed on 21 December 2024).
48. Fioraldi, A.; Maier, D.; Eißfeldt, H.; Heuse, M. AFL++: Combining Incremental Steps of Fuzzing Research. In Proceedings of the 14th USENIX Workshop on Offensive Technologies (WOOT) 2020, Online, 11 August 2020.
49. Fioraldi, A.; Maier, D.C.; Zhang, D.; Balzarotti, D. Libafl: A framework to build modular and reusable fuzzers. In Proceedings of the 2022 ACM SIGSAC Conference on Computer and Communications Security (CCS), Los Angeles, CA, USA, 7–11 November 2022; pp. 1051–1065.
50. LLVM. libFuzzer—A Library for Coverage-Guided Fuzz Testing. Available online: https://llvm.org/docs/LibFuzzer.html (accessed on 19 November 2024).
51. Wen, H.; Lin, Z.; Zhang, Y. Firmxray: Detecting bluetooth link layer vulnerabilities from bare-metal firmware. In Proceedings of the 2020 ACM SIGSAC Conference on Computer and Communications Security (CCS), Online, USA, 9–13 November 2020; pp. 167–180.

52. Shakya, A.K.; Pillai, G.; Chakrabarty, S. Reinforcement learning algorithms: A brief survey. *Expert Syst. Appl.* **2023**, *231*, 120495. [CrossRef]
53. Baktash, J.A.; Dawodi, M. Gpt-4: A review on advancements and opportunities in natural language processing. *arXiv* **2023**, arXiv:2305.03195.
54. Yun, I.; Lee, S.; Xu, M.; Jang, Y.; Kim, T. QSYM: A practical concolic execution engine tailored for hybrid fuzzing. In Proceedings of the 27th USENIX Security Symposium, Baltimore, MD, USA, 15–17 August 2018; pp. 745–761.
55. Böhme, M.; Pham, V.T.; Nguyen, M.D.; Roychoudhury, A. Directed greybox fuzzing. In Proceedings of the 2017 ACM SIGSAC Conference on Computer and Communications Security (CCS), Dallas, Texas, USA, 30 October–3 November 2017; pp. 2329–2344.
56. Ba, J.; Böhme, M.; Mirzamomen, Z.; Roychoudhury, A. Stateful greybox fuzzing. In Proceedings of the 31st USENIX Security Symposium, Boston, MA, USA, 10–12 August 2022; pp. 3255–3272.
57. Stepanov, E.; Serebryany, K. MemorySanitizer: Fast detector of uninitialized memory use in C++. In Proceedings of the 2015 IEEE/ACM International Symposium on Code Generation and Optimization (CGO), San Francisco, CA, USA, 7–11 February 2015; pp. 46–55.
58. Developers, L. Undefined Behavior Sanitizer. Available online: https://clang.llvm.org/docs/UndeïňĄnedBehaviorSanitizer.html (accessed on 19 November 2024).

future internet

MDPI

Review

Recent Advancements in Federated Learning: State of the Art, Fundamentals, Principles, IoT Applications and Future Trends

Christos Papadopoulos, Konstantinos-Filippos Kollias and George F. Fragulis *

Internet of Things & Applications Lab, Department of Electrical & Computer Engineering, University of Western Macedonia, ZEP Campus, 50100 Kozani, Greece; chrispapadopoulos998@gmail.com (C.P.); dece00063@uowm.gr (K.-F.K.)
* Correspondence: gfragulis@uowm.gr

Abstract: Federated learning (FL) is creating a paradigm shift in machine learning by directing the focus of model training to where the data actually exist. Instead of drawing all data into a central location, which raises concerns about privacy, costs, and delays, FL allows learning to take place directly on the device, keeping the data safe and minimizing the need for transfer. This approach is especially important in areas like healthcare, where protecting patient privacy is critical, and in industrial IoT settings, where moving large numbers of data is not practical. What makes FL even more compelling is its ability to reduce the bias that can occur when all data are centralized, leading to fairer and more inclusive machine learning outcomes. However, it is not without its challenges—particularly with regard to keeping the models secure from attacks. Nonetheless, the potential benefits are clear: FL can lower the costs associated with data storage and processing, while also helping organizations to meet strict privacy regulations like GDPR. As edge computing continues to grow, FL's decentralized approach could play a key role in shaping how we handle data in the future, moving toward a more privacy-conscious world. This study identifies ongoing challenges in ensuring model security against adversarial attacks, pointing to the need for further research in this area.

Keywords: federated learning; data privacy; decentralized model; adversarial attacks; IoT applications

1. Introduction

Federated learning (FL) is an innovative approach to decentralized machine learning, particularly relevant in an era characterized by modern mobile devices that gather vast amounts of user data. As highlighted by McMahan, these devices can significantly enhance the user experience by using data to train models, such as improving speech recognition or photo selection. However, due to the huge and privacy-sensitive nature of the data, central storage and traditional training methods are often impractical. FL proposes a paradigm whereby the data remain on the device, and a shared model is developed by aggregating locally computed updates. This method effectively handles unbalanced and non-IID data distributions while reducing the communication costs, making it an innovative solution in machine learning. The core of FL involves a framework allowing devices or nodes, like computers and mobile phones, to learn autonomously from their locally stored data. Instead of sending all raw data, they perform on-site training and share only model updates with a central server. This server aggregates the updates to refine a global model, which is then shared back with the devices for further improvements. Federated learning is a revolutionary advancement from traditional machine learning, where data had to be centralized. Now, model training happens directly at the data source, preserving privacy and reducing the transfer costs. FL is not only theoretical—it is enabling advances in industries like healthcare and industrial IoT, where data privacy and bandwidth limitations are critical. However, with great innovation, new challenges emerge. FL confronts privacy issues directly, but it also raises questions about model security and optimization. The models relied on previously for centralized systems are not suitable for a federated environment, so we need new algorithms and strategies. FL's decentralized approach is not merely focused on security—it considers efficiency. It reduces the data transfer overhead, making it a powerful solution in environments with limited bandwidth and computing power. Moreover, it is in line with strict data protection laws like GDPR, offering smart solutions for cross-border data transfer. As for economics, there are significant reductions in data storage, transfer, and processing costs. This study examines the domain of federated learning, highlighting its complexities, potential, and challenges. We start by defining FL and its performance, providing a strong foundation. Then, we explore how FL is already being used across mobile environments, organizations, and the IoT. We also address the challenges that come with FL's decentralized nature. Next, we contrast FL's unique features with those of traditional centralized learning. We delve into data privacy tools like differential privacy and homomorphic encryption and explore personalization strategies. We consider non-IID data in federated systems, along with the design space of FL and data distribution strategies, as well as ensuring robustness in distributed learning. We examine how FL interacts with traditional machine learning, breaking down different FL structures like horizontal and vertical FL, and we discuss federated transfer learning. We present potential threats and a full view of both the opportunities and vulnerabilities.

IID refers to independent and identically distributed data, which are commonly contrasted with non-IID data in the context of federated learning. This term refers to data in which each data point is independent of others and follows the same probability distribution. In federated learning, handling non-IID data is a significant challenge, as the data held by different devices or clients are often not uniformly distributed, leading to potential biases in the global model and slower convergence rates.

Finally, we give details regarding the algorithms and frameworks that enable FL to operate, like the Federated Averaging (FedAvg) algorithm and tools like TensorFlow and PySyft. We also address the risks—model inversion, data poisoning, and Sybil attacks—and the defenses needed to keep FL systems secure.

This survey offers a comprehensive examination of federated learning (FL), a decentralized machine learning approach that enhances data privacy and reduces communication overheads. It covers both the theoretical underpinnings and practical applications of FL in sectors like healthcare and IoT, addressing challenges such as data security, regulatory compliance, and model optimization. This paper stands out by exploring FL algorithms, frameworks, and security risks while proposing mitigation strategies. Its holistic approach caters to both beginners and experts, providing valuable insights to leverage FL's potential in real-world applications and guiding future research in this evolving field.

Our paper's major goal is to present a comprehensive overview of federated learning (FL), including the current achievements, problems, and future applications in areas such as IoT, healthcare, and data privacy. While survey articles typically summarize the state of the art, our purpose goes beyond simply gathering information. Our paper's specific goal is to examine and highlight existing difficulties in FL, as well as presenting a road map for future study. The research questions (RQ) that we examine are as follows.

RQ1: How can federated learning (FL) strike a balance between data privacy, security, and communication costs while retaining model performance?

This point is critical since FL aims to keep data decentralized while maintaining high accuracy and security standards. Understanding how to ensure this equilibrium can help to guide future algorithmic advancements.

RQ2: What security problems, such as adversarial attacks, must be addressed to ensure the viability of FL deployment in real-world applications?

With the rising number of security threats in decentralized systems, particularly in vital sectors such as healthcare, this paper aims to identify the limitations of the present security solutions and consider how future work can overcome these. These questions not only correlate with this paper's primary thesis, but they also demonstrate the survey's structure by focusing on crucial areas of FL that are yet to be examined.

This paper is structured as follows. In Section 2, we introduce federated learning by covering its background and foundational concepts. Section 3 explores the opportunities, challenges, and applications of FL across various domains. Section 4 categorizes the types of FL, such as horizontal and vertical FL. Section 5 examines the key attributes and characteristics of FL, like privacy and scalability. Section 6 discusses the algorithms and frameworks that underpin FL. Section 7 addresses potential attack strategies and mitigation techniques. Section 8 provides a critical discussion of the findings, and Section 9 concludes with future implications and directions for research.

2. Background Material—Introduction to FL

Federated learning (FL) changes machine learning by training models on devices like smartphones and IoT sensors instead of a central server. This method enhances data privacy, reduces transport costs, and meets real-time processing needs [1]. It improves privacy in healthcare and overcomes bandwidth issues in industrial IoT. FL also reduces biases and creates more inclusive models. However, ensuring the security of decentralized systems is a challenge. FL helps to comply with privacy regulations like GDPR, and its efficiency could lead to lower costs in data management. As edge computing grows, FL is key to a privacy-focused, efficient future.

2.1. FL Basics

FL pioneers a unique approach: instead of transferring data to a central point for analysis and model building [2,3], the training itself takes place where the data reside; see Figure 1.

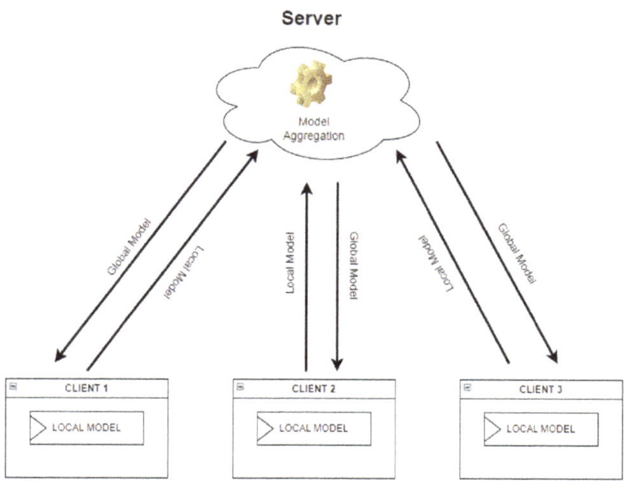

Figure 1. Federated learning architecture.

FL allows multiple users in a network to utilize their local data to contribute to an integrated, global model. This process, while ensuring data privacy, also uses the diverse and expansive nature of the data residing on these devices, leading to more robust and generalizable models.

The FL process consists of three core parts.

- Learning Algorithm and Training: The server trains a model by repeating several steps, like designing the learning algorithm, selecting clients, distributing the model, updating the client model, and server-side aggregation and model updates.

- Privacy Protection Mechanism: FL can protect users' data privacy by employing data encryption training, ensuring that the model does not reveal the original data. Additionally, encrypting the data transmission process ensures that only intermediary results without extra information are relayed during the training process.
- Incentive Mechanism: Since FL relies on participation, it is essential to offer adequate incentives to participants. The incentive mechanism strives to equitably share the benefits of FL, motivating users to participate consistently and deterring malicious actors from dominating the process.

A more analytical outline of the FL process can be provided as follows [4].

- Initialization: On a server, a global model is created.
- Model Distribution: This global model is dispatched to the various participating nodes or devices.
- Local Training: Each node dedicates itself to training this model using its reservoir of local data.
- Model Update Sharing: After this training, the nodes send back model updates to the central server.
- Aggregation: The central entity aggregates these updates, often employing techniques like Federated Averaging, as proposed by [5].
- Iteration: The previous three steps (distribution, training, and aggregation) are reiterated until the model achieves an acceptable level of performance.

Despite FL's design, issues persist, such as ensuring the twin objectives of secure and efficient communication, navigating the heterogeneity of systems, handling skewed and non-IID data, and combating malicious threats. In [6], the authors specifically underscore the importance of data security and the need for efficient communication channels that prioritize the transfer of only the most pivotal model updates, minimizing data breach risks. Several distinct concerns associated with the more conventional centralized learning approach are addressed seamlessly by FL, which can be categorized into the following three classes.

- Regulatory Hurdles: Globally, there has been a surge in regulations, such as GDPR in Europe, CCPA in California, and PDPB in India. These laws present strict rules regarding the movement and mixture of sensitive data, especially when the data protection standards vary across regions. FL addresses these regulatory complexities by minimizing data movement.
- User Privacy: Users are increasingly concerned about the privacy of their data. Applications that involve inputting sensitive information like passwords or credit card details raise expectations that such details remain on the device, shielded from external servers. FL addresses this expectation, reinforcing users' trust.
- Data Volume and Bandwidth: A growing number of devices, especially those like surveillance cameras, generate vast data volumes. Transferring this vast amount of data centrally is not only a logistical challenge but is often not economically viable. By enabling on-site training, FL substantially reduces the bandwidth demands, making it a more scalable option.

2.2. *Definitions and Alternative Nomenclature in Distributed Learning*

Federated learning is a rapidly evolving topic in machine learning, marked by the emergence of various terminologies that often overlap with or resemble FL. Understanding these terms is crucial for scholars, practitioners, and industry experts to ensure clear communication and accurate knowledge dissemination. By definition, FL is a distributed machine learning approach where models are trained across multiple devices or nodes without the need to centralize data, preserving data privacy and reducing the data transfer overheads, particularly with large, decentralized datasets [7–9].

Key related terms include the following.

- Collaborative Learning: Often used synonymously with FL, emphasizing cooperative model training without sharing raw data.
- Distributed Machine Learning (DML): A broader concept encompassing FL, focusing on distributed computations with FL's emphasis on privacy.
- Edge Learning/Training: Aligns with FL but focuses on training at the network's periphery, such as on mobile devices or IoT endpoints [10].
- On-Device Learning: Highlights training on devices like smartphones without offloading data, central to FL's paradigm.
- Decentralized Machine Learning: Encompasses any machine learning technique without a central authority, with FL focusing on decentralized data and privacy.
- Privacy-Preserving Machine Learning: Includes methods like homomorphic encryption, SMPC, and differential privacy, with FL as a key pillar.

2.3. *Integrating Security and Storage*

Here, we clarify which parts of the process described above deal with security and storage considerations, which are discussed later in the paper. FL prioritizes local data storage on devices (e.g., cellphones, IoT devices) to safeguard privacy and reduce the reliance on centralized servers. This local storage solution is critical in complying with data privacy rules (such as GDPR) and minimizing the risk of exposing sensitive data. However, it poses new issues in controlling storage restrictions on edge devices, which we will describe later. During the local training phase, the FL process uses local storage to compute updates, rather than sending raw data. Security is a critical component during the sharing of model updates. When devices send their locally trained updates back to the central server, privacy and security risks emerge. Malicious entities could intercept the updates or manipulate them to corrupt the global model (via model poisoning or adversarial attacks). Therefore, secure aggregation techniques and differential privacy mechanisms must be integrated into the FL process to ensure that updates cannot be reverse-engineered to expose sensitive data or be compromised by attackers. This security challenge relates directly to the sharing and aggregation stages of the process. In the aggregation phase, the central server aggregates the updates from multiple devices to update the global model. To secure this process, homomorphic encryption and secure multi-party computation (SMPC) are commonly used to ensure that the updates are encrypted and privacy is preserved during aggregation. These measures address both security (protecting the updates from interception) and storage efficiency (since raw data are never transferred, and only model updates are sent, minimizing the storage load on the server).

3. General Opportunities, Challenges, and Applications

Recognizing the opportunities, understanding the challenges, and identifying new applications are critical in today's technology. We investigate the broad prospects of developing technologies, as well as their specialized applications in cellphones, organizational infrastructures, and IoT, while also addressing the challenges that come with these improvements.

3.1. *Opportunities*

Federated learning allows model training across multiple devices while keeping data local. This decentralized approach offers major benefits in data privacy and training efficiency, making FL valuable for various industries. Research highlights FL's importance in machine learning and data science [11,12]. Experts like Kairouz in [13] stress the need to address issues like data handling, communication costs, and security.

3.1.1. Enhanced Security and Reduced Data Transfer Costs

With increasing data breaches, protecting data privacy is crucial, especially in sensitive fields like healthcare and personal communications [14]. FL's decentralized approach ensures that raw data remain on users' devices, minimizing security risks and enhancing trust. This infrastructure is particularly beneficial in sectors like healthcare and banking, where data-driven insights are needed without exposing raw data [15–18]. FL also reduces the costs and environmental impacts by minimizing data transfer and processing data locally [19,20].

3.1.2. Improved Model Personalization

Today's consumers, equipped with a plethora of choices, desire tailored experiences. FL is perfectly positioned to respond to this demand. By continually refining models based on individual device data, FL crafts a learning model that is inextricably linked to user behavior. As these models evolve, they intuitively align with the users' preferences, resulting in experiences that are not only personalized but deeply resonant. This level of customization is paramount in ensuring user retention and satisfaction in an increasingly competitive market [21,22].

3.1.3. Scalability

At its core, FL is designed for expansion. Its structure, which encourages the addition of devices to its network, is inherently scalable. Each device that becomes part of this network augments the collective intelligence without ever directly sharing its raw data with a centralized entity. This architecture ensures that, as the network grows, so does its diversity and richness in data, all while maintaining a lightweight and efficient structure [23].

3.1.4. Utilization of Edge Devices and Real-Time Learning

Federated learning utilizes the computing capabilities of edge devices like smartphones and IoT tools, incorporating them into its learning structure. This method helps to maximize the resources and promotes the widespread use of machine learning, leading to a more inclusive concept [24]. In dynamic sectors like autonomous driving and emergency medical response, real-time data processing is critical. FL excels in these areas by enabling models to adapt rapidly to new data, avoiding the latency associated with traditional batch updates. This capability is vital when even slight delays can have significant consequences.

3.1.5. Decentralization, Robustness, and Optimized Network Traffic

Unlike centralized systems, FL's decentralized nature improves resilience by eliminating single points of failure. Despite failures in individual nodes, the system remains functioning, demonstrating resilience [25,26]. FL distinguishes itself in a regulatory context centered on data protection by guaranteeing compliance without sacrificing data-driven insights. Its emphasis on data localization enables organizations to function within stringent regulatory constraints. FL optimizes network traffic by transmitting model updates instead of substantial raw data, ensuring effective bandwidth use and decreasing the latency [5]. The practical impact of FL across diverse sectors, from healthcare to smart cities, underscores its transformative role in data analytics.

3.2. Areas of Application

There are a number of areas of application for FL (see Table 1).

Table 1. Applications of federated learning (FL).

Application Area	Description
Smartphones	• FL's decentralized data processing revolutionizes data privacy for smartphone applications [15,27]. • Applications like predictive texting and streaming benefit without compromising user data [28].

Table 1. *Cont.*

Application Area	Description
Organizations	• FL offers a new framework for healthcare and finance sectors in managing vast amounts of confidential data [29]. • Decentralized modeling allows insights without exposing individual data, aligning with GDPR and HIPAA regulations.
Internet of Things (IoT)	• FL applications in the IoT universe enhance functionality through decentralized learning [30]. • Security benefits are achieved through data decentralization, making devices more efficient and adaptive.
Healthcare	• FL addresses the intersection of data-driven insights and ethical considerations in healthcare [31]. • Decentralized processing on healthcare databases preserves patients' data integrity while pooling insights for industry-wide patterns [32].
Personalized Advertising	• FL decentralizes the learning process, allowing advertising platforms to glean user insights without accessing granular data [33]. • Ensures robust personalization while respecting user privacy, shifting digital advertising strategies [34–36].
Automotive Sector	• FL facilitates on-device training for autonomous vehicles, revolutionizing real-time, data-driven decision-making [37]. • Potential to accelerate the transition to more efficient and safer self-driving vehicles [38].
Defense Against Financial Fraud	• FL serves as a potent tool for the banking sector in preempting financial malpractice [39]. • Collaborative model training without sharing raw data supports predictive accuracy and customer trust.
Insurance and FL	• FL enables multi-party computation and insight sharing without the direct transfer of raw data in insurance operations [40–42]. • Optimizes risk models while ensuring that individual data rights remain uncompromised [43].
Military and Police Forces	• FL enhances machine learning models for law enforcement agencies without sharing raw data. • Military adoption of FL shifts the focus from central servers to local storage on edge devices, ensuring secure, efficient data exchange.

3.3. Main Challenges

The decentralized design of FL, which emphasizes data privacy and distributed learning, differs from that of traditional, centralized machine learning models, introducing novel challenges at every stage. Pioneering research has been instrumental in outlining the numerous challenges that affect FL, and it is imperative to understand these in detail if we are to exploit the full potential of FL. While federated learning offers exciting possibilities, it represents a significant shift from traditional methodologies. This innovation, albeit promising, introduces new layers of complexity, especially in implementation. Techniques that worked well in centralized systems might not be directly applicable any longer. The expansion of FL across large and diverse networks brings challenges related to synchronization, data standardization, and real-time collaboration. Moreover, the varying capabilities and potential failures of devices, as previously mentioned, add to these complexities. To fully leverage FL, researchers and practitioners need to innovate, adapt, and create new strategies suited to this model. The inherent design of FL promotes data security. However, the very nature of distributed systems introduces multiple points of potential vulnerability. Every interaction and every data exchange, regardless of whether it is minimal, needs to be fortified against breaches. Integrating secure multi-party computation (SMC) with FL is one way to enhance the privacy and security in federated settings. However, consistently encrypting these interactions without affecting the performance poses a challenge [44].

The delivery of consistent and accurate results is challenging. Variabilities in data quality, distribution, and computational capabilities can influence models' performance. The statistical variations in data sources add to this complexity. While techniques like data preprocessing and augmentation offer some solutions, maintaining privacy while achieving large-scale optimization in FL is a complex task [45–47]. Challenges such as adapting methodologies to specific project demands, managing non-independent and identically distributed (non-IID) data, and optimizing communication are critical tasks in FL. However, as research advances, solutions to these challenges are expected to emerge, paving the way for the broader adoption of FL [48–51].

3.3.1. Communication and System Heterogeneity

Communication is fundamental to every distributed system, including federated learning (FL). In the age of big data and artificial intelligence, FL stands out due to its ability to protect data privacy while minimizing the need to transfer and process massive volumes of data, all while maintaining the advantages of machine learning. Unlike typical centralized training, FL uses collaborative model training to share parameter updates. However, its wider implementation is hampered by the significant communication and processing overheads resulting from the high computing demands and huge parameter updates sent. This problem is particularly acute in Internet of Things (IoT) applications, where edge and fog devices frequently have limited computing power, bandwidth, and data capacities. This study aims at filling this gap by providing a number of recent works conducted to improve the communication and/or computational efficiency in FL [6,44].

Communication costs are the primary restriction, and we demonstrate a 10–100× reduction in communication rounds compared to synchronized stochastic gradient descent. However, FL operates in an environment marked by diverse systems and protocols. Managing the complicated process of interaction within such a heterogenous landscape is challenging. The variabilities in storage, processing power, and communication capabilities among federated components add to this complexity. Each system might have its own limitations, capacities, and peculiarities, which can affect the overall synchronization and efficiency. While solutions like model compression and decentralized training [45] provide some benefit, implementing these solutions seamlessly across a diverse network remains a challenge.

3.3.2. Threats and Adversarial Attacks

Most digital systems have vulnerabilities, and FL, despite its advanced architecture, is not exempt. FL faces risks from adversarial attacks [52,53]. These attacks are sophisticated attempts to deceive or manipulate the learning process. The decentralized nature of FL makes it imperative to have robust defense mechanisms in place. Techniques such as secure function evaluation, homomorphic encryption, and differential privacy can be applied in federated settings to provide privacy and combat threats. These methods offer potential defenses [2].

3.3.3. Infrastructure and Bandwidth Issues

A solid infrastructure is required for FL to work properly. However, difficulties such as unreliable networks and restricted bandwidths, particularly in edge devices, might pose substantial impediments. These limits might delay model updates and training, thereby impacting real-time decision-making and overall system performance [24].

4. Types of FL

Different situations call for specialized FL strategies, leading us to identify distinct categories. In the literature, FL is usually categorized into three primary categories, which we expand upon here, together with a novel one: federated reinforcement learning (FRL). Each of these types of FL (see Figure 2) utilizes a variety of methods and techniques for model training, drawing upon the shared information sources available. The comprehension of these categories allows researchers to examine the unique characteristics and applications of each type, which in turn aids in the advancement of FL strategies [54].

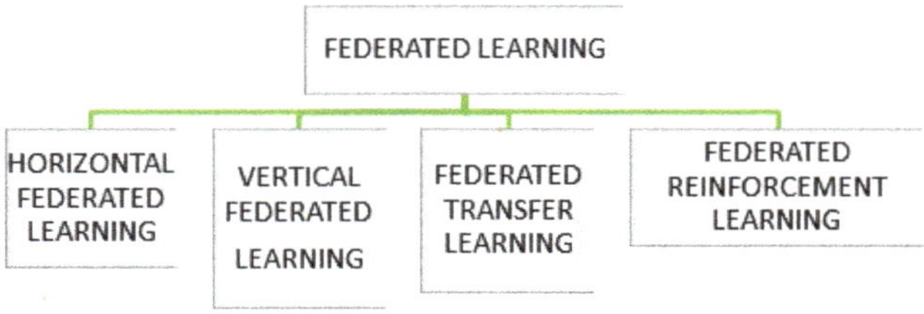

Figure 2. Types of FL.

4.1. Horizontal FL (HFL)

Machine learning traditionally relies on a centralized training paradigm, where data from various sources are pooled into a single repository. This method simplifies preprocessing, data access, and model evaluation, leading to robust performance and iterative improvements due to the data's homogeneity and volume. However, as the data distribution becomes more complex and concerns about privacy and security grow, new methodologies have emerged. One such approach is horizontal federated learning (HFL), or "sample-based" FL, designed for decentralized data. HFL is suitable for scenarios where entities collect data with shared features but from diverse samples [55].

The foundational aspect of HFL is its consistent feature space, maintained across all participating nodes or devices, while individual sample spaces or data records differ. This framework ensures that the data integrity and privacy are safe. In essence, while the data features are consistent among the participants, the need for direct data sharing is obviated, allowing entities to collaboratively refine a shared model [54]. For clearer insight into HFL's applicability, consider two geographically separated hospitals. Both institutions might capture analogous parameters for their patients—age, weight, and blood pressure, to name a few. The divergence arises from the distinct patient demographics that each caters to. In this scenario, HFL acts as a nexus, enabling these hospitals to synergistically enhance their diagnostic models. A notable advantage of this model is the implicit assurance that patient-specific information remains contained within its originating institution, supporting the principles of data privacy, fairness, and accuracy [56]. In this type, data samples from various devices are split horizontally, meaning that each device has the same labels for a subset of features. The objective is to prepare a model that ensures the protection of information in a cooperative way. The usual method of handling AI, which includes concentrating information on a server, presents several challenges—for example, high mailing costs, excessive battery usage, and risks to the protection and security of customer information. FL has gained considerable attention for its ability to build powerful models in a decentralized way, without direct access to customer information, thus ensuring security. Unlike conventional centralized AI, federated learning tends to address the difficulties presented by the non-IID data and imbalanced information presented in real-world applications—for example, mobile phone applications and mode identification trips using non-IID GPS addresses. With the increasing complexity of information gathering and division among organizations, especially when managing sensitive information, disconnected information repositories maintained by individual information owners have become prevalent. This requires the development of AI models that can be prepared without unifying all of the information. Regardless of the potential of HFL, it also faces challenges. One major concern is the potential imbalance of data among participants. Variations in the dataset's volume or diversity between entities could introduce bias in the model's performance. Addressing this requires strategies that ensure fair representation and learning, thereby upholding the integrity of the HFL methodology.

Regarding security, we note the following. In HFL, data are dispersed among numerous edge devices, like mobile phones or IoT devices, that train local models independently before providing changes to a central server. This decentralized structure provides an opportunity for hostile actors to exploit flaws by inserting poisoned or modified data into the local updates, possibly damaging the global model. Securing the communication connections between the central server and the local devices is crucial in reducing these risks. We stress the use of secure aggregation techniques, which ensure that individual device updates are encrypted and aggregated without disclosing raw data. This provides an additional degree of security against update interception or manipulation. Moreover, the importance of differential privacy, which limits the ability of adversaries to reconstruct sensitive data from the aggregated model, is highlighted. By introducing noise into local updates, differential privacy further reduces the likelihood of an attacker inferring individual data points, thereby enhancing the robustness of the overall system against adversarial attacks while maintaining privacy.

Consider a scenario whereby mobile devices collaborate to train a shared model for predictive text. If an attacker compromises a few devices and injects poisoned data into the system, the global model could learn incorrect patterns, reducing its accuracy and even spreading misinformation. This example highlights the importance of detecting malicious updates and implementing robust defense mechanisms, such as Byzantine-tolerant algorithms.

4.2. Vertical FL (VFL)

Vertical federated learning (VFL) is a specialized variant of federated learning designed for scenarios where local parties have diverse attributes within the same user cohort, unlike general FL systems that deal with numerous records sharing the same feature space. In VFL, there are two main types of participants: the active party, which initiates the training task and holds the primary label for data samples, and the passive participants, which contribute additional features for the same user set. For instance, a bank with limited transactional features can use VFL with another entity possessing complementary data to predict default risks and credit scores [34,57].

VFL differs from horizontal FL (HFL) by focusing on scenarios where entities possess complementary datasets (data from B parts), while HFL deals with entities having similar types of data but from different users (data from A parts). In VFL, parties target the same user set but with significantly different features, such as one entity having demographic data and another focusing on online behavior. A common identifier, like user IDs, allows collaboration without compromising data privacy. Throughout this process, the feature values remain undisclosed, ensuring data confidentiality. A key feature of VFL is its emphasis on combining different features of the same user set, in contrast to HFL's approach, where data are distributed across numerous users.

This cooperative approach in VFL aids in assembling AI models that use each participant's contribution, streamlining the model training process in settings where traditional averaging methods might fall short [58]. An illustrative real-world application of VFL would be the following. Consider a scenario whereby a financial institution, with abundant transactional data, partners with an e-commerce platform, which tracks users' browsing and purchasing behaviors. Historically, insights from either of these entities would remain in isolated repositories. However, VFL introduces the potential for a transformative, symbiotic relationship. Using common user identifiers, these entities can collaboratively design predictive models, giving rise to insights such as predictions of purchasing likelihoods based on a mixture of financial history and online behavior [57].

To further illustrate this concept, consider a multi-party, multi-class VFL (MMVFL) system. This framework takes into account the distribution of labels across VFL participants while ensuring data privacy. It empowers multiple entities to collaborate and share labels, thereby enhancing the overall learning experience. A more simplified approach reduces the complexity of the VFL system architecture and coordination requirements by eliminating the need for a central coordinator. Such advancements elevate the efficiency and adaptability of VFL frameworks. Nonetheless, VFL, despite being innovative, has its own complexities.

Challenges in federated learning (FL) include aligning data across different parties, upholding privacy standards, and integrating models trained on varied datasets. Hu et al. [59] stress that the goal is not merely combining data but creating actionable insights. To handle issues such as diverse and unreliable network connections, asynchronous VFL architectures are being used. These allow model updates without synchronizing data sharing. Modern VFL approaches balance protection, competition, and efficiency [60], shifting away from solely cryptographic methods.

Traditional VFL uses a central coordinator to securely aggregate the results, preventing data breaches. However, new methods propose removing this coordinator to improve the efficiency, with direct communication between the participants. While this could enhance the efficiency, it requires careful attention to security to prevent breaches and resist attacks.

In VFL, entities (such as businesses or institutions) exchange diverse aspects of the same data topic, such as demographic data from a bank paired with purchasing activity data from an e-commerce platform. This collaborative procedure poses novel security issues related to data privacy and model inversion attacks, in which attackers seek to reverse-engineer sensitive data from shared model modifications. Because the entities in VFL frequently work with complimentary datasets, it is critical that no sensitive information is exposed during model aggregation.

Homomorphic encryption and secure multi-party computation (SMPC) are often used to safeguard data in VFL, allowing organizations to perform calculations on encrypted data while never disclosing the raw data. The security vulnerabilities in VFL, especially surrounding data leakage during model updates, underline the necessity for advanced cryptographic methods, which are discussed in later sections.

In VFL, consider a bank collaborating with an insurance company, where both parties share different attributes of the same users to create a credit risk model. If either party's data are not fully encrypted or anonymized, there is a risk of model inversion, where an attacker might infer sensitive customer details from the shared model. This emphasizes the need for homomorphic encryption or secure multi-party computation (SMPC) to ensure that the shared updates do not expose any private information.

4.3. *Federated Transfer Learning*

Federated transfer learning (FTL) combines transfer learning and federated learning to adapt models trained in one context to a related task efficiently. It addresses differences in data distributions, advancing beyond traditional models that handle limited data [61,62]. FTL leverages transfer learning to apply knowledge across domains and federated learning to fine-tune models on diverse datasets without direct data sharing. This approach enhances the privacy and reduces the computational demands, marking a significant shift from traditional methods that centralize data or operate within fixed boundaries [63].

To clarify the potential of FTL, consider the domain of medical diagnostics, an area where data sensitivity and specificity are paramount. Let us assume a pre-existing machine learning model that is adept in diagnosing skin diseases based on a European demographic dataset. Historically, to adapt this model to an Asian demographic, a complete retraining process would ensue, often necessitating the transfer of high-volume, sensitive data across locations. However, with FTL, the model can be efficiently recalibrated using data from Asian hospitals, without the actual datasets ever leaving their respective institutions. This not only upholds data privacy but also capitalizes on the foundational knowledge embedded within the initial model, as shown in [64]. As with any advanced methodology, federated transfer learning (FTL) faces its own set of challenges.

A major issue in federated transfer learning (FTL) is negative transfer, where knowledge from the source domain harms the model's performance in the target domain. This requires careful validation and refinement to ensure that the transferred knowledge is beneficial. Traditional machine learning models often struggle with tasks outside their specific training data, showing poor performance with minor changes in the data distribution or objectives. FTL, however, offers dynamic adaptability, allowing models to use previous knowledge and adjust to new contexts without sharing raw data. This makes FTL more resilient and versatile compared to traditional models.

4.4. Federated Reinforcement Learning

Federated reinforcement learning (FRL) represents a complex extension of reinforcement learning (RL), where multiple agents in distinct environments are not only optimized locally but also share insights across a network. For instance, self-driving cars in different cities can learn from each other's experiences, improving their overall driving skills. However, FRL is still evolving, with challenges in creating effective communication systems and ensuring the accuracy of shared experiences across varying environments. While FRL combines RL and FL, it remains an area of ongoing research and development.

4.5. Differential Privacy and Homomorphic Encryption in FL

Differential privacy and homomorphic encryption are closely related to all forms of federated learning because they solve two of the most important issues in FL: data privacy and security.

In horizontal and vertical FL (described in the previous subsections), numerous entities or devices collaborate to train models while protecting the local data's privacy. To prevent data leaks during this procedure, differential privacy assures that individual data points are not rebuilt from shared model updates. Furthermore, homomorphic encryption enables calculations on encrypted data, which is critical when the data between different institutions must remain secure (for example, between hospitals or banks collaborating in a vertical FL environment). These techniques safeguard each participant's privacy.

Federated transfer learning (FTL) tries to adapt models across disparate datasets, such as healthcare and finance, when the data are sparse or from distinct domains. Differential privacy and homomorphic encryption are critical in allowing enterprises to exchange insights and models without disclosing the underlying private data. The safe transmission of model updates enabled by these techniques assures compliance with privacy rules such as GDPR, while also protecting the data's proprietary nature.

Some practical examples for each type of FL, demonstrating how differential privacy and homomorphic encryption are used in real-world scenarios, are as follows. For instance, in vertical FL (where two organizations may share different aspects of the same users), homomorphic encryption can provide secure computation throughout encrypted data without the need for the data to be decrypted. In horizontal FL, differential privacy ensures that user-specific data on mobile devices cannot be reconstructed from the global model.

5. Attributes and Characteristics of FL

This section explores the abilities of federated learning, with a focus on data privacy and methods such as differential privacy, secure multi-party computation, and homomorphic encryption. It also includes customization in FL, the influence of non-IID data, and the complete design area involving the data distribution, privacy, security, and robustness.

5.1. Data Privacy

FL places a heightened emphasis on data privacy. As highlighted by McMahan in [5], with the prevalence of sensitive data and the tightening of data privacy regulations, there is increased interest in innovative solutions that respect data privacy. FL aptly responds to this call, allowing machine learning models to be trained without centralizing or exposing the raw data.

5.1.1. Introduction to Data Privacy in FL

Safeguarding data privacy is crucial in today's digital life. Federated learning is at the forefront of this effort, dedicated to protecting user data through advanced techniques like secure multi-party computation (SMC) and differential privacy [39]. As the digital environment evolves with challenges like quantum computing and deepfakes, FL must enhance its privacy measures. Communication within FL, especially across numerous devices, is vital. Almanifi et al., in [45], highlight the importance of efficient data transmission and resource management. Compression techniques can help to reduce the data transmission volumes, making FL feasible even in bandwidth-limited scenarios. Building on [23], FL is promising for decentralized data frameworks and extends to ensemble models, complex collaborative filtering, and more intricate architectures. The decentralized nature of FL means that models are trained directly on edge devices or nodes, minimizing the risk of data exposure and breaches by sending only model updates or essential information to the central model.

5.1.2. Motivations for Enhanced Data Privacy

Empowering original data is a significant aspect of FL [13]. Data remain at their origin, whether generated or stored, which ensures that data owners maintain control over their sensitive information, reducing risks and legal liabilities. Mechanisms such as secure aggregation, which uses cryptographic protocols to mix model updates from different nodes [65], help to maintain privacy during the aggregation process. Differential privacy, another key technique, ensures that the output remains statistically indistinguishable regardless of the individual data's inclusion, providing strong mathematical privacy guarantees. Homomorphic encryption and SMC further emphasize FL's commitment to privacy [66]. Enhanced data privacy in FL is driven by technological, ethical, and legal considerations, particularly for sectors like healthcare and finance.

5.1.3. Differential Privacy in FL

Federated learning's decentralized approach trains models directly at the data sources, reducing the data's exposure and risks. Differential privacy adds controlled randomness to the data or model training process, ensuring that the outputs are indistinguishable, whether individual data are included or not [16]. Secure aggregation, as highlighted by [67], uses cryptographic methods to combine model updates while protecting individual contributions. Combining FL with differential privacy offers robust privacy guarantees and effective data utilization. However, balancing data privacy with model accuracy remains challenging, and ongoing research aims to refine such techniques to meet stringent privacy standards while maintaining model performance. This balance is crucial as FL evolves to address contemporary regulatory requirements [5].

5.2. Secure Multi-Party Computation (SMPC or SMC)

Secure multi-party computation (SMPC or SMC) is a critical concept within federated learning. With FL's decentralized approach, which involves training models directly at the data sources (such as edge devices or nodes), there is a growing demand for advanced techniques that can safeguard data privacy while maintaining model efficiency. SMPC directly meets this requirement. In essence, SMPC allows multiple participants, each with their private inputs, to collaboratively conduct computations and obtain a result without revealing their individual inputs to each other. In the context of FL, where data remain decentralized, SMPC's importance cannot be overstated. It allows for the collaborative training of models across multiple nodes, without the necessity to expose individual datasets [37,68]. In FL, models are trained at the data's source, ensuring minimal risks associated with data breaches and exposure. Within this framework, SMPC operates by facilitating collaborative computation across these decentralized nodes. Rather than sharing raw data, which could compromise privacy, each participant or node shares encrypted fragments of computations. These fragments, when combined, can provide a result (like a model update) without ever revealing individual data points.

While secure aggregation focuses on a mixture of updates, SMPC takes this one step further by allowing entire computations to be jointly performed, yet without the nodes having to reveal their proprietary datasets to one another. Given FL's application in data-sensitive domains like healthcare and finance, the utility of SMPC becomes even more relevant. These sectors can use SMPC within the FL framework to derive insights collaboratively from multiple sources, all while ensuring that individual data remain confidential [69]. However, SMPC, despite its strengths, is not without limitations. The complexity of collaborative computation across multiple nodes can introduce latency, especially as the number of participating nodes increases. Moreover, the cryptographic techniques underlying SMPC, while ensuring privacy, can sometimes be computationally intensive, demanding more resources and potentially affecting the efficiency of the FL process.

5.3. Homomorphic Encryption in FL

Homomorphic encryption (HE) is crucial in enhancing data security, especially within federated learning. HE allows computations on encrypted data without decryption, ensuring that the results are consistent with those from the original data once decrypted. In FL, where models are trained directly at the data sources, like edge devices or nodes, HE is essential in preserving data privacy. It enables computations and model training on encrypted data while ensuring that any information sent back to the central model remains secure and encrypted [70].

Benefits of Using Homomorphic Encryption

Enhanced Data Privacy: HE ensures that raw data remain encrypted throughout the computation process. This means that the data, even when being used for training or analysis, are never exposed in their raw form, thus significantly mitigating the risks associated with data breaches or unauthorized access.

- Flexibility in Computation: Despite the data being encrypted, HE allows for meaningful computations, ensuring that the insights or model updates derived from such computations are accurate and reflective of the original data.
- Compatibility with FL: Given the decentralized nature of FL, where data do not need to be centralized, HE fits seamlessly, ensuring that data privacy is maintained without hampering the training process.

Trade-Offs, e.g., Computational Costs:

While HE offers a robust solution to many challenges posed by data privacy, it comes with its set of trade-offs.

- Computational Intensity: The very processes that allow computations on encrypted data can be computationally intensive, necessitating more robust computational resources and potentially extending the training or analysis time.
- Increased Latency: Especially in real-time applications or scenarios where a rapid response is crucial, the additional time required for HE computations can introduce delays.
- Complexity: Implementing and managing HE can be complex, requiring specialized knowledge and potentially complicating the deployment of FL solutions in certain environments.

5.4. Federated Identity and Access Management (FIAM)

Federated identity and access management (FIAM) is crucial for cyber-security in federated learning (FL), where sensitive data are processed across many devices. FIAM adapts traditional systems to the federated context [71,72].

Authentication is vital in FL to prevent data tampering or malicious introduction. FIAM ensures that nodes are verified and authorized. Role-based access control (RBAC) within FIAM manages nodes' permissions based on their role, function, and trust level [73–75]. For example, a healthcare node may be restricted to sharing only aggregated insights, enhancing data control and preventing breaches.

5.5. Privacy-Preserving Data Aggregation

Differential privacy adds "noise" during data aggregation to protect individual data points [76,77]. k-Anonymity hides records among others to ensure privacy, while data masking alters data values to obscure true information. Secure aggregation protocols use encryption and integrity checks to maintain the privacy and accuracy of aggregated data.

5.6. Privacy Challenges and Limitations in FL

Model inversion attacks pose a risk by allowing adversaries to reverse-engineer training data from model outputs. Despite protecting the raw data, the model parameters or outputs in FL may still be vulnerable. Section 8 will discuss these attacks and countermeasures in detail.

Balancing user privacy with model accuracy is challenging. Techniques like differential privacy [66], which introduce noise to protect individual data points, can obscure genuine data patterns and reduce the predictive precision. This raises questions about the value of an extremely private model if its accuracy is compromised, and vice versa. This balance is crucial in sectors like healthcare, where both privacy and precise predictions are essential [38]. Additionally, privacy safeguards can introduce computational and communication burdens, potentially slowing model training and increasing the resource demands in constrained environments.

5.7. Best Practices and Standards

Below, we summarize the best practices and standards and give guidelines to ensure privacy in FL deployment.

- Local Data Storage: At its core, FL ensures that data remain on the user's device (like edge devices or nodes). This practice should be maintained, ensuring that raw data are never transmitted, reducing the potential for data exposure.
- Data Minimization: Only the essential data required for model training should be processed. This reduces the volume of data at risk and lessens the potential harm in the event of a breach.
- Regular Model Audits: Frequent validation and evaluation of the FL models help in identifying and addressing any potential privacy vulnerabilities.
- Differential Privacy: One should ensure the implementation of techniques like differential privacy to introduce calibrated noise into the data, ensuring that individual contributions are masked during aggregation.
- Encryption: One should always encrypt data during transmission. Techniques like homomorphic encryption, which allows computation on encrypted data without needing decryption, can be pivotal.

Emerging standards and protocols for data privacy in FL:

- ISO/IEC Standards: Various standards, particularly those of the International Organization for Standardization (ISO) and the International Electrotechnical Commission (IEC), address the privacy aspects of cloud computing and distributed systems, which are relevant to FL.
- NIST Guidelines: The National Institute of Standards and Technology (NIST) offers guidelines and practices on securing data during transmission and storage [78].
- Community-Driven Initiatives: Open-source communities and academic consortia are collaborating to define standards and protocols specific to FL, given its growing significance [79].

5.8. Non-IID Data in FL

In FL, the way in which data are distributed remains crucial for the effectiveness of the resulting models. Specifically, the challenge posed by non-IID data, which introduce unique complications in a decentralized training environment, requires careful consideration.

5.8.1. Understanding Non-IID Data

In an FL framework, non-IID data are characteristic of situations whereby the participating devices, whether clients or nodes, possess data distributions that are not a balanced representation of the broader population. Several factors can lead to this imbalance. For instance, different devices might adopt varying data collection procedures, reflecting the diversity and variability in devices. Further complicating factors include user-specific behaviors, which can create unique data environments. Challenges like device-specific characteristics and interactions could further skew the data.

5.8.2. Implications and Challenges of Non-IID Data

- Model Convergence Issues: Navigating model convergence becomes challenging with non-IID data. Wang et al. [48] shed light on this issue, highlighting that an uneven data distribution among nodes leads to slower convergence rates. This prolongs the training process and could diminish the effectiveness of the model.
- Performance Degradation: A model's real-world effectiveness is compromised when it is dominantly trained on non-representative data. In scenarios where such data are prominent, the model, when exposed to varied real-world scenarios, might underperform or yield unpredictable results.
- Biased Outcomes: A skewed data source, if dominant during training, can lead to models that are biased towards particular user groups or scenarios. Such bias not only reduces the model's broad application but also raises ethical concerns. As Briggs et al. note, data biases can inadvertently promote certain groups while marginalizing others, thus compromising the fairness and ethical nature of the model [80].

5.8.3. Non-IID: Potential Strategies

Addressing non-IID challenges also requires two approaches.

- Data Preprocessing: A foundational step towards countering data imbalances is the use of preprocessing measures. Implementing techniques like data augmentation, stratified sampling, and synthetic data generation can equalize the data distribution across nodes, ensuring a more balanced training environment.
- Model Aggregation Approaches: Aggregation techniques bear significance in a non-IID environment. Recent methodologies, such as those echoing the principles of FedAvg and FedProx, show promise. These methods aim to address the challenges posed by skewed data, enhancing both model performance and convergence.

5.8.4. Real-World Implications Across Sectors

The practicality of non-IID data settings in FL is seen in numerous sectors. First, the decentralized nature of FL, combined with non-IID data considerations, permits hospitals to collaboratively train models without compromising patients' confidentiality. Moreover, in the finance sector, FL offers a mechanism to analyze distributed financial datasets securely, ensuring that proprietary and confidential information remains within its respective entities. Lastly, IoT, with its vast array of heterogeneous devices, produces diverse datasets. FL becomes indispensable in such settings, allowing for collaborative model training that respects the unique data's origins.

5.8.5. Synchronous vs. Asynchronous Updates

Synchronous and asynchronous mechanisms are central to federated learning's model updates. In synchronous FL, a central server waits for updates from all nodes before aggregating the model. This approach faces issues such as "stale updates" when some devices lag, due to device differences and network reliability [81].

5.8.6. Privacy and Security in Non-IID Settings

Federated learning focuses on data privacy and efficient communication, but security concerns persist. These include risks to user privacy, model integrity, and data attributes, particularly when the data are unevenly distributed across nodes. The management of non-IID data in FL is complex and requires tailored solutions to address these security and privacy challenges effectively.

6. Algorithms and Frameworks in Federated Learning

Federated learning transforms machine learning by allowing model training across many devices while keeping users' data private. This section explores the algorithms and frameworks driving FL, crucial for its success and future development. FL algorithms are key in managing decentralized, unevenly distributed data and optimizing communication, unlike traditional models that rely on centralized, consistent datasets. With the growing volume of data from connected devices, FL algorithms, such as Federated Averaging (FedAvg) and Federated Stochastic Gradient (FedSGD), handle data locally and transmit only compressed model updates, enhancing the efficiency and privacy. Understanding these algorithms is vital in leveraging FL's full potential [82].

6.1. Federated Averaging (FedAvg)

Federated Averaging, or FedAvg, addresses the need for effective decentralized machine learning [5]. As data become more distributed across devices, centralizing them for training becomes impractical due to bandwidth and privacy issues. FedAvg provides a solution by allowing local model training on each device, while synchronizing through a global shared model, denoted as w_t, where t indicates the communication round. Each client uses methods like Stochastic Gradient Descent (SGD) for local updates, and these updates are averaged at the server to iteratively improve the global model. Recent evaluations of FL algorithms highlight FedAvg's performance. Nilsson et al. utilized the MNIST dataset, a standard for digit classification, to benchmark algorithms in a client–server setup [82]. Their comparative analysis, focusing on the communication efficiency and convergence, demonstrated FedAvg's strong performance, particularly with client communication limited to 10,000, under IID data conditions. This empirical evidence supports FedAvg's effectiveness in various FL scenarios.

6.1.1. Potential Benefits and Use Cases of FedAvg

FedAvg combines theoretical elegance with practical use by allowing decentralized devices to learn locally and contribute to a global model. This method reduces the need for large data transfers to a central server, saving the bandwidth and speeding up model training. It keeps raw data on devices, enhancing users' privacy compared to centralized models. FedAvg is ideal for scenarios with many IoT devices, smartphones, and medical devices, where it supports local learning while maintaining data privacy.

6.1.2. Limitations and Challenges of FedAvg

FedAvg faces challenges like differing data distributions across devices and asynchronous updates, which can impact model accuracy and introduce biases. Hyperparameter tuning is critical; misconfiguration can hinder model performance. Additionally, the distributed nature of FedAvg raises security concerns, as sharing model updates across networks can expose the system to adversarial attacks [83].

6.2. Federated Stochastic Gradient

In decentralized learning, Federated Stochastic Gradient (FSG) is a key technique, combining federated learning (FL) with stochastic gradient methods. It enhances the computational efficiency and supports resilient model training across distributed devices.

Federated Stochastic Gradient Descent (FedSGD) adapts the classical Stochastic Gradient Descent (SGD) for FL, addressing privacy and data distribution issues. In FedSGD, each device performs local SGD computations and sends updates to a central server, which aggregates them to refine the global model [84,85]. This approach avoids centralizing the data while improving the model performance.

6.2.1. Algorithmic Steps

The algorithmic procedure can be described by natural language in terms of the following steps [86].

1. Initialization: A global model is initialized, and its parameters are shared with all participating clients.
2. Local Computation: Each client computes the gradient of the model on its local data using SGD.
3. Model Aggregation: Clients send their computed gradients or model parameters to the central server.
4. Global Model Update: The central server aggregates these updates (typically by averaging) to adjust the global model.
5. Distribution: The updated global model is shared back with all clients.
6. Iterations: Steps 2–5 are repeated until convergence or for a predefined number of communication rounds.

While this mechanism may seem straightforward, several sensitivities, such as handling communication inefficiencies and stragglers and ensuring privacy, play a critical role in its actual implementation.

6.2.2. Challenges

The FedSGD algorithm is critical in decentralized machine learning, with enormous potential but practical limitations. Federated learning (FL) is based on consistent model gradient exchanges between clients and a central server, although network variability can create delays, particularly for larger models. "Stragglers," or slower nodes, further impede global model updates. Another risk is privacy, as sending model changes may mistakenly reveal sensitive information. Although techniques like differential privacy and encrypted computation offer viable solutions, integrating them with FedSGD while retaining its efficiency and accuracy is challenging [87].

6.2.3. Comparison with FedAvg

While both FedSGD and FedAvg are techniques in FL that aim to aggregate local model updates, the primary distinction is the method of aggregation. FedSGD focuses more on gradient updates, sending these to the central server for aggregation. In contrast, FedAvg sends the model parameters themselves after local training. Essentially, while FedSGD is gradient-centric, FedAvg is model-centric in its aggregation approach.

6.3. Model Aggregation Methods

In federated learning, model aggregation plays a crucial role by bringing together local updates from different devices or nodes into a single global model. The essence of FL lies in distributing the training of models across numerous devices, followed by consolidating these contributions centrally through model aggregation. This section explores various model aggregation techniques, emphasizing their strengths, challenges, and suitable contexts for application.

6.3.1. Simple Averaging

The most straightforward method of aggregation is simple averaging, prominently used in the Federated Averaging (FedAvg) algorithm [88]. In this method, updates from each client (e.g., gradient updates or model parameters) are averaged to produce the global update. Mathematically, for N clients,

$$\theta_{global} = \frac{1}{N} \sum_{i=1}^{N} \theta_i$$

where θ_i represents the model parameters from the ith client.

Advantages:

- Computational simplicity.
- Scalability to a large number of clients.

Challenges:

- Assumes IID data across clients, which is often not the case.
- Susceptibility to adversarial attacks, as malicious clients can skew the average.

6.3.2. Weighted Averaging

An evolution of the simple averaging method is weighted averaging, where each client's updates are weighted by the number of samples that it possesses. This approach gives more importance to clients with more data, which can be beneficial in non-IID settings.

$$\theta_{global} = \frac{\sum_{i=1}^{N} w_i \theta_i}{\sum_{i=1}^{N} w_i}$$

where w_i is the weight (often the number of samples) of the ith client.

Advantages:

- More robust to non-IID data scenarios.
- Reduces the impact of stragglers or clients with fewer data samples.

Challenges:

- Still vulnerable to adversarial attacks if a malicious client possesses a significant amount of data.

6.3.3. Geometric Median Aggregation

Instead of averaging, some aggregation techniques aim to find the geometric median of the model updates. The geometric median offers robustness against adversarial or Byzantine attacks, as it is less susceptible to outliers.

Advantages:

- Robustness against adversarial updates.
- Suitable for scenarios where security and integrity are paramount.

Challenges:

- Computationally more intensive than averaging methods.
- Determining the geometric median in high-dimensional spaces can be challenging.

6.3.4. Personalized Aggregation

Recent advances have led to methods for personalized model aggregation, where the global model is fine-tuned or adjusted based on individual clients' characteristics. This approach acknowledges the heterogeneity of the data and user behaviors across clients.

Advantages:

- Better model performance for individual clients.

- Addresses the diverse nature of federated data sources.

Challenges:

- Can lead to overfitting if not properly regulated.
- More complex than traditional aggregation techniques.

6.3.5. Other Aggregation Methods

Federated learning involves various model aggregation techniques that unify individual learning experiences into a global model. Basic methods like average aggregation compute the mean of the updates from client nodes, serving as a foundation for more advanced techniques. Clipped average aggregation refines this by limiting the updates within a set range to reduce distortions from outliers. Secure aggregation uses cryptographic methods like homomorphic encryption to protect client data during aggregation. Differential privacy average aggregation enhances the privacy by adding noise to the updates, balancing confidentiality with accuracy. Momentum aggregation includes past model shifts to accelerate convergence, while Bayesian aggregation applies Bayesian inference to address model parameter uncertainties. Adversarial aggregation detects and mitigates malicious updates through outlier detection and anomaly recognition. Quantization aggregation optimizes communication by compressing the model updates, and hierarchical aggregation organizes aggregation in tiers to reduce the overhead by aggregating locally before higher-level synthesis.

Model aggregation is crucial in FL in determining the effectiveness and robustness of the global model. Choosing the appropriate method depends on the federated data's characteristics, the network architecture, and the deployment needs, with new techniques continuing to be introduced as FL advances [88].

In Table 2, we provide a comparison of the key federated learning algorithms: FedAvg vs. alternatives.

Table 2. Comparison of key federated learning algorithms: FedAvg vs. alternatives.

Algorithm	Handling Non-IID Data	Minimizing Communication Costs	Enhancing Model Robustness	Key Strengths	Limitations
FedAvg	Struggles with non-IID data, as local updates may diverge significantly, slowing down model convergence.	Standard approach with moderate communication costs, but not optimized to reduce communication overhead.	Basic model robustness, but vulnerable to model poisoning and adversarial attacks.	Simple and widely used; baseline for FL performance.	Not optimized for non-IID data; lacks advanced security mechanisms.
FedProx	Modifies FedAvg by adding a proximal term to handle system heterogeneity and non-IID data better.	Similar to FedAvg, but may increase computational costs due to proximal term calculations.	Improved robustness in non-IID settings by reducing local update divergence.	Better than FedAvg for non-IID data; more resilient in heterogeneous environments.	Higher computational costs; still struggles in extremely skewed non-IID cases.
SCAFFOLD	Specifically designed to handle non-IID data by reducing client drift through variance reduction methods.	Slightly higher communication cost due to control variates exchanged between clients and the server.	Highly robust to non-IID data due to its focus on reducing local model drift.	Best for non-IID data handling; more stable convergence.	Increased communication costs; complexity in implementation.
FedOpt (FedAdam, FedYogi)	Uses adaptive optimizers (Adam/Yogi) to handle both IID and non-IID data more effectively.	Can be tuned to reduce communication frequency through adaptive learning rates, minimizing communication overhead.	Improved model robustness due to better optimization techniques.	Adaptable optimization; balances communication efficiency and accuracy.	Complexity in tuning; not as widely tested as FedAvg.

6.4. *Adaptive Learning Rates in Federated Contexts*

In machine learning, the learning rate plays a crucial role as a hyperparameter, determining the size of the steps that an optimization algorithm takes in pursuit of a minimum. If too large, it risks overshooting; if too small, it may become trapped in local minima or converge very slowly. In federated learning contexts, these challenges are accentuated due to the decentralized nature of the data and the necessity to combine diverse model updates from numerous devices. This section examines the adaptive learning rates in federated settings, exploring their importance, the algorithms customized for them, and the associated advantages and obstacles.

6.4.1. Federated Adaptive Algorithms and the Importance of Adaptive Learning in a Federated Setting

Traditional centralized learning benefits from consistent, IID data, but federated learning encounters challenges with non-IID data from diverse devices. This variability requires adaptive learning rates to handle each client's unique data and model progress. Adaptive mechanisms are essential for quicker and more stable convergence in federated settings [89,90]. Two notable adaptive algorithms in FL are as follows.

- Federated Adagrad: Enhances the Adagrad algorithm by adjusting the learning rates based on unique client data gradients, ensuring personalized optimization [91].
- Federated Adam: Builds on the Adam optimizer, which combines Adagrad and RMSprop's advantages, maintaining running averages of gradients and their squares for more balanced learning rate adaptation.

These adaptive methods promise improved convergence and stability but face challenges, such as computational overhead and synchronization issues, particularly with non-IID data. They require careful management to avoid divergence and still necessitate hyperparameter tuning. Research highlights the effectiveness of Adagrad, especially in communication-efficient strategies and diverse datasets. Future FL advancements will need to balance the adaptive learning rates' benefits with the management of computational and communication complexities [91].

6.4.2. Federated Adagrad

The Adaptive Gradient Algorithm (Adagrad) is an algorithm specifically designed to improve the convergence performance of machine learning models. It achieves this by adapting the learning rate for each parameter individually. Parameters that are updated infrequently receive larger updates, while frequently updated parameters receive smaller updates. This approach helps to address the issue of diminishing gradients, which can slow down or even prevent convergence during training. Federated Adagrad extends this adaptive learning rate mechanism to the decentralized realm of federated learning. In FL, training data are distributed across multiple devices or servers, and models are trained collaboratively without directly sharing the underlying data. Federated Adagrad enables efficient training in such scenarios by allowing each participating device to adapt the learning rate to its local model parameters.

Challenges in Federated Settings:

- The potential for greater communication overheads as both gradients and squared gradient accumulations might need to be communicated.
- Differences in the magnitude and direction of client updates, due to non-IID data, can cause issues in global aggregation.

6.4.3. Federated Adam

Adaptive Moment Estimation (Adam) is an optimization algorithm that builds upon the foundation of Stochastic Gradient Descent (SGD) by introducing adaptive learning rates for each parameter. This adaptation is achieved by considering the first and second moments of the gradients, which provide estimates of the mean and variance, respectively.

Adam utilizes these moments to dynamically adjust the learning rate for each parameter, leading to potentially faster convergence compared to standard SGD.

The federated version of Adam, known as Federated Adam, incorporates this adaptive learning rate methodology into the distributed setting of federated learning. In FL, the training data are split across multiple devices or servers, and models are collaboratively trained without directly sharing the underlying data. Federated Adam enables efficient training in such scenarios by allowing each participating device to estimate the local first and second moments of the gradients for its model parameters. These local estimates are then aggregated across devices to compute global estimates, which are subsequently used to update the learning rates for all participating devices. This approach facilitates adaptive learning in a decentralized manner, promoting faster convergence and improved model performance in FL settings.

Challenges in Federated Settings:

- Increased communication overhead as clients might need to transmit more information (both moments) to the server.
- Similar to Federated Adagrad, the non-IID nature of the data can cause aggregation discrepancies at the server level [91].

6.4.4. Asynchronous Methods and Algorithms

FL inherently relies on utilizing data from numerous devices spread across different geographies and functionalities. It is crucial that these devices are not always synchronized. This requirement calls for methods that enable devices or clients to update the global model asynchronously. This section explores the intricacies of asynchronous methods in FL, including their rationale, detailed explanations, a comparison to synchronous approaches, and the associated benefits and challenges.

The diverse array of devices involved in FL necessitates mechanisms capable of accommodating varied network conditions, computational capacities, and availability. Asynchronous methods provide flexibility in this regard, allowing updates to flow more organically, without a rigid structure. Here, we examine the complexities of asynchronous strategies in FL.

6.4.5. Motivation for Asynchronous Updates in FL

The complexities of real-world distributed systems present unique challenges that asynchronous methods can address.

Network Disparities: In environments where devices span a wide geographical area, the network speeds and stability vary drastically. A smartphone in an urban setting with 5G connectivity contrasts starkly with an IoT sensor in a remote location that is reliant on low-bandwidth connections. Asynchronous updates respect these disparities, allowing each device to communicate based on its optimal conditions [1].

Computational Constraints: The devices participating in FL range from powerful servers to resource-constrained sensors. Expecting them to process and deliver updates concurrently becomes unreasonable. Asynchronous methods provide an avenue for each device to contribute based on its computational pace.

Intermittent Availability: Devices might have sporadic connectivity or might be set to participate only at specific intervals (e.g., during low-usage times). Asynchronous updates accommodate such varied participation patterns, ensuring that every device, regardless of its schedule, contributes to the global model.

6.4.6. Explanation of Asynchronous Algorithms

Asynchronous approaches in federated learning focus on flexibility and adaptability.

- Staleness: Updates from slower clients may become outdated by the time they reach the central server, raising questions about how to weigh these older updates against newer ones.

- Decentralized Aggregation: Unlike traditional FL, which aggregates client updates in batches after receiving all or most updates, asynchronous methods continuously update the model as new data arrive.

6.5. Comparison with Synchronous Updates

- Latency: Asynchronous methods aim to reduce the latency by using the available data immediately, promoting faster model evolution.
- Communication Efficiency: They avoid waiting for stragglers, leading to potentially fewer communication rounds and quicker learning.
- Convergence: Synchronous updates offer stable convergence patterns, whereas asynchronous updates may face challenges in achieving consistent convergence.
- Scalability: Asynchronous methods support large-scale deployment better, handling more devices without significant changes [92].

6.6. Benefits and Challenges

Benefits

- Real-Time Learning: The global model adapts quickly to changes, enhancing its responsiveness and accuracy.
- Efficiency: Continuous updates optimize server resource use and minimize idle times.
- Scalability: Asynchronous methods easily manage growing networks.

Challenges

- Staleness Management: Managing outdated updates requires complex strategies.
- Overhead Complexity: Integrating diverse updates can lead to high computational overheads and complex aggregation.
- Inconsistency: The global model might reflect transient states rather than providing a consistent network-wide representation.

Embracing asynchronous updates can enhance federated learning, especially in large and diverse networks, but we require robust strategies to address its inherent challenges.

6.6.1. State-of-the-Art FL Algorithms: An Indicative Comparative Benchmark Against FedAvg

This section examines two algorithms: CO-OP and Federated Stochastic Variance Reduced Gradient (FSVRG). We discuss their core ideas, the ways in which they work, and their most important aspects. We also present improved versions of the classic algorithms discussed earlier.

Understanding the theory is only one aspect. The most important quality is how well these algorithms perform in real life. To obtain a clear picture, we explore a benchmarking analysis of real-world studies. Here, CO-OP and FSVRG are considered head-to-head with FedAvg, a popular baseline algorithm in FL.

We explore how well they scale, the types of problems that they are best suited for, and how they compare against FedAvg in real-world scenarios. The goal is to show the strengths and weaknesses of each approach, so that one can determine which of them might be the best fit for one's needs.

Federated Stochastic Variance Reduced Gradient (FSVRG)

FSVRG, introduced by [93] and inspired by the Unified Stochastic Fluctuation Reduced Slope, aims to address the inherent challenges of FL, particularly the distributed nature of the data. The core concept behind FSVRG is the mixture of an initial in-depth gradient evaluation with subsequent iterative stochastic updates on each participating client. By doing so, it captures the global data structure while considering the specific intricacies of each client's dataset, offering a balance between generalization and specialization.

Both FedSGD and FSVRG share the general goal of refining a global model through local client computations. However, the sensitivities of their methodologies offer different perspectives. While FedSGD focuses on synchronizing local updates to shape a centralized model, FSVRG integrates a preliminary variance reduction phase via comprehensive gradient calculations. This strategy enables FSVRG to handle datasets characterized by pronounced variability. Nonetheless, this additional computational layer implies that FSVRG could demand more computational resources than its FedSGD counterpart, especially during the initial gradient assessment and the ensuing stochastic rounds.

The benchmarking studies by Nilsson et al. [82] underscore the efficiency of FSVRG in federated environments. The results showed that FSVRG eventually outperformed FedAvg in terms of execution, highlighting its adaptability and capability. This empirical evidence demonstrates the strengths of FSVRG in particular contexts.

CO-OP Algorithm

The asynchronous CO-OP protocol arises as a novel approach to the complexities of distributed machine learning, particularly in dynamic environments. Instead of relying on static datasets, as is common with many existing FL frameworks, CO-OP is designed to adapt to dynamically generated data. As users interact with their mobile devices, the individual datasets of these users grow in real time, introducing an added layer of complexity.

Consider a system whereby K mobile clients are actively participating in a cooperative learning process. Each client, governed by the unique interaction patterns of its user, gathers its own set of data. Once a pre-defined threshold (B samples, known as the local batch size) is reached, the client begins the process of refining its local model, employing gradient descent techniques based on these recently accumulated data.

Traditional FL frameworks often employ a more centralized approach, wherein the server periodically prompts specific clients to contribute to model updates. CO-OP, however, champions decentralization by empowering clients to initiate model updates asynchronously. This autonomy allows clients to choose the best time and environment for local training, such as during optimal network conditions. After refining their local models, clients can then liaise with the central server, merging their updates and subsequently obtaining the revised global model.

The global model parameters on the server are denoted as w, with each client's parameters represented as w_k. Within the CO-OP framework, a critical metric is the age of the global model, indicating the update frequencies of clients. Clients monitor their own model's age, recalibrated using the CO-OP protocol. Starting with a common model w, clients gather data, fine-tune their models, and synchronize them with the server. CO-OP's age filter ensures timely and relevant client integration, avoiding outdated updates. As FL evolves, CO-OP addresses both IID and non-IID data, but empirical studies show that it faces strong competition from established algorithms like FSVRG.

6.7. Frameworks and Tools

The implementation and deployment of federated learning have undergone significant improvements thanks to the introduction of specialized frameworks and tools. These tools, designed specifically to handle the complexities of federated architectures, are crucial not only in simplifying the process but also in ensuring strong security and reliability. In the following sections, we examine the three notable frameworks that have played a key role in shaping the FL landscape: TensorFlow Federated, PySyft, and FATE.

6.7.1. TensorFlow Federated (TFF)

TensorFlow Federated arises from the lineage of the TensorFlow framework. As a specialized extension, TFF brings the strengths of TensorFlow into the domain of FL. The framework gives a comprehensive ecosystem, which means that developers have access to a vast library of functions and tools specifically crafted for federated scenarios. One of the standout features of TFF is its local simulation environment. This environment is invaluable for developers, providing them with a sandbox to iteratively refine and test their federated models without the problems of full deployment.

The advantages of TFF are numerous. Its seamless integration with TensorFlow means that developers familiar with TensorFlow can easily transition into the federated realm with minimal difficulty. Additionally, due to the widespread adoption of TensorFlow in the machine learning community, TFF benefits from extensive documentation, community-driven content, and numerous tutorials. However, every tool has its challenges. The richness of TFF can also pose challenges, especially for newcomers. The vastness of the TensorFlow ecosystem can sometimes lead to a steep learning curve. Nonetheless, the rewards upon overcoming this learning curve are substantial.

6.7.2. PySyft

In federated learning, PySyft distinguishes itself by not only providing tools for FL but also for encrypted and private machine learning. This framework expands upon popular deep learning platforms like PyTorch and TensorFlow, facilitating multi-party computation. What makes PySyft unique is its emphasis on decentralized deep learning. Its versatile API is designed with a focus on differential privacy and encrypted computation, ensuring that the privacy concerns inherent to FL are effectively addressed [94].

PySyft's versatility is a standout feature. Beyond FL, it serves as a versatile tool for practitioners interested in privacy-preserving machine learning. Its integration with PyTorch, a favorite in the deep learning community, provides a familiar environment, which is always advantageous. However, PySyft, being relatively new compared to TensorFlow, may occasionally exhibit features that are in beta or still being developed [95]. Nonetheless, the PySyft community, led by OpenMined, is vibrant, passionate, and continually pushing boundaries.

6.7.3. Federated AI Technology Enabler (FATE)

FATE is an innovation in federated learning. It handles all aspects, from preparing data to deploying the trained model. A unique feature of FATE is that it understands that data in FL can come from anywhere and take any form. Thus, FATE is built to work with all types of data sources and computing environments, regardless of their differences.

The scalability of FATE is commendable. Whether it is applied to large-scale datasets or complex models, FATE is constructed to handle them with ease. An emphasis on secure exchange protocols ensures that data security, especially during inter-party exchanges, is never compromised. However, as with any sophisticated tool, FATE comes with its own set of challenges. The broad range of features that it offers can sometimes be daunting for beginners, translating to a steeper learning curve. Nonetheless, as the community around FATE grows, and as more practitioners adopt it, it is expected that the collective knowledge will make the adoption of FATE smoother.

In Table 3, we provide a comparison of these federated learning frameworks: TFF vs. PySyft vs. FATE.

Table 3. Comparison of federated learning frameworks: TFF vs. PySyft vs. FATE.

Framework	Scalability	Data Privacy Mechanisms	Performance on Non-IID Data	Ease of Deployment	Key Strengths	Limitations
TensorFlow Federated (TFF)	Designed for small-scale simulations, but lacks production-level scalability for large, complex real-world deployments.	Provides basic privacy mechanisms like secure aggregation, but lacks integrated advanced privacy tools like differential privacy out of the box.	Handles non-IID data reasonably well for small-scale tests, but performance degrades with increasing heterogeneity.	Easy to use if familiar with TensorFlow; ideal for researchers and small-scale testing environments.	Seamless integration with TensorFlow; good for prototyping and research.	Not production-ready; limited scalability and advanced privacy features.

Table 3. *Cont.*

Framework	Scalability	Data Privacy Mechanisms	Performance on Non-IID Data	Ease of Deployment	Key Strengths	Limitations
PySyft	Scalable through integration with PyTorch; better suited for research and educational purposes but requires custom modifications for production use.	Supports differential privacy, federated averaging, and homomorphic encryption. Strong focus on privacy-preserving techniques.	Performs well with non-IID data due to its flexibility and extensive tools, but requires more manual setup and tuning for optimization.	Moderate difficulty in deployment; requires familiarity with PyTorch and more effort to configure for production environments.	Advanced privacy features; flexibility in handling diverse data types and distributions.	Complex setup for large-scale production environments; higher learning curve.
FATE (Federated AI Technology Enabler)	Designed for large-scale, production-grade deployments with scalability in mind for real-world use cases like healthcare and finance.	Integrates advanced privacy mechanisms such as differential privacy and homomorphic encryption, making it highly secure for sensitive data applications.	Optimized for handling of non-IID data in large-scale scenarios, including cross-organizational use cases (e.g., healthcare and finance).	More complex to deploy due to its extensive feature set, but highly suited for industrial applications with full production support.	Production-level scalability; strong focus on enterprise applications and data privacy.	Steeper learning curve and higher complexity in deployment; not as beginner-friendly as other frameworks.

7. Attack Strategies

Federated learning offers a promising approach to model training across multiple devices while maintaining data privacy by keeping them localized. It aims to address the privacy concerns associated with centralized machine learning models. However, FL is vulnerable to attacks, particularly model inversion attacks, which pose significant risks. Understanding these vulnerabilities and potential exploits is essential in securely deploying and scaling FL systems. This section examines various attack strategies, the risks that they present in the context of FL, and mitigation techniques to strengthen FL systems against these threats.

7.1. Contextualizing Attacks in FL

FL has revolutionized machine learning by decentralizing data processing to enhance privacy and reduce large-scale data transfer. While it keeps data local and shares model updates, this decentralized approach brings its own set of challenges. FL's multiple nodes introduce new vulnerabilities, expanding the risk of adversarial attacks. Malicious nodes can disrupt the training process by sending biased or erroneous updates, a tactic exemplified by Byzantine attacks [96]. Despite these risks, tools like Varma et al.'s "Legato" algorithm offer solutions, focusing on layerwise gradient aggregation to mitigate the impact of malicious nodes [97].

7.2. Significance of Addressing Attack Vectors

Federated learning allows the training of machine learning models on many devices without sharing raw data, enhancing the privacy but introducing new security challenges. For instance, deep learning, commonly used in FL, is susceptible to adversarial attacks, where small changes to data can mislead models, such as altering a stop sign to a yield sign in self-driving car training data [98]. As FL evolves, so must the defenses against vulnerabilities like white-box attacks, where attackers exploit model information. Researchers are developing protective measures, such as methods to detect and remove poisoned data. While FL safeguards privacy, ongoing security improvements are crucial.

7.3. Model Inversion Attacks

One of the predominant concerns in the security of FL revolves around model inversion attacks. These attacks essentially calculate the outputs of a machine learning model to infer and reconstruct its training data. As FL often deals with sensitive data distributed over multiple nodes, understanding and mitigating such attacks becomes especially vital.

7.3.1. Implications of Model Inversion in FL

One of the abilities of federated learning is data localization, where each node retains its data and only shares model updates for aggregation, thus enhancing the privacy by keeping the raw data local. However, this decentralized approach introduces vulnerabilities, particularly through model inversion attacks. Even without direct access to raw data, attackers can infer details from aggregated model updates, like piecing together a puzzle. For instance, in a healthcare FL model, such attacks could reveal sensitive patient information, undermining the trust in FL. Additionally, vulnerabilities in individual nodes could expose broader insights, emphasizing the need to address the potential security risks in FL [98].

7.3.2. Mitigating Model Inversion Attacks

Model inversion attacks, which seek to reverse-engineer and reconstruct private training data from trained models, highlight the critical need for robust mitigation strategies to protect federated learning systems. These attacks exploit the detailed information retained by overfitted models, which capture not only general patterns but also the specific sensitivities and irregularities of the training data, making them particularly vulnerable.

To mitigate these risks, it is essential to prevent models from overfitting [99]. Key strategies include the following .

- Regularization Techniques: Methods such as L1 and L2 regularization add a penalty to the loss function, discouraging models from focusing too much on any single feature and promoting a more generalized understanding of the data.
- Validation Protocols: Implementing rigorous validation checks during training helps to monitor model performance on unseen data, allowing the early detection and prevention of overfitting.
- Data Augmentation: By increasing the diversity of the training data through augmentation techniques, models are less likely to memorize specific data points and more likely to learn generalized patterns.

Recent advancements, such as the "ResSFL" framework, offer sophisticated strategies tailored to FL scenarios [100]. Integrating these strategies with fundamental modeling principles bolsters FL systems' defenses, safeguarding data privacy and resilience. Ongoing innovations will require vigilance and adaptability to stay ahead of potential threats.

7.4. Membership Inference Attacks

7.4.1. The Nature of Membership Inference

Membership inference attacks exploit machine learning models' tendency to unintentionally memorize training data. These attacks probe models with specific inputs and analyze confidence levels. High-confidence responses suggest that the input data were part of the training set, revealing a privacy vulnerability in complex models like deep neural networks [101,102].

7.4.2. Threats to Data Privacy and Impacts

These attacks pose significant privacy risks, particularly in sensitive sectors like healthcare and finance, potentially leading to bias, societal exclusion, reputational damage, and loss of trust. They also erode public confidence in technology, emphasizing the need for responsible data use [103,104].

7.4.3. Strategies to Counter Membership Inference Attacks

In machine learning, membership inference attacks have become a significant threat to data privacy. Addressing these attacks requires a strong understanding of their nature and a comprehensive defensive strategy [103].

1. Embracing Differential Privacy: One of the most effective defenses against membership inference attacks is differential privacy. Based on a strong mathematical framework, differential privacy introduces calibrated noise to a model's outputs. This could be during its training phase or even after training has been completed. The main idea is to add a degree of randomness such that attackers find it nearly impossible to determine whether a specific data point was in the training set.
2. Data Sanitization: Before any training begins, it is crucial to rigorously clean and sanitize the data. This ensures that patterns or identifiable markers are eliminated. Data anonymization techniques, such as k-anonymity, help in masking specific attributes, making datasets more homogeneous. The l-diversity approach, on the other hand, ensures that sensitive attributes in the data are diverse enough to prevent the singling out of individual records. Together, these techniques make the identification of individual data points a much more complex task.
3. Model Auditing: Data security is an ongoing challenge. To stay ahead of attackers, regular checkups are essential. These can be performed by one's own security team or outside experts. They can be considered as practice rounds against membership inference attacks. By simulating these attacks in a safe environment, we can find weaknesses in our machine learning models before they are exploited in reality. This provides us with time to fix the problems and make our defenses even stronger.
4. Regularization Techniques: A model that fits well to its training data is a model that is suitable for exploitation. Regularization techniques, like L1 and L2 regularization, add penalty terms to the model during the training process, discouraging it from becoming overly reliant on any single attribute. Techniques like dropout, where random neurons are "dropped out" during training, ensure that the model generalizes better, reducing the risk of overfitting and the consequent susceptibility to attacks.
5. Output Aggregation: Instead of relying on a single model's prediction, aggregating the outputs from multiple models can be an effective strategy. Ensemble methods, which combine predictions from different models, tend to generalize better. By pooling insights, the resulting predictions are not only more accurate but also less revealing about the specific sensitivity of the training data.
6. Reduced Model Precision: In the complicated process of machine learning, sometimes less can be more. Reducing the precision of the model weights and outputs introduces an element of controlled uncertainty, which can be used to enhance the privacy. Techniques like quantization, which limit the precision of the model parameters, create an environment where attackers, even if they gain access to the model, face significant challenges in making precise inferences about the underlying data.

   Here, "precision" refers to the number of bits used to represent a number. By reducing the precision of the model weights and outputs, we introduce a degree of vagueness into the model's calculations. This vagueness acts as a form of protection, as it makes it more difficult for attackers to extract sensitive information from the model. Even if an attacker were to gain access to the model itself, the reduced precision would blur the results, making it a challenging task to draw accurate conclusions about the training data.
7. Model Architectural Decisions: The architecture of a machine learning model can be a source of vulnerability or strength. By choosing architectures that are leaner, with fewer parameters or layers, there is less room for data leakage. The choice of architecture can serve as the first line of defense against membership inference attacks.
8. User Awareness and Education: Beyond algorithms and architectures lies the human factor. Keeping users in the loop, educating them about the risks, and ensuring that they are well informed can be as crucial as any technical measure. A well-informed

user is a vigilant user, and their understanding and cooperation can be instrumental in creating robust defense against data breaches.

Together, these strategies form a multi-layered defense system against membership inference attacks, emphasizing both technical excellence and ethical responsibility. The counteraction of membership inference attacks represents a mixture of technical rigor, strategic planning, and ethical responsibility.

7.5. Eavesdropping and Man-in-the-Middle Attacks

The continuous exchange of data across networks is inherently associated with risks as attackers aim to intercept and exploit this information. Among the most significant of these risks are those posed by eavesdropping and man-in-the-middle (MitM) attacks, which are especially concerning in scenarios involving sensitive data. Due to its decentralized structure and dependence on communication between numerous nodes, federated learning is particularly vulnerable to such security threats.

7.5.1. Characterizing Eavesdropping in a Federated Setting

The unauthorized interception of communications in cyber-security, especially within a federated learning setting, is known as eavesdropping. In contrast to centralized systems, FL allocates learning among local devices and only sends model updates to a central server. This design presents various communication points, all susceptible to interception. Experienced attackers might be able to deduce sensitive information from intercepted communications, thereby compromising FL's privacy objectives. Furthermore, man-in-the-middle (MitM) attacks present a live risk, as attackers are able to intercept, change, or reroute communications, leading to major threats to the reliability and safety of the FL procedure [105].

- Alter Model Updates: Introducing slight biases or modifications in the model updates being sent to the central server. Over time, these could skew the global model in malicious or unintended ways.
- Introduce Malicious Instructions: For federated systems that rely on dynamic model structures, attackers could potentially alter the model architectures or parameters, leading to compromised nodes.
- Data Deception: By modifying the communicated updates, attackers could deceive the central server about the nature of the data at the edge, leading to models that might be ineffectual or even counterproductive.

In federated settings, eavesdropping and man-in-the-middle (MitM) attacks present a dual threat. On one hand, there is the ongoing risk of data inference through eavesdropping, which is passive yet persistent. On the other hand, MitM attacks pose an active and potentially catastrophic threat that could undermine the core principles of FL. Effectively safeguarding against these threats necessitates an in-depth understanding of their complexities, followed by the implementation of strong countermeasures [106].

7.5.2. Potential Damages and Consequences

As federated learning becomes increasingly popular for its decentralized approach, concerns about eavesdropping and man-in-the-middle (MitM) attacks have gained significance. FL allows multiple edge devices to collaboratively learn a shared model while keeping the data local, but this distributed setup introduces vulnerabilities. Eavesdropping in FL involves the unauthorized interception of communications between client nodes and the central server. While raw data are not shared, model weights, gradients, and updates are transmitted, which an eavesdropper could exploit to infer information about the original training data. Over time, a persistent eavesdropper could develop a shadow model, approximating a client's data distribution.

MitM attacks are even more severe. An attacker could intercept, alter, and forward communications between clients and the server, manipulating gradients or model updates. This could poison the global model, causing it to degrade or behave unpredictably, potentially leading to global model drift. Such attacks can also undermine aggregation mechanisms like Federated Averaging, skewing the model in unintended directions, especially when differential privacy is involved. These attacks pose significant risks to data privacy, potentially revealing sensitive information like personal identifiable information (PII). Moreover, MitM attacks can disrupt consensus protocols in federated settings, leading to delays or halting the learning process. To protect FL systems, advanced cryptographic techniques, secure aggregation methods, and robust consensus protocols are essential [105].

7.6. Secure Communication Protocols

FL, with its decentralized design, promises new horizons in innovation and collaboration, but it also exposes systems to vulnerabilities, especially from eavesdropping and MitM threats. To counteract these vulnerabilities, the importance of secure communication protocols cannot be overstated. End-to-end encryption forms the foundation of these protocols, promising foundational privacy. By encrypting data directly at their source and only decrypting them at their destination, this mechanism ensures that intercepted communications remain unintelligible. Furthermore, the dynamic nature of modern encryption algorithms ensures that they can adapt to and combat emerging threats, providing a continually evolving protective barrier. However, encryption alone is not sufficient. This is where the Public Key Infrastructure (PKI) becomes relevant, introducing a robust framework of trust. PKI operates based on the validation provided by certificate authorities (CAs) to verify the authenticity of participants. This added layer of trustworthiness means that MitM attackers find it exceptionally difficult to impersonate genuine nodes, thanks to the rigorous verification steps that PKI entails [107].

Another crucial aspect is secure aggregation. Instead of transmitting raw model updates, which could inadvertently reveal patterns to attackers, nodes employ cryptographic techniques. They send aggregated and encrypted summaries, which remain indecipherable until they reach the central server. There, the processes of aggregation and decryption unfold. This approach ensures that individual node updates remain shielded from potential eavesdroppers. However, the pursuit of security does not end here. Continuous authentication protocols introduce dynamic trust verification. Regular authentication checks throughout communication sessions improve the security by discovering anomalies early on and preventing man-in-the-middle (MitM) attacks. Using virtual private networks (VPNs) or secure tunnels enhances the data security by encrypting and encapsulating packets, lowering the risk of eavesdropping. The human factor is also important: participants can become vulnerabilities if they are not educated about secure communication and threat recognition. Regular training and an emphasis on cyber-hygiene can transform participants into watchful defenders, preventing them from becoming vulnerabilities. A complete methodology that combines modern technology with proactive human involvement maintains the integrity and security of federated learning systems.

7.7. Data Poisoning

7.7.1. Introduction to Data Poisoning in FL

Data poisoning poses a significant threat in machine learning, particularly within federated learning (FL), where model training is decentralized. FL enhances privacy and efficiency but lacks centralized data quality controls, making it susceptible to malicious nodes injecting corrupted data or model updates. Attackers often employ subtle manipulations, making minor changes that evade detection yet degrade the model integrity over time [108]. For example, in facial recognition, slight alterations to genuine images can misguide the model. Coordinated attacks by multiple compromised nodes further amplify the risks, allowing attackers to drive the central model toward harmful objectives and undermining FL's resilience.

7.7.2. Defense Mechanisms Against Poisoning

Defending against poisoning attacks in FL demands a blend of sophisticated techniques and human vigilance. One of the primary defense pillars is model validation combined with anomaly detection. Regularly measuring the global model's performance against trusted benchmarks or validation datasets ensures that anomalies in accuracy or behavior are swiftly found. Simultaneously, by utilizing advanced statistical or machine-learning-driven anomaly detection methods, the system can monitor each node's updates. Nodes that consistently display unexpected or erratic contributions can be singled out for deeper scrutiny [109].

The Byzantine fault tolerance concept arises as a crucial asset. Initially crafted to uphold system reliability even in the face of malicious nodes, its principles can be seamlessly integrated into FL. This ensures that, even if certain nodes are compromised, the overall system remains resilient, preventing malicious inputs from derailing the global model [110].

Directly overseeing the nature of node updates offers another layer of defense. Techniques such as gradient clipping place a limit on the magnitude of updates, ensuring that no single node exerts a disproportionate influence over the model's trajectory. In the same way, normalization practices guarantee that updates from all nodes adhere to an anticipated range, negating the possibility of the model taking a drastic turn due to tainted data [111].

However, trust within a decentralized setup does not need to be all-or-nothing. Introducing reputation systems can transform trust into a dynamic attribute. Nodes earn scores reflecting their historical behaviors and contributions. Those persistently associated with questionable updates might witness a decline in their trustworthiness ratings [111]. As this system matures, nodes with dwindling trust scores could face increased scrutiny and, in severe cases, might even be sidelined to avoid influencing the global model.

7.8. Backdoor Attacks

7.8.1. Understanding the Nature of Backdoor Attacks

Backdoor attacks in cyber-security are stealthy intrusions that avoid disrupting machine learning models' performance under normal conditions. Instead, they introduce latent triggers, only activating under specific circumstances to serve an attacker's goals while undetected [112]. For instance, a facial recognition system could be subtly compromised with a backdoor that responds to a particular pattern, like a specific hat. When the trigger pattern appears, the model misidentifies the individual, potentially enabling unauthorized access. These attacks are especially dangerous because they are difficult to detect and can be triggered at critical moments, facilitating targeted disruptions and security breaches.

7.8.2. Implications of Backdoor Attacks in FL

Federated learning uses a decentralized approach to enhance the data privacy and computational efficiency. However, this decentralization also introduces vulnerabilities, particularly to backdoor attacks. In FL, nodes independently train models on local data and send updates to a centralized server, assuming that each node operates with integrity. This contrasts with centralized systems, where backdoor attacks typically involve manipulating a central dataset. FL's structure, with numerous independent nodes, increases the attack surface as each node could potentially be compromised. A malicious node can subtly introduce tainted updates, affecting the global model without immediate detection. The aggregation process in FL, notably federated averaging, is susceptible to sophisticated attackers who can craft precise updates that blend with legitimate ones. These malicious updates can embed backdoors into the global model, which then functions normally for most inputs but triggers malicious behavior for specific inputs. FL's commitment to keeping raw data localized enhances its privacy but complicates backdoor detection. Unlike centralized systems that have access to raw data for comprehensive auditing, FL's central server only receives aggregated updates, lacking the granularity needed to detect anomalies. This opacity hinders the identification of tainted contributions from individual nodes. In summary, while FL's decentralized nature offers significant benefits, it also presents unique challenges, particularly in defending against backdoor attacks. Recognizing these challenges is crucial in strengthening FL systems against such covert threats [113].

Centralized learning systems, with their unrestricted access to raw data, can employ a variety of auditing and anomaly detection tools. In contrast, FL faces limitations in this area. The central server, limited to aggregated updates, lacks the detailed insight provided by raw data. This lack of transparency complicates the identification of the origin of each update, making it difficult to determine whether a node's contribution has been compromised by an embedded backdoor [36].

7.8.3. Overcoming the Threat of Backdoor Attacks

Federated learning faces significant challenges due to backdoor attacks, necessitating robust countermeasures. The FL community is actively pursuing strategies to enhance the security, using technological advancements and collaboration. Differential privacy is a key method, introducing statistical noise to node updates to obscure data and reduce the effectiveness of backdoor triggers, thereby complicating attackers' efforts. Robust aggregation methods further strengthen FL by vetting node updates, considering both content and historical reliability. This diminishes the impact of suspicious contributions. Current countermeasures often exclude benign models from aggregation, particularly those with diverse data distributions, leading to underperformance. To solve this, DeepSight was established, which uses unique methodologies to analyze the data distribution and identify variations in the model structure and outputs. DeepSight detects and removes tainted model clusters, while the current defenses combat any leftover poisoned models. Anomaly detection is critical, requiring complex algorithms to detect irregularities in node updates. These technologies function as early warning systems for potential backdoors. Routine validation against trustworthy datasets ensures that the global model's behavior matches expectations, identifying unusual variations as potential backdoor signs. Model interpretability gives an additional degree of transparency by assisting in identifying unexplainable behaviors or biases that indicate the presence of a backdoor. FL relies heavily on a culture of transparency and collaboration. Encouraging nodes to share observations and insights while maintaining data privacy is crucial. This networked vigilance ensures a united defense against backdoors, using the collective expertise of the FL ecosystem. With innovative techniques, shared vigilance, and continuous refinement, FL can navigate the complex interaction of decentralized data processing and backdoor threats, balancing its decentralized nature with protective mechanisms [114–116].

7.9. Sybil Attacks

Sybil attacks received their name from John Douceur's 2002 work, introducing the concept within peer-to-peer networks. The term references the book Sybil, representing the idea of one entity assuming multiple identities [117]. Historically, these attacks have challenged decentralized systems, from early file sharing to blockchain. In distributed systems, where trust and authenticity are critical, Sybil attacks exploit these by creating numerous fake identities. This allows attackers to dominate decision making, sway consensus, and distort information sharing. Such manipulation degrades the trust that is essential to distributed systems, undermining their cooperative nature [118,119].

Defense Protocols Against Sybil Attacks in FL

Navigating the FL landscape necessitates not only the appreciation of its decentralized nature but also keen awareness of the underlying threats, which include Sybil attacks. As FL systems grow in complexity and adoption, ensuring the integrity and authenticity of the participating nodes becomes paramount. With this goal in mind, several defense protocols have emerged to counter the threat of Sybil attacks.

One of the foundational approaches in this regard is the implementation of strong identity verification protocols. In an FL environment, the very act of onboarding a node carries huge significance. Ensuring that every node, before it can participate and contribute updates, undergoes a rigorous identity verification process can serve as the first line of defense. This involves not only traditional authentication mechanisms but can also include cryptographic methods, hardware attestations, or even third-party verifications. The primary objective is clear: to validate the legitimacy of a node before it becomes an active participant in the learning process.

Identity verification, while vital, might not suffice on its own, especially if an attacker manages to bypass this first gate. This necessitates a second layer of defense in the form of rate limiting. By controlling and limiting the number of updates or the participation rate for newly onboarded or untrusted nodes, FL systems can diminish the potential impact of malicious entities. For instance, a new node's updates could be given lesser weight in the global model until it establishes a track record of consistent and genuine contributions. This ensures that, even if a Sybil node were to infiltrate the network, its influence would be curtailed, at least until it gains undue credibility [120].

While these proactive measures build a strong defense, they are complemented by reactive strategies centered around behavioral analysis. In FL, where data remain localized but updates are shared, monitoring the nature, pattern, and timing of these updates can reveal important information. By employing advanced analytics and machine learning techniques, it is possible to discern patterns consistent with Sybil attacks, such as suspiciously synchronized updates from multiple nodes. Detecting such anomalies in real time can allow for immediate intervention, either in the form of isolating the suspected nodes or subjecting their updates to further scrutiny.

8. Discussion

This article examines the fundamentals, methods, advancements, and uses of federated learning, with a specific emphasis on its incorporation in IoT settings. The goal was to examine the benefits that FL provides with its decentralized structure and also to recognize the difficulties and weaknesses that come with this new approach. Our paper emphasizes FL's ability to improve data privacy and efficiency in machine learning and also highlights the significant security threats linked to decentralized systems. It explores the equilibrium between customization and privacy in federated learning apps, the requirement for teamwork and standardization among FL networks, and the significance of continued alertness toward evolving cyber-threats.

The answers to the research questions stated in the Introduction are given below.

RQ1: Balancing the trade-offs between data privacy, security, and communication costs while retaining model performance calls for a comprehensive strategy in federated learning (FL). Privacy-preserving approaches, such as differential privacy and homomorphic encryption, ensure that sensitive data are protected during the training process, although they sometimes entail a cost in terms of the computing overhead or model accuracy. To address this, secure aggregation methods are used to protect model updates while not dramatically increasing the communication costs. On the other hand, methods such as FedAvg are frequently used to reduce the communication costs by reducing the frequency of data exchange, although these techniques may struggle with extremely heterogeneous, non-IID data. Integrating advanced privacy-preserving approaches with communication-efficient protocols provides a pathway to retaining robust model performance while ensuring security and cost-effectiveness in large-scale FL systems.

RQ2: Federated learning (FL) faces significant security challenges that must be addressed to ensure robust deployment in real-world applications. One of the primary concerns is adversarial attacks, where malicious actors can manipulate local model updates or inject poisoned data into the training process, ultimately degrading the global model's performance. Model poisoning and data poisoning are critical threats that expose vulnerabilities in the aggregation phase. Additionally, inference attacks, such as model inversion and membership inference, threaten the privacy of individuals by attempting to reconstruct sensitive data from shared model updates. To mitigate these risks, techniques such as homomorphic encryption, differential privacy, and secure multi-party computation (SMPC) are employed, ensuring that data remain protected even in the presence of adversaries. However, balancing these security measures with system scalability and performance remains a crucial challenge for real-world FL deployments.

Considering previous works, we point out the following. In [121], it is mentioned that FL is vulnerable to inference and poisoning attacks, with challenges in balancing efficiency and security, as privacy-preserving protocols often compromise the performance while protecting sensitive data from breaches and malicious servers. In [122], it is shown that FL faces vulnerabilities due to inference and poisoning attacks, compromising data privacy and performance. A malicious server can further threaten systems' integrity, and balancing efficiency with strong security remains a challenge due to the trade-offs in privacy-preserving protocols. In [123], the PEFL framework presented faces challenges in balancing privacy and security, with privacy-preserving methods hindering poisoning attack detection. Its reliance on homomorphic encryption creates a large computational overhead, and, while effective against specific attacks, it may not cover all vectors. Implementation is also complex. In [124], the FedPD algorithm addresses cross-client interference in open-set recognition but lacks focus on privacy or security mechanisms, a key concern in FL applications. It introduces the LPD and GDCA techniques but does not cover adversarial attacks or detailed IoT use cases. The study in [125] addresses challenges in training complex models, including biases due to the architecture and data. Its federated learning focus limits its generalizability to broader contexts. Techniques like active learning and knowledge distillation may show variable effectiveness, and the efficacy analysis lacks consideration of all relevant variables. In [126], it is shown that FL enhances privacy by keeping data local but faces challenges in ensuring complete security. Communication bottlenecks can occur, especially with large models, and the performance may lag compared to centralized models due to data heterogeneity. The need for GDPR compliance further complicates FL's implementation. Our paper offers a specific focus on advanced cryptographic techniques like homomorphic encryption, differential privacy, and SMC to address security and privacy in FL. It also extensively covers IoT applications, GDPR compliance, and defense against adversarial attacks. While not as broad as other surveys, its strength lies in addressing critical intersections among security, privacy, and legal frameworks, making it highly relevant to real-world FL challenges.

The results indicate that FL offers a promising solution to the privacy issues found in centralized machine learning models, but it also brings security issues. Some of the challenges include being vulnerable to risks such as eavesdropping and Sybil attacks, which may undermine the integrity of the learning process. Our paper confirms the theory that proactive defense mechanisms are crucial in preserving trust and security in FL networks. FL's decentralized nature naturally ensures data privacy by storing data on individual devices; however, it also demands strong security measures to manage the potential risks. This study highlights the significance of consistent surveillance, the verification of identities, and promoting a culture of cooperation and openness in order to avoid and uncover security breaches. Furthermore, the balance between providing tailored experiences and protecting data privacy is a key area of attention. With the increasing sophistication of FL algorithms, it is crucial to ensure a careful balance between these two objectives to prevent sensitive information from being compromised.

In contrast to traditional centralized models, FL implements a system whereby security is spread among several nodes, all of which may be susceptible to attacks. Prior research has identified comparable security concerns but frequently emphasized defensive tactics in response. This study builds on this discussion by promoting a proactive stance on security in FL, stressing the importance of ongoing monitoring and adaptive defense mechanisms in light of the ever-changing cyber-security environment. The results aid in explaining decentralized machine learning's value, especially for IoT applications. FL disrupts traditional beliefs about centralized data and enables the exploration of secure, privacy-focused machine learning models. Our study underscores the importance of gaining more profound insights into how personalization and privacy intersect in FL, representing a delicate equilibrium that has the potential to reshape the limits of data-driven technologies. FL's decentralized structure is ideal for industries like healthcare and urban planning, where data privacy is crucial. However, in order to exploit the full potential of FL, there is a need to create standardized protocols and frameworks to guarantee compatibility among various systems. The proactive defense tactics mentioned in our paper are crucial in safeguarding the security of FL networks, especially as they grow in popularity and attract more advanced threats.

The ethical implications of FL, particularly concerning data privacy and the potential for bias in decentralized models, warrant careful consideration. Ensuring that FL systems are designed with fairness and transparency in mind will be critical for their acceptance and success. FL's impact extends beyond the technical realm, influencing how data are handled and protected in a wide range of industries. Its success could lead to a shift in how society views data privacy, potentially driving new standards and regulations that prioritize user consent and data security.

Future Implications and Directions

In the future, it is important for research to focus on creating adaptive FL models that can respond to changing security threats. More research is necessary to examine the relationship between customizing services and safeguarding privacy, especially in critical settings such as healthcare. Moreover, exploring standardized protocols for FL systems may promote increased collaboration and compatibility, minimizing the risk of fragmentation in the FL environment. Numerous unanswered questions persist about achieving ideal personalization while safeguarding data privacy and ensuring that FL systems can withstand advanced cyber-threats. Answering these questions will be essential for the ongoing progress of FL. Further investigation into FL's wider use cases, like smart cities and autonomous systems, has the potential to reveal possibilities for decentralized machine learning. Furthermore, it will be crucial to conduct research on the regulatory consequences of FL, specifically within the topic of data protection legislation, in order to guarantee its sustainability in the long run. This paper has brought attention to FL's dual role as a valuable tool to improve data privacy and as a possible target for advanced cyber-attacks. It is essential to implement proactive defense strategies, collaboration, and standardization in order to fully exploit FL's capabilities. FL's capacity to safeguard data confidentiality while facilitating decentralized machine learning proves to be an essential advancement for big data and IoT technologies. However, its success will depend on the ongoing efforts of researchers, developers, and policymakers to address its inherent challenges. More efficient and scalable privacy-preserving mechanisms, such as homomorphic encryption and secure multi-party computation (SMC), continue to be a major research focus. The current methods are either computationally intensive or degrade the model performance. The future of FL is anticipated to involve the development of lighter encryption methods and more efficient, safer aggregation systems that can operate in real time, particularly in resource-constrained situations such as IoT. Many existing FL techniques assume IID data, although this is rarely the case in real-world applications. Because non-IID data remain one of the most significant challenges, future research should focus on developing adaptive aggregation approaches and innovative algorithms that can manage skewed data distributions across a wide range of devices. Future FL systems must be resistant to adversarial attacks such as model poisoning and data inversion, while still preserving players' trust. Research on federated trust mechanisms, such as reputation-based systems and blockchain for federated learning, could be critical to safeguarding FL settings. Communication constraints continue to be one of FL's most significant issues. Future research should concentrate on asynchronous communication protocols, model compression approaches, and adaptive learning rate optimization in order to reduce the volume of data transferred while maintaining model correctness and fairness between nodes.

As FL evolves, there is an opportunity to change how machine learning is implemented in various industries. By acknowledging the potential benefits and limitations, the FL community can lead the development of a safe, distributed, and cooperative machine learning setting.

9. Conclusions

Our paper addresses various FL topics but is constrained by the ongoing development of current research. We suggest that future research could focus on developing new FL algorithms that protect privacy and are resilient to adversarial attacks. Furthermore, there is a definite requirement for more research on the relationship between customization and confidentiality, as well as the creation of uniform procedures to support cooperation among various FL platforms. While our paper provides an extensive review of federated learning, the goal was also to identify research gaps that future work can address.

Based on our analysis of the literature and the current trends in FL, we identify the following gaps.

Gap 1: Insufficient Resistance to Adversarial Attacks. Although numerous strategies, including differential privacy and safe aggregation, have been presented, there is still no agreement on how to properly secure FL models against adversarial assaults. Research in this field is still dispersed, and existing solutions frequently compromise the performance or scalability.

Gap 2: Difficulties in Managing Non-IID Data. Non-IID data present substantial obstacles to FL's performance. Most known algorithms, such as FedAvg, assume IID data distributions, and solutions for non-IID circumstances are still in their early stages.

Gap 3: Scalability Issues in Real-World Applications. While FL has been successfully deployed in small-scale settings, there is a lack of study on its scalability over large networks, particularly in resource-constrained situations such as IoT devices.

This paper mainly targeted the current FL applications and recognized the security risks, possibly neglecting upcoming trends and future obstacles. These limitations indicate that the findings may not fully capture the future directions of FL, especially as new technologies and threats emerge. This study's emphasis on the present difficulties could also restrict its relevance to upcoming advancements in the field. In order to overcome these constraints, upcoming works should integrate new studies and investigate innovative uses of FL that are starting to become popular. Furthermore, conducting research on proactive defense strategies in actual FL implementations could offer useful perspectives.

Author Contributions: Conceptualization, C.P. and G.F.F.; methodology, C.P.; validation, C.P., K.-F.K. and G.F.F.; writing—original draft preparation, C.P.; writing—review and editing, C.P., K.-F.K. and G.F.F.; supervision, G.F.F. All authors have read and agreed to the published version of the manuscript.

Funding: This research received no external funding.

Data Availability Statement: No new data were created or analyzed in this study.

Conflicts of Interest: The authors declare no conflicts of interest.

References

1. Jiang, J.C.; Kantarci, B.; Oktug, S.; Soyata, T. Federated Learning in Smart City Sensing: Challenges and Opportunities. *Sensors* **2020**, *20*, 6230. [CrossRef] [PubMed]
2. Sikandar, H.S.; Waheed, H.; Tahir, S.; Malik, S.U.R.; Rafique, W. A Detailed Survey on Federated Learning Attacks and Defenses. *Electronicsweek* **2023**, *12*, 260. [CrossRef]
3. Liu, Y.; Zhang, L.; Ge, N.; Li, G. A Systematic Literature Review on Federated Learning: From A Model Quality Perspective. *arXiv* **2020**, arXiv:2012.01973. [CrossRef]
4. Beutel, D.; Topal, T.; Mathur, A.; Qiu, X.; Fernandez-Marques, J.; Gao, Y.; Sani, L.; Kwing, H.; Parcollet, T.; Gusmão, P.; et al. A Flower: A Friendly Federated Learning Research Framework. *arXiv* **2007**, arXiv:2007.14390.

5. McMahan, B.; Moore, E.; Ramage, D.; Hampson, S.; Arcas, Y.B.A. Communication-Efficient Learning of Deep Networks from Decentralized Data. In Proceedings of the 20th International Conference on Artificial Intelligence and Statistics, PMLR, Ft. Lauderdale, FL, USA, 20–22 April 2017; pp. 1273–1282.
6. Li, T.; Sahu, A.K.; Talwalkar, A.; Smith, V. Federated Learning: Challenges, Methods, and Future Directions. *IEEE Signal Process. Mag.* **2020**, *37*, 50–60. [CrossRef]
7. Sammut, C.; Webb, G.I. (Eds.) *Encyclopedia of Machine Learning*; Springer: Boston, MA, USA, 2010.
8. Sammut, C.; Webb, G.I. (Eds.) *Encyclopedia of Machine Learning and Data Mining*; Springer: Boston, MA, USA, 2017.
9. Manual, O.R. Federated Learning Glossary. Available online: https://www.openriskmanual.org/wiki/Federated_Learning_Glossary (accessed on 4 November 2024).
10. Papatsimouli, M.; Lazaridis, L.; Ziouzios, D.; Dasygenis, M.; Fragulis, G. Internet of things (IOT) awareness in Greece. In Proceedings of the 4th ETLTC International Conference on ICT Integration in Technical Education (ETLTC2022), Aizuwakamatsu, Japan, 25–28 January 2022; EDP Sciences: Les Ulis, France, 2022; Volume 139, p. 03013.
11. Mammen, P. Federated Learning: Opportunities and Challenges. *arXiv* **2021**, arXiv:2101.05428.
12. Zhang, T.; Gao, L.; He, C.; Zhang, M.; Krishnamachari, B.; Avestimehr, A.S. Federated Learning for the Internet of Things: Applications, Challenges, and Opportunities. *IEEE Internet Things Mag.* **2022**, *5*, 24–29. [CrossRef]
13. Bonawitz, K.; Kairouz, P.; Mcmahan, B.; Ramage, D. Federated Learning and Privacy. *Commun. ACM* **2022**, *65*, 90–97. [CrossRef]
14. Nevrataki, T.; Iliadou, A.; Ntolkeras, G.; Sfakianakis, I.; Lazaridis, L.; Maraslidis, G.; Asimopoulos, N.; Fragulis, G.F. A survey on federated learning applications in healthcare, finance, and data privacy/data security. *AIP Conf. Proc.* **2023**, *2909*, 120015.
15. Rehman, A.; Razzak, I.; Xu, G. Federated Learning for Privacy Preservation of Healthcare Data From Smartphone-Based Side-Channel Attacks. *IEEE J. Biomed. Health Inform.* **2023**, *27*, 684–690. [CrossRef]
16. Truong, N.; Sun, K.; Wang, S.; Guitton, F.; Guo, Y. Privacy Preservation in Federated Learning: An Insightful Survey from the GDPR Perspective. *Comput. Secur.* **2021**, *110*, 102402. [CrossRef]
17. Yaacoub, J.P.A.; Noura, H.N.; Salman, O. Security of Federated Learning with IoT Systems: Issues, Limitations, Challenges, and Solutions. *Internet Things Cyber-Phys. Syst.* **2023**, *3*, 155–179. [CrossRef]
18. Li, L.; Fan, Y.; Tse, M.; Lin, K.Y. A Review of Applications in Federated Learning. *Comput. Ind. Eng.* **2020**, *149*, 106854. [CrossRef]
19. Kang, D.; Ahn, C.W. Communication Cost Reduction with Partial Structure in Federated Learning. *Electronicsweek* **2021**, *10*, 2081. [CrossRef]
20. Yao, X.; Huang, C.; Sun, L. Two-Stream Federated Learning: Reduce the Communication Costs. In Proceedings of the 2018 IEEE Visual Communications and Image Processing (VCIP), Taichung, Taiwan, 9–12 December 2018; pp. 1–4. [CrossRef]
21. Jiang, Y.; Konečný, J.; Rush, K.; Kannan, S. Improving Federated Learning Personalization via Model Agnostic Meta Learning *arXiv* **2019**, arXiv:1909.12488.
22. Fallah, A.; Mokhtari, A.; Ozdaglar, A. Personalized Federated Learning with Theoretical Guarantees: A Model-Agnostic Meta-Learning Approach. *Adv. Neural Inf. Process. Syst.* **2020**, *33*, 3557–3568.
23. Bonawitz, K.; Eichner, H.; Grieskamp, W.; Huba, D.; Ingerman, A.; Ivanov, V.; Kiddon, C.; Konečný, J.; Mazzocchi, S.; McMahan, H.B.; et al. Towards Federated Learning at Scale: System Design. *arXiv* **2019**, arXiv:1902.01046. [CrossRef]
24. Abreha, H.G.; Hayajneh, M.; Serhani, M.A. Federated Learning in Edge Computing: A Systematic Survey. *Sensors* **2022**, *22*, 450. [CrossRef] [PubMed]
25. Grama, M.; Musat, M.; Muñoz-González, L.; Passerat-Palmbach, J.; Rueckert, D.; Alansary, A. Robust Aggregation for Adaptive Privacy Preserving Federated Learning in Healthcare. *arXiv* **2020**, arXiv:2009.08294.
26. Lycklama, H.; Burkhalter, L.; Viand, A.; Küchler, N.; Hithnawi, A. Rofl: Robustness of secure federated learning. In Proceedings of the 2023 IEEE Symposium on Security and Privacy (SP), San Francisco, CA, USA, 21–25 May 2023; pp. 453–476.
27. Yang, C.; Wang, Q.; Xu, M.; Chen, Z.; Bian, K.; Liu, Y.; Liu, X. Characterizing Impacts of Heterogeneity in Federated Learning upon Large-Scale Smartphone Data. In Proceedings of the Web Conference 2021, Ljubljana, Slovenia, 19–23 April 2021; pp. 935–946. [CrossRef]
28. Ek, S.; Portet, F.; Lalanda, P.; Vega, G. Evaluation and Comparison of Federated Learning Algorithms for Human Activity Recognition on Smartphones. *Pervasive Mob. Comput.* **2022**, *87*, 101714. [CrossRef]
29. Li, L.; Fan, Y.; Lin, K.Y. A Survey on Federated Learning. In Proceedings of the 2020 IEEE 16th International Conference on Control & Automation (ICCA), Singapore, 9–11 October 2020; pp. 791–796. [CrossRef]
30. Wen, J.; Zhang, Z.; Lan, Y.; Cui, Z.; Cai, J.; Zhang, W. A Survey on Federated Learning: Challenges and Applications. *Int. J. Mach. Learn. Cybern.* **2023**, *14*, 513–535. [CrossRef] [PubMed]
31. Rights (OCR), O.f.C. Summary of the HIPAA Privacy Rule. Available online: https://www.hhs.gov/hipaa/for-professionals/privacy/laws-regulations/index.html (accessed on 4 November 2024).
32. McMahan, H.B.; Moore, E.; Ramage, D.; Arcas, B.A.Y. Federated Learning of Deep Networks Using Model Averaging. *arXiv* **2016**, arXiv:1602.05629.
33. Cavdar Aksoy, N.; Tumer Kabadayi, E.; Yilmaz, C.; Kocak Alan, A. A Typology of Personalisation Practices in Marketing in the Digital Age. *J. Mark. Manag.* **2021**, *37*, 1091–1122. [CrossRef]
34. Liu, Y.; Kang, Y.; Zou, T.; Pu, Y.; He, Y.; Ye, X.; Ouyang, Y.; Zhang, Y.Q.; Yang, Q. Vertical federated learning: Concepts, advances, and challenges. *IEEE Trans. Knowl. Data Eng.* **2024**, *36*, 3615–3634. [CrossRef]

35. SiniosoGlou, I.; Xouveroudis, K.; Argyriou, V.; Lagkas, T.; Saoulidis, T.; Fragulis, G.; Goudos, S.K.; Sarigiannidis, P. Personalisation of Federated Learning Models Through Knowledge Distillation on Decentralised Data. In Proceedings of the 2023 IEEE Globecom Workshops (GC Wkshps), Kuala Lumpur, Malaysia, 4–8 December 2023; pp. 56–61.
36. Bakopoulou, E.; Tillman, B.; Markopoulou, A. FedPacket: A Federated Learning Approach to Mobile Packet Classification. *IEEE Trans. Mob. Comput.* **2022**, *21*, 3609–3628. [CrossRef]
37. Li, Y.; Tao, X.; Zhang, X.; Liu, J.; Xu, J. Privacy-Preserved Federated Learning for Autonomous Driving. *IEEE Trans. Intell. Transp. Syst.* **2022**, *23*, 8423–8434. [CrossRef]
38. Du, Z.; Wu, C.; Yoshinaga, T.; Yau, K.L.A.; Ji, Y.; Li, J. Federated Learning for Vehicular Internet of Things: Recent Advances and Open Issues. *IEEE Open J. Comput. Soc.* **2020**, *1*, 45–61. [CrossRef]
39. Yang, Q.; Liu, Y.; Chen, T.; Tong, Y. Federated Machine Learning: Concept and Applications. *Acm Trans. Intell. Syst. Technol.* **2019**, *10*, 1–19. [CrossRef]
40. Toujani, O.; Benhamza, A.; Hachaïchi, Y. The Impact of Big Data and Artificial Intelligence in the Insurance Sector. Available online: https://www.researchgate.net/publication/370340790_The_Impact_of_Big_Data_and_Artificial_Intelligence_in_the_Insurance_Sector (accessed on 4 November 2024).
41. Eling, M.; Nuessle, D.; Staubli, J. The Impact of Artificial Intelligence along the Insurance Value Chain and on the Insurability of Risks. *Geneva Pap. Risk Insur. Issues Pract.* **2022**, *47*, 205–241. [CrossRef]
42. Kumar, N.; Srivastava, J.; Bisht, H. Artificial Intelligence in Insurance Sector. *J. Gujarat Res. Soc.* **2019**, *21*, 79–91.
43. Mamiko, Y.A. *The Impact of Big Data and Artificial Intelligence (AI) in the Insurance Sector*; OECD: Paris, France, 2020.
44. Wei, K.; Li, J.; Ding, M.; Ma, C.; Yang, H.H.; Farokhi, F.; Jin, S.; Quek, T.Q.S.; Vincent Poor, H. Federated Learning with Differential Privacy: Algorithms and Performance Analysis. *IEEE Trans. Inf. Forensics Secur.* **2020**, *15*, 3454–3469. [CrossRef]
45. Almanifi, O.R.A.; Chow, C.O.; Tham, M.L.; Chuah, J.H.; Kanesan, J. Communication and Computation Efficiency in Federated Learning: A Survey. *Internet Things* **2023**, *22*, 100742. [CrossRef]
46. Singh, A.; Vepakomma, P.; Gupta, O.; Raskar, R. Detailed Comparison of Communication Efficiency of Split Learning and Federated Learning. *arXiv* **2019**, arXiv:1909.09145.
47. Ma, X.; Zhu, J.; Lin, Z.; Chen, S.; Qin, Y. A State-of-the-Art Survey on Solving Non-IID Data in Federated Learning. *Future Gener. Comput. Syst.* **2022**, *135*, 244–258. [CrossRef]
48. Wang, H.; Kaplan, Z.; Niu, D.; Li, B. Optimizing Federated Learning on Non-IID Data with Reinforcement Learning. In Proceedings of the IEEE INFOCOM 2020—IEEE Conference on Computer Communications, Toronto, ON, Canada, 6–9 July 2020; pp. 1698–1707. [CrossRef]
49. Zhao, Y.; Li, M.; Lai, L.; Suda, N.; Civin, D.; Chandra, V. Federated Learning with Non-IID Data. *arXiv* **2018**, arXiv:1806.00582. [CrossRef]
50. Siniosoglou, I.; Argyriou, V.; Lagkas, T.; Moscholios, I.; Fragulis, G.; Sarigiannidis, P. Unsupervised Bias Evaluation of DNNs in non-IID Federated Learning Through Latent micro-Manifolds. In Proceedings of the IEEE INFOCOM 2022—IEEE Conference on Computer Communications Workshops (INFOCOM WKSHPS), New York, NY, USA, 2–5 May 2022; pp. 1–6.
51. Siniosoglou, I.; Bibi, S.; Kollias, K.F.; Fragulis, G.; Radoglou-Grammatikis, P.; Lagkas, T.; Argyriou, V.; Vitsas, V.; Sarigiannidis, P. Federated Learning Models in Decentralized Critical Infrastructure. In *Shaping the Future of IoT with Edge Intelligence*; River Publishers: Aalborg, Denmark, 2023; pp. 95–115.
52. Zhang, J.; Chen, J.; Wu, D.; Chen, B.; Yu, S. Poisoning Attack in Federated Learning Using Generative Adversarial Nets. In Proceedings of the 2019 18th IEEE International Conference on Trust, Security and Privacy in Computing and Communications/13th IEEE International Conference On Big Data Science And Engineering (TrustCom/BigDataSE), Rotorua, New Zealand, 5–8 August 2019.
53. Bhagoji, A.N.; Chakraborty, S.; Mittal, P.; Calo, S. Analyzing Federated Learning through an Adversarial Lens. In Proceedings of the 36th International Conference on Machine Learning, PMLR, Long Beach, CA, USA, 9–15 June 2019; pp. 634–643.
54. Ogundokun, R.O.; Misra, S.; Maskeliunas, R.; Damasevicius, R. A Review on Federated Learning and Machine Learning Approaches: Categorization, Application Areas, and Blockchain Technology. *Inf. Int. Interdiscip. J.* **2022**, *13*, 263. [CrossRef]
55. Letizia, N. Parallelism and Horizontal Federated Learning: A Review. Available online: https://www.researchgate.net/publication/370130332_Parallelism_and_Horizontal_Federated_Learning_A_Review (accessed on 4 November 2024).
56. Huang, W.; Li, T.; Wang, D.; Du, S.; Zhang, J.; Huang, T. Fairness and Accuracy in Horizontal Federated Learning. *Inf. Sci.* **2022**, *589*, 170–185. [CrossRef]
57. Li, Q.; Thapa, C.; Ong, L.; Zheng, Y.; Ma, H.; Camtepe, S.A.; Fu, A.; Gao, Y. Vertical Federated Learning: Taxonomies, Threats, and Prospects. *arXiv* **2023**, arXiv:2302.01550. [CrossRef]
58. Zhang, X.; Yin, W.; Hong, M.; Chen, T. Hybrid Federated Learning: Algorithms and Implementation. *arXiv* **2021**, arXiv:2012.12420.
59. Hu, R.; Gong, Y.; Guo, Y. Federated Learning with Sparsification-Amplified Privacy and Adaptive Optimization. In Proceedings of the Thirtieth International Joint Conference on Artificial Intelligence, Montreal, QC, Canada, 19–27 August 2021; pp. 1463–1469. [CrossRef]
60. Zhou, Z.; Chen, H.; Li, K.; Hu, F.; Yan, B.; Cheng, J.; Wei, X.; Liu, B.; Li, X.; Chen, F.; et al. A Novel Optimized Asynchronous Federated Learning Framework. In Proceedings of the 2021 IEEE 23rd Int Conf on High Performance Computing & Communications; 7th Int Conf on Data Science & Systems; 19th Int Conf on Smart City; 7th Int Conf on Dependability in Sensor, Cloud & Big Data Systems & Application (HPCC/DSS/SmartCity/DependSys), Haikou, China, 20–22 December 2021; pp. 2363–2370. [CrossRef]

61. Jing, Q.; Wang, W.; Zhang, J.; Tian, H.; Chen, K. Quantifying the Performance of Federated Transfer Learning. *arXiv* **2019**, arXiv:1912.12795.
62. Liu, Y.; Kang, Y.; Xing, C.; Chen, T.; Yang, Q. Secure Federated Transfer Learning. *IEEE Intell. Syst.* **2020**, *35*, 70–82. [CrossRef]
63. Huang, Y.; Yang, X.; Guo, J.; Cheng, J.; Qu, H.; Ma, J.; Li, L. A High-Precision Method for 100-Day-Old Classification of Chickens in Edge Computing Scenarios Based on Federated Computing. *Animals* **2022**, *12*, 3450. [CrossRef] [PubMed]
64. Gao, D.; Liu, Y.; Huang, A.; Ju, C.; Yu, H.; Yang, Q. Privacy-Preserving Heterogeneous Federated Transfer Learning. In Proceedings of the 2019 IEEE International Conference on Big Data (Big Data), Los Angeles, CA, USA, 9–12 December 2019; pp. 2552–2559. [CrossRef]
65. Bonawitz, K.; Ivanov, V.; Kreuter, B.; Marcedone, A.; McMahan, H.B.; Patel, S.; Ramage, D.; Segal, A.; Seth, K. Practical Secure Aggregation for Privacy Preserving Machine Learning. In Proceedings of the 2017 ACM SIGSAC Conference on Computer and Communications Security, Dallas, TX, USA, 30 October–3 November 2017.
66. Liu, X.; Li, H.; Xu, G.; Lu, R.; He, M. Adaptive Privacy-Preserving Federated Learning. *Peer-Peer Netw. Appl.* **2020**, *13*, 2356–2366. [CrossRef]
67. Bonawitz, K.; Ivanov, V.; Kreuter, B.; Marcedone, A.; McMahan, H.B.; Patel, S.; Ramage, D.; Segal, A.; Seth, K. Practical Secure Aggregation for Federated Learning on User-Held Data. *arXiv* **2016**, arXiv:1611.04482.
68. Xu, M.; Ng, W.C.; Niyato, D.; Yu, H.; Miao, C.; Kim, D.I.; Shen, X.S. Stochastic Resource Allocation in Quantum Key Distribution for Secure Federated Learning. In Proceedings of the GLOBECOM 2022—2022 IEEE Global Communications Conference, Rio de Janeiro, Brazil, 4–8 December 2022; pp. 4377–4382. [CrossRef]
69. Du, W.; Atallah, M.J. Secure Multi-Party Computation Problems and Their Applications: A Review and Open Problems. Electrical Engineering and Computer Science. 11. Available online: https://surface.syr.edu/eecs/11 (accessed on 15 August 2024).
70. Ma, J.; Naas, S.A.; Sigg, S.; Lyu, X. Privacy-Preserving Federated Learning Based on Multi-Key Homomorphic Encryption. *Int. J. Intell. Syst.* **2022**, *37*, 5880–5901. [CrossRef]
71. Fremantle, P.; Aziz, B.; Kopecký, J.; Scott, P. Federated Identity and Access Management for the Internet of Things. In Proceedings of the 2014 International Workshop on Secure Internet of Things, Wroclaw, Poland, 10 September 2014; pp. 10–17. [CrossRef]
72. Alsulami, J. Towards a Federated Identity and Access Management Across Universities. Ph.D. Thesis, Embry-Riddle Aeronautical University, Daytona Beach, FL, USA, 2021.
73. Taylor, K.; Murty, J. Implementing Role Based Access Control for Federated Information Systems on the Web. *Conf. Res. Pract. Inf. Technol. Ser.* **2003**, *34*, 87–95.
74. Anggorojati, B.; Mahalle, P.N.; Prasad, N.R.; Prasad, R. Capability-Based Access Control Delegation Model on the Federated IoT Network. In Proceedings of the 2012 15th International Symposium on Wireless Personal Multimedia Communications (WPMC), Taipei, Taiwan, 24–27 September 2012; pp. 604–608.
75. Vellanki, S.; Sobolewski, M. Federated Role-based Access Control in Exertion-oriented Programming. In Proceedings of the 4th Annual Symposium on Information Assurance (ASIA'09), Albany, NY, USA, 3–4 June 2009.
76. Fisichella, M.; Lax, G.; Russo, A. Partially-Federated Learning: A New Approach to Achieving Privacy and Effectiveness. *Inf. Sci.* **2022**, *614*, 534–547. [CrossRef]
77. Asad, M.; Aslam, M.; Jilani, S.F.; Shaukat, S.; Tsukada, M. SHFL: K-Anonymity-Based Secure Hierarchical Federated Learning Framework for Smart Healthcare Systems. *Future Internet* **2022**, *14*, 338. [CrossRef]
78. Mai, V.S.; La, R.; Zhang, T.; Huang, Y.X.; Battou, A. Federated Learning with Server Learning for Non-IID Data. In Proceedings of the 2023 57th Annual Conference on Information Sciences and Systems (CISS), Baltimore, MD, USA, 22–24 March 2023.
79. Gosselin, R.; Vieu, L.; Loukil, F.; Benoit, A. Privacy and Security in Federated Learning: A Survey. *Appl. Sci.* **2022**, *12*, 9901. [CrossRef]
80. Briggs, C.; Fan, Z.; Andras, P. Federated Learning with Hierarchical Clustering of Local Updates to Improve Training on Non-IID Data. In Proceedings of the 2020 International Joint Conference on Neural Networks (IJCNN), Glasgow, UK, 19–24 July 2020; pp. 1–9. [CrossRef]
81. Sprague, M.R.; Jalalirad, A.; Scavuzzo, M.; Capota, C.; Neun, M.; Do, L.; Kopp, M. Asynchronous Federated Learning for Geospatial Applications. In *ECML PKDD 2018 Workshops*; Monreale, A., Alzate, C., Kamp, M., Krishnamurthy, Y., Paurat, D., Sayed-Mouchaweh, M., Bifet, A., Gama, J., Ribeiro, R.P., Eds.; Springer International Publishing: Cham, Switzerland, 2019; Volume 967, pp. 21–28.
82. Nilsson, A.; Smith, S.; Ulm, G.; Gustavsson, E.; Jirstrand, M. A Performance Evaluation of Federated Learning Algorithms. In Proceedings of the Second Workshop on Distributed Infrastructures for Deep Learning, Rennes, France, 10–11 December 2018; pp. 1–8. [CrossRef]
83. Sun, T.; Li, D.; Wang, B. Decentralized Federated Averaging. *IEEE Trans. Pattern Anal. Mach. Intell.* **2022**, *45*, 4289–4301. [CrossRef]
84. Li, Q.; Tai, C.; Weinan, E. Stochastic Modified Equations and Dynamics of Stochastic Gradient Algorithms I: Mathematical Foundations. *J. Mach. Learn. Res.* **2019**, *20*, 1–47.
85. Yuan, H.; Ma, T. Federated Accelerated Stochastic Gradient Descent. *Adv. Neural Inf. Process. Syst.* **2020**, *33*, 5332–5344.
86. Mekkaoui, e.K.; Mesquita, D.; Blomstedt, P.; Kaski, S. Federated Stochastic Gradient Langevin Dynamics. In Proceedings of the Thirty-Seventh Conference on Uncertainty in Artificial Intelligence, PMLR, Online, 27–30 July 2021; pp. 1703–1712.

87. Nikoloutsopoulos, S.; Koutsopoulos, I.; Titsias, M.K. Personalized Federated Learning with Exact Stochastic Gradient Descent. *arXiv* **2022**, arXiv:2202.09848.
88. Moshawrab, M.; Adda, M.; Bouzouane, A.; Ibrahim, H.; Raad, A. Reviewing Federated Learning Aggregation Algorithms; Strategies, Contributions, Limitations and Future Perspectives. *Electronics* **2023**, *12*, 2287. [CrossRef]
89. Wu, X.; Zhang, Y.; Shi, M.; Li, P.; Li, R.; Xiong, N.N. An Adaptive Federated Learning Scheme with Differential Privacy Preserving. *Future Gener. Comput. Syst.* **2022**, *127*, 362–372. [CrossRef]
90. Deng, Y.; Kamani, M.M.; Mahdavi, M. Adaptive Personalized Federated Learning. *arXiv* **2020**, arXiv:2003.13461.
91. Lydia, A.A.; Francis, F.S. Adagrad—An Optimizer for Stochastic Gradient Descent. *Int. J. Inf. Comput. Sci.* **2019**, *6*, 566–568.
92. Konečný, J.; McMahan, H.B.; Yu, F.X.; Richtárik, P.; Suresh, A.T.; Bacon, D. Federated Learning: Strategies for Improving Communication Efficiency. *arXiv* **2017**, arXiv:1610.05492.
93. Johnson, R.; Zhang, T. Accelerating Stochastic Gradient Descent Using Predictive Variance Reduction. Available online: https://proceedings.neurips.cc/paper/2013/file/ac1dd209cbcc5e5d1c6e28598e8cbbe8-Paper.pdf (accessed on 4 November 2024).
94. Ziller, A.; Trask, A.; Lopardo, A.; Szymkow, B.; Wagner, B.; Bluemke, E.; Nounahon, J.M.; Passerat-Palmbach, J.; Prakash, K.; Rose, N.; et al. PySyft: A Library for Easy Federated Learning. In *Federated Learning Systems: Towards Next-Generation AI*; Rehman, U.M.H., Gaber, M.M., Eds.; Studies in Computational Intelligence; Springer International Publishing: Cham, Switzerland, 2021; pp. 111–139.
95. Budrionis, A.; Miara, M.; Miara, P.; Wilk, S.; Bellika, J.G. Benchmarking PySyft Federated Learning Framework on MIMIC-III Dataset. *IEEE Access Pract. Innov. Open Solut.* **2021**, *9*, 116869–116878. [CrossRef]
96. Alazab, M.; Rm, S.P.; M, P.; Maddikunta, P.K.R.; Gadekallu, T.R.; Pham, Q.V. Federated Learning for Cybersecurity: Concepts, Challenges, and Future Directions. *IEEE Trans. Ind. Inform.* **2022**, *18*, 3501–3509. [CrossRef]
97. Varma, K.; Zhou, Y.; Baracaldo, N.; Anwar, A. LEGATO: A LayerwisE Gradient AggregaTiOn Algorithm for Mitigating Byzantine Attacks in Federated Learning. In Proceedings of the 2021 IEEE 14th International Conference on Cloud Computing (CLOUD), Chicago, IL, USA, 5–10 September 2021.
98. Manakitsa, N.; Maraslidis, G.S.; Moysis, L.; Fragulis, G.F. A review of machine learning and deep learning for object detection, semantic segmentation, and human action recognition in machine and robotic vision. *Technologies* **2024**, *12*, 15. [CrossRef]
99. Huang, Y.; Gupta, S.; Song, Z.; Li, K.; Arora, S. Evaluating Gradient Inversion Attacks and Defenses in Federated Learning. *Adv. Neural Inf. Process. Syst.* **2021**, *34*, 7232–7241.
100. Li, J.; Rakin, A.S.; Chen, X.; He, Z.; Fan, D.; Chakrabarti, C. ResSFL: A Resistance Transfer Framework for Defending Model Inversion Attack in Split Federated Learning. In Proceedings of the 2022 IEEE/CVF Conference on Computer Vision and Pattern Recognition (CVPR), New Orleans, LA, USA, 18–24 June 2022; pp. 10184–10192. [CrossRef]
101. Li, J.; Li, N.; Ribeiro, B. Effective Passive Membership Inference Attacks in Federated Learning against Overparameterized Models. In Proceedings of the Eleventh International Conference on Learning Representations, Virtual, 25–29 April 2022.
102. Dayal, S.; Alhadidi, D.; Abbasi Tadi, A.; Mohammed, N. Comparative Analysis of Membership Inference Attacks in Federated Learning. In Proceedings of the International Database Engineered Applications Symposium Conference, Heraklion, Greece, 5–7 May 2023; pp. 185–192. [CrossRef]
103. Suri, A.; Kanani, P.; Marathe, V.J.; Peterson, D.W. Subject Membership Inference Attacks in Federated Learning. *arXiv* **2022**, arXiv:2206.03317. [CrossRef]
104. Elhattab, F.; Bouchenak, S. Mitigating Membership Inference Attacks in Federated Learning. In Proceedings of the COMPAS'23 : Conférence Francophone En Informatique, Annecy, France, 4–7 July 2023.
105. Lyu, L.; Yu, H.; Ma, X.; Chen, C.; Sun, L.; Zhao, J.; Yang, Q.; Yu, P.S. Privacy and Robustness in Federated Learning: Attacks and Defenses. *IEEE Trans. Neural Netw. Learn. Syst.* **2022**, *35*, 8726–8746. [CrossRef]
106. Bouacida, N.; Mohapatra, P. Vulnerabilities in Federated Learning. *IEEE Access Pract. Innov. Open Solut.* **2021**, *9*, 63229–63249. [CrossRef]
107. Danquah, P.; Kwabena-Adade, H. Public Key Infrastructure: An Enhanced Validation Framework. *J. Inf. Secur.* **2020**, *11*, 241–260. [CrossRef]
108. Gupta, P.; Yadav, K.; Gupta, B.B.; Alazab, M.; Gadekallu, T.R. A Novel Data Poisoning Attack in Federated Learning Based on Inverted Loss Function. *Comput. Secur.* **2023**, *130*, 103270. [CrossRef]
109. Yin, C.; Zeng, Q. Defending Against Data Poisoning Attack in Federated Learning With Non-IID Data. *IEEE Trans. Comput. Soc. Syst.* **2023**, *11*, 2313–2325. [CrossRef]
110. Shejwalkar, V.; Houmansadr, A. Manipulating the Byzantine: Optimizing Model Poisoning Attacks and Defenses for Federated Learning. In Proceedings of the 2021 Network and Distributed System Security Symposium, Virtual, 21–25 February 2021. [CrossRef]
111. Tolpegin, V.; Truex, S.; Gursoy, M.E.; Liu, L. Data Poisoning Attacks Against Federated Learning Systems. In *Computer Security—ESORICS 2020*; Chen, L., Li, N., Liang, K., Schneider, S., Eds.; Springer International Publishing: Cham, Switzerland, 2020; Volume 12308, pp. 480–501.
112. Ozdayi, M.S.; Kantarcioglu, M.; Gel, Y.R. Defending against Backdoors in Federated Learning with Robust Learning Rate. *arXiv* **2020**, arXiv:2007.03767. [CrossRef]
113. Bagdasaryan, E.; Veit, A.; Hua, Y.; Estrin, D.; Shmatikov, V. How To Backdoor Federated Learning. In Proceedings of the Twenty Third International Conference on Artificial Intelligence and Statistics, PMLR, Online, 26–28 August 2020; pp. 2938–2948.

114. Du, M.; Jia, R.; Song, D. Robust Anomaly Detection and Backdoor At- Tack Detection via Differential Privacy. *arXiv* **2020**, arXiv:1911.07116.
115. Rieger, P.; Nguyen, T.D.; Miettinen, M.; Sadeghi, A.R. DeepSight: Mitigating Backdoor Attacks in Federated Learning Through Deep Model Inspection. In Proceedings of the 2022 Network and Distributed System Security Symposium, San Diego, CA, USA, 24–28 April 2022. [CrossRef]
116. Wu, C.; Yang, X.; Zhu, S.; Mitra, P. Mitigating Backdoor Attacks in Federated Learning. *arXiv* **2021**, arXiv:2011.01767. [CrossRef]
117. Douceur, J.R. The Sybil Attack. In *Peer-to-Peer Systems*; Druschel, P., Kaashoek, F., Rowstron, A., Eds.; Springer: Berlin/Heidelberg, Germany, 2002; Volume 2429, pp. 251–260.
118. Jiang, Y.; Li, Y.; Zhou, Y.; Zheng, X. Sybil Attacks and Defense on Differential Privacy Based Federated Learning. In Proceedings of the 2021 IEEE 20th International Conference on Trust, Security and Privacy in Computing and Communications (TrustCom), Shenyang, China, 20–22 October 2021; pp. 355–362. [CrossRef]
119. Fung, C.; Yoon, C.J.M.; Beschastnikh, I. The Limitations of Federated Learning in Sybil Settings. In Proceedings of the 23rd International Symposium on Research in Attacks, Intrusions and Defenses (RAID 2020), San Sebastian, Spain, 14–15 October 2020; pp. 301–316.
120. Fung, C.; Yoon, C.J.M.; Beschastnikh, I. Mitigating Sybils in Federated Learning Poisoning. *arXiv* **2020**, arXiv:1808.04866. [CrossRef]
121. Chen, J.; Yan, H.; Liu, Z.; Zhang, M.; Xiong, H.; Yu, S. When Federated Learning Meets Privacy-Preserving Computation. *Acm Comput. Surv.* **2024**, *56*, 1–36. [CrossRef]
122. Chen, Z.; Yang, C.; Zhu, M.; Peng, Z.; Yuan, Y. Personalized Retrogress-Resilient Federated Learning toward Imbalanced Medical Data. *IEEE Trans. Med. Imaging* **2022**, *41*, 3663–3674. [CrossRef] [PubMed]
123. Liu, X.; Li, H.; Xu, G.; Chen, Z.; Huang, X.; Lu, R. Privacy-Enhanced Federated Learning against Poisoning Adversaries. *IEEE Trans. Inf. Forensics Secur.* **2021**, *16*, 4574–4588. [CrossRef]
124. Yang, C.; Zhu, M.; Liu, Y.; Yuan, Y. FedPD: Federated Open Set Recognition with Parameter Disentanglement. In Proceedings of the IEEE/CVF International Conference on Computer Vision, Paris, France, 1–6 October 2023; pp. 4882–4891.
125. Siniosoglou, I.; Argyriou, V.; Fragulis, G.; Fouliras, P.; Papadopoulos, G.T.; Lytos, A.; Sarigiannidis, P. Applied Federated Model Personalization in the Industrial Domain: A Comparative Study. *IEEE Open J. Commun. Soc.* **2024**. [CrossRef]
126. AbdulRahman, S.; Tout, H.; Ould-Slimane, H.; Mourad, A.; Talhi, C.; Guizani, M. A Survey on Federated Learning: The Journey from Centralized to Distributed on-Site Learning and Beyond. *IEEE Internet Things J.* **2020**, *8*, 5476–5497. [CrossRef]

MDPI AG
Grosspeteranlage 5
4052 Basel
Switzerland
Tel.: +41 61 683 77 34

Future Internet Editorial Office
E-mail: futureinternet@mdpi.com
www.mdpi.com/journal/futureinternet

www.ingramcontent.com/pod-product-compliance
Lightning Source LLC
Chambersburg PA
CBHW040803250926
51850CB00007BA/1072
* 9 7 8 3 7 2 5 8 5 3 4 7 2 *